HANDBOOK OF RESEARCH METHODS IN CAREERS

HANDBOOKS OF RESEARCH METHODS IN MANAGEMENT

Series Editor: Mark N.K. Saunders, *University of Birmingham, UK*

This major series provides the starting point for postgraduate research students in business and management and associated social science disciplines. Each *Handbook* offers a definitive overview of a range of research methods appropriate for a particular subject area within business and management and allied subjects. The series aims to continue to produce prestigious high-quality works of lasting significance, providing insights into methodological issues alongside qualitative, quantitative and mixed methods. Each *Handbook* comprises original contributions by leading and up-and-coming researchers, selected by an editor who is an acknowledged international leader in their field. International in scope, these *Handbooks* provide an invaluable guide to those embarking on a research degree and to researchers moving into a new subject area.

Titles in the series include:

Handbook of Research Methods on Intuition
Edited by Marta Sinclair

Handbook of Research Methods on Human Resource Development
Edited by Mark N.K. Saunders and Paul Tosey

Handbook of Research Methods on Trust
Second Edition
Edited by Fergus Lyon, Guido Möllering and Mark N.K. Saunders

Handbook of Qualitative Research Methods on HRM
Innovative Techniques
Edited by Keith Townsend, Rebecca Loudoun and David Lewin

Handbook of Methods in Leadership Research
Edited by Birgit Schyns, Rosalie Hall and Pedro Neves

Handbook of Research Methods for Tourism and Hospitality Management
Edited by Robin Nunkoo

Handbook of Research Methods on the Quality of Working Lives
Edited by Daniel Wheatley

Handbook of Qualitative Research Methods for Family Business
Edited by Alfredo De Massis and Nadine Kammerlander

Handbook of Research Methods on Creativity
Edited by Viktor Dörfler and Marc Stierand

Handbook of Research Methods in Careers
Edited by Wendy Murphy and Jennifer Tosti-Kharas

Handbook of Research Methods in Careers

Edited by

Wendy Murphy

Associate Dean of Academic Programs and Professor of Organizational Behavior, Management Division, Babson College, USA

Jennifer Tosti-Kharas

Associate Professor of Organizational Behavior, Management Division, Babson College, USA

HANDBOOKS OF RESEARCH METHODS IN MANAGEMENT

Edward Elgar
PUBLISHING

Cheltenham, UK • Northampton, MA, USA

Published by
Edward Elgar Publishing Limited
The Lypiatts
15 Lansdown Road
Cheltenham
Glos GL50 2JA
UK

Edward Elgar Publishing, Inc.
William Pratt House
9 Dewey Court
Northampton
Massachusetts 01060
USA

Paperback edition 2022

A catalogue record for this book
is available from the British Library

Library of Congress Control Number: 2021935863

This book is available electronically in the **Elgar**online
Business subject collection
http://dx.doi.org/10.4337/9781788976725

ISBN 978 1 78897 671 8 (cased)
ISBN 978 1 78897 672 5 (eBook)
ISBN 978 1 0353 0899 6 (paperback)
Printed and bound by CPI Group (UK) Ltd, Croydon, CR0 4YY

We dedicate this book to our community of colleagues around the world who make research in careers both fascinating and rewarding.

And we want to recognize the support from our respective families while editing this collection during the pandemic. Our greatest hope is that our children—Keira, Alexa, and Jack Murphy and Lucy and Theo Kharas—find generative methods for exploring their own careers and a similar community to enable them to thrive.

Contents

About the editors

Wendy Murphy is a Professor of Management and Associate Dean of Undergraduate Academic Programs at Babson College. She earned her Ph.D. from Boston College's Carroll School of Management. Her research interests are at the intersection of careers, developmental (mentoring) networks, and work–life issues. Murphy has authored over 30 publications in academic journals such as *Academy of Management Learning & Education, Human Resource Management, Journal of Management*, and the *Journal of Vocational Behavior*, and in practitioner outlets, such as *Harvard Business Review, Sloan Management Review*, and the *Boston Business Journal*. Her book with Dr. Kathy Kram, *Strategic Relationships at Work: Creating Your Circle of Mentors, Sponsors, and Peers for Success in Business and Life*, bridges mentoring scholarship and practice.

Jennifer Tosti-Kharas is an Associate Professor of Management at Babson College. She earned her Ph.D. from New York University's Stern School of Business. Her research focuses on meaningful work, career as a calling, and unexpected career transitions, and has been published in numerous outlets, including *Academy of Management Review, Academy of Management Perspectives, Journal of Vocational Behavior*, and *Personnel Psychology*. She co-authored with Eric Lamm the forthcoming textbook, *Organizational Behavior: Developing Skills for Managers*, from Pearson Higher Education. Jen has served as a Representative-at-Large for the Careers Division of the Academy of Management, and is currently their elected Treasurer. She is currently a guest editor for a special issue of *Journal of Business Ethics* on "Ethics and the Future of Meaningful Work."

Contributors

Jos Akkermans is an Associate Professor of Sustainable Careers at the School of Business and Economics, Vrije Universiteit Amsterdam, the Netherlands. His research primarily focuses on questions related to career sustainability, career shocks, career transitions, and employability. He has published his work in leading journals in the field, including *Journal of Vocational Behavior*, *European Journal of Work and Organizational Psychology*, *Human Resource Management Journal*, and *Applied Psychology*. Jos currently serves as an Associate Editor at the *Journal of Vocational Behavior*, and he is a member of the Academy of Management Careers Division leadership team.

Mark Bailey is the Associate Professor of Design Innovation and Director of Transnational Education for the School of Design at Northumbria University, UK. He leads design-led innovation research and practice activities and a number of business/research partnerships. He has also established and co-leads the Responsible Innovation Practice research group, investigating education for knowledge creation at the intersection of disciplines. Prior to his academic career, he worked in the aerospace industry on advanced passenger and business jet aircraft designs and has also led a design consultancy. Mark contributed substantially to defining the GETM3 project and wrote important sections of the plan. As part of that project, he has undertaken a secondment to Slovenia and works mainly in the curriculum innovations workstream.

Yehuda Baruch is a Professor of Management (DSc *Technion*, FAcSS & FBAM) at Southampton Business School, University of Southampton, UK and Affiliated Professor of Management at Audencia Business School, France. His research focuses on careers and global HRM. He has published over 150 refereed papers, including in *Journal of Management*, *Academy of Management Annals*, *Human Resource Management*, *Journal of Vocational Behavior*, *Human Relations*, and *Research Policy* and 50 books and book chapters. In addition, he is formerly: VP Research EURAM, AE, *HRM*, Editor, *Group & Organization Management* and *Career Development International*; and past Chair, Careers Division of the Academy of Management.

Janine Bosak is Professor of Work and Organisational Psychology and Director of Research of the Leadership and Talent Institute (LTI) at Dublin City University Business School, Ireland. She also serves as Executive Committee Member of the European Association of Work and Organizational Psychology (EAWOP). Janine conducts research in the areas of Women and Leadership and Employee Wellbeing in Organizations. Her work has been published in various journals. As part of the GETM3 project, Janine has undertaken secondments in Slovenia and Korea.

Jon P. Briscoe is Professor and Chair in the Management Department at Northern Illinois University. His primary research revolves around self-directed and values-driven (protean) careers. In addition he studies careers in different countries and cultures. In 2004 he co-founded the Cross-Cultural Collaboration on Contemporary Careers (5C Group) with Douglas (Tim) Hall and Wolfgang Mayrhofer. The group has grown to conduct comparative research in over 30 countries. Jon is past Program Chair of the Careers Division of the Academy of Management. His teaching centers upon leadership and the development of global leaders.

Julie Brückner is a postgraduate researcher in the Department of Work, Psychology, and Strategy at Dublin City University Business School, Ireland, receiving her doctorate in 2020. Her research interests include implicit motives, leadership, and gender. Julie has undertaken a secondment in Slovenia and will spend two months on secondment in Korea as part of the GETM3 project. She contributes mainly to the employers workstream.

Matej Černe is Associate Professor of Management and Organization at the School of Economics and Business, University of Ljubljana, Slovenia. His research interests include innovation management, creativity, organizational behavior and psychology, human resource management, leadership, and multi-level issues in management. He serves as Editor-in-Chief of the *Dynamics Relationships Management Journal*, Associate Editor of *Economic and Business Review*, and an editorial board member at *The Leadership Quarterly*, *Human Resource Management Review* and *Human Resource Management Journal*. As part of the GETM3 project, Matej has undertaken a GETM3 secondment in Ireland.

Samuel Clegg is an Associate Lecturer in Entrepreneurship at the Newcastle Business School at Northumbria University, UK. He has first-hand experience working within start-ups having previously co-founded several businesses through accelerator programs and is currently the Managing Director of Highfly; a digital marketing agency based in Newcastle upon Tyne. He is also a business mentor through the Supply Chain North East regional development program. Sam plays multiple roles on the GETM3 project: contributing to all workstreams, running social media communication, building the online dissemination platform, and championing social capital development. He has undertaken secondments in Ireland, Poland, Slovenia, and Korea.

Suzanne Crane is an International Project Manager at Northumbria University, UK, with 14 years' experience in the higher education industry. Skilled in operational excellence, meeting facilitation, and project delivery: she has a Master of Arts in Professional Practice in Higher Education from Northumbria University. A member of the Association of University Administrators, and a mentor for their Postgraduate Certificate in Higher Education Administration, Management and Leadership, she is also a member of the Marie Curie Alumni Association, a Marie Sklodowska-Curie Fellow, and is currently the Co-Chair of the Northumbria University Women's Staff Network. Suzanne manages the GETM3 project's administration and organization and has visited every project partner.

Allison Creed is a Curriculum Designer and Lecturer in the Faculty of Arts at the University of Melbourne with expertise in Applied Linguistics, Education, and Organizational Coaching in undergraduate and postgraduate courses on and off-shore. Her research utilizes conceptual metaphor theory and cognitive linguistics to focus on issues in career and employability and the language of wine with articles appearing in the *British Journal of Guidance and Counselling, International Journal of Educational and Vocational Guidance*, and *Journal of Career Assessment*. She is also a Researching and Applying Metaphor (RaAM) Executive Committee member (Conference Secretary), research team member of the University of Southern Queensland ACCELL, and collaborates with the Inland Norway University of Applied Sciences Faculty of Education and University of Amsterdam Metaphor Lab.

Suzanne C. de Janasz is Professor of Management and Conflict Analysis and Resolution (a joint appointment) at George Mason University in Virginia; past positions include the Gleed Distinguished Chair of Business Administration at Seattle University, and Professor of Leadership and Organization Development at IMD in Switzerland. Her research on mentoring, work–family conflict, and leadership appears in such journals as *Harvard Business Review, Academy of Management Executive, Journal of Organizational Behavior, Journal of Vocational Behavior*, and *British Journal of Management*, and has been featured in global newspapers, online publications, and radio programs. Current projects include CEO learning, gendered negotiation, and work–family issues in the gig economy.

Michael Dickmann is a Professor of International Human Resource Management (HRM) at Cranfield University and the Director of the Cranfield Masters in Management. His research focuses on human resource strategies, structures and processes of multinational organizations, cross-cultural management, international mobility and global careers. Michael has published in a broad range of academic journals and he is the lead author of several books on international HRM and global careers. Since 2017 he is the Senior Editor-in-Chief of *The International Journal of Human Resource Management*.

Shoshana R. Dobrow is an Assistant Professor of Management at the London School of Economics. Her research examines careers—particularly the meaning of work, the sense of calling, and developmental mentoring networks—often utilizing longitudinal approaches. This work has been published in journals such as *Academy of Management Discoveries, Journal of Applied Psychology, Journal of Management, Journal of Organizational Behavior*, and *Personnel Psychology* and has been recognized with several best paper awards. Shoshana received the inaugural Mid-Career Award from the Academy of Management's Careers Division in 2020. She holds a Ph.D. in Organizational Behavior from Harvard University.

Paul Doyle is a Senior Lecturer and Head of Professional Development Programmes in Computer Science, Technological University Dublin, Ireland. His research areas include distributed systems, big data, curriculum development and technology in education. He develops and delivers flexible and blended learning courses in South Korea and China and is involved in a number of European-funded projects focusing on curriculum and education. He spent 20 years working internationally in the IT industry. Paul leads the production of the major deliverables from GETM3 using online video technology and has undertaken secondments in Korea.

Katarzyna Dziewanowska is an Assistant Professor of Marketing at the Faculty of Management, University of Warsaw, Poland. She is a member of the European Marketing Academy and Polish Scientific Association of Marketing, a visiting researcher at the Centre for Studies on Higher Education at University of California, Berkeley, and is a visiting fellow at Northumbria University, UK. Her research interests focus on consumer behavior, value co-creation, consumer experiences, and experiential marketing, as well as customer satisfaction, loyalty, and relationship marketing. Katarzyna was an original member of the GETM3 project team and leads the research workstream focused on young people. She has undertaken secondments in Ireland, the UK, Slovenia, and Korea.

Holly Slay Ferraro is an Associate Professor of Management in the Albers School of Business and Economics and an Associate Director for Faculty Professional Development in the Center for Faculty Development at Seattle University. She received her Ph.D. in Organizational Behavior from the University of Maryland, College Park. Her research examines how people grapple with dimensions of self (e.g. age, race, gender) in making career decisions. She is also interested in how organizational and institutional practices contribute to struggles with aspects of identity. Her research on midlife/midcareer transitions won a Cutting Edge Award from the Academy of Human Resource Development.

Rajashi Ghosh is an Associate Professor of Human Resource Development (HRD) and Chair of the Policy, Organization, and Leadership (POL) department in School of Education at Drexel University. Her research expertise is in mentoring, coaching, workplace incivility, and leader development. Her work has been published in several peer-reviewed journals including all AHRD journals and other high-impact outlets publishing work related to HRD such as *Journal of Vocational Behavior*, *Career Development International*, and *European Journal of Training and Development*. Rajashi has been recognized by several prestigious awards including the 2016 Early Career Scholar Award at the AHRD, the 2015–2016 Award for Outstanding Early Career Scholar Achievement from the Office of Provost at Drexel University, and the 2018–2019 Provost Fellowship at Drexel University.

Kerry Roberts Gibson is an Assistant Professor in the Management Division at Babson College. Her research focuses on interpersonal, dyadic work relationships and the mechanisms that contribute to relational growth and development. She is particularly interested in understanding how work relationships shift over time. Her research has been published in the *Academy of Management Review, Organizational Behavior and Human Decisions Processes* and on *Harvard Business Review*'s website, hbr.org.

Danna Greenberg is the Walter H. Carpenter Professor of Organizational Behavior at Babson College. Her research explores how individuals navigate the interface between their personal and professional lives and the implications this has for their thriving at work, at home, and in their communities. She has recently published a book on this topic entitled *Maternal Optimism: Forging Positive Paths Through Work and Motherhood*. Her secondary area of research focuses on academic careers and our roles as professors and scholars. Her research has been widely published including in the *Academy of Management Journal, Academy of Management Perspectives*, and *Academy of Management Learning and Education*.

Douglas T. Hall is the Morton H. and Charlotte Friedman Professor of Management Emeritus in the Questrom School of Business at Boston University. He has held faculty positions at Yale, York, Michigan State and Northwestern Universities. He has also held visiting positions at Columbia, Minnesota, the U.S. Military Academy at West Point, Boston College, the University of Canterbury (NZ), the Center for Creative Leadership, and the IESE Business School in Barcelona. His research deals with retirement, success, global careers, work–family dynamics, and leadership development.

Brian Harney MCIPD is Professor in Strategy & HRM at Dublin City University Business School, Ireland. His research focuses on the intersection of Strategy and HRM, with a particular focus on SMEs, growth, and knowledge-intensive sectors. His research has received over 15 awards and he has secured competitive funding in excess of €3 million to understand and enhance SME management and development. He currently serves on the editorial board of *HRM (US), the International Journal of HRM and Employee Relations*. Brian leads the workstream dedicated to curriculum innovation in GETM3 and has undertaken secondments in Slovenia, Poland, and the UK.

Gregory Hennessy is a management consultant with more than 25 years of experience in strategy and organizational development. He integrates human and organizational behavior, qualitative and quantitative analysis, complexity, and systems thinking to help clients solve their most difficult problems and develop strategic capability. Greg holds master's degrees in Social Science from the California Institute of Technology and in Management from MIT's Sloan School. He is earning his doctoral degree in Positive Organizational Psychology from Claremont Graduate University, where he studies the relationship between character, entrepreneurship and strategic leadership.

Joeri Hofmans is Professor of Work and Organizational Psychology at the Faculty of Psychology and Educational Sciences, Vrije Universiteit Brussel (VUB). His research focuses on the role of personality, leadership, and motivation at work, with particular emphasis on within-person fluctuations and temporal dynamics. He has published in a broad range of applied psychology journals including *Organization*

Science, Organizational Research Methods, Journal of Organizational Behavior, The Leadership Quarterly, and *Journal of Vocational Behavior*. He currently serves as an editorial board member for several journals, including *Organizational Research Methods, Journal of Vocational Behavior, Assessment*, and *European Journal of Work and Organizational Psychology*.

Robert Kaše is an Associate Professor of Management and Organization at the School of Economics & Business, University of Ljubljana, Slovenia. His research interests include organizational networks, strategic HRM, talent management, careers, compensation, and emergence. His work has been published in various HR journals. Supporting interaction between research and practice, he is a board member of the Slovenian HR Association, lecturer at executive training, and works on applied projects with corporate clients. As part of the GETM3 project, Robert has undertaken a secondment in Korea.

A. Julie Katz is a facilitator, mediator, coach, and trainer. Her work as a graduate teaching assistant (MBA program), master's degree and work in conflict analysis, and graduate studies in social work (George Mason University) incorporates her appreciation for self-determination and innovative problem solving gained through careers as the owner and creative director for a communications and marketing business, in metalwork arts, and supporting the disabilities community. Projects include gendered negotiation; participants' mediation experience; evaluating an employment program for young adults with disabilities, and a leadership training; and facilitating "belonging" with art in communities with members with disabilities.

Gábor Kismihók is the head of the Learning and Skills Analytics research group at the Leibniz Information Centre for Science and Technology (TIB). He concentrates his research efforts on matching processes between education, labor market, and individuals. Gábor regularly publishes his research in various peer-reviewed international journals and book chapters in the fields of Learning Analytics, Research Methods, Technology Enhanced Learning and Knowledge Management. In the past years he has been busy with various EU funded research projects (FP7, FP7 Marie Curie ITN, Lifelong Learning Programme) focused on employability, person–organization fit, mobile Learning Management System development, context aware educational systems and semantic technology in education.

Ilsang Ko is a Professor in the College of Business Administration, Chonnam National University (CNU), South Korea. He has an MBA from the University of Pittsburgh and a Ph.D. from the University of Colorado. His research interests are B2B electronic commerce, global collaboration, and firm's capacity and capability of IT applications. His research work has appeared in various international journals. Ilsang was an original member of the GETM3 project team, leads the participation of CNU and ensures implementation of the project activities there, including chairing the International Conferences on Global Entrepreneurial Talent Management & Social Collaboration. He has undertaken secondments in the UK, Ireland, Slovenia and Poland.

Vladimer B. Kobayashi is currently a Ph.D. candidate at the Amsterdam Business School of the University of Amsterdam under a Marie Curie ITN Fellowship. He is working as faculty at the University of the Philippines Mindanao. His research interests include applying text mining and machine learning to human resource management, organizational research, and career studies.

Colin I.S.G. Lee is an Assistant Professor at the Rotterdam School of Management, Erasmus University. His research addresses questions at the intersection of human resource management, organizational behavior, IO psychology, and career studies. Leveraging computational tools for data extraction, normalization, and processing, he provides insights into how people can be matched to work and develops methods for the dissemination of academic knowledge in his fields of interest. His work has been published in leading journals, including *Human Resource Management Review* and *Journal of Vocational Behavior*, and he has received esteemed academic awards as well as extensive media coverage.

Ague Mae Manongsong is a Ph.D. candidate in the School of Education at Drexel University. She earned her MA in I/O Psychology from CSU, Sacramento and an MA in Organizational Behavior and Evaluation from Claremont Graduate University. Her research interests center on the different applications of mentoring for the purposes of increasing the likelihood of positive leadership and career outcomes for women and women of color.

Wolfgang Mayrhofer is Full Professor and head of the Interdisciplinary Institute of Management and Organisational Behaviour, WU Vienna, Austria. He previously has held full-time positions at the University of Paderborn, Germany, and at Dresden University of Technology, Germany and conducts research in comparative international human resource management and careers, and systems theory and management and has received national and international awards for outstanding research and service to the academic community. Wolfgang has widely published, serves as editorial or advisory board member of several international journals and research centers and regularly consults with organizations in the for-profit and non-profit world.

John McMackin is Assistant Professor with the Work, Psychology and Strategy Group at DCU Business School, and Chair of the School's MSc in Talent, Leadership and HR Strategy programme. He previously served as Director of Executive and International Education for the School. His research has been published in, for example, the *Academy of Management Review*, *Human Resource Management Review*, and *Applied Cognitive Psychology*. He has been awarded a Senior Fellowship of the Higher Education Academy, in recognition of excellence in teaching and learning support. John has undertaken secondments in Slovenia as part of the GETM3 project.

Jessica R. Methot is an Associate Professor of Human Resource Management in the School of Management and Labor Relations at Rutgers University, and a Distinguished Research Professor in the Department of Management at University of Exeter Business School, UK. She received her Ph.D. in Organizational Behavior from the University of Florida Warrington College of Business. Dr. Methot conducts research at the intersection of interpersonal workplace relationships and social network dynamics, including how formal HR practices transform informal social networks, the functional and dysfunctional consequences of workplace relationships, and their temporal and multidimensional features.

Katarina K. Mihelič is Associate Professor of Management and Organization at the School of Economics & Business, University of Ljubljana, Slovenia. She studied the psychology of the workplace and her research interests include (un)ethical behavior and work–family dynamics. Her work has been published in international scholarly outlets such as *Human Resource Management, Journal of Business Ethics, Personnel Review, Business Ethics: A European Review* and *Creativity Research Journal*. Katja leads the GETM3 workstream dedicated to employers, particularly SMEs, and has undertaken a secondment in the UK.

Stefan T. Mol is Assistant Professor of Organizational Behavior and Research Methods at the Amsterdam Business School of the University of Amsterdam, the Netherlands. Stefan's research interests center on a variety of topics including but not limited to career shocks, person–environment fit, employability, refugee integration in the labor market, psychological contracts, expatriate management, and methods such as text-mining, learning analytics, and meta-analysis.

Aimilia Mylona is a master's graduate in Business Administration in the track of Human Resource Management, Vrije Universiteit Amsterdam, the Netherlands. During her education, her research focused primarily on internal and external employability. Aimilia is currently following a career in Human Resources within tech startups, while pursuing entrepreneurial ventures on career advice and guidance for young graduates.

Susan Nacey is a Professor of English as a Second/Foreign Language, and currently the Vice Dean of Research at the Faculty of Education at the Inland Norway University of Applied Sciences in Hamar/Lillehammer. She researches metaphor and other features in a wide variety of text types in English and Norwegian, especially in written and spoken learner language. She is the author of "Metaphors in learner English" (John Benjamins, 2013) and the co-editor of "Metaphor identification in multiple languages: MIPVU around the world" (John Benjamins, 2019).

Sanne Nijs is an Assistant Professor at the Department of Human Resource Studies, Tilburg University, the Netherlands. Her research primarily focuses on questions related to talent management and talent identification. Within this field, she studies topics such as the favorable and unfavorable outcomes of talent management practices. She has published her work in leading journals in the field, including *European Journal of Work and Organizational Psychology*, *Human Resource Management Review*, and *Journal of World Business*. Sanne is part of the Future of Work and

Organizational Psychology taskforce that works towards creating a healthy academic discipline.

Susan O'Donnell is Secretary to the Board and Head of Governance at Northumbria University, UK. She is a professionally qualified Risk Manager with almost 30 years' experience across a range of sectors, the last 10 years of which were in Higher Education. Her governance work spans the fields of risk and assurance, corporate governance, due diligence, safeguarding and counter terrorism. Susan supports the GETM3 Project Board to consider the management of risks and opportunities across all workstreams and has undertaken a related secondment in Ireland.

Janneke K. Oostrom is an Associate Professor at the School of Business and Economics, Vrije Universiteit Amsterdam, the Netherlands. Her research primarily focuses on questions related to employee recruitment, selection, and assessment. Within this field, she studies topics such as situational judgment testing, impression management, test fairness, and biases. She has published her work in leading journals in the field, including *Journal of Applied Psychology*, *The Leadership Quarterly*, *Journal of Research in Personality*, and *Journal of Experimental Social Psychology*. Janneke currently serves as an Associate Editor at the *International Journal of Selection and Assessment*.

Emma Parry is Professor of Human Resource Management and Head of the *Changing World of Work* Group at Cranfield School of Management, UK. Her research focuses on the impact of the external environment on people management and careers, specifically national context, technological advancement and changing workforce demographics. Emma is a Fellow of the British Academy of Management, an Academic Fellow of the Chartered Institute of Personnel and Development (CIPD) and an Honorary Fellow of the Institute for Employment Studies (IES). She has published several books and numerous papers in high quality academic journals.

Alison Pearce is Associate Professor of Strategic Entrepreneurship at Newcastle Business School at Northumbria University, UK, Affiliate Professor at Grenoble Ecole de Management, France and a Senior Fellow of the UK Higher Education Academy. One of the original cohort of British Erasmus students sent abroad in 1987 she spent 15 years living and working internationally in marketing, design and product development culminating in Head of Innovation and Business Development and running her own marketing and design consultancy. She is now the convenor of a faculty Research Interest Group and her work has been published in academic journals, industry magazines, books, blogs, and news media. An original member of the GETM3 team, Alison led the funding bid and, as Principal Investigator, now leads the project's overall implementation, undertaking secondments in Ireland, Poland, Slovenia, and Korea.

Peter Pease is a Senior Lecturer in Entrepreneurship and Psychology at Newcastle Business School, University of Northumbria, UK. His research focuses on the personal psychological resources which predict entrepreneurial success and how to nurture them. Before joining NBS, Peter spent 25 years setting up and running his own businesses in recruitment, vocational education and HR. He has had a long-standing interest in learning evaluation and research impact and is Impact Manager on GETM3, undertaking secondments in Slovenia, Ireland, Poland and Korea.

Rose Quan is Associate Professor in International Business and Strategy at Newcastle Business School at Northumbria University, UK. Her research interests include international entrepreneurship, international student and staff mobility, and international market entry strategy for MNEs and SMEs from both developed and developing countries. Her scholarly work has appeared in various international journals. Rose is co-lead of the GETM3 work stream managing networking, communication, dissemination, and training activities. She has completed secondments in Korea, Ireland, Poland, and Slovenia.

Bert Schreurs is Professor of Human Resources at the Faculty of Social Sciences and Solvay Business School, Vrije Universiteit Brussel (VUB). Prior to joining the VUB, Bert taught at Maastricht University, Utrecht University, and KU Leuven. His research focuses on work stress and motivation, career management, and self-regulation at work. He has published in various journals such as *Journal of Organizational Behavior*, *Journal of Occupational Health Psychology*, *Journal of Vocational Behavior*, *Human Resource Management Review*, and *Work & Stress*. He currently serves as an Associate Editor of *Career Development International* and is a Past Chair of the Academy of Management Careers Division.

Scott E. Seibert is a Professor and Chair of the Human Resource Management Department at Rutgers University. He earned his Ph.D. from Cornell's School of Management and Labor Relations. His research is in the areas of careers processes and career success, leadership, employee motivation, and the psychology of entrepreneurship. He has published widely in top-tier journals including the *Journal of Applied Psychology*, *Personnel Psychology*, *Journal of Management*, and *Academy of Management Journal*. He has received the Academy of Management Journal Best Paper Award and the Outstanding Publication in Organizational Behavior Award and a past Chair of the Careers Division of the Academy of Management.

Alireza Shokri is an Associate Professor in Operations and Supply Chain Management at Newcastle Business School, Northumbria University, UK. He joined academia in 2011 after working in industry for many years. His main research interest is on quality and efficiency strategies such as Lean and Lean Six Sigma (LSS) and he is currently working on various research projects including a British Academy-funded project and GETM3, where he designed and leads quality management processes.

Dimitra Skoumpopoulou is a Senior Lecturer in Newcastle Business School, Northumbria University, UK. She has over 15 years' experience being a consultant in the UK and abroad with wide-ranging experience in the implementation and use of Information Systems (IS). She offered training and support to organizations and helped businesses to introduce, develop and use IS. Her research is focused on the human aspects of IS implementation. Dimitra is co-lead of the GETM3 workstream managing networking, communication, dissemination and training activities in the project and has undertaken secondments in Slovenia and Ireland.

Brenda Stalker is a Senior Lecturer in Human Resource Development and Faculty Director of Degree Apprenticeship Programmes in Newcastle Business School at Northumbria University, UK. Building on her professional experience in corporate and executive development, she now leads the Faculty's strategy on working with employers to develop work-based learning programs to develop existing and new talent across private and public sectors. Her research published in international journals includes learning communities, talent management, international careers and work identities. Brenda was a founder member of the GETM3 project team and co-leads the workstream managing networking, communication, dissemination and training activities in the project. She has completed secondments in Ireland, Poland and Slovenia.

Huan Sun is a full-time Ph.D. candidate at Newcastle Business School, Northumbria University, UK. Her doctoral research topic is related to Chinese SMEs' innovation and sustainability. She also has an interest in practising various methods such as regional and multi-case studies. She has served as an Associate Lecturer at Northumbria University, contributed to multiple workstreams and undertaken a GETM3 secondment in Slovenia.

Jose Aldo Valencia Hernandez is a Lecturer at the Design Innovation Department and the academic lead of the Centre for Entrepreneurship, Design and Innovation, both at Maynooth University in Ireland. He also collaborates with Mi:Lab exploring ways of tackling the challenges within the higher education system through the design approach. He holds a Ph.D. in Design, Innovation & Entrepreneurship from the School of Design at Northumbria University, UK, researching designer-entrepreneurs. He has served as a business consultant in strategic design for SMEs. Aldo contributes to multiple workstreams in GETM3 and has undertaken secondments in Slovenia, Korea and Ireland.

Viktoriya Voloshyna is a Ph.D. candidate at School of Human Resource Management, at York University in Toronto. Her research interests lie in the area of career transition, professional identity transformation, and identity threat. She also focuses on topics related to power issues and status passages of various actors. She has specific interest in grounded methodology and related qualitative research approaches.

Jarno Vrolijk is currently a Ph.D. candidate at the Amsterdam Business School of the University of Amsterdam. His primary research interests lie in people analytics, natural language semantics and improving language understanding by taking advantage of different approaches.

Hannah Weisman is a Post-Doctoral Fellow at Harvard Business School. She completed her Ph.D. in Management at the London School of Economics. She uses longitudinal methods to understand how people make meaning of their work, especially in career transitions. Hannah was named a Finalist in the 2019 INFORMS/Organization Science Best Dissertation Proposal Competition for her research on the career transitions people make to pursue their callings. She has received several awards, including the Best Paper Award from the Academy of Management's Careers Division. She has also served as Student Representative for the Academy of Management's Organizational Behavior Division.

Bart Wille is Assistant Professor of Industrial-Organizational Psychology in the Faculty of Psychology and Educational Sciences at Ghent University. His research focuses on the assessment, development, and outcomes of psychological individual differences (e.g. personality traits, vocational interests, leadership styles) in the context of work and careers. He has published this work in a broad range of journals including *Journal of Applied Psychology*, *Personnel Psychology*, *Journal of Organizational Behavior*, *Organizational Research Methods*, and *Journal of Vocational Behavior*. He currently serves as an editorial board member for several journals, including *Journal of Applied Psychology*, *Journal of Vocational Behavior*, *Journal of Counseling Psychology*, and *International Journal of Testing*.

Szu-Hsin Wu is currently a Lecturer in Marketing at Dundee University's Business School in the UK. She has a multidisciplinary background, including art education, graphic design, management and marketing. Her current research interests focus on actor engagement, sustainability innovation and value co-creation. Szu-Hsin has undertaken GETM3 secondments in Slovenia and Poland and works mainly in the young people workstream.

Jeffrey Yip is an Assistant Professor of Management at the Beedie School of Business, Simon Fraser University (SFU). His research is in the areas of leadership, mentoring, and career development. At SFU, he teaches leadership and teamwork in the Executive MBA and graduate programs in business. Prior to academia, Jeffrey was a research faculty with the Center for Creative Leadership and co-founded the Halogen Foundation, an organization focused on entrepreneurship and leadership education. He holds a Ph.D. in Management from Boston University and a Master's in Human Development and Psychology from Harvard University.

Jelena Zikic is an Associate Professor and Graduate Program Director at the School of Human Resource Management, at York University in Toronto. Her Ph.D. is from the University of Toronto's Rotman School of Management. She developed her expertise in the area of career transitions of diverse populations and studies the impact of global mobility on career growth and development. Her research interests focus on career management issues of diverse populations, combining the individual as well as organizational perspective. Her work has appeared in journals such as *Journal of Organizational Behavior*, *Human Relations*, and *Journal of Vocational Behavior* among others.

Introduction to the *Handbook of Research Methods in Careers*

Wendy Murphy and Jennifer Tosti-Kharas

We are excited to introduce you to the *Handbook of Research Methods in Careers*. This Handbook serves as a comprehensive introduction to the methodologies that researchers use in the careers domain. The field of careers "explores people's lifelong succession of work experience, the structure of opportunity to work, and the relationship between careers and other aspects of life" (Academy of Management, 2020). As such, the field itself is multi-disciplinary and multi-level, as individual careers develop embedded in the context of organizations, families/societies, cultures and national geographies and as the scholars' disciplinary lenses may inform the level of analysis studied.

We felt the time was right for a handbook on careers research methods for a few reasons. First, careers as a phenomenon of study have unquestionably become more rich, dynamic, and complex than ever before. What started with a recognition that many careers are no longer unfolding within a single organization on a set, typically upward, path (e.g., Arthur & Rousseau, 1996) at the turn of the new millennium has evolved into a series of highly individualized career paths (Cappelli & Keller, 2013). The rise of novel employment relationships, like contract, freelance, and "gig" work, has changed the nature of the relationship between organizations and workers (e.g., Petriglieri, Ashford & Wrzesniewski, 2019; Spreitzer, Cameron & Garrett, 2017). Globalization has meant that people increasingly pursue expatriate assignments, and careers develop across geographical and cultural borders (Biemann, Fasang & Grunow, 2011; Tams & Arthur, 2007). The rise of technology enabled remote collaboration and work even before the rise of a global pandemic forced many to work from their homes (Spurk & Straub, 2020). A turbulent few decades, marked by terror attacks, global recessions, and that same pandemic have led countless people to make career changes, both voluntary and involuntary (Akkermans, Richardson & Kraimer, 2020; Briscoe, Henagan, Burton & Murphy, 2012; Michaelson & Tosti-Kharas, 2020). Aging Baby Boomers contemplated encore careers and transitions to retirement (Boveda & Metz, 2016), as Millennials were categorized as non-committal job-hoppers (Ng, Schweitzer & Lyons, 2010). We present this list, not as comprehensive nor exhaustive, but rather to illustrate that changes to the world around us affect our careers in numerous ways. This trend will likely continue, as the highly-anticipated "fourth industrial revolution" foretells artificial intelligence, automization, and technological unemployment, all of which will provide further shifts in people's careers (Schwab, 2016). What this means for careers scholars is that there is no shortage of interesting questions to ask, nor of innovative ways to study these questions, and we hope this Handbook can help inspire research that better helps us understand careers, now and in the future.

Second, perhaps as a natural response to the changes affecting people's actual careers, the field of careers research itself has witnessed a significant evolution. Early on, the field encompassed vocational development aiming to help people identify the starting occupation in their career – with the basic assumption that initial placement could carry one through to retirement – as well as the organizational human resource systems to help people progress along that track (see Arthur, Hall & Lawrence, 1989 for a brief history of the field from the vantage point 30 years ago). What began decades ago as a coordinated attempt to stake out careers research as a domain of study continues today as an increasingly rich exploration of how people's careers develop over time and in relationship with the world around them. Evidence of this broadening of the field can be found in the sheer number and variety of research published in our top journals and presented at conferences. Part of this variety means that, just as it is difficult to paint "careers today" with one broad brush, it is nearly impossible to talk about one dominant approach to careers research. As the questions we ask about careers get more interesting, complicated, and layered, so too do the methodological approaches we use to explore career phenomena. Careers theories draw from fields as distinct as psychology, sociology, economics, and anthropology, each of which has its own rich methodological tradition (Arthur, Hall & Lawrence, 1989; Dokko, Tosti-Kharas & Barbulescu, 2020). Novel sources of data have been enabled by the same forces of technology and globalization that shift careers themselves. Researchers are availing themselves of the breadth and depth of data archived in corporate databases and on the Internet. They are collaborating on "mega-projects" that unite vast teams of scholars to compare results across contexts. Rather than utilizing primarily quantitative *or* qualitative methods, studies combine these approaches to maximum effect. The HR Department in many companies now includes Ph.Ds whose analysis of "big data" comprised of employees' career moves yields valuable insights (e.g., Duhigg, 2016). An important point of distinction between research on careers versus other topics within the management sciences is that every researcher has a career of their own that provides an opportunity for introspection and inspiration. Auto-ethnographic and narrative analyses can help us better understand what we can draw from our own careers (Belkhir et al., 2019). We see careers research becoming more divergent – not to the point of fragmentation, but rather to the point where these diverse approaches can complement and build upon each other.

Third, as careers researchers ourselves, we saw both symbolic and practical importance to having a dedicated collection of chapters exploring the best, most cutting-edge methodologies for studying careers. Despite the recognition that careers research is a defined area of study with all the trappings of one, including specialized journals and conferences – e.g., a particularly vibrant division within the Academy of Management, standing tracks at EGOS – there has not yet been a targeted volume to explore the breadth and variety of research methods within this area. We saw handbooks like this one for fields like human resource management and leadership, and wholeheartedly believed that there was both a desire and need for such a volume for careers. Frankly, this is the handbook we wish existed when we were embarking on our own career paths, as doctoral students, forging dissertations in this area.

We hope that you, as a reader of this Handbook, find the chapters collected here to be useful in your own research on careers. For scholars who are new to the field of careers, this collection of chapters should serve as a roadmap to the breadth of research methods in careers. Our authors present their methods in detail and offer numerous actionable best practices, realistic previews, and even cautionary tales based on their vast collective experience publishing in this area. For experienced researchers, we showcase the diverse and interdisciplinary approaches to designing projects and studying careers across the spectrum of quantitative and qualitative methodologies. We have chosen scholars to contribute to this volume who are not simply experts in the given methodology, but who have a track record of publishing cutting-edge research specifically in the area of careers. Therefore, these chapters are not written as generic explorations of a given method, but are intentionally situated within careers research. Together, the 58 authors who contributed to this Handbook represent institutions and organizations across 13 countries from a range of disciplinary training and an even wider range of national origins. The diversity inherent in our authorship reflects the diversity in careers research itself and provides further evidence of the rich heritage and future of the careers field.

OVERVIEW OF CAREERS RESEARCH

This Handbook starts with an extensive review of trends in career methods by Jos Akkermans, Colin I.S.G. Lee, Sanne Nijs, Aimilia Mylona, and Janneke K. Oostrom. Their chapter maps the methodologies most commonly used in research published in careers journals in the last five years, including the strengths and weaknesses of these methods, and identifies opportunities for future research. This chapter sets the stage for each series of chapters that follow to explore different approaches in-depth. The book is then organized into three parts on measurement and design, quantitative methods, and qualitative and mixed methods.

Part I: Measurement and Design

We begin the section on Measurement and Design with a thorough overview of constructs and key theories in the careers domain by Yehuda Baruch. In this chapter, theories such as boundaryless and protean careers are identified as well as related constructs such as global careers, mentoring, and work–life balance. The resulting list serves as an encyclopedia of terms and definitions and related challenges to their study. The chapter concludes with a discussion of how to study careers, matching empirical approaches to the research question and domain of interest, and addressing the "artificial divide" between quantitative and qualitative methodologies.

As this volume demonstrates, the breadth of career studies may necessitate teams of researchers to study trends, develop theory, validate constructs, and explore cross-cultural career issues. We have two chapters each introducing large-scale, multi-country, multi-year projects from a design perspective: the 5C Group and GETM3.

The 5C Group (Cross-Cultural Collaboration on Contemporary Careers) is composed of over 60 researchers organized into 30 country teams, and it continues to grow. Chapter authors Jon P. Briscoe, Michael Dickmann, Douglas T. (Tim) Hall, Emma Parry, and Wolfgang Mayrhofer explain that their objective is to "identify, develop and empower researchers in diverse parts of the world, to bring attention to diverse populations and their 'careerscapes,' and to contribute to efforts being more inclusive in social science research." The chapter briefly outlines the group's history and development of design principles for member selection, group norms, cultural, and methodological traditions. Attention to project design and intentional collaboration has resulted in over 20 articles and book chapters and over 30 presentations on their research around the world.

GETM3 (Global Entrepreneurial Talent Management 3) is an international, interdisciplinary funded research project bringing together 16 partners from five countries: the United Kingdom, Ireland, Poland, Slovenia, and the Republic of Korea (South Korea). In this chapter, 23 co-authors outline the project objectives, design, methodology, and participant experiences to illustrate the complexity and coordination required of a large, multi-year collaboration. A key objective is to "help people develop their knowledge, skills, and careers, while building links between organizations working in different sectors of the economy, including universities, research institutes, and SMEs" (European Commission, 2019). More importantly though, the chapter demonstrates how the GETM3 project serves as a bridge across national, sectoral, disciplinary, methodological, and career life stages as a vehicle for the career development of participants AND researchers themselves.

In studying career decision making, Gregory Hennessy and Jeffrey Yip explore the phenomenon of contingent employment in today's growing "gig economy." In this chapter, we see how design choices such as context are essential in enabling the researchers to explore constructs of interest in the careers domain. The chapter overviews the literature on career decision making and takes a deep dive into career decision making heuristics discussing types, rules, and options as well as the career decision making environment. It concludes with suggestions on how to study career decisions by applying real options theory in dynamic career environments.

Mentoring serves as an important source of professional learning and development in the careers domain. In their chapter on designing and studying mentoring programs, Rajashi Ghosh and Ague Manongsong demonstrate the very construct they study in their own co-author relationship of mentor and mentee respectively. This chapter provides a review of studies on formal mentoring programs in corporations, universities, professional associations, and with entrepreneurs; critiques the design of programs and methodological rigor of this area of research from an evidence-based perspective; and suggests how to improve both the design and study of programs as interventions in the workplace.

Part II: Quantitative Methods

To begin the section on quantitative research methods in careers, Vladimer B. Kobayashi, Stefan T. Mol, Jarno Vrolijk, and Gábor Kismihók's chapter on text mining helps scholars avail themselves of the veritable bounty of textual data available today. The digitization of company personnel records coupled with data found across the Internet allows unique views into theoretical issues of interest to careers researchers. This chapter provides an approachable overview of the process of text mining and analysis, starting with acquiring the textual data, preparing the data for analysis, and then conducting the analysis. The authors provide an in-depth example of text analysis using the example of 50,000 job vacancy postings which are analyzed to shed light on salary.

Next, the chapter on conducting longitudinal research by Shoshana R. Dobrow and Hannah Weisman acknowledges that since careers by definition unfold over time, the methods we use to examine them should also build in this temporal component. Building on the authors' collective research spanning multiple years and data collections, the authors share practical advice for designing, conducting, analyzing, and ultimately publishing longitudinal research. In the process, they acknowledge the complexity inherent in managing such a project as well as the possibility of having to educate audiences less familiar with longitudinal methods as to the soundness of one's approach.

Individuals enact their careers embedded in personal and professional networks of relationships. In this chapter, Jessica R. Methot and Scott E. Seibert provide an introduction to social network analysis and develop a multi-level framework for organizing career-related network constructs. They review the study design, data collection needs, and network theory essential to exploring careers based on a social network analysis perspective. Their framework, which combines relational features (network composition, configuration, and content) and relational levels of analysis (individual, dyadic, and network), helps researchers situate their interests in this methodological toolbox. Social network analysis is a rich approach for examining a variety of topics in careers and provides many opportunities for understanding the changing nature of work.

Our understanding of contemporary careers can be improved by adopting a multi-level perspective. In this chapter, Bert Schreurs, Joeri Hofmans, and Bart Wille explain how individuals and organizations are nested within geographic boundaries, and time is nested within individuals. These complexities can be explored through multi-level modeling, which enables researchers to disentangle the effects of each level of analysis. The authors walk readers through this analysis in a step-by-step fashion, providing a clear rationale and a roadmap for fellow researchers. Finally, they discuss two opportunities for further research: individuals nested in occupations and individuals nested in romantic/partnership dyads.

Part III: Qualitative and Mixed Methods

This section begins with a chapter by Kerry Roberts Gibson and Danna Greenberg presenting an overview of the importance and relevance of grounded theory research to careers scholars. In doing so, the authors discuss a novel, understudied aspect of performing grounded theory research, whether interview, archival, or participant-observation: the relationships the researcher has with a variety of elements of the research itself. In considering the relationship of the researcher to the underlying phenomenon of interest, to their research subjects, and to the eventual audience of the work, the authors provide concrete recommendations about how to best navigate these relationships, specifically the tensions and biases that are likely to accompany them. This chapter reveals an aspect of conducting primary research that is rarely talked about, yet extremely important to manage in practice.

Qualitative, in-depth interviews offer advantages in explaining career phenomena from an insider perspective. In this chapter, Suzanne C. de Janasz and A. Julie Katz reveal how in-depth interviews produce rich data reflecting the complexity of individuals' career experiences. Researchers gain a holistic view of beliefs, attitudes, decision making, and sense-making processes when participants have the opportunity to reflect on their behavior as well as their underlying motivations. The authors explore various approaches, from unstructured to semi-structured and structured interview protocols, and discuss options and decisions around the process before, during, and after the interview itself. In doing so, they build the case for in-depth interviews as an essential methodology for building theory and understanding the unique and evolving patterns of career.

In her chapter on narrative analysis, Holly Slay Ferraro provides a comprehensive look at how careers researchers can utilize this approach to better understand how people think about their careers over time. Importantly, she describes the ability of narratives to connect individual career identities with the institutions in which they are embedded, even as these connections change and shift. Drawing upon her own research on marginalized and stigmatized communities, as well as the work of others, the author explains how narratives allow people to tell their stories, allowing us to gain insight into populations we often overlook within careers research.

Applying a mixed method approach, Allison Creed and Susan Nacey examine metaphorical language usage in career-life preparedness, an important foundation for career development. The authors explain that "metaphor identification can open a window to deeper understanding of how individuals and organizations make meaning about education and career development over the lifespan." This chapter introduces a reliable and replicable procedure for metaphor identification, which they use to investigate career guidance discourse but could be applied across other contexts or career stages. Metaphor analysis is an innovative approach to examining career narratives with the potential to reveal new or unexplored concepts in the careers domain.

Careers are complex and interdisciplinary phenomena; thus Jelena Zikic and Viktoriya Voloshyna argue that mixed methods may be the most effective research approach. In this chapter, the authors discuss the myriad benefits of integrating different data collection techniques in one study to produce insights that go beyond a single approach. They review key journals in the careers field uncovering that the vast majority of papers are from a deductive, quantitative perspective. However, careers are dynamic and difficult to separate from the rich context in which they unfold, which makes qualitative data essential for understanding the multiple influences on careers. To provide further resources, they review exemplary studies employing mixed methods. Notably, the large scale projects (5C and GETM3) introduced in the section on measurement and design support this perspective as well. Thus, the consideration of how multiple methods provide a comprehensive lens on careers is a fitting conclusion to the Handbook.

REFERENCES

Academy of Management (2020). Careers. http://www.prcoeedings.aom.org/Content.aspx?id=237#car.

Akkermans, J., Richardson, J., & Kraimer, M. (2020). The Covid-19 crisis as a career shock: Implications for careers and vocational behavior. *Journal of Vocational Behavior*, *119*, 103434.

Arthur, M. B., & Rousseau, D. M. (1996). *The Boundaryless Career: A new employment principle for a new organizational era*. Oxford, UK: Oxford University Press.

Arthur, M. B., Hall, D. T., & Lawrence, B. S. (1989). Generating new directions in career theory: The case for a transdisciplinary approach, pp. 7–25. In M. B. Arthur, D. T. Hall, & B. M. Lawrence (Eds). *Handbook of Career Theory*. Cambridge, UK: Cambridge University Press.

Belkhir, M., Brouard, M., Brunk, K. H., Dalmoro, M., Ferreira, M. C., Figueiredo, B., Scaraboto, D., Sibai, O., & Smith, A. N. (2019). Isolation in globalizing academic fields: A collaborative autoethnography of early career researchers. *Academy of Management Learning & Education*, *18*(2), 261–285.

Biemann, T., Fasang, A. E., & Grunow, D. (2011). Do economic globalization and industry growth destabilize careers? An analysis of career complexity and career patterns over time. *Organization Studies*, *32*(12), 1639–1663.

Boveda, I., & Metz, A. J. (2016). Predicting end-of-career transitions for baby boomers nearing retirement age. *The Career Development Quarterly*, *64*(2), 153–168.

Briscoe, J. P., Henagan, S. C., Burton, J. P., & Murphy, W. M. (2012). Coping with an insecure employment environment: The differing roles of protean and boundaryless career orientations. *Journal of Vocational Behavior*, *80*(2), 308–316.

Cappelli, P., & Keller, J. R. (2013). Classifying work in the new economy. *Academy of Management Review*, *38*(4), 575–596.

Dokko, G., Tosti-Kharas, J., & Barbulescu, R. (2020). Bridging micro and macro: An interdisciplinary review of theories used in career studies, pp. 25–41. In H. Gunz, M. Lazarova, & W. Mayrhofer (Eds). *The Routledge Companion to Career Studies*. London, UK: Routledge.

Duhigg, C. (2016). What Google learned from its quest to build the perfect team. *The New York Times Magazine*, February 25, 2016.

European Commission (2019). *Research and innovation – Participant portal 2020 online manual*. http://ec.europa.eu/research/participants/docs/h2020-funding-guide/cross-cutting-issues/gender_en.htm.

Michaelson, C., & Tosti-Kharas, J. (2020). A world changed: What post-9/11 stories tell us about the position of America, purpose of business, and meaning of work. *Academy of Management Review*, advanced online publication.

Ng, E. S. W., Schweitzer, L., & Lyons, S. (2010). New generation, great expectations: A field study of the Millennial Generation. *Journal of Business and Psychology*, *25*(2), 281–292.

Petriglieri, G., Ashford, S. J., & Wrzesniewski, A. (2019). Agony and ecstasy in the gig economy: Cultivating holding environments for precarious and personalized work identities. *Administrative Science Quarterly*, *64*(1), 124–170.

Schwab, K. (2016). *The Fourth Industrial Revolution*. New York: Crown.

Spreitzer, G. M., Cameron, L., & Garrett, L. (2017). Alternative work arrangements: Two images of the new world of work. *Annual Review of Organizational Psychology and Organizational Behavior*, *4*, 473–499.

Spurk, D., & Straub, C. (2020). Flexible employment relationships and careers in times of the COVID-19 pandemic. *Journal of Vocational Behavior*, *119*, 103435.

Tams, S., & Arthur, M. B. (2007). Studying careers across cultures. *Career Development International*, *12*(1), 86–98.

1. Mapping methods in careers research: a review and future research agenda

Jos Akkermans, Colin I.S.G. Lee, Sanne Nijs, Aimilia Mylona, and Janneke K. Oostrom

In their 2007 *Handbook of Career Studies*, Gunz and Peiperl described the careers literature as a Rorschach's test. Indeed, as research on careers is conducted by numerous scholars in a wide variety of disciplines (see Arthur, Hall, & Lawrence, 1989, pp. 9–10; Gunz & Peiperl, 2007, p. 3), including psychology, management, and sociology, people's perspectives of the field have long been dependent upon their discipline and niche, as well as their mindset and preconceptions. Following the Academy of Management Careers Division domain statement,[1] the field of careers research could be characterized as: "people's lifelong succession of work experiences, the structure of opportunity to work, and the relationship between careers and other aspects of life." Major topics in the field range from individual career behaviors to organizational career management, and from labor force diversity to cross-cultural careers, with a career typically being defined as "the unfolding sequence of a person's work experiences over time" (Arthur et al., 1989, p. 8).

Arguably, however, we have come a long way since Gunz and Peiperl's critique. Because of several synthetic reviews of the careers literature (e.g., Akkermans & Kubasch, 2017; Baruch, Szücs, & Gunz, 2015; Byington, Felps, & Baruch, 2019; Lee, Felps, & Baruch, 2014; Wang & Wanberg, 2017), a more consistent image has started to emerge of this diverse topic area and the relationships between its subfields. Lee et al. (2014) mapped the existing management literature on careers and found six core categories: international careers, career choice, career management, career adaptation, career success, and life opportunities. The authors conclude that there is a lack of integration between disciplines, and that, for example, management, psychology, education, and sociology could learn from each other to a much greater degree. Baruch et al. (2015) come to a similar conclusion, noting that the field of careers has focused rather narrowly on the individual career agent, for example by emphasizing topics such as career success and employability. Interestingly, the authors speculate that the dominant focus on agentic factors has been fueled by the relative ease with which these factors can be assessed with quantitative methods, and quantitative studies might be easier to publish in most journals.

In line with the reviews from Lee et al. (2014) and Baruch et al. (2015), Akkermans and Kubasch (2017) in their review of five years of careers studies found that the vast majority of them focused on micro-level concepts, and that topics such as career success, career decisions, and employability were the most frequently researched topics. They share Baruch et al.'s conclusion that quantitative studies seem to dominate the field, despite the fact that careers journals have no explicit policy on preferring quantitative over qualitative research. Wang and Wanberg (2017) looked specifically at careers research in the field of applied psychology and found similar topics that have been dominant in the field, such as career choice, career success, and career transitions. The authors also conclude that methodologies in careers research seem to have become more sophisticated since the 2000s. Finally, in a review of 23 years of research in the *Journal of Vocational Behavior*, Byington et al. (2019) again come to a similar conclusion of micro-level topics dominating the field, finding that especially the topics of career choice and worker well-being were prominent in the discourse. They add that a third, separate, category of studies appeared in their results that focused on scale development and validation.

Thus, overall, it seems that despite the inherent diversity within the field of careers (cf. Lee et al., 2014) there is actually a rather consistent picture emerging from recent review studies in terms of the topics that are at the core of the discourse. Yet, although the development of *topics* in the field of career studies has become much clearer, the development of *methods* is much less clear. The abovementioned reviews have drawn some preliminary conclusions, such as a dominant focus on quantitative research (Akkermans & Kubasch, 2017; Baruch et al., 2015), an increasing popularity of validation studies (Byington et al., 2019), and an overall increasing sophistication of methods (Wang & Wanberg, 2017). However, these claims are not yet firmly substantiated and, as such, our knowledge of the diversity and sophistication of methods used in career studies is still rather limited. Generating such an overview of methods used in careers research would benefit the development of the field because it allows us to accurately track developments in methodologies, their diversity, and their potentially increased sophistication.

For this purpose, we employ a science mapping technique, that builds on bibliometrics (i.e., the quantitative study of academic literatures) and Natural Language Processing (Zupic & Čater, 2015), to systematically examine the method sections of all papers published in five core careers journals between 2014 and 2018. Specifically, we use the VOSviewer methodology (Van Eck & Waltman, 2010, 2014) to map methods in careers research and provide an overview of the dominant categories of research methods. This approach has the advantage that it allows a broad purview of literature, forms an aid in the sensemaking process due to its interactive visualizations, and is tailored specifically to the visualization of academic documents. Unsurprisingly, it has been used in hundreds of studies, both within (e.g., Carpini, Parker, & Griffin, 2017; Markoulli, Lee, Byington, & Felps, 2017; Parker, Morgeson, & Johns, 2017; Zhao & Li, 2019) and beyond (e.g., Fergnani, 2019; Waaijer, Van Bochove, & Van Eck, 2010; Yeung, Goto, & Leung, 2017) the management literature.

METHOD

Our visualization of the methods used in careers research, was developed in four consecutive stages. First, we compiled a text corpus using the five principal careers journals in the field of management: *Career Development International* (CDI), *Career Development Quarterly* (CDQ), *Journal of Career Assessment* (JCA), *Journal of Career Development* (JCD), and the *Journal of Vocational Behavior* (JVB). From these journals, we selected all articles published between 2014 and 2018 and manually extracted the texts from the methods sections. This provided a corpus of 831 methods sections.

In the second stage, we parsed and refined the key technical terms from the methods sections. For this we used the VOSviewer software (version 1.6.11), which identifies technical terms by using Natural Language Processing, to select nouns and any preceding nouns and adjectives. As shown by Justeson and Katz (1995), this *noun phrase* selection algorithm is an effective way to identify technical terms in texts, independent of the domain.

The initial term list contained 57,702 terms. This list was then reduced to 2,048 terms, by selecting the terms that occurred in 10 or more different documents. This threshold serves to remove idiosyncratic or misspelt terms (see Van Eck, 2011). The refined term list was then coded using a coding scheme inspired by Markoulli et al. (2017) and adopted for the coding of the extracted methods sections. More specifically, we coded the terms with the following labels: "how" (i.e., data collection, analytic technique), "who" (i.e., individual actor, collective actor), "where" (i.e., location), and "what" (i.e., constructs). Terms that did not fit any of the codes were excluded. The terms that could not be coded were typically generic terms or artifacts of the use of academic article texts (e.g., "approach," "et al," "figure"). Finally, any remaining generic terms were removed using the VOSviewer relevance algorithm (Van Eck & Waltman, 2011, p. 2). This algorithm determines a term's relevance based on its distribution across the documents, and excludes 40% of the terms with the most nonspecific (i.e., generic) distribution. This led to our final list of 730 terms.

The third stage entailed the visualization of the terms, based on their relatedness. The VOSviewer determines the relatedness of terms using the *association strength* measure. For each term pair, the association strength is the ratio of co-occurrence between the two terms, over the product of the occurrence counts of the two terms (Rip & Courtial, 1984; Van Eck & Waltman, 2010). The VOSviewer then fits the association strengths in a two-dimensional image using the VOS mapping algorithm. This algorithm makes the distances between the terms on the map reflective of their respective association strengths. In other words, it minimizes the difference between the distances and the association strengths (Van Eck, Waltman, Dekker, & Van den Berg, 2010).

In the fourth and final stage, the subfields were identified using the VOS clustering algorithm (Waltman, Van Eck, & Noyons, 2010). This algorithm maximizes the sum of the association strengths between terms, while minimizing the size of the clusters, where the ratio is weighted to provide a *clustering resolution* (i.e., determines the size of the clusters). This resolution, like all other settings in the software, was left at its default value, to reduce the risk of imposing our perspective of the field on the visualization. Articles, from the original selection of 831 publications in the core careers journals, were assigned to a cluster when at least 50% of the terms extracted from its method section were located in the cluster.

FINDINGS

We found four different clusters based on the method sections of all analyzed papers. Below, we will describe each of the four clusters in detail, after which we will offer some overall observations and conclusions. Figure 1.1 shows a network visualization, where the size of the nodes represent the frequency of occurrence of a term across the 831 method sections and the distance between the terms denotes their relatedness. The full interactive map can be accessed here: http://bit.ly/map pingmethodsincareers.[2]

Green Cluster: Quantitative Methods – Applied Psychology

The first cluster is the green cluster. This cluster contains 228 terms, which makes it the largest cluster in our overview. We labeled this cluster *quantitative methods – applied psychology* as the studies within this cluster apply a range of quantitative methods and are mostly situated in the area of applied psychology, often focusing on organizational research related to proactive employee behaviors targeted at one's career or one's job. The most prominent *data collection* terms within this cluster are Utrecht Work Engagement Scale (UWES), career satisfaction scale, and time lag, and the key *data analysis terms* are common method variance, best fit, and slope. These terms relate to either the data collection (concurrent vs. longitudinal and single source vs. multiple source), often used scales, or the analysis approach (structural equation modeling and moderation analyses). Key *concepts* within this cluster are vigor, absorption, and job resource. Of all four clusters, the topics in this cluster occur in the most frequently cited papers. The five most cited articles that we linked to this cluster are those of Zacher (2014a), Tolentino, Garcia, Lu, Restubog, Bordia, and Plewa (2014), Lu, Wang, Lu, Du, and Bakker (2014), Hirschi, Herrmann, and Keller (2015), and Zacher (2014b), with citation rates ranging between 47 and 90. All five articles were published in *JVB*. Looking at the citation numbers per year, the study from Rudolph, Lavigne, and Zacher (2017b), also published in *JVB*, is the one with the highest score of 15.3 times cited per year. This study presents a meta-analysis on the relations between career adaptability and adaptivity, adapting responses, and adaptation results.

The research in this cluster is part of a relatively mature field, relying on quantitative field data in organizations, as indicated by the frequent occurrence of terms such as employee (231 times), response rate (186 times), and company (128 times). The maturity of these topics is also demonstrated by the presence of two meta-analyses

Table 1.1   Overview of the most frequent article topics per cluster in the Careers Map[a]

Cluster	Method of Data Collection	Method of Data Analysis	Sample Characteristic	Location	Concept
Quantitative Methods – Applied Psychology (Green; 228 terms)	Utrecht Work Engagement Scale (UWES)	Common method variance	Public sector	Netherlands	Vigor
	Career satisfaction scale	Best fit	Immediate supervisor	Amsterdam	Absorption
	Time lag	Slope	HR manager	Belgium	Job resource
Quantitative Methods – Vocational Psychology (Red; 219 terms)	Career decision self-efficacy scale	Estimated internal consistency reliability	Asian Indian	Southeastern United States	Self-appraisal
	Instrument development Study	Good internal consistency	American Indian	Korea	Life meaning
			Biology	Seoul	Goal selection
Qualitative Methods (Blue; 164 terms)	Interview transcript	Content analysis	Auditor	Singapore	Childhood
	Interview protocol	CCI	Interviewee		Rigor
	Interview question	Interrater reliability	Interviewer		Counseling session
Structural Equation Methods (Yellow; 119 terms)	Item level	Incremental fit index	US sample	French	Personality dimension
	Bootstrapping	MLR			Subgroup
	Observed variable	Configural invariance			

Note: [a] "Top terms" were systematically selected by identifying the terms referenced in the largest number of article titles/abstracts per cluster, per sub-category of the classification scheme. A maximum of 3 of the most frequently referenced terms were identified.

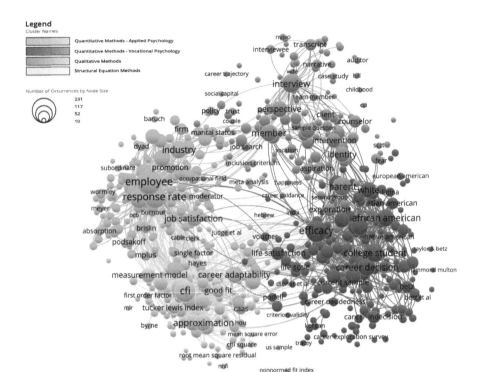

Note: For the interactive map, see: http://bit.ly/mappingmethodsincareers.

Figure 1.1   Science map of career studies methods sections

in this cluster, focusing on the antecedents and outcomes of career adaptability (Rudolph et al., 2017b) and job crafting (Rudolph, Katz, Lavigne, & Zacher, 2017a). In general, the studies build on validated models and measures, such as the Utrecht Work Engagement Scale (UWES) (Schaufeli, Bakker, & Salanova, 2006), the Job Crafting Scale (Tims, Bakker, & Derks, 2012), the Career Satisfaction Scale (Greenhaus, Parasuraman, & Wormley, 1990), and the Career Adapt-Adaptability Scale (CAAS) (Zacher, 2014a). As the CAAS is a relatively new instrument, the studies within this cluster include several validation studies (e.g., Zacher, 2014a; Öncel, 2014; Tolentino et al., 2014), explaining the frequent occurrences of the terms factor model (90 times) and single factor (43 times). In general, the methodological approaches in this cluster seem to be fairly robust, often involving longitudinal or multiple wave designs (e.g., Harju, Hakanen, & Schaufeli, 2016; Hirschi et al., 2015; Guan et al., 2014; Lu et al., 2014; Nohe & Sonntag, 2014), diary studies (e.g., Breevaart, Bakker, & Demerouti, 2014; Goh, Ilies, & Wilson, 2015; Zacher, Brailsford, & Parker, 2014; Zacher, 2015), and employee–supervisor dyads (e.g.,

Demerouti, Bakker, & Gevers, 2015). It should be noted that the vast majority of the studies with such multiple wave and multi-source designs was published in *JVB*.

The career crafting studies within the green cluster look at a broad range of predictors and outcomes of career adaptability. The most often studied predictors include personality traits (Zacher, 2014a, Tolentino et al., 2014), self-esteem (Cai et al., 2015), and the outcomes include career satisfaction (Zacher, 2014a) and perceived career growth (Waters, Briscoe, Hall, & Wang, 2014). The green cluster was also the main cluster for studies on employability (e.g., Forrier, Verbruggen, & De Cuyper, 2015; Onyishi, Enwereuzor, Ituma, & Omenma, 2015; Oostrom, Pennings, & Bal, 2016; Van der Heijden et al., 2018). The job crafting studies mostly build on the job demands-resources (JD-R) model (Bakker & Demerouti, 2017; Demerouti, Bakker, Nachreiner, & Schaufeli, 2001). The studies within this cluster concentrate on the outcomes of job crafting, with work engagement being the most often studied outcome (Breevaart et al., 2014; Demerouti et al., 2015; Harju et al., 2016; Lu et al., 2014). There are also studies in this cluster that focus on work-related attitudes, motivation, and well-being, such as Caesens, Stinglhamber, and Luypaert's (2014) study on the impact of work engagement and workaholism on well-being, Akkermans, De Lange, Van Der Heijden, Kooij, Jansen, and Dikkers' (2016) work on age and motivation, and McCallum, Forret, and Wolff's (2014) study on networking behaviors and commitment.

Red Cluster: Quantitative Methods – Vocational Psychology

The second largest cluster is the red cluster, containing 219 terms. We labeled this cluster *quantitative methods – vocational psychology* as the studies apply a range of quantitative methods and are mostly situated in the area of vocational psychology and counseling. Prominent *data collection* terms in this cluster were career decision self-efficacy scale, instrument development, and study, and the key *data analysis* terms were estimated internal consistency, reliability, and good internal consistency. The prominent *concepts* were self-appraisal, life meaning, and goal selection. The five most cited papers that were linked to the cluster are Di Fabio and Kenny (2015), Praskova, Hood, and Creed (2014), Moakler and Kim (2014), Allan, Autin, and Duffy (2014), and Navarro, Flores, Lee, and Gonzalez (2014), with citation numbers ranging between 25 and 47. Two additional articles show up when looking at the number of citations per year. Besides the article of Di Fabio and Kenny (9.4 times per year), which also has the highest number of citations per year, the studies from Fouad, Singh, Cappaert, Chang, and Wan (2016) and Lent, Ireland, Penn, Morris, and Sappington (2017) are a shared runner up with six citations per year. The top-cited papers in this cluster were published showing a larger diversity of journals compared to the green cluster, with *CDQ*, *JCA*, *JCD*, and *JVB* all being represented.

Although all studies in the red cluster use quantitative methods, there is no clear pattern or specific approach that is most dominant. The majority of studies have used correlational and regression analyses, with 20 studies in the top 50 most cited articles testing a mediation model, sometimes in multi-wave studies (e.g., Garcia,

Restubog, Bordia, Bordia, & Roxas, 2015; Houlfort, Fernet, Vallerand, Laframboise, Guay, & Koestner, 2015; Praskova et al., 2014) but also using cross-sectional designs (e.g., Allan et al., 2014; Douglass & Duffy, 2015; Ezeofor & Lent, 2014; Miller & Rottinghaus, 2014). The term moderation was also mentioned 14 times, indicating that the majority of these studies tested a mediation and/or moderation model. However, structural equation modeling techniques are rarely applied in this cluster. The emphasis in this cluster lies on reporting psychometric properties of scales (e.g., scale score, internal consistency, short form), which is in line with the counseling literature that often reports on the quality of counseling tools and techniques (cf. Whiston, Li, Goodrich Mitts, & Wright, 2017).

A detailed inspection of the map shows two distinct patterns of terms: those related to the samples and those related to the topics used in this cluster. In terms of samples, we observe the dominant use of student and young adult samples, as evidenced by terms such as college student (128 times), undergraduate student (95 times), and sophomore (60 times). In fact, 32 out of the 50 most cited papers used students (27 times) or young people (5 times), which coincides with a predominant focus on early career choices and decisions within the discipline of vocational and counseling psychology (cf. Fouad & Kozlowski, 2019). Another clear pattern in terms of samples is that the red cluster has many rather specific samples, as shown by often occurring terms such as African American (115 times), Asian American (51 times), Native American (41 times), South Korean (29 times), and Latina (32 times). Most of these studies deliberately focused on these target groups in their research, for example Moakler and Kim (2014) examined whether African American and Latina students would choose a STEM career, Sovet and Metz (2014) who compared the role of parenting style in adolescent career decision-making among French and Korean youth, and Douglass, Duffy, and Autin (2015) who compared experiences of calling among US and Indian workers. At the same time, it also points towards a rather large diversity of samples across the world, including Korea (Jung, Park, & Rie, 2015), Israel and China (Willner, Gati, & Guan, 2015), Angola and Mozambique (Lent et al., 2014), Italy (Kozan, Di Fabio, Blustein, & Kenny, 2014), and Malaysia (Lam & Santos, 2018).

In terms of the topics, the studies predominantly focus on issues related to vocational psychology and counseling, with the most prominent terms being career decision (124 times), career choice (83 times), life satisfaction (73 times), career indecision (61 times), future career (48 times), and calling (36 times). At the core of these topics is the idea of vocational/career choice and career decisions, for example Fouad et al. (2016) studied whether women would pursue and remain in an engineering career, and Willner et al. (2015) studied career decision-making profiles and their implications for career counselors. Also of note is that Career Construction theory – often in the form of career adaptability as a focal construct – and Social Cognitive Career Theory (SCCT) were often used and tested in the red cluster: among the top 50 most cited studies, 7 studies were about career adaptability, and an additional 13 studies mention SCCT. Career adaptability was studied both as an outcome (e.g., of calling (Praskova et al., 2014; Douglass & Duffy, 2015) and career decision-making

self-efficacy (Guan, Capezio, Restubog, Read, Lajom, & Li, 2016)) and an antecedent (e.g., of academic satisfaction (Duffy, Douglass, & Autin, 2015)) and life satisfaction (Buyukgoze-Kavas, Duffy, & Douglass, 2015). SCCT's premises were often
tested in different target groups, such as white and Latino engineering major students
(Lee, Flores, Navarro, & Kanagui-Muñoz, 2015), African college students (Lent et
al., 2014), and South Korean engineering students (Kim & Seo, 2014).

Blue Cluster: Qualitative Methods

The third cluster we identified is the blue cluster. This cluster was labeled the
qualitative methods cluster because it reflects the variety of methods, approaches,
and instruments mostly used in qualitative research on careers. The cluster contains
164 terms. The most prominent *data collection terms* in the blue cluster are interview transcript, interview protocol and interview question. The term interview was
mentioned a total of 135 times and consequently takes up a central position in the
map. The most prominent *data analysis terms* are content analysis, CCI (i.e., Career
Construction Interview) and interrater reliability. Key *concepts* in the blue cluster
are childhood, rigor, and counseling session, which may indicate that qualitative
research is especially prominent in the stream of research on vocational psychology
and counseling, which often use samples of young individuals. This is supported
by the map, which shows considerable overlap between the blue and red clusters.
The five most cited articles in the blue cluster are the articles of Lengelle, Meijers,
Poell, and Post (2014), Cardoso, Silva, Gonçalves, and Duarte (2014), Lewis, Harris,
Morrison, and Ho (2015), Ryba, Ronkainen, and Selänne (2015), and Nota, Santilli,
and Soresi (2016). In this top five, the number of citations ranged between 14 and
17, which is still relatively low. When zooming in on the highest number of citations
per year, the article from Nota et al. is the top cited paper with 3.5 citations per year,
closely followed by the work of Whiston et al. (2017) with 3.3 citations per year.
The top five cited studies in the blue cluster were a mix of articles published in *CDI*,
CDQ, and *JVB*.

A visual inspection of the map shows that, next to the prominent terms mentioned
in Table 1.1, the following terms take up a central position in the blue cluster: parent
(139 times), member (117 times), and perspective (103 times). Since these terms
give only limited insight into actual methods for data collection and data analysis, we
scanned the map for additional terms that help us come to a clearer understanding of
the methods used in this cluster. In terms of qualitative methods for collecting and
analyzing data, narrative analysis (38 times), case studies (20 times), focus groups
(17 times), and content analysis (17 times) were recurring terms. Assessing the interrater reliability seems to be a quality criterion that multiple authors (e.g., Shoffner,
Newsome, Minton, & Morris, 2015; McWhirter, Luginbuhl, & Brown, 2014) adopt
in order to ensure the rigor of their qualitative studies. It is interesting to note that
although content analysis and narrative analysis were mentioned rather frequently in
this cluster, the term discourse analysis was largely absent in the analyzed articles.
Of the 50 most cited articles of this cluster only the article of Simosi, Rousseau,

and Daskalaki (2015) adopted a grounded theory methodology to study how young professionals describe their career paths in the aftermath of the 2008 Financial Crisis. The Gioia methodology (Gioia, Corley, & Hamilton, 2013) and Charmaz's approach to Grounded Theory research (Charmaz, 2006) – established approaches for conducting inductive qualitative research – were not explicitly referenced frequently enough to appear on the map.

A closer analysis of the 50 most cited articles in the blue cluster shows that most interview studies (e.g., case studies, focus groups) aim to come to a deeper understanding of changes in vocational identity and/or career outcomes (e.g., Di Fabio, 2016). Accordingly, identity takes up a central position in the map. Multiple articles analyze these topics from a Career Construction perspective. Maree (2016), for example, applied the Career Construction Interview (i.e., CCI) to gain insights into the career-life related challenges black employees experience. Although the majority of these studies was interested in life stories, career transitions, and career changes, only a few authors employed a longitudinal approach, an exception being Lewis et al. (2015), who adopted a qualitative longitudinal research design to study the interplay between life-stages and career transitions for women over a four-year period. Other qualitative studies in this cluster focused on exploring career boundaries and boundarylessness (e.g., Afiouni, 2014; Okay-Somerville & Scholarios, 2014) as well as international careers and expatriation (e.g., Baruch & Forstenlechner, 2017; Shortland, 2014).

While most articles included in the blue cluster adopt a qualitative design – hence the label of the cluster – some quantitative studies (e.g., Gross-Spector & Cinamon, 2018), a meta-analysis (Whiston et al., 2017) and conceptual/review papers (e.g., Akkermans & Kubasch, 2017; Dispenza, Brown, & Chastain, 2016) were represented in the cluster. The most impactful non-qualitative studies – in terms of yearly citations – (meta-) analyzed the effectiveness of career interventions on outcomes, such as career adaptability and life satisfaction (Nota et al., 2016), and vocational identity (Whiston et al., 2017). Out of the 50 most cited articles, two articles adopted a mixed method approach: Shortland (2014) combined surveys and semi-structured interviews to investigate how female role models support women to take up expatriate assignments in a male-dominated industry, and Cinamon and Rich (2014) used mixed methods to investigate future work and family roles among at-risk Israeli adolescents.

Yellow Cluster: Structural Equation Methods

The fourth cluster we identified is the yellow cluster, which consists of 119 terms, considerably less than the 162 to 228 terms in the other clusters. We labeled this cluster *structural equation methods*, because it contains a relatively large number of articles in which (1) (confirmatory) factor analyses related to the psychometric properties of (new) measures are examined, or (2) structural relations between antecedents and outcomes of career-related variables are examined. The three most prominent *data collection* terms are item level, bootstrapping, and observed variable, and the three most prominent *data analysis* terms are incremental fit index, MLR (i.e., Multiple Linear Regression), and configural invariance. Key *concepts* are personality, dimension, and subgroup. The five most cited articles linked to this cluster are, in order of the number of citations, Santilli, Nota, Ginevra, and Soresi (2014), Wilkins, Santilli, Ferrari, Nota, Tracey, and Soresi (2014), Van den Broeck, Sulea, Vander Elst, Fischmann, Iliescu, and De Witte (2014), Fiori, Bollmann, and Rossier (2015), and Sortheix, Chow, and Salmela-Aro (2015). The study of Maggiori, Rossier, and Savickas (2017) had the highest number of citations per year, with 4.7 citations. The top five cited articles in the yellow cluster were all published in *JVB*, with the exception of one article that was published in *CDI*.

A visual inspection of the yellow cluster in the map shows that, next to the prominent terms in the table, the following terms take up a central position based on their number of occurrences: CFI (i.e., comparative fit index; 180 times), approximation (117 times), TLI (i.e., Tucker Lewis index; 79 times), and good fit (70 times). Although structural equation modeling (SEM) as a term does not take up a central place in the map, a closer inspection of the articles and terms shows that articles adopting SEM do not always use the exact same terms when describing their methods (e.g., structural equation, structural equation model, structural equation modeling and structural model). Consequently, the term SEM is underrepresented in the map. However, the frequently occurring words presented above closely relate to this particular approach.

The yellow cluster contains terms from 13 different articles in which new or adapted measures are introduced and their psychometric properties (e.g., underlying factor structures) are tested through SEM analyses. For example, Malo, Tremblay, and Brunet (2016) developed a measurement of Cognitive Adjustment at Work (CAW), Etzel and Nagy (2015) introduced and validated a three-factor model of person–environment fit, Perreira, Morin, Hebert, Gillet, Houle, and Berta (2018) developed a short version of the Workplace Affective Commitment Multidimensional Questionnaire (WACMQ-S), Morgan, de Bruin, and de Bruin (2015) developed the South-African Career Interest Inventory, and Maggiori, Nihil, Froidevaux, and Rossier (2014) introduced a new tool for people preparing for retirement, the Transition to Retirement Questionnaire (TRQ). These validation studies were mostly published in *JCA* and *JVB*.

The cluster also contains four studies in which SEM is used to test the measurement equivalence of existing measures. Carr and colleagues (Abrams, Lee, Brown, & Carr, 2015; Carr et al., 2014; Roche, Carr, Lee, Wen, & Brown, 2017) tested the measurement equivalence of the Career Indecision Profile-65 (CIP-65) between US samples, European samples, and Asian samples. Furthermore, Spurk, Abele, and Volmer (2015) examined the measurement invariance of the Career Satisfaction Scale (CSC) across different occupational groups (e.g., physicians, economists, engineers, and teachers). The remaining articles adopt SEM in both cross sectional studies (e.g., Lichtenthaler & Fischbach, 2016) and longitudinal studies (e.g., Perera & McIlveen, 2014), to test structural relations (i.e., path models) between the antecedents and outcomes of various career-related variables. For example, Santilli et al. (2014) examined a partial mediation model between career adaptability and life satisfaction through agency and hope, and Van den Broeck et al. (2014) examined whether qualitative job insecurity is related to counterproductive work behavior via autonomy, belongingness, and competence. Furthermore, Froehlich, Beausaert, Segers, and Gerken (2014) used SEM to study the effect of chronical age and informal and formal learning activities on employability, Preenen, Verbiest, Van Vianen, and Van Wijk (2015) studied the relationship between career competencies and learning, and De Vos, Forrier, Van der Heijden, and De Cuyper (2017) examined the role of occupational expertise in job search intensity.

Overall Observations and Conclusions

A number of conclusions can be drawn from the analysis of the four clusters that we found when analyzing all published papers in *JVB*, *CDI*, *CDQ*, *JCA*, and *JCD*.

Quantitative research dominates the careers field

Prior overview studies had already noted that the field of careers research is dominated by quantitative studies (e.g., Akkermans & Kubasch, 2017; Baruch et al., 2015). Our analysis of the methods used in these studies shows a similar picture as quantitative studies were clearly the most often used, being a prominent part of the green, red, and yellow clusters. However, it should be noted that there was a large diversity of quantitative approaches in these clusters, ranging from scale development, to structural equation modeling, to regression, to group comparisons. These findings shows that the methods in the field are just as diverse as the field is in terms of topics and perspectives (cf. Lee et al., 2014; Gunz & Peiperl, 2007).

Although quantitative research was clearly dominant, we did find a cluster linked to qualitative research as well. Thus, despite previous observations that qualitative research is not published very often in the field of careers (cf. Akkermans & Kubasch, 2017), our analysis shows a more nuanced picture. First, qualitative research seems to be predominantly linked to the vocational psychology and counseling literature, and much less to the applied psychology discipline. The map also shows a stronger connection between the blue and red clusters vs. the blue and green clusters. Second, the qualitative methods cluster was not only the smallest in term count, but was also linked to the articles with the fewest citations. This arguably creates a reinforcing pattern, in which there is less qualitative research in the field of career studies, and these studies also get cited less often. If we would speculate further, these findings also seem to show that quantitative and qualitative research communities are rather disconnected, even though the topics they study are often highly similar.

Methods seem to be linked to disciplines and journals

After analyzing the clusters, we found that the green and red clusters represent two distinct disciplines: although both clusters primarily used quantitative designs, the former was grounded in applied psychology whereas the latter was grounded in vocational psychology and counseling. Some of the key differences between these clusters – which fit with existing norms in the respective disciplines – were: (1) the samples (field studies and general worker samples in green vs. student, young adult, and specific target group samples in red), (2) the analysis techniques (SEM in green vs. regression in red), and (3) the most popular topics (proactive work and career behaviors in green vs. career decisions and choices in red). The separation between these two disciplines also becomes clear when looking at the map as the green and red clusters have only very few connecting terms, whereas they are both quite intimately linked to the blue and yellow clusters, with green most strongly to yellow, and red most strongly to blue. This latter observation indicates that although qualitative research and structural methods are used across disciplines, qualitative methods are more often used in vocational psychology, whereas structural methods are more often used in applied psychology. Thus, these findings imply that there is a rather big separation between the applied psychology and vocational psychology disciplines in *how* they study careers. Our findings support and expand on the conclusion from Fouad and Kozlowski (2019), who note that the mainstream psychology and vocational psychology fields remain separated from each other, a problem that was raised almost 20 years ago and still persists today. Based on our analysis, we can conclude that this does not only hold in terms of topics but also in terms of the methodological approaches used and even the primary journals published in.

Indeed, there also seems to be a difference between journals in this regard. The applied psychology (green) cluster is most strongly represented in *JVB* and *CDI*, who together make up 160 out of 207 studies in this cluster. The vocational psychology cluster is mostly represented in *JVB* and *JCA*, who together have 101 of 159 publications in the cluster (of note, *CDI* only had 1 article in the red cluster). The blue and yellow clusters have a less clear distinction of journals, which also relates to how strongly connected they are to other clusters in the map. In the qualitative methods cluster, *CDI* (21 articles), *CDQ* (22 articles) and *JCD* (23 articles) are almost identical in numbers of articles, whereas *JCA* (7 articles) did not have many articles. An explanation for the latter is that the journal is primarily aimed at assessment and measurement. Of note, *JVB* was also relatively poorly represented in the blue cluster with only 30 out of 104 articles (whereas *JVB* had the most papers in all other clusters), indicating that this journal published relatively few qualitative studies in the last five years. The structural equation methods cluster showed the most similarity with the applied psychology cluster in terms of journal outlets, as *JVB* (14 of 52 articles) and *CDI* (12 of 52 articles) together made up over half of the cluster. Interestingly, though, *JCA* was most prominent in the yellow structural equation methods cluster with 20 articles, which would fit with the journal's focus on instrument validation, where structural techniques such as confirmatory factor analyses are commonly applied. *JCD* (5 articles) and especially *CDQ* (1 article) were poorly represented in the yellow cluster, indicating that these two journals do not publish many studies that apply structural equation methods.

Methods in careers research are solid yet not always innovative
Overall, our analysis supports Wang and Wanberg's (2017) conclusion about the increased sophistication of methods in careers research, at least during the past five years. Looking at the entire spectrum of methods and techniques that were used in the studies between 2014 and 2018, we can see that studies have started to incorporate robust designs and analyses. For example, the yellow cluster represents structural methods and validation studies, and the green cluster featured a lot of studies that used SEM techniques. Furthermore, there were quite a lot of studies that used multi-wave designs, both short-term and long-term, and also multiple studies in one paper to cross-validate findings. In all, this means that the field of career studies has not only shed its reputation as a Rorschach's test in terms of topics, but also in terms of methodologies, as they have become increasingly robust in recent years.

At the same time, the vast majority of the research was still rather traditional in terms of methods and techniques. For example, we found only very few quantitative studies that used dynamic within-person designs – such as latent growth models and functional cluster analyses (Hofmans, Vantilborgh, & Solinger, 2018) – to study processes and changes over time. This would seem to be an ideal approach when studying careers, which are by definition temporal phenomena. Similarly, qualitative research in the field has mostly been static rather than adopting a dynamic design, and recently developed opportunities for analyzing large qualitative samples, for example through text mining (Kobayashi, Mol, Berkers, Kismihók, & Den Hartog, 2017), have not been mobilized yet in the field. In all, we would cautiously conclude that the field of careers is certainly making progress in terms of quality of methods, yet seems to be somewhat behind on the latest developments that are applied, for example, in organizational behavior and IO psychology research.

RESEARCH AGENDA

A career is typically defined as a *sequence* of a person's *work experiences* that *unfold over time* (Arthur et al., 1989). This definition implies that careers are, by definition, a temporal and dynamic phenomenon, in which past, current, and future experiences and expectations interact with each other to form career narratives. Although we can conclude from our analyses that researchers are increasingly adopting multiple wave designs – especially in the applied psychology quantitative cluster – we also noticed that, in general, career studies often use methodologies that imply a relatively static and isolated career. That is: studies often focus on short-term processes and developments, and they rarely take into account past and future events or expectations. Interestingly, some studies seem to theoretically embrace the dynamic nature of the career, but do not always align this with methods capable of grasping this dynamic element. We acknowledge the inherent difficulties of setting up long-term studies that can take into account prior and current work experiences, and future expectations of work experiences. Yet, as a first suggestion and in line with a recent call in career sustainability research (De Vos, Van der Heijden, & Akkermans, 2020; Van der

Heijden et al., 2020), we challenge scholars – quantitative and qualitative alike – to examine such processes in more detail. For example, a recent qualitative study by Richardson and McKenna (2020) posited that professional sports players in highly physically demanding sports (e.g., rugby, hockey) would have an inherently unsustainable career, yet found that in the long-term their status as a well-known expert often resulted in many opportunities as analysts or for public campaigns. Similarly, while some people engage in career transitions because they want to experience a change, others may be pushed into such changes unexpectedly after experiencing a career shock (e.g., getting a sudden promotion as a positive shock, or being laid off as a negative shock; cf. Akkermans, Seibert, & Mol, 2018 for a conceptualization and review).

In order to move the field forward, career scholars could focus on sequences of career experiences in their research. Different methods – depending on the specific research question – could be valuable to generate more knowledge on these sequences and transitions. For this purpose scholars could, for example, use narrative analyses in qualitative research (see Chapter 13 by Ferraro), mixed methods studies (see Chapter 15 by Zikic and Voloshyna), and long-term longitudinal data (see Chapter 8 by Dobrow and Weisman). The field of career studies could also benefit from designs used in sociology studies, as these often use longer-term panel studies, such as longitudinal data applied across different countries (e.g., Abendroth, Huffman, & Treas, 2014) using objective firm data (e.g., Briscoe & Kellogg, 2011), and examining group-based developmental trajectories (e.g., Frech & Damaske, 2019). Please note that we are not stating that all research should be temporal, as cross-sectional "snapshots" can be valuable if they fit a particular research question, such as comparing different groups or when studying highly stable predictors of career outcomes (e.g., personality).

A second suggestion for future research in the field of careers is that we would advocate for a stronger cross-over of knowledge and methods between disciplines. In line with previous reviews (e.g., Fouad & Kozlowski, 2019), we found a rather strict distinction between the disciplines of applied psychology and vocational psychology, as evidenced by their almost complete separation in the map. Although the research questions and topics are generally highly similar – for example studying career success, career decision-making, and career transitions – the approach to studying these research questions differs considerably. Perhaps the best example is the topic of career adaptability, which was prominent in both the applied psychology (e.g., Waters et al., 2014; Zacher, 2014a) and vocational psychology (e.g., Duffy et al., 2015; Praskova et al., 2014) cluster. However, the two disciplines tend to use different methods (e.g., SEM vs. regression), with different samples (e.g., organizational vs. student samples) and focus on different topics (e.g., personality and career success vs. calling and academic satisfaction). More cross-over between disciplines would benefit the field of careers both in terms of consolidating our knowledge of topics as well as methodological approaches. In terms of the latter, when testing mediation and moderation models, studies in vocational psychology can borrow insights from applied psychology in terms of structural equation methods. Conversely, applied psychology scholars could learn from vocational psychologists in terms of using specific samples and contexts in their research.

In our conclusions and future research suggestions, we have offered various suggestions for mobilizing particular research methods in the field of career studies. However, we want to emphasize that this should not be a goal in itself. Rather, the research question is always leading in the choice of methods. An interesting observation in our results, though, is that certain methodologies seem to be more common in certain disciplines and journals. While this could of course be related to the types of research questions asked, we would speculate that an important reason for this is also the norms and "culture" in a particular discipline, and the policies of the journals that publish the articles. In the field of careers, for example, there seems to be a trend of journals from applied psychology to consider studies with cross-sectional self-report data only in exceptional circumstances,[3] likely being a key driver of the increase in multiple wave studies in the green cluster. As a final call for future research, we would urge both the people executing the research and those publishing the research that they are aware of such norms and cultures, and assess whether the chosen methods are the most appropriate ones for answering a particular research question. This could open up opportunities for more interdisciplinary research on careers.

NOTES

1.   https://car.aom.org/about-us/new-item2.
2.   The map can be viewed on any computer that has the free Java software installed (presently requires version 8 or higher). Once opened, the map file automatically connects to the map data over the user's Internet connection and displays the interactive map. For more information, please see the VOSviewer manual: http://www.vosviewer.com/download/f-x2y2.pdf.
3.   See e.g., https://onlinelibrary.wiley.com/page/journal/20448325/homepage/forauthors.html for a description of the *Journal of Occupational and Organizational Psychology* deals with cross-sectional self-report data.

REFERENCES

Abendroth, A.-K., Huffman, M. L., & Treas, J. (2014). The parity penalty in life course perspective: Motherhood and occupational status in 13 European countries. *American Sociological Review, 79*(5), 993–1014. doi:10.1177/0003122414545986

Abrams, M. D., Lee, I. H., Brown, S. D., & Carr, A. (2015). The career indecision profile: Measurement equivalence in the United States and South Korea. *Journal of Career Assessment, 23*(2), 225–235. doi:10.1177/1069072714535028

Afiouni, F. (2014). Women's careers in the Arab Middle East: Understanding institutional constraints to the boundaryless career view. *Career Development International, 19*(3), 314–336. doi:10.1108/CDI-05-2013-0061

Akkermans, J., De Lange, A. H., Van Der Heijden, B. I. J. M., Kooij, D. T. A. M., Jansen, P. G. W., & Dikkers, J. S. E. (2016). What about time? Examining chronological and subjective age and their relation to work motivation. *Career Development International, 21*(4), 419–439. doi:10.1108/CDI-04-2016-0063

Akkermans, J., & Kubasch, S. (2017). #Trending topics in careers: A review and future research agenda. *Career Development International, 22*(6), 586–627. doi:10.1108/CDI-08-2017-0143

Akkermans, J., Seibert, S. E., & Mol, S. T. (2018). Tales of the unexpected: Integrating career shocks in the contemporary careers literature. *SA Journal of Industrial Psychology, 44*, e1503. doi:10.4102/sajip.v44i0.1503

Allan, B. A., Autin, K. L., & Duffy, R. D. (2014). Examining social class and work meaning within the psychology of working framework. *Journal of Career Assessment, 22*(4), 543–561. doi:10.1177/1069072713514811

Arthur, M. B., Hall, D. T., & Lawrence, B. S. (1989). *Handbook of career theory*. New York: Cambridge University Press.

Bakker, A. B., & Demerouti, E. (2017). Job demands–resources theory: Taking stock and looking forward. *Journal of Occupational Health Psychology, 22*(3), 273–285. doi:10.1037/ocp0000056

Baruch, Y., & Forstenlechner, I. (2017). Global careers in the Arabian Gulf: Understanding motives for self-initiated expatriation of the highly skilled, globally mobile professionals. *Career Development International, 22*(1), 3–22. doi:10.1108/CDI-12-2015-0164

Baruch, Y., Szücs, N., & Gunz, H. (2015). Career studies in search of theory: The rise and rise of concepts. *Career Development International, 20*(1), 3–20. doi:10.1108/CDI-11-2013-0137

Breevaart, K., Bakker, A. B., & Demerouti, E. (2014). Daily self-management and employee work engagement. *Journal of Vocational Behavior, 84*(1), 31–38. doi:10.1016/j.jvb.2013.11.002

Briscoe, F., & Kellogg, K. C. (2011). The initial assignment effect: Local employer practices and positive career outcomes for work–family program users. *American Sociological Review, 76*(2), 291–319. doi:10.1177/0003122411401250

Buyukgoze-Kavas, A., Duffy, R. D., & Douglass, R. P. (2015). Exploring links between career adaptability, work volition, and well-being among Turkish students. *Journal of Vocational Behavior, 90*, 122–131. doi:10.1016/j.jvb.2015.08.006

Byington, E. K., Felps, W., & Baruch, Y. (2019). Mapping the *Journal of Vocational Behavior*: A 23-year review. *Journal of Vocational Behavior, 110*, 229–244. doi:10.1016/j.jvb.2018.07.007

Caesens, G., Stinglhamber, F., & Luypaert, G. (2014). The impact of work engagement and workaholism on well-being: The role of work-related social support. *Career Development International, 19*(7), 813–835. doi:10.1108/CDI-09-2013-0114

Cai, Z., Guan, Y., Li, H., Shi, W., Guo, K., Liu, Y., ... Hua, H. (2015). Self-esteem and proactive personality as predictors of future work self and career adaptability: An examination of mediating and moderating processes. *Journal of Vocational Behavior, 86*, 86–94. doi:10.1016/j.jvb.2014.10.004

Cardoso, P., Silva, J. R., Gonçalves, M. M., & Duarte, M. E. (2014). Narrative innovation in life design counseling: The case of Ryan. *Journal of Vocational Behavior, 85*(3), 276–286. doi:10.1016/j.jvb.2014.08.001

Carpini, J. A., Parker, S. K., & Griffin, M. A. (2017). A look back and a leap forward: A review and synthesis of the individual work performance literature. *Academy of Management Annals, 11*(2), 825–885. doi:10.5465/annals.2015.0151

Carr, A., Rossier, J., Rosselet, J. G., Massoudi, K., Bernaud, J.-L., Ferrari, L., ... Roche, M. (2014). The career indecision profile: Measurement equivalence in two international samples. *Journal of Career Assessment, 22*(1), 123–137. doi:10.1177/1069072713492930

Charmaz, K. (2006). *Constructing grounded theory. A practical guide through qualitative analysis*. Thousand Oaks, CA: Sage Publications.

Cinamon, R. G., & Rich, Y. (2014). Work and family plans among at-risk Israeli adolescents: A mixed-methods study. *Journal of Career Development, 41*(3), 163–184. doi:10.1177/0894845313507748

De Vos, A., Forrier, A., Van der Heijden, B., & De Cuyper, N. (2017). Keep the expert! Occupational expertise, perceived employability and job search: A study across age groups. *Career Development International, 22*(3), 318–332. doi:10.1108/CDI-12-2016-0229

De Vos, A., Van der Heijden, B. I. J. M., & Akkermans, J. (2020). Sustainable careers: Towards a conceptual model. *Journal of Vocational Behavior, 117*, 103196. doi:10.1016/j.jvb.2018.06.011

Demerouti, E., Bakker, A. B., & Gevers, J. M. P. (2015). Job crafting and extra-role behavior: The role of work engagement and flourishing. *Journal of Vocational Behavior, 91*, 87–96. doi:10.1016/j.jvb.2015.09.001

Demerouti, E., Bakker, A. B., Nachreiner, F., & Schaufeli, W. B. (2001). The job demands–resources model of burnout. *Journal of Applied Psychology, 86*(3), 499–512. doi:10.1037/0021-9010.86.3.499

Di Fabio, A. (2016). Life design and career counseling innovative outcomes. *Career Development Quarterly, 64*(1), 35–48. doi:10.1002/cdq.12039

Di Fabio, A., & Kenny, M. E. (2015). The contributions of emotional intelligence and social support for adaptive career progress among Italian youth. *Journal of Career Development, 42*(1), 48–59. doi:10.1177/0894845314533420

Dispenza, F., Brown, C., & Chastain, T. E. (2016). Minority stress across the career–lifespan trajectory. *Journal of Career Development, 43*(2), 103–115. doi:10.1177/0894845315580643

Douglass, R. P., & Duffy, R. D. (2015). Calling and career adaptability among undergraduate students. *Journal of Vocational Behavior, 86*, 58–65. doi:10.1016/j.jvb.2014.11.003

Douglass, R. P., Duffy, R. D., & Autin, K. L. (2015). Living a calling, nationality, and life satisfaction: A moderated, multiple mediator model. *Journal of Career Assessment, 24*(2), 253–269. doi:10.1177/1069072715580324

Duffy, R. D., Douglass, R. P., & Autin, K. L. (2015). Career adaptability and academic satisfaction: Examining work volition and self efficacy as mediators. *Journal of Vocational Behavior, 90*, 46–54. doi:10.1016/j.jvb.2015.07.007

Etzel, J. M., & Nagy, G. (2015). Students' perceptions of person–environment fit: Do fit perceptions predict academic success beyond personality traits? *Journal of Career Assessment, 24*(2), 270–288. doi:10.1177/1069072715580325

Ezeofor, I., & Lent, R. W. (2014). Social cognitive and self-construal predictors of well-being among African college students in the US. *Journal of Vocational Behavior, 85*(3), 413–421. doi:10.1016/j.jvb.2014.09.003

Fergnani, A. (2019). Mapping futures studies scholarship from 1968 to present: A bibliometric review of thematic clusters, research trends, and research gaps. *Futures, 105*, 104–123. doi:10.1016/j.futures.2018.09.007

Fiori, M., Bollmann, G., & Rossier, J. (2015). Exploring the path through which career adaptability increases job satisfaction and lowers job stress: The role of affect. *Journal of Vocational Behavior, 91*, 113–121. doi:10.1016/j.jvb.2015.08.010

Forrier, A., Verbruggen, M., & De Cuyper, N. (2015). Integrating different notions of employability in a dynamic chain: The relationship between job transitions, movement capital and perceived employability. *Journal of Vocational Behavior, 89*, 56–64. doi:10.1016/j.jvb.2015.04.007

Fouad, N. A., & Kozlowski, M. B. (2019). Turning around to look ahead: Views of vocational psychology in 2001 and 2019. *Journal of Career Assessment, 27*(3), 375–390. doi:10.1177/1069072719841602

Fouad, N. A., Singh, R., Cappaert, K., Chang, W.-H., & Wan, M. (2016). Comparison of women engineers who persist in or depart from engineering. *Journal of Vocational Behavior, 92*, 79–93. doi:10.1016/j.jvb.2015.11.002

Frech, A., & Damaske, S. (2019). Men's income trajectories and physical and mental health at midlife. *American Journal of Sociology, 124*(5), 1372–1412. doi:10.1086/702775

Froehlich, D. E., Beausaert, S., Segers, M., & Gerken, M. (2014). Learning to stay employable. *Career Development International, 19*(5), 508–525. doi:10.1108/CDI-11-2013-0139

Garcia, P. R. J. M., Restubog, S. L. D., Bordia, P., Bordia, S., & Roxas, R. E. O. (2015). Career optimism: The roles of contextual support and career decision-making self-efficacy. *Journal of Vocational Behavior, 88*, 10–18. doi:10.1016/j.jvb.2015.02.004

Gioia, D. A., Corley, K. G., & Hamilton, A. L. (2013). Seeking qualitative rigor in inductive research: Notes on the Gioia methodology. *Organizational Research Methods, 16*(1), 15–31. doi:10.1177/1094428112452151

Goh, Z., Ilies, R., & Wilson, K. S. (2015). Supportive supervisors improve employees' daily lives: The role supervisors play in the impact of daily workload on life satisfaction via work–family conflict. *Journal of Vocational Behavior, 89*, 65–73. doi:10.1016/j.jvb.2015.04.009

Greenhaus, J. H., Parasuraman, S., & Wormley, W. M. (1990). Effects of race on organizational experiences, job performance evaluations, and career outcomes. *Academy of Management Journal, 33*(1), 64–86. doi:10.2307/256352

Gross-Spector, M., & Cinamon, R. G. (2018). Assessing adults' career exploration: Development and validation of the vocational and maternal identity exploration scales. *Journal of Career Development, 45*(1), 19–33. doi:10.1177/0894845316667846

Guan, M., Capezio, A., Restubog, S. L. D., Read, S., Lajom, J. A. L., & Li, M. (2016). The role of traditionality in the relationships among parental support, career decision-making self-efficacy and career adaptability. *Journal of Vocational Behavior, 94*, 114–123. doi:10.1016/j.jvb.2016.02.018

Guan, Y., Guo, Y., Bond, M. H., Cai, Z., Zhou, X., Xu, J., ... Ye, L. (2014). New job market entrants' future work self, career adaptability and job search outcomes: Examining mediating and moderating models. *Journal of Vocational Behavior, 85*(1), 136–145. doi:10.1016/j.jvb.2014.05.003

Gunz, H., & Peiperl, M. (2007). *Handbook of career studies*. Los Angeles, CA: Sage Publications.

Harju, L. K., Hakanen, J. J., & Schaufeli, W. B. (2016). Can job crafting reduce job boredom and increase work engagement? A three-year cross-lagged panel study. *Journal of Vocational Behavior, 95–96*, 11–20. doi:10.1016/j.jvb.2016.07.001

Hirschi, A., Herrmann, A., & Keller, A. C. (2015). Career adaptivity, adaptability, and adapting: A conceptual and empirical investigation. *Journal of Vocational Behavior, 87*, 1–10. doi:10.1016/j.jvb.2014.11.008

Hofmans, J., Vantilborgh, T., & Solinger, O. N. (2018). k-Centres functional clustering: A person-centered approach to modeling complex nonlinear growth trajectories. *Organizational Research Methods, 21*(4), 915–930. doi:10.1177/1094428117725793

Houlfort, N., Fernet, C., Vallerand, R. J., Laframboise, A., Guay, F., & Koestner, R. (2015). The role of passion for work and need satisfaction in psychological adjustment to retirement. *Journal of Vocational Behavior, 88*, 84–94. doi:10.1016/j.jvb.2015.02.005

Jung, H., Park, I.-J., & Rie, J. (2015). Future time perspective and career decisions: The moderating effects of affect spin. *Journal of Vocational Behavior, 89*, 46–55. doi:10.1016/j.jvb.2015.04.010

Justeson, J. S., & Katz, S. M. (1995). Technical terminology: Some linguistic properties and an algorithm for identification in text. *Natural Language Engineering, 1*(1), 9–27. doi:10.1017/S1351324900000048

Kim, M. S., & Seo, Y. S. (2014). Social cognitive predictors of academic interests and goals in South Korean engineering students. *Journal of Career Development, 41*(6), 526–546. https://doi.org/10.1177/0894845313519703

Kobayashi, V. B., Mol, S. T., Berkers, H. A., Kismihók, G., & Den Hartog, D. N. (2017). Text mining in organizational research. *Organizational Research Methods*, *21*(3), 733–765. 1094428117722619. doi:10.1177/1094428117722619

Kozan, S., Di Fabio, A., Blustein, D. L., & Kenny, M. E. (2014). The role of social support and work-related factors on the school engagement of Italian high school students. *Journal of Career Assessment*, *22*(2), 345–354. doi:10.1177/1069072713493988

Lam, M., & Santos, A. (2018). The impact of a college career intervention program on career decision self-efficacy, career indecision, and decision-making difficulties. *Journal of Career Assessment*, *26*(3), 425–444. doi:10.1177/1069072717714539

Lee, C. I. S. G., Felps, W., & Baruch, Y. (2014). Toward a taxonomy of career studies through bibliometric visualization. *Journal of Vocational Behavior*, *85*(3), 339–351. doi:10.1016/j .jvb.2014.08.008

Lee, H.-S., Flores, L. Y., Navarro, R. R., & Kanagui-Muñoz, M. (2015). A longitudinal test of social cognitive career theory's academic persistence model among Latino/a and white men and women engineering students. *Journal of Vocational Behavior*, *88*, 95–103. doi:10 .1016/j.jvb.2015.02.003

Lengelle, R., Meijers, F., Poell, R., & Post, M. (2014). Career writing: Creative, expressive and reflective approaches to narrative identity formation in students in higher education. *Journal of Vocational Behavior*, *85*(1), 75–84. doi:10.1016/j.jvb.2014.05.001

Lent, R. W., Ireland, G. W., Penn, L. T., Morris, T. R., & Sappington, R. (2017). Sources of self-efficacy and outcome expectations for career exploration and decision-making: A test of the social cognitive model of career self-management. *Journal of Vocational Behavior*, *99*, 107–117. doi:10.1016/j.jvb.2017.01.002

Lent, R. W., Taveira, M. D. C., Pinto, J. C., Silva, A. D., Blanco, T., Faria, S., & Gonçalves, A. M. (2014). Social cognitive predictors of well-being in African college students. *Journal of Vocational Behavior*, *84*(3), 266–272. doi:10.1016/j.jvb.2014.01.007

Lewis, K. V., Harris, C., Morrison, R., & Ho, M. (2015). The entrepreneurship–motherhood nexus: A longitudinal investigation from a boundaryless career perspective. *Career Development International*, *20*(1), 21–37. doi:10.1108/CDI-07-2014-0090

Lichtenthaler, P. W., & Fischbach, A. (2016). Job crafting and motivation to continue working beyond retirement age. *Career Development International*, *21*(5), 477–497. doi:10.1108/ CDI-01-2016-0009

Lu, C.-Q., Wang, H.-J., Lu, J.-J., Du, D.-Y., & Bakker, A. B. (2014). Does work engagement increase person–job fit? The role of job crafting and job insecurity. *Journal of Vocational Behavior*, *84*(2), 142–152. doi:10.1016/j.jvb.2013.12.004

Maggiori, C., Nihil, R., Froidevaux, A., & Rossier, J. (2014). Development and validation of the transition to retirement questionnaire. *Journal of Career Assessment*, *22*(3), 505–523. doi:10.1177/1069072713498684

Maggiori, C., Rossier, J., & Savickas, M. L. (2017). Career adapt-abilities scale – short form (CAAS-SF): Construction and validation. *Journal of Career Assessment*, *25*(2), 312–325. doi:10.1177/1069072714565856

Malo, M., Tremblay, I., & Brunet, L. (2016). Cognitive adjustment as an indicator of psycho-logical health at work: Development and validation of a measure. *Journal of Vocational Behavior*, *92*, 33–43. doi:10.1016/j.jvb.2015.11.005

Maree, J. G. (2016). Career construction counseling with a mid-career black man. *Career Development Quarterly*, *64*(1), 20–34. doi:10.1002/cdq.12038

Markoulli, M. P., Lee, C. I. S. G., Byington, E., & Felps, W. A. (2017). Mapping human resource management: Reviewing the field and charting future directions. *Human Resource Management Review*, *27*(3), 367–396. doi:10.1016/j.hrmr.2016.10.001

McCallum, S. Y., Forret, M. L., & Wolff, H.-G. (2014). Internal and external networking behavior: An investigation of relationships with affective, continuance, and normative commitment. *Career Development International*, *19*(5), 595–614. doi:10.1108/CDI-08 -2013-0101

McWhirter, E. H., Luginbuhl, P. J., & Brown, K. (2014). ¡Apóyenos! Latina/o student recommendations for high school supports. *Journal of Career Development*, *41*(1), 3–23. doi:10 .1177/0894845312470511

Miller, A. D., & Rottinghaus, P. J. (2014). Career indecision, meaning in life, and anxiety: An existential framework. *Journal of Career Assessment*, *22*(2), 233–247. doi:10.1177/ 1069072713493763

Moakler, M. W., & Kim, M. M. (2014). College major choice in STEM: Revisiting confidence and demographic factors. *Career Development Quarterly*, *62*(2), 128–142. doi:10.1002/j .2161-0045.2014.00075.x

Morgan, B., de Bruin, G. P., & de Bruin, K. (2015). Constructing Holland's hexagon in South Africa: Development and initial validation of the South African career interest inventory. *Journal of Career Assessment*, *23*(3), 493–511. doi:10.1177/1069072714547615

Navarro, R. L., Flores, L. Y., Lee, H.-S., & Gonzalez, R. (2014). Testing a longitudinal social cognitive model of intended persistence with engineering students across gender and race/ ethnicity. *Journal of Vocational Behavior*, *85*(1), 146–155. doi:10.1016/j.jvb.2014.05.007

Nohe, C., & Sonntag, K. (2014). Work–family conflict, social support, and turnover intentions: A longitudinal study. *Journal of Vocational Behavior*, *85*(1), 1–12. doi:10.1016/j.jvb .2014.03.007

Nota, L., Santilli, S., & Soresi, S. (2016). A life-design-based online career intervention for early adolescents: Description and initial analysis. *Career Development Quarterly*, *64*(1), 4–19. doi:10.1002/cdq.12037

Okay-Somerville, B., & Scholarios, D. (2014). Coping with career boundaries and boundary-crossing in the graduate labour market. *Career Development International*, *19*(6), 668–682. doi:10.1108/CDI-12-2013-0144

Öncel, L. (2014). Career adapt-abilities scale: Convergent validity of subscale scores. *Journal of Vocational Behavior*, *85*(1), 13–17. doi:10.1016/j.jvb.2014.03.006

Onyishi, I. E., Enwereuzor, I. K., Ituma, A. N., & Omenma, J. T. (2015). The mediating role of perceived employability in the relationship between core self-evaluations and job search behaviour. *Career Development International*, *20*(6), 604–626. doi:10.1108/CDI-09-2014-0130

Oostrom, J. K., Pennings, M., & Bal, P. M. (2016). How do idiosyncratic deals contribute to the employability of older workers? *Career Development International*, *21*(2), 176–192. doi:10.1108/CDI-08-2015-0112

Parker, S. K., Morgeson, F. P., & Johns, G. (2017). One hundred years of work design research: Looking back and looking forward. *Journal of Applied Psychology*, *102*(3), 403–420. doi:10.1037/apl0000106

Perera, H. N., & McIlveen, P. (2014). The role of optimism and engagement coping in college adaptation: A career construction model. *Journal of Vocational Behavior*, *84*(3), 395–404. doi:10.1016/j.jvb.2014.03.002

Perreira, T. A., Morin, A. J. S., Hebert, M., Gillet, N., Houle, S. A., & Berta, W. (2018). The short form of the workplace affective commitment multidimensional questionnaire (WACMQ-S): A bifactor-ESEM approach among healthcare professionals. *Journal of Vocational Behavior*, *106*, 62–83. doi:10.1016/j.jvb.2017.12.004

Praskova, A., Hood, M., & Creed, P. A. (2014). Testing a calling model of psychological career success in Australian young adults: A longitudinal study. *Journal of Vocational Behavior*, *85*(1), 125–135. doi:10.1016/j.jvb.2014.04.004

Preenen, P., Verbiest, S., Van Vianen, A., & Van Wijk, E. (2015). Informal learning of temporary agency workers in low-skill jobs: The role of self-profiling, career control, and job challenge. *Career Development International*, *20*(4), 339–362. doi:10.1108/CDI-12-2013-0158

Richardson, J., & McKenna, S. (2020). An exploration of career sustainability in and after professional sport. *Journal of Vocational Behavior, 117*, 103314. doi:10.1016/j.jvb.2019.06.002

Rip, A., & Courtial, J. (1984). Co-word maps of biotechnology: An example of cognitive scientometrics. *Scientometrics, 6*(6), 381–400. doi:10.1007/bf02025827

Roche, M. K., Carr, A. L., Lee, I. H., Wen, J., & Brown, S. D. (2017). Career indecision in China: Measurement equivalence with the United States and South Korea. *Journal of Career Assessment, 25*(3), 526–536. doi:10.1177/1069072716651623

Rudolph, C. W., Katz, I. M., Lavigne, K. N., & Zacher, H. (2017a). Job crafting: A meta-analysis of relationships with individual differences, job characteristics, and work outcomes. *Journal of Vocational Behavior, 102*, 112–138. doi:10.1016/j.jvb.2017.05.008

Rudolph, C. W., Lavigne, K. N., & Zacher, H. (2017b). Career adaptability: A meta-analysis of relationships with measures of adaptivity, adapting responses, and adaptation results. *Journal of Vocational Behavior, 98*, 17–34. doi:10.1016/j.jvb.2016.09.002

Ryba, T. V., Ronkainen, N. J., & Selänne, H. (2015). Elite athletic career as a context for life design. *Journal of Vocational Behavior, 88*, 47–55. doi:10.1016/j.jvb.2015.02.002s

Santilli, S., Nota, L., Ginevra, M. C., & Soresi, S. (2014). Career adaptability, hope and life satisfaction in workers with intellectual disability. *Journal of Vocational Behavior, 85*(1), 67–74. doi:10.1016/j.jvb.2014.02.011

Schaufeli, W. B., Bakker, A. B., & Salanova, M. (2006). The measurement of work engagement with a short questionnaire: A cross-national study. *Educational and Psychological Measurement, 66*(4), 701–716. doi:10.1177/0013164405282471

Shoffner, M. F., Newsome, D., Minton, C. A. B., & Morris, C. A. W. (2015). A qualitative exploration of the STEM career-related outcome expectations of young adolescents. *Journal of Career Development, 42*(2), 102–116. doi:10.1177/0894845314544033

Shortland, S. (2014). Role models: Expatriate gender diversity pipeline or pipe-dream? *Career Development International, 19*(5), 572–594. doi:10.1108/CDI-10-2013-0123

Simosi, M., Rousseau, D. M., & Daskalaki, M. (2015). When career paths cease to exist: A qualitative study of career behavior in a crisis economy. *Journal of Vocational Behavior, 91*, 134–146. doi:10.1016/j.jvb.2015.09.009

Sortheix, F. M., Chow, A., & Salmela-Aro, K. (2015). Work values and the transition to work life: A longitudinal study. *Journal of Vocational Behavior, 89*, 162–171. doi:10.1016/j.jvb.2015.06.001

Sovet, L., & Metz, A. J. (2014). Parenting styles and career decision-making among French and Korean adolescents. *Journal of Vocational Behavior, 84*(3), 345–355. doi:10.1016/j.jvb.2014.02.002

Spurk, D., Abele, A. E., & Volmer, J. (2015). The career satisfaction scale in context: A test for measurement invariance across four occupational groups. *Journal of Career Assessment, 23*(2), 191–209. doi:10.1177/1069072714535019

Tims, M., Bakker, A. B., & Derks, D. (2012). Development and validation of the job crafting scale. *Journal of Vocational Behavior, 80*(1), 173–186. doi:10.1016/j.jvb.2011.05.009

Tolentino, L. R., Garcia, P. R. J. M., Lu, V. N., Restubog, S. L. D., Bordia, P., & Plewa, C. (2014). Career adaptation: The relation of adaptability to goal orientation, proactive personality, and career optimism. *Journal of Vocational Behavior, 84*(1), 39–48. doi:10.1016/j.jvb.2013.11.004

Van den Broeck, A., Sulea, C., Vander Elst, T., Fischmann, G., Iliescu, D., & De Witte, H. (2014). The mediating role of psychological needs in the relation between qualitative job insecurity and counterproductive work behavior. *Career Development International, 19*(5), 526–547. doi:10.1108/CDI-05-2013-0063

Van der Heijden, B., De Vos, A., Akkermans, J., Spurk, D., Semeijn, J., Van der Velde, M., & Fugate, M. (2020). Sustainable career across the lifespan: Moving the field forward. *Journal of Vocational Behavior, 117*, 103344. doi:10.1016/j.jvb.2019.103344

Van der Heijden, B. I. J. M., Notelaers, G., Peters, P., Stoffers, J. M. M., De Lange, A. H., Froehlich, D. E., & Van der Heijde, C. M. (2018). Development and validation of the short-form employability five-factor instrument. *Journal of Vocational Behavior, 106,* 236–248. doi:10.1016/j.jvb.2018.02.003

Van Eck, N. J. (2011). *Methodological advances in bibliometric mapping of science.* Rotterdam, the Netherlands: Erasmus Research Institute of Management.

Van Eck, N. J., & Waltman, L. (2010). Software survey: VOSviewer, a computer program for bibliometric mapping. *Scientometrics, 84*(2), 523–538. doi:10.1007/s11192-009-0146-3

Van Eck, N. J., & Waltman, L. (2011). Text mining and visualization using VOSviewer. Retrieved from http://arxiv.org/abs/1109.2058

Van Eck, N. J., & Waltman, L. (2014). Visualizing bibliometric networks. In Y. Ding, R. Rousseau, & D. Wolfram (Eds.), *Measuring scholarly impact: Methods and practice* (pp. 285–320). Cham: Springer International Publishing.

Van Eck, N. J., Waltman, L., Dekker, R., & Van den Berg, J. (2010). A comparison of two techniques for bibliometric mapping: Multidimensional scaling and VOS. *Journal of the American Society for Information Science and Technology, 61*(12), 2405–2416. doi:10.1002/asi.21421

Waaijer, C. J. F., Van Bochove, C. A., & Van Eck, N. J. (2010). Journal editorials give indication of driving science issues. *Nature, 463,* 157. doi:10.1038/463157a

Waltman, L., Van Eck, N. J., & Noyons, E. C. M. (2010). A unified approach to mapping and clustering of bibliometric networks. *Journal of Infometrics, 4*(4), 629–635. doi:10.1016/j.joi.2010.07.002

Wang, M., & Wanberg, C. R. (2017). 100 years of applied psychology research on individual careers: From career management to retirement. *Journal of Applied Psychology, 102*(3), 546–563. doi:10.1037/apl0000143

Waters, L., Briscoe, J. P., Hall, D. T., & Wang, L. (2014). Protean career attitudes during unemployment and reemployment: A longitudinal perspective. *Journal of Vocational Behavior, 84*(3), 405–419. doi:10.1016/j.jvb.2014.03.003

Whiston, S. C., Li, Y., Goodrich Mitts, N., & Wright, L. (2017). Effectiveness of career choice interventions: A meta-analytic replication and extension. *Journal of Vocational Behavior, 100,* 175–184. doi:10.1016/j.jvb.2017.03.010

Wilkins, K. G., Santilli, S., Ferrari, L., Nota, L., Tracey, T. J. G., & Soresi, S. (2014). The relationship among positive emotional dispositions, career adaptability, and satisfaction in Italian high school students. *Journal of Vocational Behavior, 85*(3), 329–338. doi:10.1016/j.jvb.2014.08.004

Willner, T., Gati, I., & Guan, Y. (2015). Career decision-making profiles and career decision-making difficulties: A cross-cultural comparison among US, Israeli, and Chinese samples. *Journal of Vocational Behavior, 88,* 143–153. doi:10.1016/j.jvb.2015.03.007

Yeung, A. W. K., Goto, T. K., & Leung, W. K. (2017). The changing landscape of neuroscience research, 2006–2015: A bibliometric study. *Frontiers in Neuroscience, 11,* 120. https://doi.org/10.3389/fnins.2017.00120

Zacher, H. (2014a). Career adaptability predicts subjective career success above and beyond personality traits and core self-evaluations. *Journal of Vocational Behavior, 84*(1), 21–30. doi:10.1016/j.jvb.2013.10.002

Zacher, H. (2014b). Individual difference predictors of change in career adaptability over time. *Journal of Vocational Behavior, 84*(2), 188–198. doi:10.1016/j.jvb.2014.01.001

Zacher, H. (2015). Daily manifestations of career adaptability: Relationships with job and career outcomes. *Journal of Vocational Behavior, 91,* 76–86. doi:10.1016/j.jvb.2015.09.003

Zacher, H., Brailsford, H. A., & Parker, S. L. (2014). Micro-breaks matter: A diary study on the effects of energy management strategies on occupational well-being. *Journal of Vocational Behavior, 85*(3), 287–297. doi:10.1016/j.jvb.2014.08.005

Zhao, H., & Li, C. (2019). A computerized approach to understanding leadership research. *The Leadership Quarterly*, *30*(4), 396–416. https://doi.org/10.1016/j.leaqua.2019.06.001

Zupic, I., & Čater, T. (2015). Bibliometric methods in management and organization. *Organizational Research Methods*, *18*(3), 429–472. doi:10.1177/1094428114562629

PART I

MEASUREMENT AND DESIGN

2. Constructs in careers research: an overview of the multiple constructs and challenges in the careers domain
Yehuda Baruch

INTRODUCTION

Careers as a field of studies is characterized by an abundance of constructs and terminologies. Part of the variety of concepts and terminologies stem from the many disciplinary perspectives upon which careers studies build. The major disciplines have been identified as: psychology, social psychology, sociology, anthropology, economics, political science, history, and geography (Arthur, Hall, & Lawrence, 1989). Whereas this diversity contributes to the richness, innovation and creativity within the field, these multiple perspectives could muddle the current knowledge, and manifest a certain lack of direction (Arnold & Cohen, 2008; Baruch, Szücs, & Gunz, 2015; Lee, Felps, & Baruch, 2014).

One characteristic of an academic discipline is a cyclical process whereby conceptual works and theories are suggested, adopted and further develop the discipline. Through this continuous process, there is an accumulation of data (e.g. narrative, numerical data) and knowledge (using appropriate analysis) which is both theoretical (Shepherd & Suddaby, 2017) and practical (Rynes, Bartunek, & Daft, 2001). This leads the disciplinary literature to the point where models and concepts are considered theoretically developed, making it an established discipline. Career studies are no different, and there is a continuous process of development of new concepts, ideas and models. These are summarized in handbooks (Arthur et al., 1989; Gunz & Peiperl, 2007), encyclopedias (e.g. Greenhaus & Callanan, 2006) and review articles (Sullivan, 1999; Sullivan & Baruch, 2009; Baruch & Bozionelos, 2011). The field benefitted also from specific meta-analytical coverage of career success and its meaning (Ng, Eby, Sorensen, & Feldman, 2005: Spurk, Hirschi, & Dries, 2019).

Many of the wide range of constructs forming Career Studies as a discipline are represented by metaphors, and tend to focus on career agents (Baruch et al. 2015). There is an ever-increasing plethora of terminologies, probably due to the multiple fields upon which the discipline builds, and the increased number of scholars with interest in the subject. Surprisingly, most of the concepts that were introduced to the literature tend to gather momentum and recognition by the growing number of scholars interested in career studies, rather than fade away. The field expands rapidly, with several clearly established constructs, though some ideas do not catch momentum.

Others appear to attract attention, but do not persist, failing to make a lasting difference to the field (Arnold & Cohen, 2008).

The aim of this chapter is to address the question: *What is it in Careers that we study and how do we study Careers?* I introduce the many constructs and theories covered by the field, trying to identify the main constructs, and discuss related challenges in their study. I refer to either specific career constructs, or constructs that relate to or strongly correspond with career studies. The former includes constructs like boundaryless, protean, kaleidoscope, for example; the latter are areas like global careers, work–life balance, diversity, alternative work arrangements, and so on.

HISTORICAL CONTEXT

The study of careers in modern time started with the Chicago studies (Hughes, 1937), exploring careers from sociological perspectives, and continued to the typical careers as shaped by and taking place in stable organizations (Whyte, 1956; Wilensky, 1961). The criteria for success was climbing up the ladder (Townsend, 1970). The idealization of the "organization man" ended by the end of the 20th century, with the emergence of the new psychological contract (Rousseau, 1995) and boundaryless career (DeFillippi & Arthur, 1994) as metaphorically suggested by Osterman's (1996) title: *Broken Ladders: Managerial Careers in the New Economy*. Most of the constructs presented in this chapter were introduced to the literature during the last few decades, many of them relate to the so-called "New Careers" (Sullivan & Baruch, 2009). Due to the individualization of career and their management, the protean career (Hall, 1996; 2004) captured significant attention. The protean and boundaryless theories offer complementary perspective on new careers (Briscoe, Henagan, Burton, & Murphy, 2012), where individuals with a protean career orientation would find it easier to fulfill their careers in a boundaryless environment.

Disciplinary Positioning

Before moving to the specific constructs that characterize the field, a word on the big divide within the discipline: *Career management* and *career counseling*. I use the "and" rather than "vs.", because I believe that one should learn from both, and these two streams of scholarship should be mutually fertilizing each other. In practice, though, both communities tend to work in isolation, sometime ignoring the scholarship of the other stream, either for ignorance or for lack of interest.

Career counseling is a field within vocational psychology, and is about guiding individuals through their careers, where client–counselor relationships are critical to the career, and these relationships evolve over time (Cardoso, Silva, Gonçalves, & Duarte, 2014; McMahon, 2016). According to Walsh and Osipow (2014), there are seven methodological approaches, which are typically employed under the career counseling area: The Trait-and-Factor approach, the Person-Centered approach, the Psychodynamic approach, the Developmental approach, the Social

Learning approach, the Social Psychological approach, and Computer Assisted Career Counseling. Lastly, career counseling tends to build on qualitative work (e.g. McMahon, 2016).

The other stream, *Career management*, is led by scholars from management disciplines that explore careers from the management point of view (Greenhaus et al., 2019). For example, how individuals and organizations plan and manage careers, what types of careers exist – for example, organizational, entrepreneurial, self-directed – and their characteristics. Such careers can be within or outside organizations (Hall, 2002), local or global (Dickmann & Baruch, 2011), in the private or public realm. Scholars explore careers from multiple perspectives – individual, organizational and society, where each entity plays a role in the process of evolving as a career and labor market ecosystem (Baruch, 2015; Baruch & Rousseau, 2019).

WHAT CONSTRUCTS ARE USED, APPLIED AND UTILIZED IN CAREER STUDIES

The main aim of this chapter is to introduce an overview of career concepts and terminology that is used within the field. I start by following earlier work that covered this terminology up to 2012 (Baruch et al., 2015), and add more recent additions to the literature that emerged later.

Earlier Findings

Baruch et al. (2015) have identified the career terms or constructs which appeared in the literature until 2012. They used the Delphi method with 12 careers experts, which resulted in a quite diverse list of 50 career terms that have shaped the discipline. The most popular ones were the following, based on the H-index measure:

Career Success

Career success has a dual meaning and is considered from dual perspectives: There is a distinction between intrinsic and extrinsic success indicators. Intrinsic career success reflects the self-perception of individuals, such as career/job satisfaction, fulfillment, following a calling, etc. In contrast, extrinsic career success reflects measurable objective indicators of success, the most common of which are income and hierarchical progression. Many works explore the different perspectives and meaning of career success – for further reading see Heslin (2005), Ng et al. (2005) and Spurk et al. (2019).

Career Stage/Phase

Careers, by definition, follow several stages. Within organizations, individuals will follow a progression, which can be internal within the employing organization, external to another organization or another type of employment. The moves can be multidirectional. For example, internal moves can be up the ladder, lateral or demotion related. External can be into another organization at a similar, higher or lower position, same area or different, to self-employment (e.g. to consultancy, to entrepreneurship), or to end employment altogether (Baruch, 2004a). The seminal work of Super (1957) explained how during the life span of a person, people develop and implement self-concept in one or more careers (or vocations). It was followed by several frameworks, focusing on stable models. Super later described the life span, life-space theory (1980) combining the psychology of individual development during life and social role theory for the understanding of multiple role career progress. An integrated model by Baruch (2004b, p. 54) suggested the following stages, where career may be reflected on and changed, repeating some of the stages in a second, third or more career cycles. The stages are:

(a)   Foundation
(b)   Career entry
(c)   Advancement
(d)   Re-evaluation
(e)   Reinforcement
(f)   Decline
(g)   Retirement.

Boundaryless Career

The boundaryless career is perhaps the most discussed "new career" theory, introduced by DeFillippi and Arthur (1994) and Arthur and Rousseau (1996) to represent a transition from traditional careers, which are structured and stable, to contemporary careers, which are driven by the breakdown of multiple boundaries that structured the traditional career systems. These can be organizational, geographical, social and psychological, to mention the most prominent. The concept of boundaryless career was contested (e.g. Inkson, Gunz, Ganesh, & Roper, 2012; Rodrigues, Guest, & Budjanovcanin, 2016), and in reality one should bear in mind that this is a metaphor, as certain boundaries always exist. Yet, contemporary career scholarship suggests that many of the traditional boundaries are more permeable and there is more dynamism in the system, including the ability to make non-traditional career moves and the acceptance of career transitions. For further reading see Arthur (2008; 2014).

Career Exploration

Career exploration can take place at any stage of career, and in varying circumstances. Mostly in the early career stage, later during transitions that take place when moving to another career stages, or when individuals opt for a second career or another major career change. For further reading see Blustein (1997).

Career System

Career system takes us from an individualistic approach to a view of the career as a system, involving individuals and organizations. Each organization, each institution, profession, and so on forms a career system with its own characteristics, which can be dynamic (Baruch, 2004a; Nicholson, 1996). Career system perspective uses the interaction across sociological and organizational frameworks, beyond the individual psychology perspective of careers. For further reading see Baruch (2004b).

Subjective/Objective Career

These are the two major ways career success is being measured. One is normative, depending on the viewpoint, norms and values of the person. It is how the individual perceives his or her career – progress, satisfaction, well-being, and so on, and how others evaluate such career achievements. The other one is descriptive, measurable, and defined according to certain set criteria (usually level of hierarchy, position of power, etc. and level of income). For further reading see Ng et al. (2005) and Spurk et al. (2019).

Career Track/Pattern/Stream

Career systems include various tracks and patterns, sometimes called career paths, through which people develop and progress in their careers.

Employability (and Career)

Employability is the ability of a person to find employment, and is more broadly defined as "a psycho-social construct that embodies individual characteristics that foster adaptive cognition, behavior, and affect, and enhance the individual-work interface" (Fugate, Kinicki, & Ashforth, 2004, p. 15). It is a multidimensional construct, and is influence by a myriad of factors (Van der Heijde & Van der Heijden, 2006). For a comprehensive explication of employability see Fugate, Van der Heijden, De Vos, Forrier, and De Cuyper (2021). Within the study of careers, employability is typically used as the perception of an individual's capability of finding a job (Rothwell & Arnold, 2007). Significant attention has been given to the study of graduates' employability and the role of employability within national and global labor markets.

Protean Career

The term "Protean Career" (Hall, 2004) captures the changing nature of employees' viewpoints on contemporary careers: "The Protean career is a process which the person, not the organization, is managing. It consists of all the person's experiences in education, training, work in several organizations, changes in occupational field, etc." (Hall, 1976, p. 201). Thus, the Protean career construct describes the experiences of employees as they assume the responsibility for planning, managing, enacting and evaluating their careers (Hall, 2004).

Career Self-management

In distinction from organizational career management, which is conducted by the employer, individual people – employees, self-employed, unemployed – can take the task of managing their own career, which can follow their own strategic aims and visions (Greenhaus et al., 2019). Such a self-managed career can be within the current employer structure or externally, can be local or global (e.g. self-initiated expatriation), and so on. The individual takes the initiative, sets targets, develops strategies, and takes actions to propel their career.

Career Plateau

Not all aspirations can be fulfilled when aiming to progress on organizational ladders, and not every career has a ladder to climb. The phenomenon was described by Ference, Stoner, and Warren (1977) as an organizational phenomenon. Only very few can become CEOs, many professions have a very flat structure. People who have reached a certain level and not moved beyond it are positioned in a career plateau. Career plateau is recognized as an important career phase (Feldman & Weitz, 1988) as it influences most employees – very few would continue hierarchical progression throughout their entire career.

Career Anchor

Career anchors (Schein, 1978; 1985) are the perceived abilities, values, attitudes and motives of individuals. These anchors – self-perceived talents and qualities – determine career aspirations and directions, serving to guide, constrain, stabilize, reinforce and develop people's careers. The list of Schein's eight anchors is as follows (the last three were added in his 1985 version):

Technical competencies
Managerial competencies
Security and stability
Entrepreneurial/creativity
Autonomy/independence
Dedication to a cause (e.g. service)
Pure challenge
Life style.

Career Resilience

Introduced by London (1983) and popularized by Waterman, Waterman, and Collard (1994), career resilience is the individual quality of keeping one's career when facing adverse circumstances and challenges, like redundancy, external crises. People with strong career resilience have the ability to adapt to changing circumstances.

Career Adaptability

The construct of career adaptability (Super & Knasel, 1981) was defined as "readiness to cope with changing work and working conditions" (p. 195) – originally to deal with transition from education to employment, and later to many challenges throughout career (Savickas, 1997).

Portfolio Career

In today's contemporary labor market, individuals can provide for a wide range of skills, understandings, and qualities to a varied portfolio of positions, juggling across several jobs and roles. Portfolio careers were introduced by Handy (1994). Some of those opting for a portfolio career do it to suit their needs and life-style, others do it out of lack of choice (Mallon, 1998).

Career Capital

Career capital comprises the resources and relationships that can positively influence career-related outcomes (Inkson & Arthur, 2001). They overlap with the competencies introduced by the Intelligent Career – see below.

Intelligent Career

Intelligent careers (Arthur, Claman, & DeFillippi, 1995) is a framework that focuses on three major career competencies:

Knowing why – values, attitudes, internal needs (motivation) identity; what motivates people to choose (and remain) in a certain career, job, and life style.
Knowing how – what comprises career competencies: skills, expertise, capabilities; tacit and explicit knowledge, and experience that enables high quality performance.
Knowing whom – networking, connections, relationships.

The Intelligent Career framework was later expanded by Jones and DeFillippi (1996), to include an additional three competencies: "knowing what" (opportunities, threats, and requirements), "knowing where" (entering, training and advancing), and "knowing when" (timing of choices and activities).

Post-corporate Career

Introduced by Peiperl and Baruch (1997), the Post-corporate Career integrates both the individual and the organizational perspectives when going through a transition. The framework considers traditional and contemporary career models to set out a vision of future careers that differs from the past, in particular following the development of horizontal links that transcend geographic and organizational boundaries.

Career Calling

In relation to work and its meaning varies across people and cultures, Wrzesniewski, McCauley, Rozin, and Schwartz (1997) suggested that for many, an inner "calling" determines their career choice and the resources they put in their career. It was later developed by Hall and Chandler (2005), who explored career as a calling to explain psychological success at work.

Career Logic

Career logic is a "distinctive pattern of work role transitions" (Gunz, Jalland, & Evans, 1998, p. 22), where, for organizations, a career logic is an institutional logic concerned with "internal boundary structure" (Gunz, Evans, & Jalland, 2000, p. 28). There are three types of career logic: command-centered, constructional and evolutionary. A command-centered career logic consists "of moving between a series of similar managerial posts that differ mainly in the size of their responsibilities and in prestige" (Gunz et al., 1998, p. 22). Constructional career logic consists of a variety of different experiences. The evolutionary career logic refers to career patterns that are new to the firm and/or the labor market, and led by individuals. Different career logics will fit with different types of organizational structures and strategies.

Multidirectional Career

Multidirectional careers (Baruch, 2004a) are careers that can take a non-traditional direction, not necessarily entering an organization and following a clear progression path. The concept reflects on a trend portrayed as a transition from the traditional career system labeled "linear career system" into a "multidirectional career system." Baruch suggested possible explanations for the reasons and nature of the phenomenon.

Career Imprints

Career imprints are defined as a "set of capabilities and connections, coupled with the confidence and cognition that a group of individuals share as a result of their career experiences at a common employer during a particular period in time" (Higgins, 2005, p. 4). They can be the specific shape of careers of executives at sectoral level, manifesting the relevance of organizational culture in developing future leaders. These imprints can be business related or value/political based (Wang, Du, & Marquis, 2019).

Kaleidoscope Career

Using a novel framework of authenticity, balance and challenge, Mainiero and Sullivan (2006) explain why so many people, in particular in the US, are opting out of the high-powered, high-stress 'rat race' into entrepreneurship careers. The use of the kaleidoscope metaphor manifests that careers are dynamic and in motion; as life changes, careers are altered to adjust to these changes, and vice versa, creating multiple patterns.

Sustainable Careers

Similar to physical sustainability, career sustainability can be considered a particular form of human sustainability, which comprises the capacity to learn, adapt, create, test and maintain one's adaptive capability in leading one's own career. De Vos and Van der Heijden's edited book (2015) offers multiple perspectives on the nature and meaning of career sustainability.

Career Impatience

Veiga (1981) identified two career motives that are central to a manager's desire for a career move, one of them is career impatience (the other one fear of stagnation). This is one of the few non-positive career constructs and metaphors that characterizes career studies (for a counter-balance framework see the dark side of careers – Baruch and Vardi, 2016). Lack of patience may trigger a move, but this could be a premature move or a move in the wrong direction.

Customized Career

Customized careers (Valcour, Bailyn, & Quijada, 2007) are non-traditional career patterns that defy the conventional timing of career and non-traditional employment relationships where people can set for themselves a career that fits best to their own specific needs and conditions.

Career Boundary

Simply a boundary that defines career, like organizational/professional/national boundary (working in one organization or profession or nation) – such boundaries that, under the boundaryless career, can be crossed more easily in the contemporary career system.

Career Habitus

Career habitus is a habitus (see Bourdieu's work) which "fits" to a particular career field (Mayrhofer et al., 2004). Applying the concept of career habitus enables various levels of analysis to understand careers in various contexts, in particular global careers.

Nomadic Careers

Another verbal metaphor of careers that might be simply a different label of the boundaryless careers, where people move in search of career opportunities (Tremblay, 2003). The label did not catch continued attention in the literature (for an exception see Rouvrais, Remaud, & Saveuse, 2020). This type of constant career movement is typical in the "gig economy" (Lowe, 2018).

Butterfly Career

This is another type of career metaphor that did not catch strong attention – associated with the boundaryless career, where individuals tend to "taste" different options and careers, no longer bound to a single organization, sector or profession. Introduced by McCabe and Savery (2007), it characterizes individuals that "flutter" between sectors according to opportunities and personal choice to develop their career prospects.

Apart from the above terms identified, other terminologies suggested were less prominent or broader, and included several general terms and very specific terms. The general ones were: *Career action; Career as story; Career field; Career studies; Employment security; Gendered careers; Life design; Life projects; Occupational careers; Psychological success; Time and careers;* and *Work and careers.*

Very specific terms listed were: *Blended life course; Career (meta)competencies; Career communities; Career learning cycles; Career preparedness;* and *Flexicurity.*

The list was not claiming to be all-inclusive, due to the nature of the Delphi method. For example, some concepts were missing, like Career fitness (e.g. Forret & Sullivan, 2002; Sukiennik, Bendat, Raufman, & Sikiennik, 2013), Proactive career, Dual career couples and Career ownership. In particular, one specific construct that later gained recognition as a theory or framework is "*Career construction*" (Savickas, 2013), a relatively new addition to the myriad of concepts, theories and metaphors that characterize career studies.

LABELING OF CAREER THEORIES AND CONCEPT: THE USE OF CAREER METAPHORS

A number of scholars used metaphors to explicate and manifest certain types of careers or career construct. Inkson (2006) argued how metaphors contribute to and enhance the study of careers. In the study of career constructs (Baruch et al., 2015), it was identified that some half of the current career concepts, theories and constructs are represented by a metaphor, as listed above, for example, "Protean career," using a metaphor from Greek mythology, or "Butterfly career," a metaphor from biology, or the "Kaleidoscope career," using the man-made object metaphor.

A general issue missing from the constructs above due to the way the Delphi method was conducted is organizational career management practices (OCM/P), where many specific practices exist and influence careers. Among these I consider the following as important constructs in career studies, in particular for career management:

Mentoring (Kram, 1985), which gained significant attention with proven impact (Allen & Eby, 2007) and related constructs, like reverse mentoring (Murphy, 2012) is such a phenomenon. Mentoring is a well-established organizational practice, which contributes to both mentor and mentees, and is well documented in the career studies literature, mostly associated with positive outcomes.

Organizational career counseling, which can be provided by a direct supervisor, by an external counselor, or by the HR Department is another practice that aims to help individuals to identify their career options and help them to progress in their careers.

Common career paths are found in many organizations, where people follow a distinct path. It can be a plateau career or fast-track/high-flyer track.

Dual ladder (parallel hierarchy for professional staff) is a case where in certain organizations or sectors there exist career paths that fit different populations. A person can progress as a manager or as a professional (e.g. engineer), or in hospital, there is a career ladder for doctors, for nurses, for support staff. This enables people to progress in their profession rather than opt for a managerial administrative career.

Lateral moves to create a cross-functional experience are useful where in terms of hierarchy a person reaches their plateau, but can nevertheless move sideways and benefit from further learning and challenging, fulfilling a career.

Succession planning (Rothwell, Jackson, Ressler, Jones, & Brower, 2015) is another organizational practice where the HR Department can generate an organizational-wide plan to identify for each person, or each person in a certain level and above, where they may progress to, if they move, who may replace them, what needs to occur before individuals are promoted and so on.

OTHER AND MORE RECENT CONCEPTS AND THEORIES

The above list does not cover "global career(s)," which is a parallel concept where many careers takes place in a global environment, and specific careers like expatriate careers (hence later repatriation) attract a wide range of writing in the career area. Some of these are organizational-based, others are self-initiated expatriation (which to a certain extent overlap with the migration literature). Self-initiated expatriation can take place at the individual level (Al Ariss & Crowley-Henry, 2013) but also within organizations (Altman & Baruch, 2012).

Similarly, with the exponential growth in the Internet economy, virtual careers are growing and many find their vocation to be exclusively within the virtual world.

With the increased attention on entrepreneurial activities, there is an increased attention on entrepreneurial careers (Dyer, 1995). With the high relevance of work engagement, related terms like "career engagement" (e.g. Nilforooshan & Salimi, 2016; Hirschi & Jaensch, 2015) have attracted further study.

The happenstance learning theory (Krumboltz, 2009) has gained significant attention in the career counseling literature. It builds on or is similar to a certain extent with the chance-event career concept. This theory suggests that not all of one's career future needs to be strictly planned, and people should be open to a variety of activities that may introduce to them interesting and beneficial career options. This theory addresses the way individuals opt for and follow their different career paths as they go through life events.

The dynamics of constructs in career studies continues to evolve. New terminology emerges as new thinking flourishes, for example, "career resourcing" (Nigam & Dokko, 2019), which can help in the creation of new professions or occupations, or quite generic terms like "flexible careers" (Tomlinson, Baird, Berg, & Cooper, 2018). There are also sectorial perspectives, such as careers in high-tech, careers in the public sector, and academic careers (Baruch & Hall, 2004).

The more recent career theory that captures the dynamic nature of contemporary careers and associated different actors and entities in the career landscape is the career ecosystem, mentioned above (Baruch, 2015; Baruch & Rousseau, 2019). It provides a comprehensive overarching concept to incorporate the multiple actors, and multiple levels of analysis necessary to capture career systems. In the career ecosystem the *Actors* in are individuals, institutions and nations. The nature of career transactions is such that *interconnectedness* is complex and psychological contracting is a critical factor. *Interactions* are most notably the exchange of labor for wages, as well as other transactions across actors. In the context of *Interdependency*, firms depend on employees to survive, perform and thrive; and on governments to enable them to conduct their business. Overall, the career ecosystem theory offers new ways to understand the complex and complicated nature of careers and their management.

Clustering

Career studies can be clustered according to many possible considerations. A meta-analysis exploring career studies according to the disciplinary field identified several focused topics of interest (Lee et al., 2014). Findings indicate that scholarly work in the field of career tends to cluster in line with six focused fields, including international careers, career management, career choice, career adaptation, individual and relational career success, and life opportunities. Another clustering of career studies is along the level-of-analysis continuum between individual/organizational and society/national level.

Other Streams

Role of chance event: Chance events are "factors that have the unique qualities of being unpredictable and unplanned for" (Rice, 2014, p. 446). Chance events can lead to 'career shocks' that may alter career trajectories (Blokker et al., 2019). The event can be positive or negative, and its outcomes can also be positive or negative (Rice, 2014; Zhou, Guan, Xin, Mak, & Deng, 2016). It is challenging to identify the role of chance events in the making of a successful career (Hu et al., 2015). A chance event is an unexpected, accidental or unplanned event that may significantly influence career development and progress, either in a positive or a negative way. Nevertheless, most career development literature has focused on the active and rather rational (conscious) role of agents in shaping careers (Brew, Boud, Lucas, & Crawford, 2017), and shares a limited perspective on the unexpected side of career development. Despite the long-term cover of chance events in the career development literature since the 1950s, empirical studies on the matter are still lacking (Bright, Pryor, Chan, & Rijanto, 2009; Pryor & Bright, 2011). Few studies have emerged that cover this aspect of careers (Grimland, Vigoda-Gadot, & Baruch, 2012; Kindsiko & Baruch, 2019).

The dark side of careers (Baruch & Vardi, 2016) has emerged as a field only recently, building on the idea that alongside enthusiasm and positive perspectives, human nature may be associated with a dark side too – for example, the dark side of social capital (Gargiulo & Benassi, 1999). In this regard, careers are similar to several fields where the dark side starts to gain attention only later. For example, the study of the dark triad of leadership (psychopathy, narcissism, and Machiavellianism), as presented by Cohen (2018). This new stream is expected to unveil the less positive side of careers and their management in the current dynamic world.

HOW TO STUDY CAREERS – METHODS TO FIT

Career studies cut across a variety of disciplines and levels of analysis. At the individual level, each person has a career, but the planning and management of careers varies with their level, profession, sector, and work domain, to name a few factors. Career management studies explore individuals and organizations as well as their interrelationship, and may include multiple players. In career counseling, the involved players are typically two: the client and the counselor.

The progress of careers and the success or failure in careers is determined by multiple factors, with various stakeholders involved. A broad view of career studies depicts careers as a global ecosystem of labor markets where many actors interact (Baruch, 2015). As a result, the careers literature is multifaceted. It draws from and contributes to a variety of research fields. Among these the most prominent are management, psychology, sociology, economics, and education.

This diversity of research domains reflects the reality that career studies can benefit from multi-disciplinary and inter-disciplinary studies, which necessitate multiple methodologies. This brings another major divide – the artificial divide, I argue: Qualitative versus quantitative methods. The reason I suggest it is an artificial or at least unnecessary argument is that to my view, the purpose of using research is to generate new knowledge. New knowledge can be developed via the use of either quantitative methods, qualitative methods or both (mixed-method). For many purposes, the utilization of qualitative and quantitative methods is complementary. Further, using both is highly recommended to gain a comprehensive knowledge about any phenomenon (Johnson & Onwuegbuzie, 2004).

Career studies mostly rely on research methods from the social and behavioral sciences. For empirical work this covers quantitative and qualitative methodologies. The former utilize statistics and the latter narrative analysis. Statistical analysis extracts knowledge from relationships between various variables, when data are collected via questionnaire-based surveys or secondary data, for example. Qualitative methodology explores narrative, for example from case studies, interviews, vignettes, and diary methods. Qualitative researchers may use the Gioia method (Gioia, Corley, & Hamilton, 2013), or critical incident technique (Cassell & Symon, 2004), for example.

Conducting quantitative analysis, the career field moved, like many other OB/HRM studies, from high reliance on cross-sectional studies to a more complex methodology in terms of data collection (multi-source) and data analysis – from correlational to regression, structural equation modeling, and Bayesian analysis, to name a few.

New tools are constantly being developed – for example, sequential analysis of careers: Careers can be defined as sequences of positions occupied by an individual during the course of a lifetime (Super, 1980). For the empirical analysis of career sequences, optimal matching analysis (OMA) has received the most attention in the social sciences (Aisenbrey & Fasang, 2010; Dlouhy & Biemann, 2015; van der Laken, Bakk, Giagkoulas, van Leeuwen, & Bongenaar, 2018). In OMA, each individual's career is first converted into a string with a limited number of different states. The optimal matching algorithm computes the similarity for each pair of sequences in a sample as the number of operations that is required to transform one sequence into another (Biemann & Datta, 2014). Most applications of OMA are followed by a cluster analysis, which identifies clusters of similar sequences in the distance matrix.

When considering factors that would be relevant for the decision of methodology choice in studying careers, scholars should contemplate the following: Reliability and validity of measurements in the quantitative method, in particular in using questionnaire surveys – development, design distribution and data collection. Measures used should be properly validated (e.g. Dobrow & Tosti-Kharas, 2011). New tools like new scales should be user-friendly and easy to compile.

Another issue worthy of attention is a realistic evaluation of the strength of findings in terms of statistical significance, population sample and representation (see for guidance, for example on sample size, in Saunders, Lewis, & Thornhill, 2016).

There are further methodologies that can be used, some are frequently applied, others less so. Laboratory studies and experiments are rife in general organizational behavior studies, but less so in careers, as the timeframe and related concepts are wider.

Network analysis is more often applied in career studies, as it is important both to identify elements of career competence and capital (e.g. "know whom" of the intelligent career), or to identify the prominence of individuals within a system.

More approaches that can be useful for knowledge creation in the field of careers are case studies, ethnographic and action research, which fit for qualitative work, as suggested by Swanson and Fouad (2014).

Lastly, significant knowledge can be gained from covering existing literature – either conducting meta-analysis, which is very much a quantitative approach, or from a qualitative perspective, studying conceptual work and literature reviews, in particular systematic reviews (Denyer & Tranfield, 2009).

Final note: Research Ethics. Like any research, scholars should aim to collect and analyze data adhering to strict ethical guidelines. These should be followed, bearing in mind the need to gain new knowledge, but keeping integrity and safeguarding the rights of the participants.

CAVEATS AND LIMITATIONS

Most of the past work on careers has focused on OECD and Western geo-locations and culture. There is under-representation of career studies in the Far-East, South America and Africa.

Publication bias may also restrict knowledge creation within the field. This takes place when studies that did not reach significant results are not published, because journals tend to accept for publication only studies that report strong and significant results (Homberg & Bui, 2013). The problem is widely recognized in other fields, for example medicine (Dickersin, Scherer, & Lefebvre, 1994) and is considered to be persistent (Dwan, Gamble, Williamson, & Kirkham, 2013). Similarly, replication studies are rarely published, and it is difficult to ascertain whether or not past knowledge is valid. Again, both issues are not unique to career studies, but should be borne in mind when new theories are developed.

CONCLUSION

In this chapter, I covered the variety of concepts and terminologies that characterize the careers field. They stem from the many disciplinary perspectives upon which careers studies build. In terms of disciplinary positioning I have pointed out the duality within the discipline: *Career management* and *career counseling* as two related sub-fields that can benefit from mutual learning. I listed many theories and concepts, though no list can be fully inclusive and the field continues to progress.

New perspectives emerge, such as the more recent attention to the dark side of careers or to the gig-economy, alongside the continuous attention to organizational careers. Specific attention was devoted to the academic issue of methodology – how can careers be studied, which tools are available and are a fit for career scholarship. I hope the reader will find it useful for prompting further research in the field.

REFERENCES

Aisenbrey, S., & Fasang, A. E. (2010). New life for old ideas: The 'second wave' of sequence analysis bringing the 'course' back into the life course. *Sociological Methods & Research, 38*(3), 420–462.

Al Ariss, A., & Crowley-Henry, M. (2013). Self-initiated expatriation and migration in the management literature: Present theorizations and future research directions. *Career Development International, 18*(1), 78–96.

Allen, T. D., & Eby, L. T. (Eds.) (2007). *The Blackwell Handbook of Mentoring: A Multiple Perspective Approach.* Malden, MA: Blackwell.

Altman, Y., & Baruch, Y. (2012). Global self-initiated corporate expatriate careers: A new era in international assignments? *Personnel Review, 41*(2), 233–255.

Arnold, J., & Cohen, L. (2008). The psychology of careers in industrial and organizational settings: A critical but appreciative analysis. In G. P. Hodgkinson & J. K. Ford (Eds.), *International Review of Industrial and Organizational Psychology.* Chichester: Wiley, Vol. 23, pp. 1–44.

Arthur, M. B. (2008). Examining contemporary careers: A call for interdisciplinary inquiry. *Human Relations, 61*(2), 163–186.

Arthur, M. B. (2014). The boundaryless career at 20: Where do we stand, and where can we go? *Career Development International, 19*(6), 627–640.

Arthur, M. B., Claman, P. H., & DeFillippi, R. J. (1995). Intelligent enterprise, intelligent careers. *Academy of Management Executive, 9*(4), 7–22.

Arthur, M. B., Hall, D. T., & Lawrence, B. S. (Eds.) (1989). *Handbook of Career Theory.* Cambridge: Cambridge University Press.

Arthur, M. B., & Rousseau, D. M. (1996). The boundaryless career as a new employment principle. In M. G. Arthur & D. M. Rousseau (Eds.), *The Boundaryless Career.* New York: Oxford University Press, pp. 3–20.

Baruch, Y. (2004a). Transforming careers: From linear to multidirectional career paths: Organizational and individual perspectives. *Career Development International, 9*(1), 58–73.

Baruch, Y. (2004b). *Managing Careers: Theory and Practice.* Harlow: FT–Prentice Hall/ Pearson.

Baruch, Y. (2015). Organizational and labor market as career eco-system. In A. De Vos & B. I. J. M. Van der Heijden (Eds.), *Handbook of Research on Sustainable Careers.* Cheltenham, UK and Northampton, MA, USA: Edward Elgar Publishing, pp. 164–180.

Baruch, Y., & Bozionelos, N. (2011). Career issues. In S. Zedeck (Ed.), *APA Handbook of Industrial & Organizational Psychology.* Washington, DC: APA Publications, pp. 67–113.

Baruch, Y., & Hall, D. T. (2004). The academic career: A model for future careers in other sectors? *Journal of Vocational Behavior, 64*(2), 241–262.

Baruch, Y., & Rousseau, D. M. (2019). Integrating psychological contracts and their stakeholders in career studies and management. *The Academy of Management Annals, 13*(1), 84–111.

Baruch, Y., Szücs, N., & Gunz, H. (2015). Career studies in search of theory: The rise and rise of concepts. *Career Development International, 20*(1), 3–20.

Baruch, Y., & Vardi, Y. (2016). A fresh look at the dark side of contemporary careers: Toward a realistic discourse. *British Journal of Management, 27*(2), 355–372.

Biemann, T., & Datta, D. (2014). Analyzing sequence data: Optimal matching in management research. *Organizational Research Methods, 17*(1), 51–76.

Blokker, R., Akkermans, J., Tims, M., Jansen, P., & Khapova, S. (2019). Building a sustainable start: The role of career competencies, career success, and career shocks in young professionals' employability. *Journal of Vocational Behavior.* 112, 172–184.

Blustein, D. L. (1997). A context-rich perspective of career exploration across the life roles. *The Career Development Quarterly, 45*(3), 260–274.

Brew, A., Boud, D., Lucas, L., & Crawford, K. (2017). Responding to university policies and initiatives: The role of reflexivity in the mid-career academic. *Journal of Higher Education Policy and Management, 39*(4), 378–389. doi:10.1080/1360080X.2017.1330819.

Bright, J. E., Pryor, R. G., Chan, E. W., & Rijanto, J. (2009). Chance events in career development: Influence, control and multiplicity. *Journal of Vocational Behavior, 75*(1), 14–25. doi:10.1016/j.jvb.2009.02.007

Briscoe, J. P., Henagan, S. C., Burton, J. P., & Murphy, W. M. (2012). Coping with an insecure employment environment: The differing roles of protean and boundaryless career orientations. *Journal of Vocational Behavior, 80*(2), 308–316.

Cardoso, P., Silva, J. R., Gonçalves, M. M., & Duarte, M. E. (2014). Innovative moments and change in career construction counseling. *Journal of Vocational Behavior, 84*(1), 11–20.

Cassell, C., & Symon, G. (Eds.) (2004). *Essential Guide to Qualitative Methods in Organizational Research.* London: Sage.

Cohen, A. (2018). *Counterproductive Work Behaviors: Understanding the Dark Side of Personalities in Organizational Life.* New York: Routledge.

DeFillippi, R. J., & Arthur, M. B. (1994). The boundaryless career: A competency-based perspective. *Journal of Organizational Behavior, 15*, 307–324.

Denyer, D., & Tranfield, D. (2009). Producing a systematic review. In D. Buchanan & A. Bryman (Eds.), *The Sage Handbook of Organizational Research Methods.* Thousand Oaks, CA: Sage, pp. 671–689.

De Vos, A., & Van der Heijden, B. I. J. M. (Eds.) (2015). *Handbook of Research on Sustainable Careers.* Cheltenham, UK and Northampton, MA, USA: Edward Elgar Publishing.

Dickersin, K., Scherer, R., & Lefebvre, C. (1994). Systematic reviews: Identifying relevant studies for systematic reviews. *The BMJ, 309*(6964), 1286–1291.

Dickmann, M., & Baruch, Y. (2011). *Global Careers.* New York: Routledge.

Dlouhy, K., & Biemann, T. (2015). Optimal matching analysis in career research: A review and some best-practice recommendations. *Journal of Vocational Behavior, 90*, 163–173.

Dobrow, S. R., & Tosti-Kharas, J. (2011). Calling: The development of a scale measure. *Personnel Psychology, 64*(4), 1001–1049.

Dwan, K., Gamble, C., Williamson, P. R., & Kirkham, J. J. (2013). Systematic review of the empirical evidence of study publication bias and outcome reporting bias: An updated review. *PloS One, 8*(7), e66844.

Dyer Jr, W. G. (1995). Toward a theory of entrepreneurial careers. *Entrepreneurship Theory and Practice, 19*(2), 7–21.

Feldman, D. C., & Weitz, B. A. (1988). Career plateaus reconsidered. *Journal of Management, 14*(1), 69–80.

Ference, T. P., Stoner, J. A., & Warren, E. K. (1977). Managing the career plateau. *Academy of Management Review, 2*(4), 602–612.

Forret, M. L., & Sullivan, S. E. (2002). A balanced scorecard approach to networking: A guide to successfully navigating career changes. *Organizational Dynamics, 31*(3), 245–258.

Fugate, M., Kinicki, A. J., & Ashforth, B. E. (2004). Employability: A psycho-social construct, its dimensions, and applications. *Journal of Vocational Behavior, 65*(1), 14–38.

Fugate, M., Van der Heijden, B. I. J. M., De Vos, A., Forrier, A., & De Cuyper, N. (2021). Is what's past prologue? A review and agenda for contemporary employability research. *Academy of Management Annals*. https://doi.org/10.5465/annals.2018.0171.

Gargiulo, M., & Benassi, M. (1999). The dark side of social capital. In R. T. A. J. Leenders & S. M. Gabbay (Eds.), *Corporate Social Capital and Liability*. Boston, MA: Springer, pp. 298–322.

Gioia, D. A., Corley, K. G., & Hamilton, A. L. (2013). Seeking qualitative rigor in inductive research notes on the Gioia methodology. *Organizational Research Methods*, *16*(1), 15–31.

Greenhaus, J. H., & Callanan, G. A. (2006). *Encyclopedia of Career Development*. Thousand Oaks, CA: Sage.

Greenhaus, J. H., Callanan, G. A., & Godshalk, V. M. (2019). *Career Management for Life* (5th edn). New York: Routledge.

Grimland, S., Vigoda-Gadot, E., & Baruch, Y. (2012). Career attitudes and success of managers: The impact of chance event, protean and traditional careers. *International Journal of Human Resource Management*, *23*(6), 1074–1094.

Gunz, H., Evans, M. G., & Jalland, R. M. (2000). Career boundaries in a boundaryless world. In M. Peiperl, M. B. Arthur, R. Goffee, & T. Morris (Eds.), *Career Frontiers: New Conceptions of Working Lives*. New York: Oxford University Press, pp. 24–53.

Gunz, H. P., Jalland, R. M., & Evans, M. G. (1998). New strategy, wrong managers? What you need to know about career streams. *Academy of Management Perspectives*, *12*(2), 21–37.

Gunz, H. P., & Peiperl, M. A. (Eds.) (2007). *Handbook of Career Studies*. Thousand Oaks, CA: Sage.

Hall, D. T. (1976). *Careers in Organizations*. Pacific Palisades, CA: Goodyear.

Hall, D. T. (1996). *The Career is Dead – Long Live the Career*. San Francisco, CA: Jossey-Bass.

Hall, D. T. (2002). *Careers In and Out of the Organization*. Thousand Oaks, CA: Sage.

Hall, D. T. (2004). The protean career: A quarter-century journey. *Journal of Vocational Behavior*, *65*(1), 1–13.

Hall, D. T., & Chandler, D. E. (2005). Psychological success: When the career is a calling. *Journal of Organizational Behavior*, *26*(2), 155–176.

Handy, C. (1994). *The Age of Paradox*. Boston, MA: Harvard Business School Press.

Heslin, P. A. (2005). Conceptualizing and evaluating career success. *Journal of Organizational Behavior*, *26*(2), 113–136.

Higgins, M. (2005). *Career Imprints. Creating Leaders Across an Industry*. San Francisco, CA: Jossey-Bass.

Hirschi, A., & Jaensch, V. K. (2015). Narcissism and career success: Occupational self-efficacy and career engagement as mediators. *Personality and Individual Differences*, *77*, 205–208.

Homberg, F., & Bui, H. T. M. (2013). Top management team diversity: A systematic review. *Group & Organization Management*, *38*(4), 455–479.

Hu, W. C., Thistlethwaite, J. E., Weller, J., Gallego, G., Monteith, J., & McColl, G. J. (2015). 'It was serendipity': A qualitative study of academic careers in medical education. *Medical Education*, *49*(11), 1124–1136. doi:10.1111/medu.12822.

Hughes, E. C. (1937). Institutional office and the person. *American Journal of Sociology*, *43*, 404–443.

Inkson, K. (2006), *Understanding Careers: The Metaphors of Working Lives*. Thousand Oaks, CA: Sage.

Inkson, K., & Arthur, M. B. (2001). How to be a successful career capitalist. *Organizational Dynamics*, *30*(1), 48–61.

Inkson, K., Gunz, H., Ganesh, S., & Roper, J. (2012). Boundaryless careers: Bringing back boundaries. *Organization Studies*, *33*(3), 323–340.

Johnson, R. B., & Onwuegbuzie, A. J. (2004). Mixed methods research: A research paradigm whose time has come. *Educational Researcher*, *33*(7), 14–26.

Jones, C., & DeFillippi, R. J. (1996). Back to the future in film: Combining industry and self-knowledge to meet the career challenges of the 21st century. *Academy of Management Perspectives*, *10*(4), 89–103.

Kindsiko, E., & Baruch, Y. (2019). Careers of PhD graduates: The role of chance events and how to manage them. *Journal of Vocational Behavior*, *112*, 122–140.

Kram, K. E. (1985). *Mentoring at Work: Developmental Relationships in Organizational Life*. Glenview, IL: Scott Foresman.

Krumboltz, J. D. (2009). The happenstance learning theory. *Journal of Career Assessment*, *17*(2), 135–154.

Lee, C. I. S. G., Felps, W., & Baruch, Y. (2014). Toward a taxonomy of career studies through bibliometric visualization. *Journal of Vocational Behavior*, *85*(3), 339–351.

London, M. (1983). Toward a theory of career motivation. *Academy of Management Review*, *8*, 620–630.

Lowe, T. S. (2018). Perceived job and labor market insecurity in the United States: An assessment of workers' attitudes from 2002 to 2014. *Work and Occupations*, *45*(3), 313–345.

Mainiero, L. A., & Sullivan, S. E. (2006). *The Opt-Out Revolt: Why People are Leaving Companies to Create Kaleidoscope Careers*. Palo Alto, CA: Davis-Black.

Mallon, M. (1998). The portfolio career: Pushed or pulled to it? *Personnel Review*, *27*(5), 361–377.

Mayrhofer, W., Iellatchitch, A., Meyer, M., Steyrer, J., Schiffinger, M., & Strunk, G. (2004). Going beyond the individual: Some potential contributions from a career field and habitus perspective for global career research and practice. *Journal of Management Development*, *23*(9), 870–884.

McCabe, V. S., & Savery, L. K. (2007). 'Butterflying' a new career pattern for Australia? Empirical evidence. *Journal of Management Development*, *26*(2), 103–116.

McMahon, M. (2016). Working with storytellers: A metaphor for career counselling. In M. McMahon (Ed.), *Career Counselling*. New York: Routledge, pp. 35–46.

Murphy, W. M. (2012). Reverse mentoring at work: Fostering cross-generational learning and developing millennial leaders. *Human Resource Management*, *51*(4), 549–573.

Ng, T. W. H., Eby, L. T., Sorensen, K. L., & Feldman, D. C. (2005). Predictors of objective and subjective career success: A meta-analysis. *Personnel Psychology*, *58*(2), 367–408.

Nicholson, N. (1996). Career systems in crisis: Change and opportunity in the information age. *Academy of Management Perspectives*, *10*(4), 40–51.

Nigam, A., & Dokko, G. (2019). Career resourcing and the process of professional emergence. *Academy of Management Journal*, *62*(4), 1052–1084.

Nilforooshan, P., & Salimi, S. (2016). Career adaptability as a mediator between personality and career engagement. *Journal of Vocational Behavior*, *94*, 1–10.

Osterman, P. (1996). *Broken Ladders: Managerial Careers in the New Economy*. New York: Oxford University Press.

Peiperl, M. A., & Baruch, Y. (1997). Back to square zero: The post-corporate career. *Organizational Dynamics*, *25*(4), 7–22.

Pryor, R., & Bright, J. (2011). *The Chaos Theory of Careers: A New Perspective on Working in the Twenty-First Century*. New York: Routledge.

Rice, A. (2014). Incorporation of chance into career development theory and research. *Journal of Career Development*, *41*(5), 445–463. doi:10.1177/0894845313507750.

Rodrigues, R., Guest, D., & Budjanovcanin, A. (2016). Bounded or boundaryless? An empirical investigation of career boundaries and boundary crossing. *Work, Employment and Society*, *30*(4), 669–686.

Rothwell, A., & Arnold, J. (2007). Self-perceived employability: Development and validation of a scale. *Personnel Review*, *36*(1), 23–41.

Rothwell, W. J., Jackson, R. D., Ressler, C. L., Jones, M. C., & Brower, M. (2015). *Career Planning and Succession Management: Developing Your Organization's Talent – for Today and Tomorrow*. Santa Barbara, CA: Praeger.

Rousseau, D. M. (1995). *Psychological Contracts in Organizations*. Thousand Oaks, CA: Sage.

Rouvrais, S., Remaud, B., & Saveuse, M. (2020). Work-based learning models in engineering curricula: Insight from the French experience. *European Journal of Engineering Education*, *45*(1), 89–102.

Rynes, S. L., Bartunek, J. M., & Daft, R. L. (2001). Across the great divide: Knowledge creation and transfer between practitioners and academics. *Academy of Management Journal*, *44*(2), 340–355.

Saunders, M., Lewis, P., & Thornhill, A. (2016). *Research Methods for Business Students* (7th edn.). Harlow, UK: Pearson.

Savickas, M. L. (1997). Career adaptability: An integrative construct for life-span, life-space theory. *The Career Development Quarterly*, *45*(3), 247–259.

Savickas, M. L. (2013). Career construction theory and practice. In S. D. Brown & R. W. Lent (Eds.), *Career Development and Counseling: Putting Theory and Research to Work*. Hoboken, NJ: John Wiley & Sons, vol 2, pp. 147–183.

Schein, E. H. (1978). *Career Dynamics: Matching Individual and Organizational Needs*. Reading, MA: Addison-Wesley.

Schein, E. H. (1985). *Career Anchors: Discovering your Real Values*. San Francisco, CA: University Associate Inc.

Shepherd, D. A., & Suddaby, R. (2017). Theory building: A review and integration. *Journal of Management*, *43*(1), 59–86.

Spurk, D., Hirschi, A., & Dries, N. (2019). Antecedents and outcomes of objective versus subjective career success: Competing perspectives and future directions. *Journal of Management*, *45*(1), 35–69.

Sukiennik, D., Bendat, W., Raufman, L., & Sikiennik, D. (2013). *The Career Fitness Program: Exercising your Options*. Harlow, UK: Pearson Education.

Sullivan, S. E. (1999). The changing nature of careers: A review and research agenda. *Journal of Management*, *25*(3), 457–484.

Sullivan, S. E., & Baruch, Y. (2009). Advances in career theory and research: A critical review and agenda for future exploration. *Journal of Management*, *35*(6), 1542–1571.

Super, D. E. (1957). *The Psychology of Careers*. New York: Harper & Row.

Super, D. E. (1980). A life-span, life-space approach to career development. *Journal of Vocational Behavior*, *16*(3), 282–298.

Super, D. E., & Knasel, E. G. (1981). Career development in adulthood: Some theoretical problems and a possible solution. *British Journal of Guidance & Counselling*, *9*, 194–201.

Swanson, J. L., & Fouad, N. A. (2014). *Career Theory and Practice: Learning through Case Studies*. London: Sage.

Tomlinson, J., Baird, M., Berg, P., & Cooper, R. (2018). Flexible careers across the life course: Advancing theory, research and practice. *Human Relations*, *71*(1), 4–22.

Townsend, R. (1970). *Up the Organization*. New York: Knopf.

Tremblay, D. G. (2003). New types of careers in the knowledge economy. *Communications & Strategies*, *49*(1), 81–105.

Valcour, M., Bailyn, L., & Quijada, M. (2007). Customized careers. In M. A. Peiperl & H. P. Gunz (Eds.), *Handbook of Career Studies*. Thousand Oaks, CA: Sage, pp. 188–210.

Van der Heijde, C. M., & Van der Heijden, B. I. J. M. (2006). A competence-based and multidimensional operationalization and measurement of employability. *Human Resource Management*, *45*, 449–476.

van der Laken, P., Bakk, Z., Giagkoulas, V., van Leeuwen, L., & Bongenaar, E. (2018). Expanding the methodological toolbox of HRM researchers: The added value of latent bathtub models and optimal matching analysis. *Human Resource Management*, *57*(3), 751–760.

Veiga, J. F. (1981). Plateaued versus nonplateaued managers: Career patterns, attitudes, and path potential. *Academy of Management Journal*, *24*(3), 566–578.

Walsh, W. B., & Osipow, S. H. (2014). *Career Counseling: Contemporary Topics in Vocational Psychology*. New York: Routledge.

Wang, D., Du, F., & Marquis, C. (2019). Defending Mao's dream: How politicians' ideological imprinting affects firms' political appointment in China. *Academy of Management Journal*, *62*(4), 1111–1136.

Waterman, R. H. Jr, Waterman, J. A., & Collard, B. A. (1994). Toward a career-resilient workforce. *Harvard Business Review*, *72*(4), 87–95.

Whyte, W. H. (1956). *The Organization Man*. Philadelphia, PA: University of Pennsylvania Press.

Wilensky, H. L. (1961). Careers, life-styles, and social integration. *International Social Science Journal*, *12*, 553–558.

Wrzesniewski, A., McCauley, C., Rozin, P., & Schwartz, B. (1997). Jobs, careers, and callings: People's relations to their work. *Journal of Research in Personality*, *31*(1), 21–33.

Zhou, W., Guan, Y., Xin, L., Mak, M. C. K., & Deng, Y. (2016). Career success criteria and locus of control as indicators of adaptive readiness in the career adaptation model. *Journal of Vocational Behavior*, *94*, 124–130. doi:10.1016/j.jvb.2016.02.015.

3.   The 5C Group: developing and sustaining a cross-cultural team

Jon P. Briscoe, Michael Dickmann, Douglas T. Hall, Emma Parry, and Wolfgang Mayrhofer

INTRODUCTION: GROUP, LEADERSHIP, AND TASK

This chapter will review the genesis and ongoing operation of the 5C Group: The Cross-Cultural Collaboration on Contemporary Careers (see 5c.careers). While methodological considerations will be outlined, the main goal of this chapter is to describe how we collectively design and manage a complex, cross-cultural group to achieve not just research goals, but also the developmental goals of the group members as well as social impact. Other writings on the project cover our early stages (Briscoe, Chudzikowski, Demel, Mayrhofer, and Unite, 2012), reflections on its contributions to one of the key areas in the field (Briscoe, Dickmann, Hall, Parry, Mayrhofer, and Smale, 2018), and our emic stance when it comes to understanding careers across the globe (Mayrhofer et al., 2016).

The 5C project is unique in its scale, especially in the careers field. It currently involves 30 country teams (and growing) and over 60 researchers. A review of the literature shows that very few cross-cultural studies in the careers field go beyond even a few countries (Briscoe, Dickmann, and Parry, 2020). Notable similar projects in other realms of social science and management research include, among others, the GLOBE project on leadership (House, Hanges, Javidan, Dorfman, and Gupta, 2004), CRANET (Parry, Stavrou, and Morley, 2011), the World Values Survey (http://www.worldvaluessurvey.org/wvs.jsp) and the European Values Study (https://europeanvaluesstudy.eu/). The Hofstede (Hofstede, 1980; Hofstede, Hofstede, and Minkov, 2010) and Schwartz (2006) studies on cultural values also come to mind, although each of them are primarily coordinated by their namesakes with cooperation from partners, not necessarily co-equal involvement.

We strongly believe that understanding careers across cultural contexts is critical. The great majority of empirical research—but even more importantly theory—finds its genesis in Western Europe and the United States as the core of so-called WEIRD countries—Western, Educated, Industrial, Rich, Democratic—that do not, on the other hand, constitute the majority of people (Henrich, Heine, and Norenzayan, 2010). As has been explored elsewhere, this results in a situation in which a fraction of the world tries to not only understand, but also define the rest of the world's career challenges and opportunities.

Even with careful methods and research strategies that hopefully produce accurate and locally representative results, if they are driven by only Western researchers, they do not appreciate, and/or produce capacity in local populations to define and conduct relevant research from an emic perspective.

Thus, in our work, beyond producing theory and research that is hopefully useful, we aimed to also identify, develop and empower researchers in diverse parts of the world, to bring attention to diverse populations and their "careerscapes," and to contribute to efforts being more inclusive in social science research.

In the remainder of this chapter we will discuss various phases of our research to date, and across those phases we will describe research strategies and methods (broadly), leadership, and group development and maintenance (see Table 3.1). Because these three factors are interconnected we managed them together, sometimes explicitly, sometimes implicitly, and sometimes not at all due to a lack of awareness or appreciation of the issues at hand as well as a lack of insight and mere capacity in terms of energy and time. Looking back allows us to harvest lessons learned. We will group them along three distinct, yet fuzzy development periods: Phase 1 denotes the early stage of the endeavor with a focus on setting up the collaboration and getting started with interview data; Phase 2 involves enlarging the scope both in terms of participating countries and moving from interview to survey data; the transition to Phase 3 signals yet another development step with considerations about next steps.

PHASE 1: THE EARLY STAGES

Forming a Team

The genesis of the idea for a cross-cultural group on careers started with Jon Briscoe's developing passion for careers (which had not been focal in his doctoral studies), and nascent interest in the world beyond his home country. He had gone to a meeting at EGOS (European Group for Organizational Studies) in Barcelona in 2002, which he later found out was the first time a track in EGOS had been devoted to careers. This was stimulating—intellectually, empirically, culturally and socially. One early impression was that Europeans really emphasized context while Americans emphasized the individual. The conference sessions in fact reflected this European predilection, requiring the track to meet as a group for two days versus attending myriad hand-picked sessions. This allowed some depth to develop relationships and understanding.

On the other side of the Atlantic, Jon had been happily extending his relationship with his dissertation chair at Boston University, USA, Douglas T. Hall (Tim). Uninterested in careers as a primary topic in his doctoral training, Jon became a "believer" when he started his own career as a professor and more importantly, saw how careers represented an intersection of so many life dimensions for his working MBA students. Jon contacted Tim who agreed to pursue theoretical and empirical work on careers with his former student.

This nexus of interest in careers (protean careers primarily) and international research generated an idea of testing protean careers across countries. As such, Jon

Table 3.1   *Developmental issues in the lifecycle of the 5C Group*

	Phase 1 Forming the Collaboration and Beginning Research	Phase 2 Enlarging the Size and Scope of the Team and the Research	Phase 3 Strategic and Institutional Growth
Team Issues	Member Recruitment and Selection	Shifting from a tilt toward personality and values to seeking skills and expertise as well	Expanding beyond first person interaction
	Norm Establishment	Keeping the norms while remaining open minded	Institutionalizing norms while adapting to larger scale
	Emergence of Ritual and Symbol	Finding your place in a large group	
Research Issues	Forming Questions	Forming new questions	Establishing transcendent questions
	Research Strategy	From qualitative to quantitative	
	Choosing Method and Approach	Choosing and testing constructs and instruments	
	Country Selection	Broadening the scope	
	Sample Selection of People/ Occupation		
	Data Collection	From interviews to surveys	
	Data Analysis	From micro to macro	
Leadership Issues	Establishing and Modeling Guiding Values	Clarifying and practicing shared and specialized leadership roles	Leadership succession
	Eliciting Broad Participation	Managing and coordinating subgroups versus one team	Tension between looking inward and outward
	Establishing Rules	Continuity versus change	Establishing strategy based upon purpose versus outward success
	Developing the Psychological Contract	Encouraging creativity and contribution	Legitimization of the group outwardly
	Establishing a "Secure Base"	Managing tension between instrumentality and community	
	Conflict Resolution		

needed partners. He reached out first to Tim to gauge interest and then at a meeting of the Academy of Management in 2003 to Wolfgang Mayrhofer from WU Vienna, Austria, whom he had met at EGOS. These decisions were based upon a confidence in their skills, character, and social compatibility. The next summer at EGOS and the Academy of Management meetings, social meetings were planned with a few potential partners to explore opportunities. After this initial partnering, we slowly expanded the circle to invite doctoral students and more associates and a first formal meeting was held before the Academy of Management Meeting in Hawaii in 2005.

Identifying partners

Selection of partners was and remains perhaps the single most important decision to be made in our research journey. Partners combine to create a "secure base" (Waters and Cummings, 2000) from which the world can be viewed and interpreted. From the beginning, the initial three partners (Jon, Tim, Wolfgang) were very reflective and explicit about the values we were looking for in our partners.

We aimed to identify people who were relatively non-instrumental—meaning they valued the research and collegial journey as much as the outcome destination, especially in terms of expected publications. We strongly focused on being developmental, meaning we encouraged new researchers (doctoral students and early career academics) to participate in order to grow. Partners' growth remains a key part of the group culture and an outcome that is co-equal if not more important than research outcomes. We wanted people who cared about career actors, meaning the ultimate end users of our research and the communities in which they live. This priority takes precedence over "sexier" research that might generate headlines but lacks practical utility. Interest in careers was sought, a bit more than research skills, with the assumption that it would sustain and positively influence "commitment to the cause," while additional research skills could, if necessary, be acquired. As research stages progressed, more specificity in skills was sometimes required. A practical necessity was to be able to speak and communicate effectively in English.

Team dynamics
Beyond selecting partners, group maintenance involved establishing norms, boundaries and rituals. For example, a norm existed that not providing data meant not being part of the group. This norm, along with the selection norms mentioned above, also served as a boundary that both restricted and enabled behavior, for example in terms of participation and being engaged. Another boundary was that the leadership team had to approve of new members and then the group had to meet those new members and have a mutual (with the potential new member) approbation. There were times when a friend would be nominated or an outsider would try to join that had no apparent interest in careers and/or was not deemed as compatible with the core norms and values of 5C and the gatekeeping function worked effectively.

A norm of encouraging participation was always important, but we worked especially hard in the early years to not only encourage but expect this by having everyone report and present their findings and ideas. Another norm, reflecting participation was that anyone who volunteered for a task could take it on—such as developing a coding framework or creating a conference proposal. Other norms include meeting two times a year, usually for two days each. A norm that developed from experience was having our meetings, if possible at all, before versus after adjacent conferences; otherwise our energy and focus became depleted.

A ritual that is not too unusual was simply sharing meals or building into the meeting program a half day of joint social activities. Both partly became memorable based upon their sometimes exotic or fun locations, such as a dinner with a fantastic view on the Greek island of Spetses, taking part in the ball of WU (University of Vienna) in the imperial palace, or residing in a condo on the Pacific Ocean Beach with a crab feast dinner. They were times where we could rest from a busy day's work. Wolfgang emerged as the social facilitator of the group and was creative in developing new icebreakers for each meeting. He, more than others seemed to recognize the necessity of checking in with one another, and giving some permeability to rigid boundaries that normally separate work and personal lives. Over many years we learned of births, deaths, children, first homes, publications, and so on. Having rituals that go beyond work was important to creating a sense of community.

Methodological Concerns

At some point before the first formal 5C meeting, as we did more planning for theory and methods, we came to realize that testing protean career theory around the world would merely meet the goal of testing one theory, developed in the U.S., in countries that may or may not even frame careers in a similar fashion. This would be squarely against the basic thought of moving beyond ethnocentric research based on WEIRD assumptions. For our purposes, we realized we had to first understand how careers were viewed in local cultures. This seemed to demand a qualitative approach, given the prevalence of Western frameworks in the careers arena.

Triggered by our initial meeting in Hawaii, a consecutive set of meetings allowed us to discuss as a larger team how to design our research. We wanted to know what people value in their careers and how they manage their careers, in different countries. We framed these two queries around "career success" and "career transitions." We developed an interview guide that in addition to seeking context and background information asked interviewees how they defined career success, and about one or more crucial career transitions. The focus on career transition was used to see how contextual factors and personal factors framed how the interviewee approached, managed, and learned from (or not) their transition.

A parenthetical note—while we chose qualitative research for theoretical reasons, it turned out to be an ideal (if sometimes difficult) way to collaborate because it demanded that everyone bring their findings to the table and discuss them with the group. This was a good way to build relationships and establish a deeper common team identity.

Sampling occupations

We realized that we could not interview enough people to generalize across populations, so we tried to be both strategic and theoretically grounded about selective sampling. We settled on three broad occupational groups: business management, nurses, and manual labor. We chose these based upon the mobility that each occupation might experience, their existence across the globe as well as the degree of structure that might be imposed upon each occupation. We aimed to interview an equal number of men and women in each occupation. Finally, we decided to look at individuals in their early career stages (out from graduation or apprenticeship at least five years) and late career stages (less than ten years to retirement). We reasoned that, consistent with other research (Levinson, 1978; 2011) the early career is a time of pressure but also opportunity, in which we could see formative issues in careers, across people. In turn, focusing upon the later career stages allowed us to see more of a repository of career experience and outcomes.

Country sampling

Trying to decide how to sample countries we considered Hofstede's work (Hofstede, 1980; Hofstede, Hofstede, and Minkov, 2010). However, the Hofstede framework categorized countries on a series of 2x2 matrices such as individualism (high/low) and masculinity/femininity, which was not helpful for determining sampling regions. Hofstede's research also had certain limitations such as using only IBM employees and only employees who could speak English. We therefore turned to Schwartz's (2006) research in part because his methods seemed less problematic but also because he presented a framework with seven cultural regions: Africa and the Middle East, Confucian Asia, Eastern Europe, English Speaking, Latin America, South Asia, and Western Europe (Schwartz views Israel as unique from these regions). These regions are based upon variation across seven culture value orientations: affective autonomy/intellectual autonomy versus embeddedness, hierarchy versus egalitarianism, and mastery versus harmony. The GLOBE framework (House et al., 2004) also existed at the time, and closely parallels and further specifies cultural regions akin to Schwartz's 2006 framework, however we did not initially utilize this framework.

We implemented our research plan by conducting interviews in at least one country of each region: Africa and Middle East—South Africa and Israel; Confucian Asia—China and Japan; Eastern Europe—Serbia; English Speaking—United States; Latin America—Costa Rica and Mexico; South Asia—Malaysia; and Western Europe—Austria and Spain.

Data analysis

Analyzing qualitative data across countries is a difficult process. In order to be able to compare results non-English speakers needed to translate emerging themes into English. After writing an initial report from each country, the research team had a two-day meeting to discuss and compare notes.

This meeting was held on the beautiful Greek island of Spetses in July of 2006. We chose this venue because it was the site of the annual meeting of the International Association of Cross-Cultural Psychology. We presented various country results from the 5C project which helped the members obtain reimbursement from their universities. We combined research meetings with conference participation, and the idyllic setting and wonderful Greek seafood meals contributed greatly to our motivation and creativity. This meeting cemented for us the idea that the process was at least as important as any research deliverables. Another benefit of this meeting was that Shalom Schwartz, whose model we had used in selecting countries, was the keynote speaker, and we had the opportunity to meet with him and obtain his helpful feedback and suggestions for our research.

A critical part of this stage was to de-emphasize status, language skill, and personality and invite and urge all members to participate in the dialogue. This represents an N-Way approach (Brett, Tinsley, Janssens, Barsness, and Lytle, 1997) which also parallels our defining of the research questions and methods. An N-Way approach tries to avoid having a dominant voice or view and asks each research member to contribute their perspective.

From the conceptual categories that emerged from analyses during this meeting, we created a detailed coding guide and each country team agreed to code their data according to it. Most but not all countries encoded this process using N-vivo analysis software.

The tangible outcomes of this phase of the research, which we refer to as "Phase 1" were an edited book (Briscoe, Hall, and Mayrhofer, 2012) and several articles, which we won't detail here as we are addressing building a cross-cultural team primarily. The intangible results of this phase were that we had a common framework we could refer to and we had a feeling of having accomplished something useful and of becoming a cohesive work group.

Leadership and group dynamics issues
There are several leadership issues related to Phase 1. Probably the most important one is value clarity and value expression. Identifying the values that guided our effort allowed us to understand boundaries in relation to what is worthy of group effort, who is appropriate as a research partner, and how to govern learning processes and resolve interpersonal or group conflicts. Values need to be expressed, challenged and discussed at regular intervals because like any living group, circumstances change and values and boundaries that may have been appropriate before may need to be revisited, adjusted, or understood in new ways.

Another leadership task is providing gravity to the group, in terms of providing a secure base and a role of authority, which inevitably involves status, role, and power differences to a degree. Academics, while sometimes really opinionated, are not much different from the general population of workers in terms of wanting direction, or, wanting to follow someone else's lead versus being disruptive, or original. The formal leaders in Phase 1 (Jon, Tim, Wolfgang) had to balance providing "gravity" with encouraging innovation, expression, voice and participation. Without giving attention to this tension, it is not hard to imagine leaders becoming consumed with authority, status and power and defeating the N-Way approach that is so vital if taking a qualitative and/or theory generating approach not only across cultures, but also across a diverse set of biases, skills and personalities.

An important aspect in our view is sharing leadership roles, both formally and informally. Jon, Tim, and Wolfgang acted in concert in general, but certainly had their own opinions, strengths and weaknesses. At times one person may be taking formal charge of a meeting while another person is providing vital group maintenance functions, such as Wolfgang's icebreakers. One may have more skills with organizing, one with motivating, and another with recruiting. These strengths evolve based upon group task and size. It is our view that having more than a single leader dilutes the likelihood of status and power going to the head of a single person as well as being seduced into a research track or framework that is overly idiosyncratic, quixotic or simply wrong-headed.

Of course, leadership emerges in every meeting and interaction with the group at large. Junior faculty or doctoral students would suggest and pursue innovations in research design, coding, writing, and so on. Opportunities were given to help sponsor and highlight some who have fewer opportunities for the spotlight.

Coordination of the group is a real task. Meetings must be arranged, reservations made, publishers communicated with, and so on. One person doing this by themselves is not sustainable. Structure versus consideration (Judge, Piccolo, and Ilies, 2004) becomes a salient issue. Group building, brainstorming and other organic necessities of a thriving group must be balanced against deadlines, the need for frameworks, rules of operation, and so on. This again is helped by having a group of formal leaders and informal leaders who can take turns leading and letting a given leader rest.

Another issue that is important but not obvious perhaps beforehand is "running interference" or managing exceptions with the formal and informal group. In some ways, group and organizational leadership parallels parenting. You hope to give your children roots and wings. You hope to provide them with a secure base with which to approach the world. Status and power differences will exist, as will individual *and* cultural variation in how conflict should be handled. Sometimes as formal and informal leaders, individually or together, we might have to entertain grievances that might be overly awkward for the group to face together. We might have to reassure a very valued team member that their contribution was needed and appreciated in spite of messages received or implied from another team member. Any team doing good work will develop passion and express emotion in good and also hard ways, and leading such a group requires some parent-like instincts and sympathies.

A final and very important function of group leadership in such a setting is leading change and guiding the group in facing the challenge of the "death" and "rebirth" of the group, albeit in different forms. At a meeting in Costa Rica we were all hitting our stride, getting along, and being productive. The question came up of "do we need to add more members?" The common sentiment was "no" if not "no!" We were a happy bunch who had learned to value one another and work synergistically. Wolfgang, however, was not in agreement and identified this as a critical juncture if we were to continue to advance the work. Wolfgang won the day.

PHASE 2: BROADENING THE SCOPE

Expanding the Team

As we had decided to press forward with our research, we shifted our focus to testing some of the variables we had identified across our qualitative sample from Phase 1, beyond a small collection of countries. This would mean the need to add more countries, and more members.

In some cases, interested acquaintances would approach a member of the 5C team, in other cases a member of the team would identify potential collaborators. When a potential team member self-identified or was identified, they would be sent a letter outlining the "psychological contract" informally, including our values and research goals, and in return they would be asked to supply a letter of interest addressed to the group leadership (Jon, Tim, and Wolfgang).

While a lot of our "pitch" and expectation of behavior involved group norms and goals, we were explicit in transactional ways as well. One of our promises, which has been more problematic than anticipated in execution, is that the initial four main articles that came out of the research would list every contributor if they provided the necessary data from their country. This proved difficult for various reasons such as articles getting accepted under different pretenses than were assumed by submitting authors (e.g. journal rules about listing multiple authors), articles assumed to be publishable that were less "ready for primetime" than we presumed, and data becoming available in an unpredictable and non-linear matter.

Beyond our anticipated four "main" articles, we set up and over time modified publication guidelines for further articles. For example, any country team was free to use their own data for any purpose, but if an author(s) wanted to use other countries' data they must first invite such countries' teams to participate in the analysis. Beyond that we defined what would constitute a meaningful contribution to obtaining data, analyzing it, and producing it in written form. In spirit these guidelines ring true with our culture, in practice it becomes a bit unwieldy and worries of social loafing and equity in contribution have at times surfaced.

It is also significant to note that our selection criteria for team members expanded slightly to seek out more individuals with specific statistical and macro skills as they would be needed in defining and conducting the coming research activities.

Finding partners was sometimes difficult depending upon the country region, with geographic proximity being a fair gauge for difficulty, with countries beyond Western Europe and English-speaking harder to find partners in. In some cases, we would court them, shopping for potential colleagues by viewing university websites and so on. In some cases, even still, partners have done tremendous work but have not been able to meet in person due to financial or logistical limitations.

Socially, as the group continued to grow, it was not as easy to know every person in-depth. This changed the operating realities of the group and discussion (and disagreement) was sometimes based more on a contest of ideas and less on personal diplomacy. This was both good and bad. Some personalities and some cultural perspectives were more low or high context and so we struggled at times to sort out ideas from theoretical perspective, differences in training, cultural styles and personalities. This was even more complicated (yet helped) by trying to adhere to our values of being developmental, egalitarian and striving for pro-social impact.

As the group grew, instrumentality became harder to screen out. We realize that ego and a need for achievement are needed to do good work, but we did not want to emphasize personal gain or reputation at the expense of the larger group. Again, relative anonymity made it a little easier for some people to be tempted to treat others as a means to an end. We tried to handle this by revisiting core values as important decisions were made. Along with a greater importance of instrumentality came more productivity, which was not unwelcome to most, if not all members of the group.

Leadership Evolution

We had anticipated a very orderly transition of leadership going into Phase 2—but, the reality became very different. Jon had been doing a lot of the titular leadership work and a great deal of coordination tasks, and had become burned out. However, he had not adequately communicated this, perhaps due to ambivalence about relinquishing a more central role, perhaps due to being unsure about how to discuss a transition. Besides, he was not sure if Wolfgang or Tim would want to take up the mantle.

Enter a broken toe. Jon had planned on announcing to the team that he did not wish to be the operational point person on Phase 2 at our next meeting, held in conjunction with the EGOS meeting in Gothenburg, Sweden in 2011. He anticipated a group discussion about how to move forward. Jon broke his toe right before his trip to Sweden and decided to avoid travel. He informed Wolfgang by email that he hoped to not be the point person on this phase. He assumed that Wolfgang would take up the mantle. To his surprise, Wolfgang called him at some point from Sweden letting him know that he had approached two of our newer members, Michael Dickmann and Emma Parry of Cranfield University's School of Management in the UK and asked if they would be willing to lead the group. He was calling for Jon's approval. The conversation was real-time and a response was needed. Surprised that Wolfgang had done this rather than take the role, Jon said yes, although without being completely at peace with it.

Michael, who had been approached by Wolfgang, had only joined the group two years earlier. Building on his experience as consultant and HR director, he brought a new discipline to team meetings and was able to facilitate difficult conversations with more facility than had been experienced by the group in the past. Emma brought organizational skills to the research itself such as database management and the coordination of tasks.

While the changes were welcome to most, Jon became confused about his role and experienced intermittent anxiety about who was leading the group. Emma and Michael also experienced some frustration with this. As a simple example, a new member showed up to a meeting and Jon and others did not know who this person was. It was a simple communications issue about who should be notified about a new member, and Emma felt put in a bad position by Jon's frustration over being caught by surprise.

In retrospect, Jon's anxiety was much like an entrepreneur's who having had an idea and started a company, is not completely happy about the turn of events required to bring the company to a more operational level.

Leadership roles were vague, as Jon, Tim and Wolfgang were the ostensible leaders of the group and acted as gatekeepers for new members, but Michael and Emma were running the meetings and essentially running the group. Jon's anxiety and desire to remain in the leadership role behind the scenes created tension, which was evident to others in meetings.

This latent conflict culminated in a more explicit way where roles were challenged and discussed over dinner amongst the now five leaders in Philadelphia in 2014.

Jon's point of view was that while Michael and Emma were doing a fine job with the project's second phase, they were taking on more overall leadership than he felt was warranted. Emma, as a task-focused individual, felt that she was simply trying to "get things done." Wolfgang added that the expanded group benefitted from more facilitation and guidance. In addition, Emma and Michael expressed that they had given a lot to the project and felt that even after this phase of the project was over, they wanted to remain vital to the team's leadership. At some point during the night, Tim (a key mentor of Jon as a reminder) and Wolfgang talked separately to Jon. In a non-judgmental way Tim said he had wondered how Jon would handle it when "he wasn't the owner of the group" anymore. Jon's latent conflict had come to the surface and he wasn't ready to let it go yet. He took a cab back to the hotel while the others walked, and Wolfgang volunteered to go with him. At some point during the ride, Jon expressed that it would be easier to perhaps walk away. Wolfgang said "it might be easier for you, but it would not be easier for the group." Incidentally, Emma had a similar conversation with Michael, suggesting that she might just leave the group, but was persuaded to stick it out. Both agreed that the vision and membership of 5C were fantastic, that they could feel a high level of energy and community spirit but that we would need to clarify the formal and informal leadership roles.

As it turned out, this night was a turning point. The meetings later that week were reportedly more comfortable for others present, and the expression of differences seemed to be all that was needed to start resolving the conflict. Jon became more accepting of shared leadership roles and more appreciative instead of conflicted about the contributions of Emma and Michael. An irony of this extended transition phase is that Jon was actually working against the norms of participation and development that he helped establish. There was a lack of appreciation for how much his identity was fused with the group and a boundary had now come to help him distinguish between his personal and formal connection to the group. Incidentally, clearer roles now enabled others to more openly express their appreciation of Jon's founding function and enduring commitment to 5C.

At some point, it was proposed by Wolfgang that rather than a single leader, there would be a "Steering Committee" of five co-equal leaders. Michael and Emma continued to manage the research operations for Phase 2, Jon managed membership, and all five provided "wisdom" and perspective to the team. When difficult issues arose whether in the public space of the group or in private, each of the leadership team was respected and turned to.

As the leadership group exists at this writing, it is an unusual and in some ways remarkable group. We have specialized, mostly organically, but sometimes out of negotiation into roles that add value for the group. Tim, as the most experienced (now retired but very active in the research) team member and as a respected pioneer in the field of careers, provides gravity to the group. His perspective, values, and ideas are respected and turned to. Wolfgang eschews formal authority but beyond being a socialization specialist has enormous informal influence on the group and seems to serve the role of asking hard questions (what should we be doing) and guiding the group through the answers to those questions. Michael is an expert at conducting our long two-day meetings and organizing closure and outcomes. Emma helps design the research, keeps everyone on task and serves as a guardian and steward of the data. Jon participates in discussions and serves to welcome and sustain new members, resolve conflict and continually focus on the mission and values of the 5C effort when practical decisions are being considered.

Within the leadership team, the five sets of personalities, biases, egos, values and skills balance one another. If left to one person to lead, the group would have had problems at any point along the way. Having a single leader also does not communicate to the group at large that their ideas are welcome and that they have freedom to shape the future of the team community and the research. This structure allowed careful reactions and thoughtful exchange with respect to the "big topics" such as overall vision, evolving mission and the balancing of short- versus long-term issues.

Age and status have played an important role. Early in the group life, while Jon had youthful energy and was at an establishment phase in his career, Tim and Wolfgang were well-established and could offer fatherly or brotherly like perspective and when necessary, a gentle nudge. Michael, who was at a similar career stage to Jon, and Emma, who was younger but beyond her early career, brought hunger to the project and a desire to add value.

Research

As the qualitative stage changed to a quantitative one, we were faced with different and also difficult questions. We had sorted out the sampling strategy in Phase 1 but now we strived to get at least two countries per each of the GLOBE study's designated ten regions. This sampling strategy meant we gradually increased the number of countries and teams in the group by nearly three-fold.

Conceptual focus
The initial decision was where to focus conceptually. We had qualitative data on career success and career transitions, but the career success categories were less complex and also seemed to have traction in the careers field, so we decided to focus upon that area.

Some very difficult meetings were held developing a basic model from which to ask questions, develop research questions, and decide which scales would be most appropriate. This was complicated because we had team members with varying degrees of tenure in terms of 5C membership who were newly navigating the group, and we had 20–30 people in many of these meetings with strong opinions on research constructs, scales, and so on. Our values of participation, equality and development that offered everyone a voice did not always offer closure to the group at the end of a long session. That said, the eventual products were group products. Michael's facilitation skills were priceless in bringing organization and focus to these meetings.

Survey design

A first step after identifying scales was to translate them from English to the focal language in each non-English speaking country using Brislin's (1970) technique. After this, Emma coordinated the field testing of the surveys in each country to see how the scales performed and if adjustments or alternatives were needed. Simultaneously, a sub-team began constructing and testing a new career success scale, using over sixty items (meanings of career success) refined from the qualitative study (Briscoe et al., 2014).

An innovation Robert Kaše (a partner from Ljubljana University in Slovenia who joined in Phase 2) developed was to use an online card sort technique instead of exploratory scale development to develop clusters of meaning, first in several countries (at least one in each GLOBE cluster) individually, then across 13 samples combined. This saved temporal and financial resources as exploratory factor analysis would have required huge samples and time. Other members willingly stepped in to support this work.

The career success scale was validated across a larger sample of countries and confirmatory factor analysis was used to confirm a final factor structure and seven distinct meanings of career success that were universally valid and shared across the 30 countries in the eventual survey (Briscoe et al., 2017).

With the scale in hand, and Emma's work to test the other survey items complete, we were ready to launch the survey. This process had taken us about four years. At times, this had seemed almost endless but had some very positive learning effects. Many 5C members, too many to name, had at different times given highly pertinent insights. Some of these were driven by particular research interests and the group discussed and explored what was exciting, what would energize members and what was practical. We learned that the country contexts were highly diverse, which gave rise to limits in terms of survey design. The democratic principles—together with a strong value not to "outvote" people and to take all ideas seriously—in a large group meant that it felt that we moved ahead at a snail's pace, just to potentially slither back. Within the process some frustration was building (after about 18 months) as more action-driven 5C members wanted to move ahead more quickly. At this stage the community building and integration activities of the group became invaluable and, together with a strong vision, allowed us to continue on the path.

Sampling

Country sampling was not difficult other than finding appropriate and willing partners. Deciding which occupations to sample was more difficult. In the end we decided to focus upon managers, professionals, clerical/retail workers, and manual labor. Again, as with willingness to collect data, availability in all countries of these four samples was a basic requirement, In addition, managers (business) were chosen because the great majority of the group worked in business schools and felt an obligation to create research relevant to our students; professionals crossed a wide array of occupations that required more and more specialized schooling; clerical/retail represented a group that did not necessarily need advanced training and whose career mobility might vary; finally, manual labor was included because, as we had found in the qualitative study, this work varies greatly across countries in terms of regulation and job mobility. We hoped that our sample would be relevant to "non-elites" in terms of representing more than educated and privileged employees in different countries.

Data collection
Data collection varied and was difficult. Panels of participants could be purchased from providers like Qualtrics, but this was expensive. In only two cases did a country turn to such options, primarily due to researchers' time constraints or the sheer difficulty of getting cooperation via normal channels. Some country teams could easily gather data from huge sections of students or were having the advantage of publicly announcing the project through media. Other country teams were forbidden from giving extra credit for research participation or for paying respondents for research assistance. It truly varied and as such, these differences, combined with iterative recruitment of new members, meant the results came in a staggered fashion.

Analysis and dissemination
One practical difficulty with the staggered fashion is that subgroups would form, ready to submit a paper for conference presentation, for example. The sub-team would get a head start from the larger group and a small in-group would naturally form around the paper. While this was natural, and acceptable, it meant that contrary to our psychological contract of all members being co-authors, in some cases we had tiers of authors before people even gathered data or had a chance to express preferences.

A key bottleneck at the analysis stage was that only a fraction of the full team had the statistical and macro-theoretical skills (e.g. societal indicators, macro-economics, institutional theory) to appropriately analyze large samples and employ global level constructs from outside our own survey measures.

TRANSITIONING INTO PHASE 3

Leadership and Coordination Issues in Phase 2 Going Into Phase 3

The leadership issues in transitioning to Phase 2 have been discussed and some of the coordination issues have been touched upon. Most of the same leadership issues that were introduced in Phase 1 remained relevant, but their scale changed. Logistical issues would require at least a full-time staff person to coordinate, so they were split amongst several of the team members. Leadership issues were shared amongst the aforementioned steering committee of five who had learned to function in more supplementary ways.

As the analysis and outputs in Phase 2 rapidly proliferate and we anticipate "what's next" there are two core themes that the entire 5C group deals with, themes of opportunity, tension, and challenge: culture/goal adaptation and mission reflection.

Adapting Our Culture and Goals

The core of the original group culture has survived and adapted from Phase 1 to Phase 2, but it has shown some stress fractures. For example, the obvious reward of material output and entrepreneurship has resulted in sometimes inevitable "haves" and "have nots" at least as far as some subprojects are concerned. Some of the team leaders on different articles were unable to participate in other articles for example. As mentioned earlier, more instrumentality has emerged, even while the expressed sentiment of the larger group favors learning, community, development and positive impact as core values.

As Schein notes (2010) entrepreneurial organizations who thrive on an initial set of values and basic assumptions must adapt as they enter their midlife where basic priorities are preserved, but must also be adapted to the challenges of internal integration and external adaptation.

Structure and systems are two factors that will need attention, so that as the group grows yet more and requites more coordination, the coordination always enables rather than defeats collaboration and community, when possible.

Reflection upon Mission

The key challenge for the next phase in our mind is having a "rallying cry" around which the whole group can energize and find focus and motivation. The community itself has probably been the biggest motivation and the process that it generates and protects, more than the outputs, but outputs represent tangible goals around which to focus said community.

Method/construct versus mission

Phase 1 was motivated by discovery which was intellectually satisfying. Phase 2 was motivated by achievement and bringing to fruition the foundational constructs discovered in Phase 1. Both phases were motivated by community, connection and development. The next phase may need to be something beyond execution of research strategies and methods—perhaps a mission to impact our field and communities in ways that decisively add value and take a less descriptive and a more generative or proactive role in impacting the world.

Intimacy versus impact

At times the intimacy of the community may be at odds with a wider impact. For example, commercializing products from the group or seeking visibility seem like obvious possibilities, but given the finite energy full-time researchers have in their careers, there are at times what feel like zero-sum gains to be reckoned with (between community and instrumentality). To be sure this may be a false dilemma, but it is a tension, nonetheless.

Inward versus outward

A closely related theme to the one above is balancing a focus on the group and community itself, versus outreach to our scholarly communities, students, organizational stakeholders, and the world at large. Shifting to a more outward focus may threaten some energy devoted to the community, but it also might fulfill some of the explicit and implicit mission of the community and not necessarily be a threat to the group. For example, collaboration with other careers groups that may emerge could be fruitful, or consortia such as CRANET in Human Resource Management or GLOBE in leadership.

Specialization versus holism

Within the group a tension exists between group processes and subgroup projects and foci. To what degree do we benefit from smaller, specialized activities versus common projects that have served as a glue? Can the culture adapt to develop specialization and innovation and still instill a community or mission-first attitude? Can subgroups thrive and add to a common identity if not working in the context of the whole 5C community?

Local versus global

A final tension is the focus upon local regions and countries versus the global collection of countries. In Phase 1, the qualitative research really lent itself to stories and patterns which lent themselves well to narrative and local examples. Phase 2 has allowed us to examine the world in a more holistic way and compare sets of countries in fairly broad ways. As the team grows and our ability to look at things holistically grows, we must balance this ability against highlighting very local and specific life stories, careers, and interventions.

Leadership continuity versus change

As we go into Phase 3 we are again facing a new leadership challenge. In the last years life has intervened for some of the five leaders of 5C—be it the normal progression through life stages, health issues, new roles at our respective universities or simply competitive and work pressures. At the same time, there are some new and fantastically thoughtful, innovative and visionary emerging informal leaders in the group. We need to find ways to balance the opportunities of the various options to ensure the continued robust community and outward success of 5C.

CONCLUSION

Our experience in forming the 5C Group demonstrates that defining and researching important scholarly questions in the careers field is both possible and desirable. An important aspect of this is in our case was forming not just a group, but a community of people who are values as ends in and of themselves, not just a means to an end.

REFERENCES

Brett, J. M., Tinsley, C. H., Janssens, M., Barsness, Z. I., and Lytle, A. L. 1997. New approaches to the study of culture in I/O psychology. In P. C. Earley and M. Erez (Eds.), *New Perspective On International/Organizational Psychology*: 75–129. San Francisco: Jossey-Bass.

Briscoe, J. P., Chudzikowski, K., Demel, B., Mayrhofer, W., and Unite, J. 2012. The 5C project: our story and our research. In J. P. Briscoe, D. T. Hall, and W. Mayrhofer (Eds.), *Careers Around the World*: 39–56. New York and London: Routledge Taylor and Francis Group.

Briscoe, J. P., Dickmann, M., Hall, D. T. T., Parry, E., Mayrhofer, W., and Smale, A. 2018. Career success in different countries: reflections on the 5C project. In M. Dickmann, V. Suutari, and O. Wurtz (Eds.), *The Management of Global Careers. Exploring the Rise of International Work*: 117–148. London: Palgrave.

Briscoe, J. P., Dickmann, M., and Parry, E. 2020. Careers across countries. In H. Gunz, M. Lazarova, and W. Mayrhofer (Eds.), *The Routledge Companion to Career Studies*: 293–309. London: Routledge.

Briscoe, J. P., Hall, D. T., and Mayrhofer, W. (Eds.) 2012. *Careers Around the World*. New York and London: Routledge Taylor and Francis Group.

Briscoe, J. P., Kaše, R., Dries, N., Dysvik, A., Unite, J., Adeleye, I., Andresen, M., Apospori, E., Babalola, O., Bagdadli, S., Kakmak-Otluoglu, K. O., Casado, T., Cerdin, J-L., Cha, J-S., Chudikowski, K., Dello Russo, S., Eggenhofer-Rehart, P., Fei, Z., Gianecchini, M., Gubler, M., Hall, D. T., Imose, R., Rosnita, I., Khapova, S., Kim, N., Lehmann, P., Lysova, E., Madero, S., Mandel, D., Mayrhofer, W., Bogicevic Milikic, B., Mishra, S., Naito, C., Reichel, A., Saher, N., Saxena, R., Schleicher, N., Schramm, F., Shen, Y., Smale, A., Supangco, V., Suzanne, P., and Taniguchi, M. 2017. *Minding the Gap (s): Development and Validation of a Cross-Cultural Measure of Subjective Career Success*. Paper presented at 3rd Global Conference of International Human Resource Management, New York, New York, May 19, 2017.

Briscoe, J. P., Kaše, R., Dries, N., Dysvik, A., Unite, J., Övgü Çakmak-Otluoğlu, K., Adeleye, I., Bagdadli, S., Babalola, O., Cerdin, J-L., Cha, J-S., Chudikowski, K., Fei, Z., Gianecchini, M., Kim, N., Mayrhofer, W., Mishra, S. K., Reichel, A., Rosnita, I., Saxena, R., Supangco, V., and Verbruggen, M. 2014. A cross-culturally generated measure of perceived career success: results of a three-stage study. In J. Humphreys (Ed.), *Best Paper Proceedings*, 74th Academy of Management Annual Meeting, Philadelphia, PA.

Brislin, R. W. 1970. Back-translation for cross-cultural research. *Journal of Cross-cultural Psychology*, 1(3): 185–216.

Henrich, J., Heine, S. J., and Norenzayan, A. 2010. Most people are not WEIRD. *Nature*, 466(7302): 29.

Hofstede, G. 1980. *Culture's Consequences. International Differences in Work-Related Values*. Newbury Park: Sage.

Hofstede, G. H., Hofstede, G. J., and Minkov, M. 2010. *Cultures and Organizations. Software of the Mind: Intercultural Cooperation and its Importance for Survival* (3rd ed.). New York: McGraw-Hill.

House, R. J., Hanges, P. J., Javidan, M., Dorfman, P. W., and Gupta, V. (Eds.) 2004. *Culture, Leadership, and Organizations: The GLOBE Study of 62 Societies*. Thousand Oaks, CA: Sage.

Judge, T. A., Piccolo, R. F., and Ilies, R. 2004. The forgotten ones? The validity of consideration and initiating structure in leadership research. *Journal of Applied Psychology*, 89(1): 36–51.

Levinson, D. J. 1978. *The Seasons of a Man's Life*. New York: Random House Digital.

Levinson, D. J. 2011. *The Seasons of a Woman's Life: A Fascinating Exploration of the Events, Thoughts, and Life Experiences That All Women Share*. New York: Ballantine Books.

Mayrhofer, W., Briscoe, J. P., Hall, D. T., Dickmann, M., Dries, N., Dysvik, A., Kaše, R., Parry, E., and Unite, J. 2016. Career success across the globe: insights from the 5C project. *Organizational Dynamics*, 45(2): 197–205.

Parry, E., Stavrou, E., and Morley M. (Eds.) 2011. The Cranet International Research Network on Human Resource Management, Special Issue of *Human Resource Management Review*, 2(1).

Schein, E. H. 2010. *Organizational Culture and Leadership* (Vol. 2). New York: John Wiley and Sons.

Schwartz, S. H. 2006. A theory of cultural value orientations: explication and applications. *Comparative Sociology*, 5(2–3): 137–182.

Waters, E., and Cummings, E. M. 2000. A secure base from which to explore close relationships. *Child Development*, 71(1): 164–172.

4. Managing a mega-project to explore and enhance careers: insights from Global Entrepreneurial Talent Management 3

Alison Pearce, Brian Harney, Mark Bailey, Katarzyna Dziewanowska, Janine Bosak, Peter Pease, Brenda Stalker, Dimitra Skoumpopoulou, Paul Doyle, Samuel Clegg, Alireza Shokri, Suzanne Crane, Susan O'Donnell, Rose Quan, Ilsang Ko, Katarina K. Mihelič, Robert Kaše, Matej Černe, Huan Sun, Julie Brückner, Szu-Hsin Wu, Jose Aldo Valencia Hernandez, and John McMackin

INTRODUCTION

Contemporary careers are changing, and they face many challenges. This creates a pressing need for innovative research that is cross-cultural and multidisciplinary. Many forces influence careers: shifting expectations, new technology, and institutional and cultural factors that define career success (Kaše et al., 2020). The European Union recognized the significance of enhancing career capabilities to drive innovation and competitiveness, allocating some 6.16 billion euros to researcher training and development under the Horizon 2020 program. This chapter details insights from the Global Entrepreneurial Talent Management 3 project (GETM3). GETM3 is an international, interdisciplinary, research and innovation project which received over one million euros from Research Innovation and Staff Exchange (RISE) Horizon 2020 Marie-Skłodowska-Curie Actions (MSCA), coupled with matched Korean Research Foundation funding. RISE funds short-term, international exchanges of personnel between academic, industrial, and commercial organizations worldwide to develop research capacity. A key objective is to "help people develop their knowledge, skills, and careers, while building links between organizations working in different sectors of the economy, including universities, research institutes, and SMEs" (European Commission, 2019). The goal of providing an infrastructure for individuals to work and research in other countries is to "make the whole world a learning environment" and "break down barriers between academia, industry, and business."

In this introduction we provide an overview of the GETM3 project, exploring its approach and origins, then outlining the project design, methodology, key levers of implementation, before detailing participant experiences. In so doing our focus is not simply to situate the project within the context of career research, but equally, to illuminate how the project itself serves to bridge national, sectoral, disciplinary, methodological, and career life stages as a vehicle for career development. The chapter gives examples of guiding principles and underlying values on the way to best practice. It offers pragmatic reflections on the origins, emergence, and evolution of a research collaboration exploring careers on a grand scale.

Context and Rationale

GETM3 is a multidisciplinary project bringing together 16 partners from five countries: the United Kingdom, Ireland, Poland, Slovenia, and the Republic of Korea (South Korea). The project was conceived in 2016 and began in 2017. It involves more than 100 staff conducting over 290 month-long international mobility secondments (relocations) across academia and industry. The project team was designed to be multidisciplinary composite of academics, university staff, consultants, and practitioners. The goal for the project was to improve understanding of career expectations, trajectories, and challenges, especially for young employees and their managers/employers. The word *entrepreneurial* refers to entrepreneurial skills as manifest in creativity, exploration, and positive change. As per the European Commission, the focus is not limited to new ventures, start-ups, and new jobs but also covers "an individual's ability to turn ideas into action" (European Commission, 2008, p. 7). Focusing on young entrepreneurial talent in particular, careers are understood as a series of ongoing learning cycles founded on career evolution and life-long learning (Dziewanowska et al., 2019), as opposed to distinct stages of development (Donald et al., 2019; Craig & Hall, 2011). The project is innovative in its multi-stakeholder approach, working with three stakeholder groups: young people as current students and future graduates, higher education institutions with educators of the future, and employers as future wealth creators. By drawing on insights from students, educators, and employers, the project calls for research to move beyond single stakeholder perspectives and adopt multiple perspectives and approaches.

The GETM3 project examines work that is transnational, trans-sectoral, and trans-generational. Three unique features of the GETM3 project are worth outlining. First, the explicit incorporation of industry partners ensures that GETM3 retains a focus on industry engagement and enhancing practice (described in detail later). This is timely in the context of calls to explore how an understanding of the functioning careers can lead to more effective talent management practice (Crowley-Henry et al., 2019). Second, a multi-level, cross-comparative focus highlights the ecosystem in which career opportunities and challenges are embedded (Baruch & Rousseau, 2018). Recent research notes the need for "a more fine-grained and nuanced consideration of context in our understanding of career success schemas, as a foundation for understanding subjective career success across national cultures" (Kaše et al., 2020, p. 424). The international, comparative focus of GETM3 reflects the global intensity of career challenges. It also links with the European Union and Korean Research Foundation's agenda, including the Bologna Process (harmonization of European HE systems), which solidified a shift to student mobility (Brabrand & Dahl, 2009). This relates to the third feature of GETM3, setting up infrastructure and funds for international mobility. RISE funding is that it affords "a unique opportunity for individuals to expand their horizons, enlarge their networks, receive innovative research training, and develop new career opportunities". (European Commission, 2017). Researcher mobility is key to achieving GETM3 objectives because it strengthens collaboration and knowledge sharing amongst participants, but also brings opportunities for field work and exposure to different work styles and contexts (national culture and economy, sectors, disciplines). It therefore improves the opportunity to study careers from different perspectives. By facilitating collaboration between experienced and less experienced researchers, as well as between older and younger employees, the project seeks to foster knowledge exchange, accelerate the accumulation of experience, and build research and entrepreneurial capacity.

In terms of research, the GETM3 project brings to light knowledge deficiencies via a multidisciplinary lens. From the perspective of students and younger graduates there is much to learn about career expectations including demand for the likes of flexible work arrangements, meaningful mentorship programs, and corporate purpose (Fuller, 2016). Donald and colleagues (2019) argue that student views on career trajectories and graduate employability remain poorly understood. From an employer's perspective, the World Economic Forum predicts the top skills employers will require in 2022 are analytical thinking and creativity while active learning and learning strategies are both on the rise (World Economic Forum, 2018). The future of work requires a shift in thinking to a "post-generational mindset" able to identify behaviors that unite and build strength across generations (Koulopoulos & Keldsen, 2014). Finally, in order to navigate such changes, educators are to engage and embrace entrepreneurship by building "theoretical foundations, bridging disciplines and communities (research and practice), and increasing critical thinking perspectives" (Fayolle et al., 2016, p. 896). In order to show how these challenges were explored, it is first necessary to describe the formation of the GETM3 consortium and project.

Take Your Partners! Origins of the Research Proposal

GETM3 is the latest in a series of five highly successful overlapping international collaborations conducted over a period of 11 years across higher education and industry. During this time, a unique network of diverse personal and professional relationships developed among individuals operating in the United Kingdom, Ireland, Poland, Slovenia, and the Republic of Korea, where historically "geographical distance has been compounded by psychological distance" (Bridges, 1986, p. 22). The collaboration began with a small, experimental, student mobility cooperation of seven partners. This group was funded by the Education Cooperation Programme, a part of the Industrialized Countries Instrument, an EU collaboration agreement among the EU and Australia, New Zealand, Japan and the Republic of Korea. Securing this funding started a remarkable series of increasingly complex, ambitious projects which received over four million euros from the European Union and the Korean Research Foundation. A pattern of sustained relationships and foundation of trust and understanding has emerged at the heart of this success. A global employability network was formed as a loose collaboration of researchers from different social sciences. Commonalities, intersections, and synergies were identified, as well as a desire to recognize and accommodate cultural differences and norms. This critical foundation of the 16-partner consortium that is GETM3.

Blood, Sweat, and Tears: Successful Funding Strategy

While working together, the partners devised a "strategy" for funding success. They called it blood, sweat, and tears to signify the following action guidelines respectively: focus on relationships before tasks, work with passion, and let go of sacred cows. Partners were carefully selected based on past experience and trusted recommendations. Special notice was taken of passion for understanding careers, especially enabling the potential of young people. This made it possible to convey to funders a clear vision and purpose (Hollensbe et al., 2014). The early design and use of a logo in the GETM3 funding bid demonstrated this sense of vision and coherence. The group established a project-specific culture while working within the various constraints and norms of partner institutions, and remaining cognizant of funder requirements. The project team worked pragmatically across boundaries and, like entrepreneurs, piggy-backed resources (Burgelman, 1983b; Herr & Anderson, 2005). The leadership team at the University of Northumbria in Newcastle (United Kingdom) managed the bidding process and application, strategically delegating content to subject-matter experts. The final submission was a 60-page narrative and plan supported by a detailed four-year staff mobility plan. The motivational catalyst for GETM3 was nearing completion of an existing project and a desire to sustain invested, successful relationships. The significant workload and effort to pull the submission together reinforced the culture of collaboration and desire for achievement. The team submitted their final document one hour before the deadline. They attributed the success of their submission to practicing Burgelman's (1983a) "strategic neglect": "the more or less deliberate tendency of [strategic entrepreneurs] to attend only to performance criteria on which the venture's survival is critically dependent" (p. 234). The project was ambitious, and failure at first attempt was expected.

Strategic Entrepreneurship: Infrastructure for Success

Securing international funding has increasingly become a key strategy for higher education institutions. Burgelman's (1983a) theory of strategic entrepreneurship identifies autonomous strategic behavior in which "entrepreneurial participants (…) conceive new (…) opportunities (…), mobilize corporate resources for these new opportunities, and (…) create momentum for their future development". Individuals engaging in such behavior *attempt to escape* (p. 65) the presiding structural context.

For GETM3, this meant working with peers in other faculties and institutions, rather than exclusively within respective hierarchies. Autonomous strategic behavior is "purposeful from the perspective of the actors who engage in it" (Burgelman, 1983b, p. 1350). It is conceptually equivalent to entrepreneurial activity, yet it delivers part of an existing strategy. New managerial approaches and innovative administrative arrangements are required to facilitate collaboration among participants (the strategic entrepreneurs) and their organizations.

The first year of the GETM3 project was spent establishing new policies and processes (see the vignette later in the chapter). Strategic entrepreneurs admit to being "just smart enough to hire people smarter than themselves" (Thornberry, 2001, p. 532), hence the importance of partner choice. The individual entrepreneur, or in this case the project leader, must set in motion a virtuous circle by convincing people that the innovation they want to pursue is in their own interest (Burgelman & Hitt, 2007). It is critical to a project's success that an ecosystem of interested partners develops a collective interest around the entrepreneurial leader. The total collective benefit that results from "leveraging off the self-interest" (p. 351) of the individual entrepreneur can be substantial, even though this collective interest may not have formed part of the original idea.

Engagement and 'Multisociation': Bypassing Traditional Distinctions

The aim of GETM3 is to provide innovative research and enhanced impact by producing evidence-based, actionable, knowledge and artifacts (Argyris, 1993; Gubbins et al., 2018; Voss, 2019). According to Smith and DiGregorio (2002), "bisociation" occurs when two previously unrelated matrices of information or knowledge are combined to create novelty. The intent of GETM3 is to exceed this through "*multisociation,*" a unique concept developed for the purpose of this project. It emerged from a plan to apply theory, concepts, and approaches from one discipline to several others. One example is applying Lean Six Sigma to every aspect of the project, including research, management, and in the production of integrated deliverables (see later in the chapter). Another is using design thinking from the design of the project through to the co-creation of project deliverables with multiple stakeholders (cf. Rouse, 2019). One example is an exercise to explore career expectations and skills required for jobs that do not yet exist (Bailey et al., 2018).

Reflecting its interdisciplinary focus, the project team avoided explicit focus on quantitative/qualitative distinctions or ideological preferences for methodologies. Constant philosophical introspection can become a distraction (Reason & Bradbury, 2006), while problems in judging managerial knowledge and writing are "ingrained and remarkably counter-productive" (Pfeffer & Sutton, 2006, p. 27). Instead, a pragmatic focus on impact resulted in an inclusive approach to knowledge and understanding. Knowledge from different sources as a form of multiple triangulation was selected for its relevance to researcher development, enhanced understanding of careers, and external impact. These fundamental assumptions in turn informed the design of the project as detailed in the next section.

RESEARCH DESIGN

Complex mega-projects like GETM3 have distinctive characteristics which present challenges for management (König et al., 2013; Anzai et al., 2012; Van Rijnsoever and Hessels, 2011). These include: (i) outcomes that are often ill-defined, as reflecting the nature of research; (ii) the balance between maintaining a strategic focus and respecting disciplinary integrity; (iii) a diverse and temporary team of independent partners based in multiple international locations; (iv) interdisciplinary research teams drawn from disparate disciplines and methodological backgrounds; and (v) the involvement of stakeholders from multiple sectors (higher education, large companies, SMEs, NGOs, government agencies, etc.). It is acknowledged that management methodologies for complex research projects are under-developed (König et al., 2013; Anzai et al., 2012), as is management of interdisciplinary research projects in general (König et al., 2013). All this points to the imperative of putting in place key guiding principles and underlying values to inform research design, including democracy, diplomacy, impact, gender, learning objectives, and plans for dissemination.

Multidisciplinary Research: Democracy through Design

Multidisciplinary research is problematic, in part because universities remain organized in disciplinary silos that respond to and perpetuate research funding streams and academic communities of self-gratification, thereby mitigating against collaboration. (Exceptions include designated multidisciplinary research centers.) A silo approach rarely reflects the realities of practical real-world challenges. A key dilemma for the GETM3 project is that its ultimate beneficiaries, employers and graduate talent, predominantly reside within this real world. Key stakeholder concerns do not relate to theoretical advancement of knowledge within a closely guarded disciplinary domain. Instead, their concerns are how to inform careers and enhance the management of talent in business. Based on this logic, the GETM3 approach to multidisciplinary research was established around pragmatism. Two practices were adopted for the multidisciplinary research design: (a) co-creative knowledge creation and exchange events, termed *sandpits*; and (b) Integrated Academic Practice (IAP), an approach allowing portfolios of Research & Innovation, Learning & Teaching, and Knowledge Exchange to work in harmony to deliver reciprocal values that benefit the academy, students, and society (Bailey & Smith, 2016).

The UK's Engineering and Physical Sciences Research Council (EPSRC, 2019) defines a sandpit as "intensive discussion forums where free thinking is encouraged to delve into the problems on the agenda to uncover innovative solutions." Within the design and delivery of the GETM3 project, the team adopted a creative, design-led approach that embedded quarterly sandpits within the program funding and governance. Sandpit meetings were scheduled on a quarterly basis rotating around partner institutions with sixteen taking place in four years. Sandpits allowed key protagonists to convene around the prosaic matters of project management, but each host institution was left to design and facilitate meetings whose purpose was to "uncover innovative solutions" (ibid.).

Sandpits have been hosted in a variety of ways to engage graduate talent and employers in action research focused on delivering data that will inform the core research questions of the GETM3 program. Sandpits were built around multisociation, that is, a plan to apply theory, concepts, and approaches from one discipline to several others. The role of design thinking proved beneficial in mediating between disciplinary and practice experience and expectations (Bailey et al., 2019; Voss, 2019). Design thinking provided a structure and resources to facilitate discussion, debate, and creativity between disciplinary and experience experts within a "safe environment" (Bailey & Smith, 2010). Because most subject expertise in GETM3 came from disciplines other than design, participants have been willing and curious to engage with a design-led approach which seeks to democratize idea ownership,

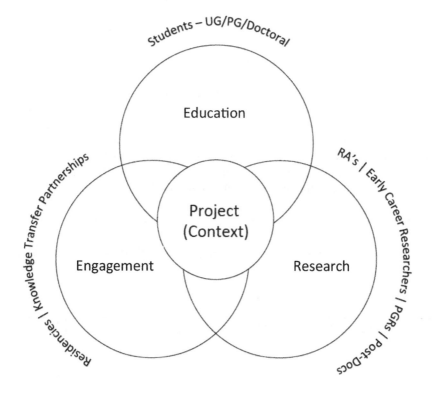

Note: PGR postgraduate researcher / RA research assistant / UG undergraduate.
Source: Bailey & Smith (2016).

Figure 4.1   *A model for integrated academic practice*

as well as to externalize and build on concepts and emerging possibilities without judgment or fear of criticism.

The same democratic approach underpins Integrated Academic Practice (IAP) employed in GETM3's engagement with students and recent graduates. In this approach participants are valued as co-researchers engaged in generative research at the front end of design (Sanders & Stappers, 2008). Importantly, and unusually for management research, student knowledge, experience, and ideas are valued as equally relevant and informative as those of seasoned academics or industrial practitioners. As illustrated in Figure 4.1, the model employed places project-based activity at the center of inquiry.

GETM3 used the IAP approach to engage multiple groups of students and postgraduates in a series of creative workshops exploring the critical question of "how universities should prepare graduates for jobs that do not yet exist?" (Bailey et al., 2018). Illustrative of the diversity and democracy of such an approach, in one such set of workshops, the cohort comprised 17 students representing eight nationalities. Participants had studied in six different countries, and their work had focused on 12 different subjects including mathematics, fine art, journalism, software engineering, sociology, and design. They had between zero and 10 years of professional employment experience, and the workshop had close to an equal number of participants by gender.

The raw data generated by each subsequent iteration of the workshops provide researchers with an evolving understanding of the fundamental concerns of graduate talent as they approached their future careers. Researchers fed these integrated outputs into recommendations and integrated outputs of the GETM3 program. Deliverables such as an Employer Toolkit will offer practical tools to enable employers and employees to find mutually beneficial middle-ground, enabling both to flourish in an unpredictable and rapidly changing world.

Designing International Research: Diplomacy and Work Packages

The GETM3 project consists of seven "work packages" (WPs) or workstreams (see Table 4.1).

Table 4.1   *GETM3 work packages*

WP1	WP2	WP3	WP4	WP5	WP6	WP7
Project management	Young people attitudes	Higher education institutions	Employer talent management	Research outputs and integration	Networking, dissemination, communication, researcher development	Research ethics and management

A detailed research design was required for the three WPs aimed at understanding stakeholder perspectives (see Table 4.2). These work packages were: WP2, focused

Table 4.2   *GETM3 research design*

WP2			WP3			WP4		
WP2	Other WPs	Individual research***	WP3	Other WPs	Individual research***	WP4	Other WPs	Individual research***
Student and graduate development* (major research stream)	WP 3&4**	Research within the scope of GETM3	Researching higher education* (major research stream)	WP 2&4**	Research within the scope of GETM3	Employer global talent management challenges* (major research stream)	WP 2&3**	Research within the scope of GETM3

Notes:
Integration across the following issues: generations, stakeholders, countries, disciplines, sectors, gender, WPs.
*main module (major research stream) addresses research objectives from the grant proposal.
**modules with additional questions/statements from other WPs in order to achieve triangulation of perspectives.
***every secondee/participant may submit individual research proposal within the scope of GETM3 (to be approved by WP leaders).

on student and graduate development and led by the University of Warsaw; WP3, focused on researching higher education and led by Dublin City University; and WP4, focused on resolving challenges to employers in global talent management, led by the University of Ljubljana. The research design for each WP was based on three key components, as follows:

1. The objectives of each WP were stated in the bid and grant agreement. WP leaders were responsible for preparing the research module that included a description of a sample, a method (e.g., such as a survey), tools (e.g., a questionnaire), and the type of study (e.g., cross-sectional).
2. Integration of perspectives. In order to achieve triangulation of perspectives, it was possible to add modules, emerging from other WPs to the main research stream of a particular WP. For example, WP1 could prepare a module addressing gender issues which are included in WP4.
3. Individual researcher interests. Over 100 participants were involved in GETM3, representing many interests, skills, and backgrounds (from engineers, to designers, and researchers, to technical personnel). The research design reflected this diversity in two ways:
   a. Each participant or research secondee was required to contribute to overall project objectives. Depending on their interests, they could discuss their tasks with the relevant WP leader. Assigned tasks could vary from desk research to data collection and analysis.
   b. Each participant could propose their own research project to conduct with the cooperation of other project participants. Such proposals were considered and approved by relevant WP leaders. This enabled deeper understand-

ing of global entrepreneurial talent management issues from a variety of perspectives, while balancing the achievement of both project deliverables and individual research interests.

In order to achieve a required level of understanding and cooperation among WP leaders, various forms of communication were used. Crucial agreements were made during face-to-face discussions that took place during the sandpit events detailed above. All WPs feed into an integration work package, WP5 led by the Technological University Dublin, which received state-of-the-art evidence from four key areas: (i) integrating interdisciplinary research, (ii) integrating multiple sectors, (iii) integrating diverse stakeholders, and (iv) integrating international research teams. The research design was also informed by the publication strategy and designed to meet EU and institutional requirements as well as facilitate meeting project objectives (i.e., international networking and collaboration). Flexibility was key to addressing new issues and questions that came up as the project moved forward and as new participants joined the initiative.

Reflecting Gender in Multicultural Research

Previous research exploring the theme of entrepreneurship has been criticized as being "about men, by men, and for men" (Holquist & Sundin, 1991, p. 1). GETM3 was committed to: (a) promote and ensure gender consciousness and equality throughout the management and research process, and through the participation of GETM3 stakeholders; and (b) embed gender as a key focal dimension in the research and work packages, consistent with Horizon 2020 gender equality guidelines (European Commission, 2019). In doing so, the GETM3 project recognized the critical role of gender for research excellence, in adding value quality and creativity in outcomes, in greater responsiveness to social needs, and in producing goods, technology, and services suited to potential markets (European Commission, 2019; Stanford University, 2019).

To address gender in project management and networking, a gender champion was appointed to monitor all gender aspects on both WP1 and the project steering committee (PSC) at the start of the project. WP leader and researcher roles were allocated as evenly as possible, with females somewhat more represented. Gender mainstreaming was a standing theme on the PSC agenda and for the sandpits, with gender being considered and recorded in a project log on the project portal by each GETM3 project partner at planning, implementation, and evaluation stages. A GETM3 Gender Policy was formulated by the gender champion as a key deliverable of WP1. This process was supported by an adapted Five-Step Gender Proofing Process template (Crawley & O'Meara, 2002) which set forth five points to address and incorporate into organization strategy: (i) different needs and experiences; (ii) related implications for the activity; (iii) how to ensure equal participation and outcomes for the sexes; (iv) a person responsible for implementation; and (v) how to measure success of the activity. In addition, a process known as "member checking" allowed a project member to challenge another's gender consciousness. The collection of participant bio data further supported gender mainstreaming. The WP leaders and steering committee were critical throughout this process. They encouraged sharing and dissemination of best practices and lessons learned, within and across WPs, and also identified potential amendments to the gender policy, which was considered a working document and subject to change. They also pro-actively addressed equal participation in research secondments. Men outnumbered women at the start of the project, so leaders examined reasons for the gender imbalance and designed steps to overcome it, using open dialogue around family commitments and how best to provide support.

To address gender in research content, gender was incorporated across all WPs as a key focal variable in research design, analysis, findings, and practical recommendations. GETM3 was very conscious of the gendered framing of entrepreneur identities and related activities portrayed in both academic and practitioner literature (Ahl & Marlow, 2012; Marlow & Martinez Dy, 2018). By including project deliverables such as a White Paper on transcending gender, and a GETM3 gender policy in the Horizon 2020 funding application, the project team clearly demonstrated their commitment to gender as a key priority and held themselves accountable. These are two critical success factors for gender equality initiatives (Kossek et al., 2006; Fortune & SHRM, 2001).

Out of the Ivory Tower: Ensuring Research Impact

Research impact is critical not only to employer stakeholders, but increasingly also to the careers of academics. The debate around the research vs. practice divide in management studies is not new. Nonetheless, academic career trajectories continue to be determined primarily by publications in highly ranked journals (DeNisi et al., 2014). There is a sense of gradual shift in policy, away from impact in academia measured purely by citations, toward a more holistic assessment (Aguinis et al., 2019). For example, the UK Research Excellence Framework (UKREF), in which the research quality of UK universities is assessed every seven years, is placing increasing emphasis on research impact; and various attempts are being made to bridge the research vs. practice divide. The evidence-based management movement (Briner, 1998; Rousseau, 2012) has gained traction, as have initiatives to make management research useful for practitioners (Tkachenko et al., 2016; Bansal et al., 2012). Leading academics in different countries are addressing this concern, including with respect to entrepreneurship (Wiklund et al., 2019). However, a problem with evidence-based management is that it tends to focus on how to impact or disseminate findings after research has been completed, a kind of post hoc engineering. Addressing such deficiencies, GETM3 has taken a rigorous approach to achieving impact by engaging with potential beneficiaries of the research at every step of the process.

Notably at the outset, the GETM3 project appointed an Impact Champion tasked with writing the funding bid and ensuring that those working on the project understand what impact means in the context of GETM3. Achieving impact was made an integral part of the research design by adopting the impact management framework developed by Reed (2016) in Figure 4.2. The inclusion of a UKREF exemplary case study as a contracted output ensured impact as a priority. Impact reinforcement became an ongoing part of quarterly sandpit meetings, which were used for impact training around analysis of research motivations, stakeholder analysis, and likely impacts.

Publics and Stakeholder Analysis Template

Name of organization, group or segment of the public	Likely interest in your research H/M/L	What aspects of your research are they likely to be interested in (or why are they likely not interested)?	What level of influence might they have on your capacity to generate impact (to facilitate or block) and/or what level of impact (positive or negative) might they derive from the research? H/M/L	Comments on level of influence (to facilitate or block impact) and/or likely impact (positive or negative) e.g. times or contexts in which they have more/less influence over the outcomes of your research, ways they might block or facilitate your research or impact, types of benefit they might derive from the research

Figure 4.2   Stakeholder and public analysis template

For motivation, researchers considered how to make the world a better place by helping people make better decisions, by improving well-being, teaching and learning, and by reducing staff turnover or helping small companies compete for talent. Impact was evaluated in terms of: significance, as judged by the degree to which it influences policies, practices, products or perceptions; and reach, as determined by the extent of impact and the diversity of those impacted. Stakeholders were listed, wants and needs identified, assumptions challenged, and means of capturing feedback considered.

Early and significant benefits accrued as a result of the emphasis on impact. These include enhanced cohesion among WPs through the common theme of impact, illuminating crossover between stakeholders. Results were presented to stakeholders and dissemination events organized with employer groups. Employers were consulted about the tools being developed and about the potential drafting of several potential UKREF impact case studies. Arguably, the greatest benefit has been developing an impact mindset which has informed project research decisions and early career researchers who will take this approach into their futures.

Capturing the Learning: the Never-Ending Journey

Career development is integral to societal, educational, and performance measures for which academics and their universities are increasingly held accountable (Zacher et al., 2019). Providing evidence of research capacity development on an individual and collective basis is a key requirement of EU funding for GETM3. An interdisciplinary team skilled in learning and innovation processes undertook design and delivery of a learning system. This involved procedures and tools to support and provide evidence for ongoing and final reports to key stakeholders, including funders, host organizations, and project participants.

The primary means to enhance career development was participation in the international secondment opportunities. This required a system to facilitate and capture the learning from these experiences. The project team therefore designed the following instruments:

1. Learning Platform – a dynamic online collaborative learning environment, which provides access to a repository of learning and research resources and outputs from ongoing research activity within the project.
2. Personal/Professional Development Matrix – all secondees receive a subscription to the VITAE researcher development website (https://www.vitae.ac.uk/) to access learning resources to support their professional development. The Vitae Researcher Development Framework (RDF) outlines characteristics of excellent researchers and provides a structure to inform, develop, and record learning gained by individual members. All project members perform a self-assessment using the Vitae RDF at the beginning and end of the project, to inform a quantitative and qualitative analysis of researcher development.
3. Individual Research Development Learning Record (IRDLR) – an online tool developed using MoveON mobility software. Participants complete an individual development plan, creating a reflective record of their individual learning journey before, during, and after their secondment. Motivating secondees to record their learning can be challenging. Therefore, workshops are included in the sandpit events, and country team leaders are tasked with ensuring their own secondees' submissions.

Initial analysis of a sample of completed IRDLRs conducted mid-way through the project indicated opportunities which did enhance career development (Stalker et al., 2019). International secondments increased participant confidence and competence in developing their networks, familiarizing with foreign cultures, expanding their research horizons by activities such as delivering research seminars in host institutions, and opening new collaborations with international partners.

There is clear evidence that participation in the project has elicited a reflective approach to understanding and reimagining secondees' own careers. Many took the opportunity to develop new professional skills beyond research, and to transfer learning back to their own institutions. For some, this contributed to achieving a promotion or identification of other opportunities which previously did not exist. Overall, there is early strong evidence of increased confidence in cross-cultural communication and in forming new working relationships. As suggested throughout this chapter, the quarterly sandpits are critical in building social capital to sustain these new long-distance relationships, and this has been reflected in the addition of a new, informal work package dedicated purely to activities building social capital. All of these interactions are institutionally and culturally patterned, and as one participant commented, "there is no way to read that in a book."

Innovative Dissemination and Communication for Diverse Audiences

A final core aspect of research design involves strategies for communication and dissemination. GETM3 is an international, virtual project where team members are "dispersed geographically and working in different organisations" (Binder, 2016, p. 1). This means running a virtual team with the additional challenges of geo-location, language, power-distance, culture, and technology preferences (Neeley, 2015). With over 100 participants across 16 universities, companies in five different countries, three major stakeholder groups, and a powerful funder, success of the project depends on communicating and disseminating information to multiple stakeholders.

An open culture of information-sharing and communication is required to ensure that appropriate, timely and engaging information is available to all stakeholders. This culture aids management effectiveness and overall group task performance in virtual teams (Warkentin & Beranek, 1999). Communication failure could isolate key contributors and reduce project effectiveness (Leenders et al., 2003). A multi-factor communication approach was taken, targeting stakeholders as follows: internal project stakeholder (active members in management, administration, and research mobilities); funding and institution stakeholders (the European Commission, the Korean Research Foundation, and organizations where members work); stakeholder targets for dissemination (project research output went to three groups: higher education institutions, students/young graduates, and businesses).

Different stakeholders required information at various times and in varying formats for communication to be effective. A single communication strategy would fail to meet demands of all identified stakeholders. The following three principles were considered paramount: information timeliness, format appropriateness, and effectiveness of the communication approach.

For internal project stakeholders, a centralized repository acted as a project management tool, mobility secondment tracker, project archive, confidential data repository, and a collaborative space where the team could share and edit online single-source documents. This eliminated any need for privately held, conflicting information from multiple contributors, and it allowed collaboration for participants across different time zones.

Social media are used to provide updates from participants currently on a secondment, keeping the project vibrant for those not currently active or seconded themselves. Private groups on Facebook and WhatsApp allow multimedia sharing across the project team without involving other non-research stakeholders. More traditional communication is used for funding and institutional stakeholders: a website for official updates, public Facebook and LinkedIn pages for information dissemination, and reports/presentations for project deliverables. Dissemination-targeted stakeholders are presented with a multimedia-rich, multi-tiered, web portal which gives information in varying formats and levels of detail using keywords and multiple paths. A top-down approach is used with interactive PDF documents linking to multimedia outputs interlinked through a series of keywords. These keywords allow material to be navigated using a stakeholder, pedagogical, or functional point of view. Output is also multi-tiered with headline information linking to more detailed summary video material, and eventually to a full seminar delivery of the research. Academic papers further support the seminar information providing a more rigorous academic backbone.

This innovative, stakeholder-centered approach uses readily available technology for communication. Stakeholders can access accurate, up-to-date, material tailored to their needs and in a format which suits them. Finally, with the use of private group, social-media applications, constant posting and updating on activities helps keep the project in the minds of team members, ensuring momentum throughout the project lifetime.

PROJECT IMPLEMENTATION

"Vision without execution is just hallucination" is a truism attributed to everyone from Edison to Einstein and even back to an ancient Japanese proverb. "Strategy without tactics is the slowest route to victory," said Sun Tzu, legendary Chinese military strategist. Call it execution or tactics, without implementation any project is worthless. Implementation has been referred to as *grunt work* (as opposed to cerebral strategizing), but we can attest to the fact that making it happen is so much more difficult than thinking it up in the first place. Our funder knows this too, and so included a significant section on implementation in the mandatory bid structure. In this section, we describe principles for and experiences in managing the project to ensure efficient and effective implementation, in light of the complexity of *doing* research on an international scale, on budget, on time, and meeting all contracted deliverables.

Plan, Do, Check, Act: Quality Management in Research

Multidisciplinary expertise has been core to GETM3 project success, especially with respect to quality management. Lean Six Sigma ensures efficient, effective, project delivery on schedule and on budget, to the satisfaction of external funders. From the initial bid stage, the team emphasized controlling and managing quality as essential to minimize the risk of disruption and failure. Total Quality Management (TQM) philosophy was used for this purpose, as well as for continuous performance improvement and to encourage stakeholder involvement (Jimenez-Jimenez et al., 2015). Project success is based on core TQM principles such as teamwork, stakeholder satisfaction, continuous improvement, transparency, and full engagement with all involved. In order to promote a TQM culture, the *Plan, Do, Check, Act* (PDCA) model was used during the project life cycle. This cycle, also known as the quality loop, is a model widely deployed for continuous problem solving and optimization. It was therefore considered suitable for quality management in this complicated, multidisciplinary, multi-sectoral, international project (Guo et al., 2018). It was used at the strategic level for the management team and WP leads to review progress at the mid-point evaluation, and at the operational level for each activity requiring output review, such as a secondment. Figure 4.3 illustrates how PDCA was applied. At both levels, PDCA helped prevent disruption and eliminate risk.

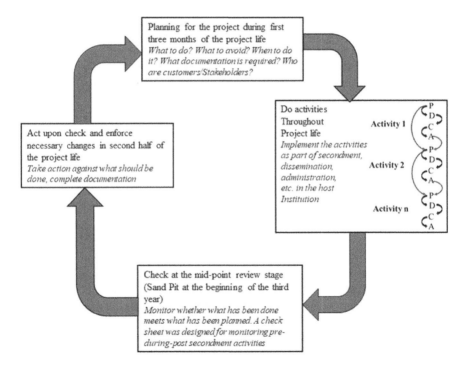

Figure 4.3   PDCA model for the GETM3 project

At the operational level, each secondee is asked to work through a checklist of items before, during, and after their secondment, to ensure their activities follow EU guidelines. Secondment experiences are shared verbally and documented on the learning platform. PDCA is also used at sandpit events to inform possible future changes in project planning and management.

Herding Cats: Reflections on Introducing and Managing Key Processes

In the realm of university research the focus is often purely on the academic, neglecting project and administrative staff (Harney et al., 2014). A key benefit of the GETM3 project is that it aims to develop inclusion of managers, administrators, and technicians through international exchanges and mobilities. Sandpit events bring all constituents together, while in terms of governance the project steering committee and advisory board similarly have diversity of representation. The reflective vignette below captures the practical experience and challenges for a project coordinator from the co-ordinating institution.

Reflection Vignette

"I know someone who needs your experience." That is how it started: a colleague with whom I had worked in the past put me in touch with the Project Leader for GETM3 at Northumbria University. The project had already been running for a year, and there were specific and immediate challenges I needed to resolve within the first few weeks of taking on the role of Project Manager. Using my previous experience and knowledge, I created new online communication processes and monitoring procedures for the project to address these issues. Within three weeks of starting work, I traveled to a quarterly project meeting in Slovenia to present them to the wider Project Team. But then to persuade them to use them!

Up until this point, I had met only project team members from my own institution. Most others had known each other, professionally and personally for a number of years. I was the outsider, the unknown, the "administrator" in a room of academics and researchers. I had to present my ideas, new systems and processes framed by EU regulation and policy. "Northumbria are making things up," "I can't ask my colleagues to share their data with everyone in the project." "Another process!?" The reaction was disappointing but not unexpected – the group had not had time to get to know me, my background, expertise and knowledge. With the opportunity to interact with colleagues both inside and outside of a formal work setting – and by offering to help them, I built rapport, demonstrated my professional expertise, and began to establish myself as one of the team. However, once back in our respective institutions, it was still difficult to get buy-in from all participants.

Approaching the halfway point, the Mid-Term Evaluation Meeting for the project took place in Warsaw where, after a day-long Sunday rehearsal, progress to date was presented to the project advisor from the EU Commission's Research Executive Agency.

During the event, colleagues praised the contribution I was making, and after presenting my online management system to the EU Adviser, I was directly complimented for my presentation and work which were highlighted as "exemplary." This event significantly increased my influence, authority, and reputation in the wider project team. It was a turning point: I had sufficiently built up the social capital needed to establish rapport with, and respect and engagement from, my new colleagues. As people got to know me and started to engage in the systems I had introduced, there was faster buy-in for further process improvements and implementation. However, I also recognize that my personal leadership style and ability to work across cultures have allowed me to create and maintain project team cohesion and keep the "cats" within project regulation boundaries. Ultimately, this will enhance our success.

Turning Risks into Opportunities

The wide geographic reach of international projects means that constantly fluctuating geo-political risks can have a direct bearing on planned activities. Project-specific risks can also impact activities, timetables, travel, and relationships (Richardson & Zikic, 2007). Allocating responsibility to a dedicated risk officer, coupled with continuous risk assessment, were critical to obtaining GETM3 funding. In the context of GETM3 (which is co-ordinated in the UK and involves South Korea) the ebb and flow of recent tensions between USA and North Korea, coupled with extended swells of Brexit uncertainties, present ongoing risks that could have critically impacted the project's fundamental landscape and direction of travel. More recently the coronavirus outbreak has mandated scenario planning and ongoing consultation with institutional and national travel advisories. Other external factors such as match funding for project expansion remained uncertain in the project's early stages. Similarly, critical incidents such as the unexpected loss of key staff and partner withdrawal could have threatened the achievement of contracted project deliverables. Instead, through careful management and the maintenance of open communication and positive networks, these events actually led to project expansion and new engagements. The indirect impact of internal and external risks created personal uncertainties, leading to delays in decision-making (e.g., attracting secondees), as individuals assessed their own personal risk for threats and opportunities ahead. Personal risk assessment can be further complicated by differing individual perceptions of risk, and by risk appetite across the range of project partners around the globe. The challenge is to turn these threats into opportunities. Such a journey may result in outcomes different from those originally planned, but in so doing may serve to strengthen partner relationships, skills and openness which can benefit the project – and future projects – overall. Successful risk management for international research projects requires entrepreneurial skills also needed in other parts of a project: horizon scanning, agility, commitment, flexibility, creative thinking, and resilience under pressure.

Transnational Work: Creating Value through Managing Mobility

"Higher education was always more internationally open than most sectors" (p. 3), and "faculty mobility has long been a positive professional norm" (p. 64) (Marginson & van der Wende, 2007). A global survey conducted by the International Association of University (IAU, 2010) revealed that 87% of universities in 115 countries included internationalization as one of their strategic goals.

Career management competence through transnational mobility may impact well-being, worker job attainment, and long-term career success (Churchman & King, 2009). Many academic staff have experienced transnational cooperation between international institutions (Pearce & Quan, 2015), either individually or collectively, as in the GETM3 project. Studies show that managing worker mobility is increasingly becoming a global concern. Working in a foreign country brings many challenges: linguistic, culturally, and professional. Workers must adjust to these differences (Markee, 1997). Language difficulty is an obvious challenge which affects performance (Biggs, 1998; Quan et al., 2013). There may be negative aspects of exposure to another culture, due to a lack of social support, or value differences between home and host countries. Adaptation to cultural change is stressful (Taha & Cox, 2016). Transnational work requires cross-cultural awareness, understanding of changes in cultural identity, building self-esteem, and willingness to acquire knowledge of a new culture (Lea & Stierer, 2011).

Dziewanowska, Quan, and Pearce (2018) analyzed the experience of GETM3 secondees. Despite similar opportunities given to all, secondees experienced different results and had varied levels of success in creating value for themselves and their organizations, as well as in responding to project objectives. This is in line with value creation literature which states that value is a subjective, relative, preferential, interactive, higher, abstract construct of a cognitive and affective nature (Sánchez-Fernández & Iniesta-Bonillo, 2006). The value creation process is affected by personal circumstances, personality, previous experience, needs, and expectations. The presence of other people – hosts and fellow secondees – can enable or inhibit value creation. The process is ongoing and continues long after a particular secondment ends. Revisiting experiences and reflecting upon them has proven to result in obtaining more value. However, the assumption is that all international experiences are automatically positive. The subjectivity and variability of the experience makes it less manageable by organizations and more reliant on the *selection* of individuals, with previous performance clearly indicative of future effectiveness. This is an important consideration for international career development. Failure to create value from an international secondment has resulted from secondee overestimation of their abilities and proclivities, or under-estimation of the challenge, before departure. Poor engagement with a host, and a focus on maintaining contact with a home institution while away, can undermine effectiveness. Some have failed to prioritize relationship over task due to undervaluation of the importance (and difficulty) of building social capital. The GETM3 project revolves around minimum 30-day secondment periods which drive the funding model. These have been significantly more effective when split or combined for multiple visits, making them more flexible and feasible, and allowing early familiarization to translate into operational effectiveness later. An initial value-creation strategy to involve as many secondees as possible by recruiting a different person for each secondment soon changed into an approach of allocating multiple secondments to trusted and effective participants. Potential for success is enhanced if both individuals and organizations are open to failure, and if there is a TQM process guiding the experience for everyone.

Trans-sectoral Work: Bringing Industry and Academia Together

At the core of GETM3 are trans-sectoral partnerships between industry and academia. They offer different knowledge-sharing opportunities in terms of technology and know-how (De Wit-de Vries et al., 2018). In the design of GETM3, such opportunities are not one-off "transactional" occurrences but are embedded in the quarterly sandpit meetings, project outputs, and international mobility plans. Funder regulations stipulate that intra-European mobility secondments must be trans-sectoral, that universities must send staff to industry and vice versa. This produces a win–win situation for both stakeholder groups. Industry can obtain knowledge and learn best practices garnered from state-of-the-art research, and find ways to build competitive advantage (Partha & David, 1994). Scholars can obtain insight on pressing industry challenges and identify new research needs (D'Este & Perkmann, 2011) from contemporary real-life industry situations. This provides an opportunity for demand-driven, engaged scholarship as opposed to supply driven research, thereby maximizing impact. Such partnerships represent a way to coordinate innovation communities beyond organizational boundaries (Mascarenhas et al., 2018). In the Republic of Korea, transferring between academic and industry is a common career path.

When researchers and practitioners nurture collaboration across sectors in management, they contribute to reducing the science–practice gap (Banks et al., 2016). Over a period of four or five years, GETM3 offers the potential for participants to build permanent bonds rather than temporary acquaintance. Participating industry organizations include long-standing strategic partners of the universities as well as new partners. Deliberately chosen to provide the broadest possible business representation, they range from international manufacturers to SME support entities to micro start-ups across all five countries. They provide a rich context for in-depth research on careers (Skoumpopoulou et al., 2019).

Based on a reflection of GETM3 experience, the following key factors have been identified as critical to an engaging and thriving academic-industry partnership:

1. *Prior relationship and building a solid trust base.* Existing industry–academia cooperation (e.g., previous shorter projects, participation of employees in the university's education programs) can be successfully extended in joint research projects. Trust between stakeholders is developed through building social capital which facilitates greater cooperation (Mascarenhas et al., 2018) and this goal has been built into the sandpit events.

2. *Designated partner liaison.* GETM3 borrowed the role of key account manager from industry: local, named individuals in each university were appointed from the start to serve as liaison with industry partners and represent their interests. This protected the business from unreasonable demands and assured their benefit, thereby preserving the local partnership. In most cases, this role is mirrored in the businesses. The management of public money requires a bureaucracy for accountability.

3. *Regular communication.* Good, pro-active communication is essential (De Wit-de Vries et al., 2018) and takes various forms according to those involved. It is facilitated by key account managers, who control the communication channel as required. Face-to-face involvement is supported by budgeting for travel to international meetings. Technology use is widespread, ensuring project task fulfillment and participation by academic leads.

4. *Flexibility.* Universities are large diversified organizations with multiple stakeholders which can render decision-making slow and complex. A publicly funded research project entails bureaucracy, continuous reporting, and periodic evaluation by a remote body. These aspects are different from how commercial organizations run, so flexibility is required by project managers. Industry experience in academia can make this easier.

5. *Opportunity for primary research.* Industry partners open doors to researchers and enable primary data collection for qualitative and quantitative research. Gathering data needs to comply with the highest ethical research standards and may also involve non-disclosure agreements. For this purpose, a project coordinator in the company identifies relevant audiences and connects them with the researchers. Industry partners generously open their doors to researchers during sandpit events, which brings practitioners and researchers together.

The activities above take time and require personal engagement from corporate and higher education partners, which can increase workloads and resource needs. Early recognition of the importance of these activities contributes to project success.

Advancing Understanding through Innovative Methodologies

The success of international mega-projects usually depends on intensity, quality, and participant interaction. Such projects offer learning and development through relational exchange. GETM3 was engineered to facilitate individual and institutional development by enriching their developmental networks (Dobrow et al., 2012) and providing opportunities for career insights.

The project introduced three innovative design features that provide individual development through interaction. Sandpits require physical co-location of project participants and are organized to allow for ample social interaction and relational exchange. A mobility plan of simultaneous secondments creates time periods when two participants are on secondment at the same location and time. By rule of physical proximity and the same hosts, these secondments allow researchers to meet and interact and engage in relational exchange (Contractor et al., 2006). Rotation around five countries ensures repeated interaction even with individuals who cannot travel. Further, secondees are placed so that professors work with less experienced researchers, and they learn from one another.

These innovative design features and their potential to affect personal and professional development through relational exchange can be addressed with particular types of social network analysis not often used in career research – two-mode network analysis and co-occurrence analysis (Borgatti et al., 2018; De Nooy et al., 2018). A particular strength of the project is longitudinal application as the sandpits and secondments unfold over time. In essence, a two-mode network analysis examines two different sets of actors (i.e., individuals and events) and relations between them. GETM3's two-mode network features a first type of node (individual project participant), a second type of node (a sandpit or a secondment at a particular time–location point), and relations between them. For example, participant X was on a secondment in place X on date Y, or participant X was present at the sandpit Z. This two-mode network can be transformed into a one-mode co-occurrence network, with only project participants as actors and co-occurrences at events as ties. For example, if two participants participated at three of the same sandpits, they have a higher co-occurrence score than two participants who participated at three separate sandpits (zero co-occurrences). The likelihood of interaction and relational exchange is much higher in the former. Co-occurrence networks can be further analyzed with specialized methods (see De Nooy et al., 2018), while co-occurrence scores can serve as input for other types of analyses such as regression.

It is valuable to use co-occurrences as potential for enhancing relational networks and opportunities for experiential insights. Relating them to actual individual professional and personal development – also at an institutional and international level – at project closure will contribute to its overall evaluation. Data collection and analysis can continue beyond. This represents a new approach to examining how large, mobility-based, international projects can affect the career development of project participants, with implications for project design and funding decisions.

Another form of methodological innovation, bibliometric methods, uses citations as the basis for evaluating the impact of a particular document. It enables researchers interested in reviewing a specific field to obtain an objective overview of the area (Zupic & Čater, 2015). Two types of bibliometric analysis have been used: document co-citation, which explores relationships and interactions between different researchers, revealing the intellectual traditions within a field (Vogel, 2012); and bibliographic coupling, which enables the identification of emergent topics (Van Raan, 2005). These approaches enabled the team to create a network-graphic representation of the intellectual structure, and of the scientific communication of research on entrepreneurial talent management and its various sub-domains, identifying the core theories used to inform the field and the current state of the art.

The words *entrepreneurial* (or *entrepreneurship*) and *talent management* were selected as keywords for search in the Web of Science Core Collection, resulting in 55 primary articles directly related to the topic (see Figure 4.4).[1] Most are journal

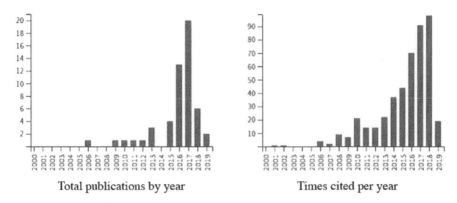

Total publications by year   Times cited per year

Source: Web of Science Core Collection 2019, https://clarivate.com/webofsciencegroup/solutions/web
-of-science-core-collection/.

Figure 4.4   Bibliometric data of primary articles

articles in the fields of either entrepreneurship or human resource management, and
most were published in the last decade, clearly indicating an increase in the popularity of such overlap in areas studied.

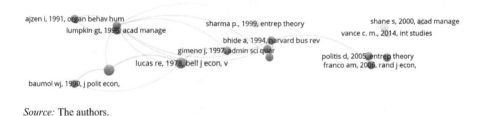

Source: The authors.

Figure 4.5   Co-citation results visualization

The networks portraying key documents, thematic clusters, and their connections
were then visualized using the VosViewer software.[2] Co-citation analysis results,
focused on the foundations of the field overlapping between entrepreneurship and
talent management, revealed four clusters (see Figure 4.5). The first (pink) is about
entrepreneurial orientation and the theory of planned behavior. The second (blue)
takes an economics perspective on entrepreneurship. The third (yellow) displays the
foundation of entrepreneurship theory, and the fourth (red) involves the interplay
between entrepreneurship and management (touching upon topics such as strategy,
knowledge diffusion, and learning).

Source: The authors.

Figure 4.6   *Bibliographic coupling results visualization*

Bibliographic coupling results, concentrated on current trends and hot topics in the field, identified four clusters (Figure 4.6). The most impactful (pink) revolves around finance and risk assessment. The second (blue) is about talent, entrepreneurial performance, and investments. The third (green) is about intrapreneurship and the fourth (yellow) about the cultural background predictors of success.

Taken together, these analyses demonstrate the potential to enhance the understanding of the connection between entrepreneurialism and talent management. Connections to finance, strategic entrepreneurship (Burgelman, 1983a), and personal–cultural antecedents clearly represent viable options for further research on how to manage one's career as an entrepreneurial person, which will inform younger people entering the workforce today and in the future.

Career Implications of Working in International Project for PhD Students

GETM3 provides instrumental career development for early-stage researchers in the form of (a) tangible and intangible resources and (b) networking through trans-sectoral, transgenerational, and transnational exchange, thus improving professional, transferable, and personal skills of researchers (Stalker et al., 2019). First, GETM3's unique international mobility opportunities develop early-stage, professional, research skills in a cross-cultural and inclusive environment. For example, embedded in secondment experiences, researchers apply various qualitative and quantitative research methods such as interviews, focus groups, action research, and surveys, in collaboration with experienced experts.

Second, GETM3 promotes the development of transferable skills through a variety of formats. This includes cooperating and communicating in multicultural teams and practicing presentation skills by disseminating research outputs at international conferences. Stimulating intellectual exchange across 16 organizations in five countries, the project also nurtures essential skills such as adaptability, cultural integration, networking, and leadership.

Since the development of professional, transferable skills is significant, GETM3 enhances the personal development of early-stage researchers. Confidence and a sense of belonging were built by active engagement in project activities and international interactions that followed. The project encouraged early-stage researchers to tap into a worldwide network of academics and business partners. Professional, personal, and emotional support was forthcoming, and this can be especially valuable for PhD students. For instance, the personal network of GETM3 participants evolved exponentially, enabling a community of practice for knowledge-sharing among global project partners in the private and academic sectors. Enthusiasm for collaboration shown at all levels helped junior scholars develop social capital at the outset of their careers.

In conclusion, GETM3's inclusive project culture not only advanced various professional skills but also enriched the life experience of the early-stage researchers involved. International collaboration such as this has a multitude of positive implications for the employability of PhD students and their career development.

CONCLUSION

The purpose of this chapter has been to outline the benefits and challenges of a mega-project exploring the entrepreneurial nature of careers. It would be false to suggest everything has progressed in the linear and rational way initially intended. Indeed, the strategically entrepreneurial way in which the management team and most participants respond to opportunities and difficulties is part of overall project success. There is little doubt that the systematic identification of key issues identified in the underpinning, design, methodology, and implementation helped navigate challenges, and has also enhanced project impact. Although at the time of this summary, the GETM3 project is only three years through four years of implementation, it has already achieved the dual benefit of researching entrepreneurial careers as well as building and enhancing entrepreneurial career capacity.

ACKNOWLEDGMENTS

The Global Entrepreneurial Talent Management 3 (GETM3) project receives funding from the European Union's Horizon 2020 research and innovation program under Marie Skłodowska-Curie grant agreement No 734824. This chapter was written by academic, industry and managerial members of the GETM3 team at Northumbria University and Highfly Ventures Ltd. (UK), Dublin City University and Technological University Dublin (Ireland), Warsaw University (Poland), Ljubljana University (Slovenia), and Chonnam National University. It was enabled by the GETM3 Overview session presented as part of the Dublin sandpit/HR Division International Conference, January 2019, at Dublin City University, Ireland.

NOTES

1. As of July 1, 2019, Google Scholar showed 18 indexed documents that specifically mention GETM3, all authored by project participants.
2. Due to cutting off less impactful documents, only key representatives of each cluster are visualized.

REFERENCES

Aguinis, H., Cummings, C., Ramani, R., & Cummings, T. G. (2019). An A is an A: the new bottom line for valuing academic research. *Academy of Learning and Education*, 34(1), 170–172.

Ahl, H., & Marlow, S. (2012). Exploring the dynamics of gender, feminism and entrepreneurship: advancing debate to escape a dead end. *Organization*, 19, 543–562.

Anzai, T., Kusama, R., Kodama, H., & Sengoku, S. (2012). Holistic observation and monitoring of the impact of interdisciplinary academic research projects: an empirical assessment in Japan. *Technovation*, 32, 345–357.

Argyris, C. (1993). On the nature of actionable knowledge. *The Psychologist*, 6(1), 29–32.

Bailey, M., Dziewanowska, K., Harney, B., Mihelic, K., Pearce, A., & Spencer, N. (2018). Beyond disciplines: can design approaches be used to develop education for jobs that don't yet exist? *Proceedings of the E&PDE 2018 20th International Conference on Engineering and Product Design*, London.

Bailey, M., Harney, B., & Pearce, A. (2019). Designing a design thinking approach to HRD. *International Journal of HRD Practice, Policy and Research*, 4(2), 9–23. doi: 10.22324/ ijhrdppr.4.202.

Bailey, M., & Smith, N. (2010). Safe environments for innovation – developing a new multidisciplinary masters programme, in W. Boks et al. (Eds.) *DS 62: Proceedings of E&PDE 2010, the 12th International Conference on Engineering and Product Design Education – When Design Education and Design Research meet ....* Strathclyde: The Design Society Institution of Engineering Designers, pp. 60–65.

Bailey, M., & Smith, N. (2016). Making it work: integrated academic practice, in E. Boya (Ed.) *Proceedings of 20th DMI: Academic Design Management Conference; Inflection Point: Design Research Meets Design Practice*. Boston: The Design Management Institute, pp. 2346–2363.

Banks, G. C., Pollack, J. M., Bochantin, J. E., Kirkman, B. L., Whelpley, C. E., & O'Boyle, E. H. (2016). Management's science–practice gap: a grand challenge for all stakeholders. *Academy of Management Journal*, 59(6), 2205–2231.

Bansal, P., Bertels, S., Ewart, T., MacConnachie, P., & O'Brien, J. (2012). Bridging the research–practice gap. *The Academy of Management Perspectives*, 26, 73–92.

Baruch, Y., & Rousseau, D. M. (2018). Integrating psychological contracts and ecosystems in career studies and management. *Academy of Management Annals*, 13(1), 84–111.

Biggs, J. (1998). Assessment & classroom teaching: a role for summative assess. *Assessment in Education*, 5(1), 103–110.

Binder, J. (2016). *Global Project Management: Communication, Collaboration and Management Across Borders*, 2nd edition. London: Routledge.

Borgatti, S. P., Everett, M. G., & Johnson, J. C. (2018). *Analyzing Social Networks*. London: Sage.

Brabrand, C., & Dahl, B. (2009). Using the SOLO taxonomy to analyze competence progression of university science curricula. *Higher Education*, 58(4), 531–549.

Bridges, B. (1986). Western Europe and Korea: an awakening relationship. *Global Economic Review*, 15(2), 21–33. doi: 10.1080/12265088608422757.

Briner, R. B. (1998). What is an evidence-based approach to practice and why do we need one in occupational psychology. *Proceedings of the 1998 British Psychological Society Occupational Psychology Conference*. The British Psychological Society, Leicester, UK, 39–44.

Burgelman, R. A. (1983a). A process model of internal corporative venturing in the diversified major firm. *Administrative Science Quarterly*, 28, 223–244.

Burgelman, R. A. (1983b). Corporate entrepreneurship and strategic management: insights from a process study. *Management Science*, 29(12), 1349–1364.

Burgelman, R. A., & Hitt, M. A. (2007). Entrepreneurial actions, innovation and appropriability. *Strategic Entrepreneurship Journal*, 1, 349–352.

Churchman, D., & King, S. (2009). Academic practice in transition: hidden stories of academic identities. *Teaching in Higher Education*, 14(5), 507–516.

Contractor, N. S., Wasserman, S., & Faust, K. (2006). Testing multitheoretical, multilevel hypotheses about organizational networks: an analytic framework and empirical example. *Academy of Management Review*, 31(3), 681–703.

Craig, E., & Hall, D. (2011). The new organizational career: too important to be left to HR?, in R. J. Burke, & C. L. Cooper (Eds.) *Reinventing HRM: Challenges and New Directions*. London: Routledge, pp. 115–132.

Crawley, M., & O'Meara, L. (2002). *Gender Impact Assessment Handbook*. Belfast: Gender Equality Unity.

Crowley-Henry, M., Benson, E. T., & Al Ariss, A. (2019). Linking talent management to traditional and boundaryless career orientations: research propositions and future directions. *European Management Review*, 16(1), 5–19.

D'Este, P., & Perkmann, M. (2011). Why do academics engage with industry? The entrepreneurial university and individual motivations. *The Journal of Technology Transfer*, 36(3), 316–339.

DeNisi, A. S., Wilson, M. S., & Biteman, J. (2014). Research and practice in HRM: a historical perspective. *Human Resource Management Review*, 24, 219–231.

De Nooy, W., Mrvar, A., & Batagelj, V. (2018). *Exploratory Social Network Analysis with Pajek: Revised and Expanded Edition for Updated Software* (Vol. 46). Cambridge: Cambridge University Press.

De Wit-de Vries, E., Dolfsma, W. A., van der Windt, H. J., & Gerkema, M. P. (2018). Knowledge transfer in university–industry research partnerships: a review. *The Journal of Technology Transfer*, 44(4), 1236–1255.

Dobrow, S. R., Chandler, D. E., Murphy, W. M., & Kram, K. E. (2012). A review of developmental networks: incorporating a mutuality perspective. *Journal of Management*, 38(1), 210–242.

Donald, W. E., Baruch, Y., & Ashleigh, M. (2019). The undergraduate self-perception of employability: human capital, careers advice, and career ownership. *Studies in Higher Education*, 44(4), 599–614.

Dziewanowska, K., Quan, R., & Pearce, A. (2018). Capturing the value of international mobility in higher education. *Global Entrepreneurial Talent Management Conference*, University of Warsaw, Poland, April 17, 2018.

Dziewanowska, K., Petrylaite, E., Balas Rant, M. & Clegg, S. (2019). Personal Career Success in the Eyes of Nascent Entrepreneurs Internationally, *International Journal of HRD Practice, Policy and Research*, 4(2), 25–44.

EPSRC (2019). *Sandpits*. https://epsrc.ukri.org/funding/applicationprocess/routes/network/ideas/whatisasandpit/.

European Commission (2008). Entrepreneurship in Higher Education: Final report of the Expert Group. https://ec.europa.eu/growth/content/final-report-expert-group-entrepreneurship-higher-education-especially-within-non-business-0_en.

European Commission (2017). Research and Innovation Staff Exchange (RISE): Bridging R&I Sectors in Europe and Worldwide. https://ec.europa.eu/research/mariecurieactions/news/research-and-innovation-staff-exchange-rise-bridging-ri-sectors-europe-and-worldwide_en.

European Commission (2019). *Research and Innovation – Participant Portal 2020 Online Manual*. http://ec.europa.eu/research/participants/docs/h2020-funding-guide/cross-cutting-issues/gender_en.htm.

Fayolle, A., Verzat, C., & Wapshott, R. (2016). In quest of legitimacy: the theoretical and methodological foundations of entrepreneurship education research. *International Small Business Journal*, 34(7), 895–904.

Fortune & SHRM (2001). Impact of diversity initiatives on the bottom line. A SHRM survey of the Fortune 1000 (S12–S14) in Keeping Your Edge: Managing a Diverse Corporate Culture. www.fortune.com/sections.

Fuller, J. (2016). How to hire a millennial. http://www.hbs.edu/recruiting/blog/post/how-to-hire-a-millennial.

Gubbins, C., Harney., B., van der Werff, L., & Rousseau, D. M. (2018). Enhancing the trustworthiness and credibility of HRD: evidence-based management to the rescue? *Human Resource Development Quarterly*, 29(3), 193–202.

Guo, Y., Gao, H., Cai, Z., Zhang, S., & Hu, F. (2018). Continuous improvement of industrial engineering education based on PDCA method and structural importance. *Proceeding of the 2018 IEEE IEE International Conference on Industrial Engineering and Engineering Management*, Bangkok, Thailand, December 2018.

Harney, B., Monks, K., Alexopoulos, A., Buckley, F., & Hogan, T. (2014). Research scientists as knowledge workers: contract status and employment opportunities. *International Journal of Human Resource Management*, 25(16), 2219–2233.

Herr, K., & Anderson, G. L. (2005). *The Action Research Dissertation: A Guide for Students & Faculty*. Thousand Oaks: Sage.

Hollensbe, E., Wookey, C., Hickey, L., George, G., & Nichols, C. V. (2014). Organizations with purpose. *Academy of Management Journal*, 57(5), 1227–1234.

Holquist, E., & Sundin, C. (1991). The growth of women's entrepreneurship – push or pull factors? *Paper presented to the European Institute for Advanced Studies in Management Conference on Small Business*, University of Durham Business School. http://www.EIASM.be.

International Association of University (IAU) (2010). Internationalisation of higher education: An evolving landscape, locality and globally. https://www.iau-aiu.net/Global-survey-on-Internationalization.

Jimenez-Jimenez, D., Martinez-Costa, M., Martinez-Lorente, A. R., & Ahmed Dine Rabeh, H. (2015). Total quality management performance in multinational companies, a learning perspective. *The TQM Journal*, 27(3), 328–340.

Kaše, R., Dries, N., Briscoe, J. P., Cotton, R. D., Apospori, E., Bagdadli, S., Çakmak-Otluoğlu, K. Ö., Chudzikowski, K., Dysvik, A., Gianecchini, M., Saxena, R., Shen, Y., Verbruggen, M., Adeleye, I., Babalola, O., Casado, T., Cerdin, J.-L., Kim, N., Mishra, S. K., Unite, J., & Fei, Z. (2020). Career success schemas and their contextual embeddedness: a comparative configurational perspective. *Human Resource Management Journal*, 30(3), 422–440. doi: 10.1111/1748-8583.12218.

König, B., Diehl, K., Tscherning, K., and Helming, K. (2013). A framework for structuring interdisciplinary research management. *Research Policy*, 42, 261–272.

Kossek, E. E., Lobel, S. A., & Brown, J. (2006). Human resource strategies to manage workforce diversity: examining "the business case," in P. Prasad, & J. K. Pringle (Eds.) *Handbook of Workplace Diversity*. London: Sage, pp. 53–74.

Koulopoulos, T., & Keldsen, D. (2014). *The Gen Z Effect: The Six Forces Shaping the Future Of Business*. Brookline, MA: Bibliomotion Inc.

Lea, M. R., & Stierer, B. (2011). Changing academic identities in changing academic work-places: Learning from academics' everyday professional writing practices. *Teaching in Higher Education*, 16(6), 605–616.

Leenders, R., van Engelen, J., & Kratzer, J. (2003). Virtuality, communication, and new product team creativity: a social network perspective. *Journal of Engineering and Technology Management*, 20(1–2), 69–92.

Marginson, S., & van der Wende, M. (2007). *Globalisation & Higher Education, Education Working Paper No.8*, Centre for Educational Research and Innovation (CERI), OECD Directorate for Education. www.oecd-ilibrary.org/education/oecd-education-working-papers.

Markee, N. (1997). *Managing Curricular Innovation*. Cambridge: Cambridge University Press.

Marlow, S., & Martinez Dy, M. (2018). Is it time to rethink the gender agenda in entrepreneurship research? *International Business Journal*, 36, 3–22.

Mascarenhas, C., Ferreira, J. J., & Marques, C. (2018). University–industry cooperation: a systematic literature review and research agenda. *Science and Public Policy*, 45(5), 708–718.

Neeley, T. (2015). Global teams that work. *Harvard Business Review*, 93(10), 74–81.

Partha, D., & David, P. A. (1994). Toward a new economics of science. *Research Policy*, 23(5), 487–521.

Pearce, A., & Quan, R. (2015). International staff mobility in higher education: to what extent could intra-European entrepreneurial approach be applied to Sino–CEE initiatives? *Journal of East European Management Studies*, 20(2), 226–254.

Pfeffer, J., & Sutton, R. I. (2006). *Hard Facts, Dangerous Half-Truths and Total Nonsense: Profiting from Evidence-Based Management*. Boston, MA: Harvard University Press.

Quan, R., Smailes, J., & Fraser, W. (2013). The transition experiences of direct entrants from overseas higher education partners into UK universities. *Teaching in Higher Education*, 18(4), 414–426.

Reason, P., & Bradbury, H. (2006). Preface to *The Handbook of Action Research: The Concise Paperback Edition*, London: Sage, pp. xxi–xxxii.

Reed, M. (2016). *The Research Impact Handbook*. Huntly, UK: Fast Track Impact.

Richardson, J., & Zikic, J. (2007). The darker side of an international academic career. *Career Development International*, 12(2), 164–186.

Rouse, E. (2019). Where you end and I begin: understanding intimate co-creation. *Academy of Management Review*, 45(1), 181–204. https://journals.aom.org/doi/10.5465/amr.2016.0388.

Rousseau, D. M. (2012). *The Oxford Handbook of Evidence-Based Management*. Oxford: Oxford University Press.

Sánchez-Fernández, R., & Iniesta-Bonillo, M. A. (2006). Consumer perception of value: literature review and a new conceptual framework. *Journal of Consumer Satisfaction, Dissatisfaction and Complaining Behavior*, 19(1), 40–58.

Sanders, E. B. N., and Stappers, P. J. (2008). Co-creation and the new landscapes of design. *Co-design*, 4(1), 5–18.

Skoumpopoulou, D., Stalker, B. & Kohont, A. (2019). Talent management in European SMEs: case analysis between Slovenia and Poland, *International Journal of HRD Practice, Policy and Research*, 4(2), 45–64.

Smith, K. G., & DiGregorio, D. (2002). Bisociation, discovery, and the role of entrepreneurial action, in M. A. Hitt, R. D. Ireland, S. M. Camp, & D. L. Sexton (Eds.) *Strategic Entrepreneurship: Creating a New Mindset*. Oxford: Blackwell Publishers, pp. 129–150.

Stalker, B., Quan, R. & Skoumpopoulou, D. (2019). Impactful learning: exploring the value of informal learning experiences to improve the learning potential of international research projects, *International Journal of Human Resource Development Practice, Policy and Research*, 4(2), 83–101.

Stanford University (2019). *Gendered Innovations.* http://genderedinnovations.stanford.edu/what-is-gendered-innovations.html.

Taha, N., & Cox, A. (2016). Social network dynamics in international students' learning. *Studies in Higher Education*, 41(1), 182–198.

Thornberry, N. (2001). Corporate entrepreneurship: antidote or oxymoron? *European Management Journal*, 19(5), 526–533.

Tkachenko, O., Hahn, H.-J., & Peterson, S. (2016). Theorizing the research–practice gap in the field of management: a review of key frameworks and models, in C. Hughes, & M. W. Gosney (Eds.) *Bridging the Scholar–Practitioner Gap in Human Resources Development.* Hershey, PA: IGI Global, pp. 101–119.

Van Raan, A. (2005). For your citations only? Hot topics in bibliometric analysis. *Measurement: Interdisciplinary Research and Perspectives*, 3(1), 50–62.

Van Rijnsoever, F. J., & Hessels, L. K. (2011). Factors associated with disciplinary and inter-disciplinary research collaboration. *Research Policy*, 40, 463–472.

Vogel, R. (2012). The visible colleges of management and organization studies: a bibliometric analysis of academic journals. *Organization Studies*, 33(8), 1015–1043.

Voss, C. (2019). Guidepost: towards an actionable and pragmatic view of impact. *Academy of Management Discoveries*, AMD-2019-0113.

Warkentin, M., & Beranek, M. (1999). Training to improve virtual team communication. *Information Systems Journal*, 9(4), 271–290.

Wiklund, J., Wright, M., & Zahra, S. A. (2019). Conquering relevance: entrepreneurship research's grand challenge. *Entrepreneurship Theory and Practice*, 43(3), 419–436. doi: 1042258718807478.

World Economic Forum. (2018). *Future of Jobs Report 2018.* Geneva: Centre for the New Economy and Society.

Zacher, H., Rudolph, C. W., Todorovic, T., & Amman, D. (2019). Academic career development: a review and research agenda. *Journal of Vocational Behaviour*, 110, 357–373. https://doi.org/10.1016/j.jvb.2018.08.006.

Zupic, I., & Čater, T. (2015). Bibliometric methods in management and organization. *Organizational Research Methods*, 18(3), 429–472.

5. Career decision making

Gregory Hennessy and Jeffrey Yip

INTRODUCTION

Career decision making is a process without simple answers. In particular, career decisions have become more challenging, with increased career mobility and the rise of contingent employment in today's "gig economy" (Amir & Gati, 2006; Arthur, Khapova, & Wilderom, 2005; Barley, Bechky, & Milliken, 2017; Petriglieri, Ashford, & Wrzesniewski, 2019). Further, demographic predictions suggest that people born today are more likely to live past 100 years, with careers that could span more than 60 years (Gratton & Scott, 2017). This increasing longevity, the prevalence of options through career platforms (e.g., LinkedIn), the rise of dual-career couples, and the growing acceptance of multiple career arcs add up to a changing decision making environment that is ripe for new methods and research.

Career decisions do not occur in a vacuum. They are indeterminably shaped by interpersonal relationships (such as in dual-career couples), the availability of alternatives, and levels of uncertainty in career environments. Yet, to date, models have focused primarily on the individual decision maker, without due consideration of a person's network of relationships or organizational environment. In this chapter, we review research on career decision making and provide recommendations for future research. First, we review existing research on career decision making styles and decision making difficulties. This stream of research reflects a focus on individual differences in decision making – a dominant theme in career research. In the second section, we propose and unpack two possible and arguably generative directions for future research: decision making heuristics and decision making environments. We present insights from the broader psychological literature on judgment and decision making and the implications of these insights for careers research.

CAREER DECISION STYLES

Some of the earliest work in career decisions centered on the process of guiding students toward a suitable career. Instruments such as the Occupational Alternatives Questionnaire (Zener & Schnuelle, 1976) and the Career Maturity Inventory (Crites, 1973; Crites & Savickas, 1996) are still helping students understand and prepare for the process of choosing a career (for example, Kent State University, 2019). In the wake of clearer guidance around the process, researchers have found that people exhibit predictable patterns of behavior when faced with a career decision. More importantly, differences in these patterns of behavior, otherwise known as career decision making styles, have consequences on decision quality and outcomes (Driver, 1979; Hardin & Leong, 2004; Parker, de Bruin, & Fischhoff, 2007).

Michael Driver (1979) was among the first to examine the role of decision making styles in careers and organizational behavior, and he defined decision making styles as habitual patterns individuals use in decision making. Building on Driver's research, Scott and Bruce (1995, p. 820) specified decision making styles as "the learned habitual response pattern exhibited by an individual when confronted with a decision situation." They noted that decision styles are not a personality trait, but a habit-based style, and therefore referred to their assessment as the General Decision-Making *Style* inventory. Researchers continued to clarify the role of styles in career decision making, leading Gati, Landman, Davidovitch, Asulin-Peretz, and Gadassi to label their framework Career Decision-Making *Profiles* (2010) to underscore the complex, multidimensional patterns that arise.

Decision styles are not mutually exclusive. Research has found that while people rely on a primary style, other modalities are not precluded (Driver, Brousseau, & Hunsaker, 1998; Harren, 1979; Singh & Greenhaus, 2004). In other words, people tend to rely on a primary style across most situations, but they may, on occasion, use a combination of styles or a non-dominant style. More specifically, research suggests career decisions are made using an opposing bilateral model in which decisions are made by relying on either primarily intuitive or rational processes (Epstein, 1994; Kahneman, 2003). These two thinking modalities have been described by Kahneman (2003) as "thinking fast" (Type I processing) and "thinking slow" (Type II processing).

Until relatively recently, research into career decision making has been dominated by those employing rational models (Type II processing). Rational career decision making relies on evidence and reason to match desired career characteristics to occupations (e.g., Gati, 1986; Pitz & Harren, 1980). Such models value "reason, logic, objectivity, and independence" (Hartung & Blustein, 2002, p. 43) as the means to reach an optimal match. More specifically, rational decision making involves "a thorough, comprehensive, dispassionate and generally solitary process of weighting, evaluating and eliminating alternatives to arrive at an optimal choice" (Ceschi, Costantini, Phillips, & Sartori, 2017, p. 17).

Limitations of Intuitive and Rational Decision Styles

There is growing evidence that intuitive styles can be ineffective under some conditions as they are more susceptible to bias than rational styles (Klein, 1998). The best contemporary models integrate the two types, where the strengths of one offset the shortcomings of the other. Most notably, Savickas and colleagues (2009) developed a comprehensive model for career management in the modern era, based upon five presuppositions about people and their work lives, namely contextual possibilities, dynamic processes, non-linear progression, multiple perspectives, and personal patterns. Murtagh, Lopes, and Lyons (2011) propose an "other-than-rational" career decision making approach, where positive emotions, happenstance, and self-regulation can guide career decision making.

In the context of career decision making, a rational style relies on thorough information searches and logical evaluation of alternatives, while an intuitive style relies on subjective experience and emotions (Scott & Bruce, 1995). These styles are independent of cognitive abilities (Thunholm, 2004) and predict self-ratings of decision quality above and beyond the Big Five personality traits (Wood & Highhouse, 2014).

The bilateral model of decision making, applied to careers, has limitations. First, rationality and intuition are not opposite ends of a single continuum. In the context of career decision making, it is quite likely that people use both rationality and intuition as complementary modalities, and as Epstein (1994) asserts, both types play highly influential roles in the determination of behavior. Whether rationality or intuition predominates is a function of the nature of the task, situation, and individual differences in decision making style. Second, current measures of intuition and rationality focus on the individual as the source of information. This stops short of considering how relationships affect decision making. Third, empirical research reveals that career decision making is neither exclusively rational nor intentional (Krieshok, Black, & McKay, 2009). Given the limits of rationality, the abundance of non-conscious processes, and the complex interplay between the two, career decision makers inevitably run into difficulties. Recent research by Yip, Li, Ensher, and Murphy (2020) have examined this limitation and uncovered the role of spirituality and advice-taking as additional modalities that are related but distinct from rationality and intuition.

DECISION MAKING DIFFICULTIES

Difficulties in and barriers to career decision making have been a centerpiece of research for some time (Hilton, 1962). Investigators have looked at a gamut of factors, especially the evaluation of variables influencing the decision, the decision process, the process for implementing the decision, and the decision context, including cognitive as well as behavioral considerations (Jepsen & Dilley, 1974). Many studies of career decision difficulties begin with a decision making framework as their organizing logic (e.g., the Career Decision Making Difficulties Questionnaire by Osipow and Gati, 1998); others end up with decision making-related problems as the central issue in career management (Kelly & Lee, 2002; O'Hare & Tamburri, 1986).

Comprehensive taxonomies have described a wide range of factors shaping career decision making difficulties (e.g., Campbell & Cellini, 1981; Kelly & Lee, 2002; Kelly & Pulver, 2003; Savickas & Jarjoura, 1991), and problems arising from decision making commonly emerge as prominent features. Gati, Krausz, and Osipow's Career Decision-Making Difficulties Questionnaire (CDDQ, 1996; see also, Gati & Saka, 2001) has been a vital assessment and taxonomy of difficulties that can lead a person to make a less-than-optimal career choice. Others use the decision making process itself to tease apart differences among other factorial dimensions, such as

Salomone's (1982) distinction between indecisive students and indecisive mid-career adults. Indecision, it turns out, is perhaps the greatest career decision difficulty of all.

Measures of Career Indecision

Difficulties in career decision making often manifest as indecision. Osipow, Carney, and Barak's (1976) Career Decision Scale was an early measure of indecision at the very start of one's career – the effort to identify a vocation. Larson, Toulouse, Ngumba, Fitzpatrick, and Heppner (1994) identify four areas of indecision for young adults: subjective career distress and obstacles, active problem-solving, academic self-efficacy, and career myths. Though geared toward college students, these same items have analogies for mid- or late-career workers. For example, academic self-efficacy could be interpreted as self-efficacy more broadly for experienced workers, and indeed, tools like the Career Decision-Making Self-efficacy Scale (Taylor & Betz, 1983) and its successor, the Career Decision Self-efficacy Scale (Betz, Klein, & Taylor, 1996) demonstrate a progression toward broader application.

Even with the insights garnered from these early studies, research interest in the types, sources, and antecedents of career indecision have remained steady. Germeijs and De Boeck's (2002) Indecisiveness Scale instituted a measure that spans modes of indecision, including career indecisiveness. An even more recent assessment, the Career Indecision Profile (Brown et al., 2012; Hacker, Carr, Abrams, and Brown, 2013), associates career choice difficulties with another set of four areas: neuroticism/negative affectivity, choice/commitment anxiety, lack of readiness, and interpersonal conflicts. Similarly, Meyer and Winer (1993) found that neuroticism and anxiety have strong associations with indecision, based on an investigation using the Career Decision Scale (Osipow, Carney, Winer, Yanico, & Koschier, 1976) and the Sixteen Personality Factor Questionnaire (Cattell & Eber, 1962). In the same vein, the Career Decidedness Scale (Lounsbury, Tatum, Chambers, Owens, & Gibson, 1999) demonstrates the association between personality and career decidedness more broadly. More recently, Gati and colleagues (2011) demonstrated that the "Big Five" personality traits of neuroticism, agreeableness, perfectionism, and the need for cognitive closure are positively associated with career decision making difficulties, while extraversion, openness to experience, and career decision self-efficacy are inversely related to them.

Despite growing research on career indecision, the mechanisms of indecision have yet to be unpacked. The challenge of career indecision is complicated by the fact that the barriers faced by decision makers are not immediately visible. In any problem-solving context, there may be a difference between the actual state of things and the perception of that state (Hennessy & Latre, 1996). More specifically, Holland, Johnston, and Asama (1993) underscored the role of individual traits in career decision making in their Vocational Identity Scale, which distinguishes a person's deeply-rooted and stable pattern of abilities, goals, and interests (*vocational identity*) from more malleable ones that may be shaped by current career aspirations and roles (*career identity*). A promising direction is the development of frameworks for understanding how individuals assess and respond to career indecision; for example, the Strategies of Coping with Career Indecision framework (Lipshits-Braziler, Gati, & Tatar, 2016).

Future Research

Given the trend toward multiple and longer career arcs, the need for research on career decision difficulties is becoming increasingly important. Longitudinal analyses will be an essential tool for examining how career decision difficulties change over time. To begin with, knowing whether difficulties are temporary or chronic is essential (Brown & Rector, 2008). This distinction brings into focus differing underlying mechanisms that require fundamentally different paths for unblocking the decision process (Fuqua & Hartman, 1983). Namely, acute indecision typically arises from circumstantial factors, such as insufficient data, contradictory information (Jaensch, Hirschi, & Freund, 2015), and heightened emotional states. A better understanding of temporary indecisiveness would require research on the content of information presented to the decision maker and other circumstantial factors. The temporal dimension of indecision is critical in differentiating between chronic and acute decision making difficulties (Hall, 1992). Research on career difficulties across the different life stages and how they evolve over time is a promising direction for future research.

DECISION MAKING HEURISTICS

A heuristic is a strategy for making decisions more quickly by discounting or ignoring available or discoverable information (Gigerenzer & Gaissmaier, 2011). For example, a basic heuristic tied to satisficing (Simon, 1955, 1957) would be to select the first option that "works" – one that meets a set of criteria "well enough" (Klein, 1998). Heuristics reduce effort by (a) examining fewer cues, (b) reducing the effort of retrieving cue values, (c) simplifying the weighting of cues, (d) integrating less information, and (e) examining fewer alternatives (Shah & Oppenheimer, 2008). Among traditional rationalists, heuristics are perceived as second-rate shortcuts since they do not make use of all the information that is available (Dean & Sharfman, 1993, 1996, Gino, Moore, & Bazerman, 2009; Pitz & Harren, 1980). However, contextual factors such as the presence of uncertainty, risk, and opportunities to learn can affect what sort of strategy makes the most sense (Gigerenzer, 2016). In particular, career decisions are often made under a condition of uncertainty. In such situations, heuristics may be more effective at getting to a high-quality decision (Gigerenzer, 2016; Newell & Simon, 1972) than applying an analytical process that requires information that is not readily available to the decision maker.

The call to apply heuristics to career decision making can be traced back at least three decades (Fitzgerald & Rounds, 1989; Gelatt, 1989; Heppner & Frazier, 1992). One of the first heuristics proposed is sequential elimination (Gati, 1986) in which occupational alternatives are evaluated as sets of characteristics. Characteristics are considered in turn, and options deemed insufficient in that characteristic are eliminated, until only a handful of options remain. It is an application of Tversky's (1972) elimination-by-aspects choice theory to career decision making.

Research on decision making reveals that people regularly use simplifying heuristics in making judgments in some circumstances (Kahneman & Tversky, 1972, 1973; Tversky & Kahneman, 1973, 1974, 1980). Such heuristics are cognitive processing short cuts, and they typically avoid making major mistakes but often fail to reach the "optimal" decision. Decisions made using heuristics have been observed to be inconsistent and prone to systematic biases because some aspects of the decision are not adequately weighed or considered at all (Pitz & Harren, 1980). The fact that heuristics are sometimes employed in even relatively simple decisions underscores the limits of rational models to explain actual behavior (Tversky & Kahneman, 1973, 1974, 1980).

Moreover, people do not just have access to a single approach or option for solving their problems. Heuristics can be used when they offer advantageous short cuts to a solution, while more sophisticated decision strategies can be employed when the situation warrants (Gigerenzer & Selten, 2002). A crucial factor in whether heuristics or complex rational strategies are more effective is whether the context involves risk or uncertainty (Qin & Simon, 1990). A decision faces *risk* when the comprehensive set of potential future states are known, and there is certainty as to the associated outcomes and their probabilities. *Uncertainty* prevails when the states, outcomes, and probabilities are not just unknown but are unknowable. In such circumstances, optimization is mathematically impossible and heuristics have an advantage, often outperforming complex "rational" strategies (Gigerenzer & Brighton, 2009).

Types of Heuristics

By definition, heuristics are procedural, and they tend to have a search-like quality about them with three fundamental elements (Gigerenzer & Todd, 1999): (1) *Search rules* that specify the path within the information space that the search will follow, (2) *Stopping rules* that specify when to conclude the search, and (3) *Decision rules* that specify how the final decision will be reached.

Several considerations influence the selection of a particular heuristic or the development of a new one for career decision making. First, heuristics are developed and refined through learning (Rieskamp & Otto, 2006). This suggests that career decision heuristics will evolve over a person's lifespan. Second, heuristics can be shared across individuals through social processes, including imitation and teaching (e.g., Snook, Taylor, & Bennell, 2004). This underscores the practical benefits of research into career heuristics. Third, heuristics can be applied in a broad range of circumstances and can take a wide range of forms. Gigerenzer and Gaissmaier's (2011) categorization offers a useful bridge to the career decision making literature. Their categories, along with examples of how they might be applied to different career situations, appear in Table 5.1.

Table 5.1   Examples of heuristics

Class of Heuristic	
1.	*Take-the-first heuristic*	Possible class of heuristic used by experienced career-decision makers
	Choose the first alternative that comes	(i.e., those in a second or third career arc) whose extensive latent
	to mind.	knowledge about the world and self might shape the career decision.
2.	*Take-the-Best*	Possible heuristic class used by those who have a strong sense of what
	A model of how people infer which of	career they want or, more generally, what is important to them.
	two alternatives has a higher value on	
	a criterion, based on binary cue values	
	retrieved from memory.	
3.	*Mapping Heuristic*	Possible heuristic used by young adults who have very few
	Tally the number of relevant cues with	preconceived ideas about their career. Also, potentially the class used
	positive values. Among the options with	by later career adults who are simply substantially uncertain about
	the highest number of positive cues,	their next career. In either case, applying the heuristic could support
	choose the one with the highest median	learning about career options and goals.
	criterion value.	

Heuristic Rules

The relevance and consequence of the above heuristics have yet to be studied in the career decision making context. They present generative possibilities for future research. A starting point will be to consider how established criteria fit into a heuristic context. Of the three types of rules in heuristics (i.e., search, stopping, and decision), decision rules obviously have the closest connection to career decision making. For example, a criterion eliminating career options that require more than 50% travel is easily seen as a heuristic decision rule. However, there remains much more to learn about how heuristics are applied by actual people making career decisions. It might turn out that previously unconsidered frameworks and taxonomies prove to be more helpful in practice. As a specific example, we next discuss real options as heuristic decision rules in career decision making.

Real Options as Heuristic Rules

Career decisions, especially those made early in a career, have an investment-like quality to them. Just like any other investment, choosing a career involves making an initial expenditure in exchange for a future stream of payments. The initial expenditure involves committing time, money, or other resources to gain the qualifications needed to enter the career. Payments received include not only income, but also perks, status, and other rewards associated with the chosen career. Taken together, this pattern of expenditures and payments is no different from the countless financial investments evaluated every day in the standard course of business, so it is worth considering how the "career as an investment" lens might shape career decision heuristics.

Consider the case of a recent MBA graduate with two offers from management consulting firms. Firm A is the premier firm, globally recognized as a thought leader in many industries, with an extensive list of highly desirable client relationships. Firm B is a respected but second-tier firm, with select areas of excellence and several sought-after clients. Firm A compensates new hires at 10% below the industry average, whereas Firm B pays 10% above it. From a strict NPV (Net Present Value) point of view, the obvious choice is to take Firm B's offer.

Nonetheless, many choose Firm A. How does Firm A get away with it? Why would top students from the best business schools take what is "obviously" an inferior offer? The answer is, at least in part, "option value." The experience of being at Firm A creates value above and beyond the direct compensation. In particular, being ex-Firm A creates career options that are fundamentally unavailable to departing or former employees of Firm B. Such real options-based career decisions are played out each year among MBA graduates around the world. However, you do not have to be an MBA graduate to recognize that sometimes the seemingly inferior choice delivers value through the doors that open up later. In today's labor context where lifetime employment is rare and individuals manage their own career progression, incorporating the value of potential career paths is more important than ever.

Real options are a logical structure for evaluating decisions like this where potential choices have one or more "options" to change the decision in the future and, as in the case just described, they have the potential to offer tremendous explanatory power in career decision making. In finance, the application of real options determines the appropriate price of investment alternatives that have such options embedded in them. It is a level of quantification and calculation that is uncommon and usually uncalled for in career decision making. Instead, the opportunity to integrate real option thinking into career decisions research is to consider how its lessons can be incorporated into career decision heuristics and into heuristic decision rules in particular. Table 5.2 provides specific examples of how common option types (Copeland & Antikarov, 2002; Guthrie, 2009; Kodukula & Papudesu, 2006, Trigeorgis & Reuer, 2017) might be translated into career decision research, especially heuristics models.

Research into heuristic-based decision making and the integration of real options into heuristic decision rules offers the promise of opening up new perspectives on career decision making. More importantly, real option heuristics brings to the foreground the role of time and discounting in career decision making – a factor that is relatively under-studied and growing in importance as people work ever longer. Moreover, real options theory addresses important aspects of career uncertainty by considering the value of opportunity generation across career alternatives. It mirrors the thinking employed by people with long time horizons and high aspirations who are inclined toward career paths that create future value.

Table 5.2   *Real options types*

Real Option Type	Description	Avenues for research
1. Expand/Invest	A career path where the immediate value of the path is marginal or negative, but it contains value derived from the expansion of career path choices in the future.	The option to expand is likely to be attractive to high-aspiration individuals with a long-term view of their career – decision makers who may be willing to accept a negative or low NPV (Net Present Value) in the short term in exchange for the potential of high growth in the future. For example, many entry-level sales jobs offer compensation heavily tied to sales performance. Even a good salesperson may find it difficult to earn an acceptable income for some time, but over time, sales staff can become some of the best paid staff.
2. Contract/Abandon	A career path with uncertain outcomes but the possibility for exiting the path at a future time without incurring significant loss.	The option to contract can be salient among individuals whose priorities lay outside career considerations (e.g., with intentions to start a family, providing care to family members), have vocational aspirations that simply cannot be addressed in the current career decision, or are generally uncertain about their ability to commit to a career.
3. Wait/Defer	A career path that affords delaying choices further into the future.	The option to wait is built-in to any position that offers good-enough rewards, a schedule that is not too demanding, and little chance of being laid-off.
4. Gather Information	A career path with the opportunity to gather information needed for subsequent job and career decisions.	The option to gather information is most valuable to those without a clear sense of vocation or with a high need for data in the decision making process. Temporary employment, including internships, are jobs with information gathering value that goes beyond the immediate compensation.
5. Test Ideas	A career path that accommodates or even rewards testing of ideas associated with future career decisions.	The option to test ideas is most valuable to those interested in careers that involve breaking new ground or disrupting established practices. Someone with a specific entrepreneurial endeavor in mind might find value in taking a job that affords them the opportunity to test ideas or observe related ideas being tested.
6. Obtain/Find Resources	A career path with the opportunity to obtain or find resources needed for future career decisions.	The option to obtain or find resources is most valuable to those interested in careers that will require resources beyond those immediately available to the decision maker. For example, those with entrepreneurial ambitions may choose a first career that puts them in contact with those having the resources that will be needed.

DECISION MAKING ENVIRONMENTS

Research on career decision making has focused primarily on the individual as a unit of analysis, leaving the influence of context unaddressed. The individual-centric model of decision making, while useful, does not adequately represent the effect of situational and environmental factors on career decisions. Further, research on career decision making has relied primarily on cross-sectional and survey-based methods. The influence of the organizational environment is often theorized but not empirically examined in research on careers (Hall & Yip, 2014).

A layering of the influence of context invites at least two streams of multi-level research into career decision making. First, researchers could examine the role of organizational practices and policies and their influence on career decision making. For example, Hall and Yip (2016) identified a typology of organizational career cultures. An inductive analysis of the decision environments that people operate in is necessary to assess the context's influence on career decision making styles. Future research in this area could include the use of qualitative and unobtrusive measures of decision making. In particular, qualitative methods could be employed to surface the contextual nature of decision making styles, including how decision environments influence it.

Second, a focus on decision making environments could surface decision making's relational nature. Relationships are influential environmental factors in career decision making, and they need further consideration. For example, career decisions are often heavily influenced by other people's perspectives and advice. Decision makers rely on counsel to gain perspective (Heath & Gonzalez, 1995; Schotter, 2003) in the service of making better decisions (Harvey & Fischer, 1997). Other studies have found that family members have a significant influence on decision making processes (Fouad et al., 2010) in both eastern and western cultures (Fouad, Fitzpatrick, & Liu, 2011). To the extent that a person has a relational self-construal, career decision making is likely dependent on relational influence from significant others (Cross, Bacon, & Morris, 2000).

The relational nature of decision making should not be underestimated. Career decisions are uniquely shaped by relational considerations, such as career decision making in dual-career couples (Hall & Richter, 1988; Kater, 1985; Lysova, Korotov, Khapova, & Jansen, 2015) or family responsibilities for parenting (Dunn, Rochlen, & O'Brien, 2013). Research on mentoring relationships has shown that relational approaches to career decision making are distinct from individual ones (Sosik & Lee, 2002). A crucial distinction is approaching a career decision from another person's perspective versus relying on their logic or intuition. More specifically, from a relational perspective, mentors can provide career advice, offer emotional support, and serve as role models (Ensher & Murphy, 2011; Ragins & Cotton, 1999). Importantly, it works. A robust body of research has actively supported the relationship between mentoring and career success (Allen, Eby, Chao, & Bauer, 2017; Wen, Chen, Dong, & Shu, 2019). For example, Lease (2004) examined the impact of mentoring on career decision making difficulties among students and found that mentoring was influential in framing their choices. Among other benefits, advice-taking can offer the advice-seeker perspective on solutions, problem reformulation, validation, and legitimization (Cross, Borgatti, & Parker, 2001). Relational decision making, specifically through advice-taking, is well-established as a decision resource. People rely on advice as a means to gain perspective on their decision (Heath & Gonzalez, 1995; Schotter, 2003) and to arrive at better outcomes (Harvey & Fischer, 1997).

Alongside the rise of systems thinking in the 1990s, the family context gained attention as a source for career decision making difficulties (Bradley & Mims, 1992; Kinnier, Brigman, & Noble, 1990; Larson, 1995; Larson & Wilson, 1998), though its origins can be traced back a decade earlier to Bratcher (1982). A central problem is that enmeshment in the family system may make it difficult for a person to differentiate their career desires and expectations from those of the family, especially in the case of young adults still living with their parents (Zingaro, 1983). More broadly, the family context can have both beneficial and harmful effects on effective career decision making (Hargrove, Creagh, & Burgess, 2002). Advances in social network analysis could be particularly useful in research on family environments and relational influences on decision making. For example, Kilduff (1992) applies network analysis to study the impact of friendship networks on career decisions. Volpe and Murphy (2011) extend a social network perspective to understand how the networks of professional working women might predict their career exit decisions, but a lot more could be done to uncover antecedents, consequences, and mechanisms associated with the family context.

Finally, research on decision making environments is likely to underscore the role of risk, uncertainty, and complexity in career decisions. As described above, heuristics are particularly useful in environments of high risk and uncertainty (e.g., Qin & Simon, 1990). When faced with uncertainty, prioritizing down to a small set of decision criteria can lead to better decisions than accounting for all possible criteria and methodically analyzing the circumstances. Moreover, given the uncertainty inherent in career decisions, especially the ongoing rapid evolution of the workplace, prior career decisions and experience may not be useful guides to future outcomes. Some aspects of the changing workplace environment are now being made public thanks to discussion boards (e.g., Reddit) and public websites featuring employee feedback (e.g., Vault and Glassdoor), which provide a rich but as yet largely untapped source of data about career decision making environments. With the availability of such data, researchers could examine how broader contexts affect career decision making and difficulties, applying approaches such as chaos theory (Bright, Pryor, & Harpham, 2005; McKay, Bright, & Prior, 2005) and system dynamics (Flynn et al., 2014) to explore career decision making as a part of a complex, adaptive career development system.

CONCLUSION

In this chapter, we examine current and possible directions for research on career decision making. From our review of the literature and contemporary methods, we propose that more research is needed in understanding career decision making as a heuristic-driven process, to supplement the current emphasis on personality and motivation. This requires methods that can capture decision making processes and information as they occur in real-time. By doing so, researchers can begin to unpack the different ways people make sense of uncertain career environments and decisions. We suggest that real options theory opens the door to evaluating career decisions not just as point-in-time decisions but as decisions that shape future choices. The more one appreciates the complexity and uncertainty inherent in the career decision making context; the more one faces the limitations of traditional "rational" decision making processes.

REFERENCES

Allen, T. D., Eby, L. T., Chao, G. T., & Bauer, T. N. (2017). Taking stock of two relational aspects of organizational life: Tracing the history and shaping the future of socialization and mentoring research. *Journal of Applied Psychology, 102*(3), 324–337.

Amir, T., & Gati, I. (2006). Facets of career decision-making difficulties. *British Journal of Guidance & Counselling, 34*(4), 483–503.

Arthur, M. B., Khapova, S. N., & Wilderom, C. P. (2005). Career success in a boundaryless career world. *Journal of Organizational Behavior, 26*(2), 177–202.

Barley, S. R., Bechky, B. A., & Milliken, F. J. (2017). The changing nature of work: Careers, identities, and work lives in the 21st century. *Academy of Management Discoveries, 3*(2), 111–115.

Betz, N. E., Klein, K., & Taylor, K. (1996). Evaluation of a short form of the Career Decision Self-Efficacy Scale. *Journal of Career Assessment, 4*, 47–57.

Bradley, R. W., & Mims, G. A. (1992). Using family systems and birth order dynamics as the basis for a college career decision-making course. *Journal of Counseling and Development, 70*(3), 445–448.

Bratcher, W. E. (1982). The influence of the family on career selection: A family systems perspective. *Personnel & Guidance Journal, 61*(2), 87–91.

Bright, J. E., Pryor, R. G., & Harpham, L. (2005). The role of chance events in career decision making. *Journal of Vocational Behavior, 66*(3), 561–576.

Brown, S. D., Hacker, J., Abrams, M., Carr, A., Rector, C., Lamp, K., ... & Siena, A. (2012). Validation of a four-factor model of career indecision. *Journal of Career Assessment, 20*(1), 3–21.

Brown, S. D., & Rector, C. C. (2008). Conceptualizing and diagnosing problems in vocational decision making. In S. D. Brown & R. W. Lent (Eds.), *Handbook of Counseling Psychology* (4th ed., pp. 392–407). Hoboken, NJ: John Wiley & Sons.

Campbell, R. E., & Cellini, J. V. (1981). A diagnostic taxonomy of adult career problems. *Journal of Vocational Behavior, 19*(2), 175–190.

Cattell, R. B., & Eber, H. W. (1962). *The Sixteen Personality Factor Questionnaire.* Champaign, IL: Institute for Personality and Ability Testing.

Ceschi, A., Costantini, A., Phillips, S. D., & Sartori, R. (2017). The career decision-making competence: A new construct for the career realm. *European Journal of Training and Development, 41*(1), 8–27.

Copeland, T., & Antikarov, V. (2002). *Real Options: A Practitioner's Guide.* New York, NY: Texere LLC.

Crites, J. O. (1973). *Theory and Research Handbook for the Career Maturity Inventory.* Monterey, CA: CTB/McGraw-Hill.

Crites, J. O., & Savickas, M. L. (1996). Revision of the career maturity inventory. *Journal of Career Assessment, 4,* 131–138.

Cross, R., Borgatti, S. P., & Parker, A. (2001). Beyond answers: Dimensions of the advice network. *Social Networks, 23*(3), 215–235.

Cross, S. E., Bacon, P. L., & Morris, M. L. (2000). The relational-interdependent self-construal and relationships. *Journal of Personality and Social Psychology, 78,* 791–808.

Dean Jr, J. W., & Sharfman, M. P. (1993). Procedural rationality in the strategic decision-making process. *Journal of Management Studies, 30*(4), 587–610.

Dean Jr, J. W., & Sharfman, M. P. (1996). Does decision process matter? A study of strategic decision-making effectiveness. *Academy of Management Journal, 39*(2), 368–392.

Driver, M. J. (1979). Individual decision-making and creativity. In S. Kerr (Ed.), *Organizational Behavior* (pp. 59–94). Columbus, OH: Grid Publishing.

Driver, M. J., Brousseau, K. E., & Hunsaker, P. L. (1998). *The Dynamic Decision Maker.* San Francisco, CA: Jossey-Bass Publishers.

Dunn, M. G., Rochlen, A. B., & O'Brien, K. M. (2013). Employee, mother, and partner: An exploratory investigation of working women with stay-at-home fathers. *Journal of Career Development, 40*(1), 3–22.

Ensher, E. A., & Murphy, S. E. (2011). The Mentoring Relationship Scale: The impact of mentoring stage, type, and gender. *Journal of Vocational Behavior, 79,* 253–266.

Epstein, S. (1994). Integration of the cognitive and psychodynamic unconscious. *American Psychologist, 49,* 707–724.

Fitzgerald, L. F., & Rounds, J. B. (1989). Vocational behavior, 1988: A critical analysis. *Journal of Vocational Behavior, 35,* 105–163.

Flynn, T., Tian, Y., Masnick, K., McDonnell, G., Huynh, E., Mair, A., & Osgood, N. (2014, December). Discrete choice, agent based and system dynamics simulation of health profession career paths. In *Proceedings of the 2014 Winter Simulation Conference* (pp. 1700–1711). Piscataway, NJ: IEEE Press.

Fouad, N. A., Cotter, E. W., Fitzpatrick, M. E., Kantamneni, N., Carter, L., & Bernfeld, S. (2010). Development and validation of the family influence scale. *Journal of Career Assessment, 18*(3), 276–291.

Fouad, N., Fitzpatrick, M., & Liu, J. P. (2011). Persistence of women in engineering careers: A qualitative study of current and former female engineers. *Journal of Women and Minorities in Science and Engineering, 17*(1), 69–96.

Fuqua, D. R., & Hartman, B. W. (1983). Differential diagnosis and treatment of career indecision. *The Personnel and Guidance Journal, 62*(1), 27–29.

Gati, I. (1986). Making career decisions: A sequential elimination approach. *Journal of Counseling Psychology, 33*(4), 408–417.

Gati, I., Gadassi, R., Saka, N., Hadadi, Y., Ansenberg, N., Friedmann, R., & Asulin-Peretz, L. (2011). Emotional and personality-related aspects of career decision-making difficulties: Facets of career indecisiveness. *Journal of Career Assessment, 19*(1), 3–20.

Gati, I., Krausz, M., & Osipow, S. H. (1996). A taxonomy of difficulties in career decision making. *Journal of Counseling Psychology, 43*(4), 510–526.

Gati, I., Landman, S., Davidovitch, S., Asulin-Peretz, L., & Gadassi, R. (2010). From career decision-making styles to career decision-making profiles: A multidimensional approach. *Journal of Vocational Behavior, 76,* 277–291.

Gati, I., & Saka, N. (2001). Internet-based versus paper-and-pencil assessment: Measuring career decision-making difficulties. *Journal of Career Assessment, 9*, 397–416.

Gelatt, H. B. (1989). Positive uncertainty: A new decision-making framework for counseling. *Journal of Counseling Psychology, 36*(2), 252–256.

Germeijs, V., & De Boeck, P. (2002). A measurement scale for indecisiveness and its relationship to career indecision and other types of indecision. *European Journal of Psychological Assessment, 18*(2), 113–122.

Gigerenzer, G. (2016). Introduction: Taking heuristics seriously. In A. Samson (Ed.), *The Behavioral Economics Guide 2016* (pp. v–xi). Retrieved from http://www.behavioraleconomics.com.

Gigerenzer, G., & Brighton, H. (2009). Homo heuristicus: Why biased minds make better inferences. *Topics in Cognitive Science, 1*(1), 107–143.

Gigerenzer, G., & Gaissmaier, W. (2011). Heuristic decision making. *Annual Review of Psychology, 62*, 451–482.

Gigerenzer, G., & Selten, R. (Eds.) (2002). *Bounded Rationality: The Adaptive Toolbox.* Cambridge, MA: MIT Press.

Gigerenzer, G., & Todd, P. M. (1999). *Simple Heuristics that Make Us Smart.* Oxford: Oxford University Press.

Gino, F., Moore, D. A., & Bazerman, M. H. (2009). See no evil: When we overlook other people's unethical behavior. In R. M. Kramer, A. E. Tenbrunsel, & M. H. Bazerman (Eds.), *Social Decision Making: Social Dilemmas, Social Values, and Ethical Judgments* (pp. 241–263). New York, NY: Psychology Press.

Gratton, L., & Scott, A. (2017). The corporate implications of longer lives. *MIT Sloan Management Review, 58*(3), 63–70.

Guthrie, G. A. (2009). *Real Options in Theory and Practice.* New York: Oxford University Press.

Hacker, J., Carr, A., Abrams, M., & Brown, S. D. (2013). Development of the Career Indecision Profile factor structure, reliability, and validity. *Journal of Career Assessment, 21*, 32–41. http://dx.doi.org/10.1177/1069072712453832.

Hall, D. T. (1992). Career indecision research: Conceptual and methodological problems. *Journal of Vocational Behavior, 41*(3), 245–250.

Hall, D. T., & Richter, J. (1988). Balancing work life and home life: What can organizations do to help? *Academy of Management Perspectives, 2*(3), 213–223.

Hall, D. T., & Yip, J. (2014). Career cultures and climates in organizations. In B. Schneider & K. M. Barbera (Eds.), *The Oxford Handbook of Organizational Climate and Culture* (pp. 215–234). Oxford: Oxford University Press.

Hall, D. T., & Yip, J. (2016). Discerning career cultures at work. *Organizational Dynamics, 45*(3), 174–184.

Hardin, E. E., & Leong, F. T. L. (2004). Decision-making theories and career assessment: A psychometric evaluation of the decision-making inventory. *Journal of Career Assessment, 12*, 51–64.

Hargrove, B. K., Creagh, M. G., & Burgess, B. L. (2002). Family interaction patterns as predictors of vocational identity and career decision-making self-efficacy. *Journal of Vocational Behavior, 61*(2), 185–201.

Harren, V. A. (1979). A model of career decision-making for college students. *Journal of Vocational Behavior, 14*, 119–133.

Hartung, P. J., & Blustein, D. L. (2002). Reason, intuition, and social justice: Elaborating on Parsons' career decision-making model. *Journal of Counseling and Development, 80*, 41–47.

Harvey, N., & Fischer, I. (1997). Taking advice: Accepting help, improving judgment, and sharing responsibility. *Organizational Behavior and Human Decision Processes, 70*, 117–133.

Heath, C., & Gonzalez, R. (1995). Interaction with others increases decision confidence but not decision quality: Evidence against information collection views of interactive decision making. *Organizational Behavior and Human Decision Processes*, *61*(3), 305–326.

Hennessy, G., & Latre, J. (1996). Clarifying variables: Actual, perceived and desired. *The Systems Thinker*, *7*(5), June/July. Retrieved from: https://thesystemsthinker.com/clarifying -variables-actual-perceived-and-desired/

Heppner, P. P., & Frazier, P. A. (1992). Social psychological processes in psychotherapy: Extrapolating basic research to counseling psychology. In S. D. Brown & R. W. Lent (Eds.), *Handbook of Counseling Psychology* (pp. 141–175). New York, NY: John Wiley & Sons.

Hilton, T. L. (1962). Career decision-making. *Journal of Counseling Psychology*, *9*(4), 291–298.

Holland, J. L., Johnston, J. A., & Asama, N. F. (1993). The Vocational Identity Scale: A diagnostic and treatment tool. *Journal of Career Assessment*, *1*(1), 1–12.

Jaensch, V. K., Hirschi, A., & Freund, P. A. (2015). Persistent career indecision over time: Links with personality, barriers, self-efficacy, and life satisfaction. *Journal of Vocational Behavior*, *91*, 122–133.

Jepsen, D. A., & Dilley, J. S. (1974). Vocational decision-making models: A review and comparative analysis. *Review of Educational Research*, *44*(3), 331–349.

Kahneman, D. (2003). A perspective on judgment and choice: Mapping bounded rationality. *American Psychologist*, *58*(9), 697–720.

Kahneman, D., & Tversky, A. (1972). Subjective probability: A judgment of representativeness. *Cognitive Psychology*, *3*(3), 430–454.

Kahneman, D., & Tversky, A. (1973). On the psychology of prediction. *Psychological Review*, *80*(4), 237–251.

Kater, D. (1985). Management strategies for dual-career couples. *Journal of Career Development*, *12*(1), 75–80.

Kelly, K. R., & Lee, W. C. (2002). Mapping the domain of career decision problems. *Journal of Vocational Behavior*, *61*(2), 302–326.

Kelly, K. R., & Pulver, C. A. (2003). Refining measurement of career indecision types: A validity study. *Journal of Counseling & Development*, *81*(4), 445–453.

Kent State University (2019). Career Maturity Inventory. https://www.kent.edu/career/career -maturity-inventory.

Kilduff, M. (1992). The friendship network as a decision-making resource: Dispositional moderators of social influences on organizational choice. *Journal of Personality and Social Psychology*, *62*(1), 168–180.

Kinnier, R. T., Brigman, S. L., & Noble, F. C. (1990). Career indecision and family enmeshment. *Journal of Counseling & Development*, *68*(3), 309–312.

Klein, G. A. (1998). *Sources of Power: How People Make Decisions*. Cambridge, MA: MIT Press.

Kodukula, P., & Papudesu, C. (2006). *Project Valuation Using Real Options: A Practitioner's Guide*. Plantation, FL: J. Ross Publishing.

Krieshok, T. S., Black, M. D., & McKay, R. A. (2009). Career decision making: The limits of rationality and the abundance of non-conscious processes. *Journal of Vocational Behavior*, *75*(3), 275–290.

Larson, J. H. (1995). The use of family systems theory to explain and treat career decision problems in late adolescence: A review. *The American Journal of Family Therapy*, *23*(4), 328–337.

Larson, J. H., & Wilson, S. M. (1998). Family of origin influences on young adult career decision problems: A test of Bowenian theory. *American Journal of Family Therapy*, *26*(1), 39–53.

Larson, L. M., Toulouse, A. L., Ngumba, W. E., Fitzpatrick, L. A., & Heppner, P. P. (1994). The development and validation of coping with career indecision. *Journal of Career Assessment, 2*(2), 91–110.

Lease, S. H. (2004). Effect of locus of control, work knowledge, and mentoring on career decision-making difficulties: Testing the role of race and academic institution. *Journal of Career Assessment, 12*(3), 239–254.

Lipshits-Braziler, Y., Gati, I., & Tatar, M. (2016). Strategies for coping with career indecision. *Journal of Career Assessment, 24*(1), 42–66.

Lounsbury, J. W., Tatum, H. E., Chambers, W., Owens, K. S., & Gibson, L. W. (1999). An investigation of career decidedness in relation to "Big Five" personality constructs and life satisfaction. *College Student Journal, 33*(4), 646–652.

Lysova, E. I., Korotov, K., Khapova, S. N., & Jansen, P. G. (2015). The role of the spouse in managers' family-related career sensemaking. *Career Development International, 20*(5), 503–524.

McKay, H., Bright, J. E., & Pryor, R. G. (2005). Finding order and direction from chaos: A comparison of chaos career counseling and trait matching counseling. *Journal of Employment Counseling, 42*(3), 98–112.

Meyer, B. W., & Winer, J. L. (1993). The career decision scale and neuroticism. *Journal of Career Assessment, 1*(2), 171–180.

Murtagh, N., Lopes, P. N., & Lyons, E. (2011). Decision making in voluntary career change: An other-than-rational perspective. *The Career Development Quarterly, 59*(3), 249–263.

Newell, A., & Simon, H. A. (1972). *Human Problem Solving.* Englewood Cliffs, NJ: Prentice Hall.

O'Hare, M. M., & Tamburri, E. (1986). Coping as a moderator of the relation between anxiety and career decision making. *Journal of Counseling Psychology, 33*(3), 255–264.

Osipow, S. H., Carney, C. G., & Barak, A. (1976). A scale of educational-vocational undecidedness: A typological approach. *Journal of Vocational Behavior, 9*, 233–243. http://dx.doi .org/10.1016/0001-8791(76)90081-6.

Osipow, S. H., Carney, C. G., Winer, J. L., Yanico, B. J., & Koschier, M. (1976). *Career Decision Scale* (3rd edn., rev.). Odessa, FL: Psychological Assessment Resources.

Osipow, S. H., & Gati, I. (1998). Construct and concurrent validity of the career decision-making difficulties questionnaire. *Journal of Career Assessment, 6*(3), 347–364.

Parker, A. M., de Bruin, W. B., & Fischhoff, B. (2007). Maximizers versus satisficers: Decision-making styles, competence, and outcomes. *Judgment and Decision Making, 2*(6), 342–350.

Petriglieri, G., Ashford, S. J., & Wrzesniewski, A. (2019). Agony and ecstasy in the gig economy: Cultivating holding environments for precarious and personalized work identities. *Administrative Science Quarterly, 64*(1), 124–170.

Pitz, G. F., & Harren, V. A. (1980). An analysis of career decision making from the point of view of information processing and decision theory. *Journal of Vocational Behavior, 16*(3), 320–346.

Qin, Y., & Simon, H. A. (1990). Laboratory replication of scientific discovery processes. *Cognitive Science, 14*(2), 281–312.

Ragins, B. R., & Cotton, J. L. (1999). Mentor functions and outcomes: A comparison of men and women in formal and informal mentoring relationships. *Journal of Applied Psychology, 84*(4), 529–550.

Rieskamp, J., & Otto, P. E. (2006). SSL: A theory of how people learn to select strategies. *Journal of Experimental Psychology: General, 135*(2), 207–236.

Salomone, P. R. (1982). Difficult cases in career counseling: II: The indecisive client. *The Personnel and Guidance Journal, 60*(8), 496–500.

Savickas, M. L., & Jarjoura, D. (1991). The Career Decision Scale as a type indicator. *Journal of Counseling Psychology, 38*(1), 85–90.

Savickas, M. L., Nota, L., Rossier, J., Dauwalder, J. P., Duarte, M. E., Guichard, J., ... & Van Vianen, A. E. (2009). Life designing: A paradigm for career construction in the 21st century. *Journal of Vocational Behavior, 75*(3), 239–250.

Schotter, A. (2003). Decision making with naive advice. *American Economic Review, 93*(2), 196–201.

Scott, S. G., & Bruce, R. A. (1995). Decision-making style: The development and assessment of a new measure. *Educational and Psychological Measurement, 55*(5), 818–831.

Shah, A. K., & Oppenheimer, D. M. (2008). Heuristics made easy: An effort-reduction framework. *Psychological Bulletin, 134*(2), 207–222.

Simon, H. A. (1955). A behavioral model of rational choice. *The Quarterly Journal of Economics, 69*(1), 99–118.

Simon, H. A. (1957). *Models of Man: Social and Rational.* New York, NY: John Wiley & Sons.

Singh, R., & Greenhaus, J. H. (2004). The relation between career decision-making strategies and person–job fit: A study of job changers. *Journal of Vocational Behavior, 64*(1), 198–221.

Snook, B., Taylor, P. J., & Bennell, C. (2004). Geographic profiling: The fast, frugal, and accurate way. *Applied Cognitive Psychology: The Official Journal of the Society for Applied Research in Memory and Cognition, 18*(1), 105–121.

Sosik, J. J., & Lee, D. L. (2002). Mentoring in organizations: A social judgment perspective for developing tomorrow's leaders. *Journal of Leadership Studies, 8*(4), 17–32.

Taylor, K. M., & Betz, N. E. (1983). Applications of self-efficacy theory to the understanding and treatment of career indecision. *Journal of Vocational Behavior, 22,* 63–81.

Thunholm, P. (2004). Decision-making style: Habit, style or both? *Personality and Individual Differences, 36*(4), 931–944.

Trigeorgis, L., & Reuer, J. J. (2017). Real options theory in strategic management. *Strategic Management Journal, 38*(1), 42–63.

Tversky, A. (1972). Elimination by aspects: A theory of choice. *Psychological Review, 79*(4), 281–299.

Tversky, A., & Kahneman, D. (1973). Availability: A heuristic for judging frequency and probability. *Cognitive Psychology, 5*(2), 207–232.

Tversky, A., & Kahneman, D. (1974). Judgment under uncertainty: Heuristics and biases. *Science, 185*(4157), 1124–1131.

Tversky, A., & Kahneman, D. (1980). Causal schemas in judgments under uncertainty. *Progress in Social Psychology, 1,* 49–72.

Volpe, E. H., & Murphy, W. M. (2011). Married professional women's career exit: Integrating identity and social networks. *Gender in Management, 26*(1), 57–83.

Wen, P., Chen, C., Dong, L., & Shu, X. (2019). The role of mentoring in protégés' subjective well-being. *Journal of Career Development, 46*(2), 171–183.

Wood, N. L., & Highhouse, S. (2014). Do self-reported decision styles relate with others' impressions of decision quality? *Personality and Individual Differences, 70,* 224–228.

Yip, J., Li, H., Ensher, E. A., & Murphy, S. E. (2020). Beyond logic and intuition: Development and validation of a career discernment scale. *Journal of Career Development.* https://doi.org/10.1177/0894845319897824

Zener, T. B., & Schnuelle, L. (1976). Effects of the self-directed search on high school students. *Journal of Counseling Psychology, 23*(4), 353–359.

Zingaro, J. C. (1983). A family systems approach for the career counselor. *Personnel & Guidance Journal, 62*(1), 24–27.

6. Designing and studying mentoring programs: review and discussion

Rajashi Ghosh and Ague Mae Manongsong

Mentoring programs are an important source of professional learning and development for employees across their careers. For mentees, participation in mentoring programs is an antecedent to career benefits such as socialization, leader development, and promotions (Eby et al., 2013). Even mentors are reported to accrue career benefits including increased job satisfaction, organizational commitment, reduced turnover intent, and improved subjective ratings of job performance (Ghosh & Reio, 2013). Thus, it is not surprising that many organizations, from Fortune 500 companies to higher education institutions, have instituted formal mentoring programs (Weinberg & Lankau, 2011). However research on mentoring in the careers domain has not kept pace with the proliferation of mentoring programs across organizational contexts.

While several studies have been conducted to identify benefits from participating in mentoring programs, there is a lack of review work providing a summary of the typical features of mentoring programs studied in the literature and analyzing how one designs and studies such programs. We could find only three papers that reviewed studies on formal mentoring programs (e.g., Ehrich, Hansford, & Tennent, 2004; Underhill, 2006; Zhang et al., 2016). Ehrich and colleagues synthesized the findings on positive and problematic outcomes of mentoring for mentors, mentees, and organizations. They also identified mentoring program features across the three disciplines of education, business, and medicine (Ehrich et al., 2004). Underhill (2006) conducted a meta-analysis of studies that used experimental, quasi-experimental, or survey design with a control or a comparison group to provide a critical analysis of career outcomes for mentored and non-mentored individuals. Finally, Zhang et al. (2016) conducted a systematic review of mentoring programs for newly graduated nurses and summarized the findings reported on mentoring program features and outcomes.

The value of this current review is fivefold. First, we provide a broad snapshot of studies conducted on formal mentoring programs with different types of participants that include employees in corporate organizations, faculty and students in universities, members of professional associations, and entrepreneurs. Second, we extend the literature by critiquing the use of established theoretical foundations or lack thereof in designing formal mentoring programs. Third, we present an assessment of the methodological rigor of the studies included in the review in terms of research design. Fourth, we synthesize findings on key mentoring program features to guide how they can be most effectively designed for individuals across varied organizational contexts. And, fifth, we refer to data from recent studies we conducted on formal mentoring programs to inform the discussion of the articles reviewed in this chapter.

METHOD

We used Google search to locate articles on "formal mentoring" and "formal mentoring programs" and identified highly cited articles published within the past 20 years. There was no restriction on the population included in the sample with regards to industry and discipline, although a majority of the articles reviewed focused on organizational/work contexts or higher education. There was also no restriction with regards to location of the sample; although the majority utilized United States-based samples. The selection criteria included studies that: (1) collected and analyzed data from participants of a mentoring program(s); (2) described critical components of a formal mentoring program; (3) reported outcomes associated with participation in a formal mentoring program. These included empirical studies with regards to mentoring program effectiveness. Exclusion criteria included (1) editorials; (2) review articles on formal mentoring; (3) studies that did not focus on a formal mentoring program, but collected data from formal mentors and mentees from different organizations; (4) and articles focused on informal mentoring. In total, 34 empirical articles were selected. For each article, we reviewed the study purpose, theoretical framework, research design, sample, variables under investigation, and findings. In addition, we reviewed the formal mentoring program features including program purpose, participants, matching, mentoring functions utilized in the dyad, duration of program, frequency of interaction, and whether participation was voluntary, and so on.

FINDINGS AND DISCUSSION

We present our findings in four parts: (1) use of theory; (2) research designs; (3) research concepts and variables; and (4) mentoring program goals and features. For each part, we present a summary and critique of the contributions made by the studies included in our review.

Use of Theory

A majority of the studies reviewed referred to traditional mentoring theory, which conceptualizes mentoring as a hierarchical one-directional relationship between a senior and a junior individual and delineates two primary kinds of support from mentors: (1) career support; and (2) psycho-social support (Kram, 1983). Career support includes offering coaching, sponsorship, networking opportunities, and stretch assignments that can prepare mentees to achieve career goals, whereas psycho-social support functions include "those aspects that enhance an individual's sense of competence, identity, and effectiveness in a professional role" (Kram, 1985, p. 32) such as friendship, acceptance, and counseling. Although the seminal study by Kram (1983) identified these mentor support functions in informal mentoring relationships, researchers have applied the traditional perspective of mentoring to study formal mentoring relationships (Allen, Eby, & Lentz, 2006a, 2006b; Allen, Russell, & Maetzke, 1997; Carter & Youssef-Morgan, 2019; Chao, 2009; Chun et al., 2010; Chun, Sosik, & Yun, 2012; Ragins, Cotton, & Miller, 2000).

Few studies referred to the underlying theoretical frameworks to justify antecedents, outcomes, or the context in which the formal mentoring relationships were being studied. For instance, Raabe and Beehr (2003) referred to leader–member exchange to compare mentor–mentee relationships with supervisor–subordinate relationships. Weinberg and Lankau (2011) referred to similarity-attraction theory and career and life stage theories to argue that the disadvantages of gender differences between mentors and mentees dissipate over the lifespan of the relationship. Similarly, Lankau, Riordan, and Thomas (2005) and Menges (2016) drew from similarity-attraction theory to explore the effect of perceived similarity between mentor and mentee on mentoring receipt. In contrast, Wanberg, Welsh, and Kammeyer-Mueller (2007) used the interpersonal process model from social psychology to examine the extent to which mentor–mentee self-disclosure impacted mentoring receipt. Muir (2014) used identity theory to explore the impact of formal mentoring program participation on leader identity development. Wang, Tomlinson, and Noe (2010) and Chun et al. (2010) referred the theoretical perspectives on trust to explore the effect of mentor trust on mentoring receipt. Finally, Srivastava (2015) used social network theory to delineate the core mechanisms linking formal mentoring to network change, whereas Chun et al. (2012) referred the relational perspective of mentoring to examine transformational leadership as an outcome for mentors and well-being and commitment as outcomes for both mentors and mentees.

To our knowledge, the articles we reviewed did not typically explore how a particular theoretical perspective can inform the design of a formal mentoring program. Only, the study by Bosch, Ramachandran, Luévano, and Wakiji (2010) described the advantages of a group-based mentoring program that was guided by the peer mentoring perspective and the study by Gibb (1999), which identified applications of both social exchange and communitarianism theories in conducting a longitudinal case study of a formal mentoring program's design and implementation over a two-year period. We need more studies that can examine mentoring programs designed based on certain theoretical frameworks, since program features can be evidence-based. Recently, we conducted a study with our colleagues (e.g., Ghosh, Hutchins, Rose, & Manongsong, 2019a) where we collected data from the participants of a formal mentoring program grounded in the relational mentoring perspective (Ragins, 2011) to provide a mutual exchange of learning, support and skill development. Participants were faculty members of a professional association in the field of workplace learning and development. In this qualitative study, our focus was to understand how participants were experiencing mutuality. As several program features (e.g., matching as per complimentary expertise, switching of mentor/mentee roles, documentation of mutual learning goals in agreement forms) were designed to foster mutual learning and growth, we explored the challenges and facilitating factors that influenced the participants' experiences of mutuality so that findings could guide improvements in the program design.

Research Designs

Most of the articles we reviewed used a quantitative research design to study formal mentoring programs. Cross-sectional survey design seems to be the most typical choice of method (e.g., Allen & Eby, 2008; Allen et al., 1997; Allen et al., 2006a; Allen et al., 2006b; Barrera, Braley, & Slate, 2010; Bean, Lucas, & Hyers, 2014; Bisk, 2002; Chun et al., 2010; Menges, 2016; Raabe & Beehr, 2003; Ragins et al., 2000; Smith, Howard, & Harrington, 2005; Solansky, 2010; Wang et al., 2010; Waters, McCabe, Kiellerup, & Kiellerup, 2002) with a few exceptions that used longitudinal survey research design (e.g., Carter & Youssef-Morgan, 2019; Chun et al., 2012; Lankau et al., 2005; Wanberg, Kammeyer-Mueller, & Marchese, 2006; Wanberg et al., 2007; Weinberg & Lankau, 2011) and a handful of others that used experimental design (e.g., Egan & Song, 2008; Seibert, 1999; Srivastava, 2015). A key strength of these studies was the collection of dyadic data from matched mentor–mentee pairs and sample sizes ranging from 60 to 100. However, given a majority of the findings are based on cross-sectional survey research, any implications for causality should be interpreted with caution. While experimental designs are desirable to claim causality, it is challenging to conduct experimental studies with formal mentoring programs. Since these programs are situated in real-life work contexts instead of in laboratory settings, organizations often hesitate to allow researchers to randomly assign employees into treatment and control groups to avoid unintended concerns about fairness. Longitudinal survey designs are a reasonable substitute that can test causality to some extent, if researchers can control for attrition of sample size over time.

Among the studies we reviewed, a small number used a qualitative research design (e.g., Bell & Treleaven, 2011; Bosch et al., 2010; Chao, 2009; Eby & Lockwood, 2005; Muir, 2014; White, Brannan, & Wilson, 2010; Wilson, Sanner, & McAllister, 2010a; Wilson, Brown, & White, 2010b) and only a couple of studies took advantage of a mixed method research design (e.g., Parise & Forret, 2008; Srivastava, 2015) to study the impact of formal mentoring programs. Future studies should use more mixed methods research (MMR) designs to understand the process and outcomes of formal mentoring programs. While quantitative studies can help us identify trends and patterns about the impact of formal mentoring programs, qualitative studies can help shed light on the nuances of those outcomes for different types of participants (e.g., minority, women etc.) and contexts. Most importantly, qualitative studies can illuminate the key relational processes in formal mentoring and give voice to the formal mentoring program participants through exploring their lived experiences. MMR can allow researchers to take advantage of the benefits of both quantitative and qualitative research designs. Recently, the lead author of this chapter conducted a convergent mixed-methods design study with colleagues where matched mentor–mentee pairs were surveyed and those who served both as mentors and mentees in the program were interviewed to gain deeper insights into the functioning of the program and its impact on the participants' psychological capital and employee engagement (e.g., Ghosh, Shuck, Cumberland, & D'Mello, 2019b). Use of both quantitative and qualitative data collection methods helped to examine both the process (e.g., key features of successful mentoring relationships) and possible outcomes associated with participation in formal mentoring (e.g., psychological capital and employee engagement), thereby expanding the breadth and range of the research inquiry.

Research Concepts and Variables

The studies we reviewed examined a variety of concepts and variables. Qualitative studies included a focus on the positive and negative mentoring experiences of both the mentee and the mentor. In particular, the concepts explored centered on matching, benefits, challenges, and quality (Bell & Treleaven, 2011; Bosch et al., 2010; Eby & Lockwood, 2005; White et al., 2010; Wilson et al., 2010a; Wilson et al., 2010b). Overall, such studies demonstrated that well-paired dyads (matches that met the needs of the mentee) who had clear and open communication were successful (Bell & Treleaven, 2011; Eby & Lockwood, 2005; White et al., 2010; Wilson et al., 2010b); mentees learned and received career support and psycho-social support (Eby & Lockwood, 2005; Wilson et al., 2010a), while mentors experienced mutuality (e.g., they shared the responsibility of mentoring, learned from their mentees, and felt personal gratification; Bosch et al., 2010; Eby & Lockwood, 2005; Wilson et al., 2010b). However, only one article focused on the specific development of an ability or skill; Muir (2014) found that participants developed leadership skills and a leader identity through participation in a formal mentoring program.

The remaining empirical articles utilized quantitative designs. We categorized the independent and dependent variables examined in these studies (see Table 6.1). The independent variables, generally, fell into one of three categories: individual, dyadic, and structural (e.g., program-related) variables. The dependent variables examined could be classified as individual, dyadic, and organizational outcomes. In the following sections, we further elaborate on our review findings about these variables.

Independent variables
A few studies we reviewed collected individual-level data (i.e., from either the mentor or mentee) to examine the impact of demographics, personality, and other mentor or mentee characteristics (Allen et al., 1997; Bisk, 2002; Morrison et al., 2014; Smith et al., 2005). In general, demographics (gender, age, education, and mentor traits) impacted the perception of benefits of participation in a formal mentoring relationship (Allen et al., 1997; Bisk, 2002; Smith et al., 2005); however, there were some inconsistent findings. For instance, with regard to the impact of gender on mentoring outcomes, one article found that mentor commitment positively impacted perception of mentoring quality especially for male protégés (Allen & Eby, 2008),

Table 6.1   Independent and dependent variable categorization

Constructs	Independent Variables			Dependent Variables			Mediators and Moderators		References
	Individual	Dyadic	Program Components	Individual	Dyadic	Organizational	Mediators	Moderators	
Age*	X								Allen et al. (1997); Bisk (2002)
Benefited from mentoring (in general)++				X					Bisk (2002)
Career commitment						X			Ragins et al. (2000)
Duration^			X						Waters et al. (2002)
Education*	X								Bisk (2002)
Emotional intelligence**		X							Chun et al. (2010)
Environment (proximity between pair)			X						Allen et al. (2006b)
Facilitation (high and low)			X						Egan & Song (2008)
Frequency of interaction^			X		X			X	Allen et al. (2006b); Chao (2009); Weinberg & Lankau (2011)
Gender/gender composition*	X	X						X	Allen et al. (1997); Allen & Eby (2008); Morrison et al. (2014); Weinberg & Lankau (2011)
Goal clarity						X			Wanberg et al. (2006)
Information shared between pair++				X					Solansky (2010)
Internal Locus of Control								X	Wang et al. (2010)

Constructs	Independent Variables			Dependent Variables			Mediators and Moderators		References
	Individual	Dyadic	Program Components	Individual	Dyadic	Organizational	Mediators	Moderators	
Job satisfaction						X			Egan & Song (2008); Raabe & Beehr (2003); Ragins et al. (2000); Seibert (1999)
Liking							X		Lankau et al. (2005)
Matching^			X				X		Allen et al. (2006a); Ragins et al. (2000)
Mentor commitment							X		Allen et al. (2006a)
Mentor effectiveness++				X					Weinberg & Lankau (2011)
Mentor traits	X								Smith et al. (2005)
Mentoring program (in general)			X						Barrera et al. (2010)
Mentoring relationship quality++				X	X				Allen et al. (2006b); Allen & Eby (2008)
Mentoring satisfaction				X	X				Allen et al. (1997); Chao (2009); Wanberg et al. (2007)
Mentoring support, functions, activities			X		X				Allen et al. (1997); Allen et al. (2006b); Carter & Youssef-Morgan (2019); Chun et al. (2012); Lankau et al. (2005); Morrison et al. (2014); Raabe & Beehr (2003); Seibert (1999); Wanberg et al. (2006); Waters et al. (2002)
Organizational commitment						X			Chun et al. (2012); Egan & Song (2008); Raabe & Beehr (2003); Seibert (1999); Wanberg et al. (2006);
Organization-based self-esteem						X			Ragins et al. (2000)
Perceived business success++				X					Waters et al. (2002)

Constructs	Independent Variables			Dependent Variables			Mediators and Moderators		References
	Individual	Dyadic	Program Components	Individual	Dyadic	Organizational	Mediators	Moderators	
Perceived mentor responsiveness								X	Wanberg et al. (2007)
Perceived program effectiveness					X				Allen et al. (2006a); Bean et al. (2014)
Perceived similarity	X								Lankau et al. (2005); Wanberg et al. (2006)
Personality*	X								Menges (2016); Wanberg et al. (2006)
Person–organization fit						X			Egan & Song (2008)
Procedural justice						X			Ragins et al. (2000)
Profit++				X					Waters et al. (2002)
Program evaluation			X						Bean et al. (2014)
Program purpose^			X						Ragins et al. (2000)
Program understanding							X		Allen et al. (2006a)
Promotion++				X					Morrison et al. (2014)
Psychological Capital							X		Carter & Youssef-Morgan (2019)
Relationship sustainability			X		X				Chao (2009)
Retention/turnover intentions						X			Barrera et al. (2010); Raabe & Beehr (2003); Ragins et al. (2000); Wanberg et al. (2006)
Satisfaction with opportunities for promotion						X			Ragins et al. (2000)
Satisfaction with program			X						Ragins et al. (2000)

Constructs	Independent Variables			Dependent Variables			Mediators and Moderators		References
	Individual	Dyadic	Program Components	Individual	Dyadic	Organizational	Mediators	Moderators	
Self-disclosure	X								Wanberg et al. (2007)
Self-esteem+				X					Seibert (1999); Waters et al. (2002)
Training^			X						Allen et al. (2006a); Allen et al. (2006b)
Transformational leadership++				X					Chun et al. (2012)
Trust (affective and cognitive)	X							X	Chun et al. (2010); Wang et al. (2010)
Trust+				X					Chun et al. (2010)
Voluntary participation^			X						Allen et al. (2006a); Allen et al. (2006b); Ragins et al. (2000)
Willingness to mentor++				X					Allen et al. (1997)
Work stress						X			Seibert (1999)
Work/job performance						X			Carter & Youssef-Morgan (2019); Egan & Song (2008); Wanberg et al. (2006)

Note: * Mentor/mentee characteristic; ** Trainable knowledge, skill, or ability; + Life domain variable; ++ Career-driven variable; ^ Design-related variable.

while another article found that gender did not have a significant effect on promotional rates of faculty members participating as mentees (Morrison et al., 2014). The conflicting findings with regards to gender may indicate a difference between the impact of one's demographics on perception of success (or other outcome variable) versus objective performance (or other data that is not self-reported).

Some studies we reviewed collected dyadic level data on independent variables, meaning data was collected on the same construct for both the mentor and mentee and/or the independent variable was operationalized as a relational construct. A dyadic approach to mentoring is aligned with the notion of both parties (mentor and mentee) learning, growing, and developing in mentoring relationships (Ragins, 2011). Variables in the review included perceptions on a psychological construct (such as perceived similarity between the pairs), trainable skills and abilities (emotional intelligence), as well as mentor/mentee characteristics (demographics, personality etc.) operationalized at the dyadic level (i.e., gender composition, similarity in personality) (e.g., Chun et al., 2010; Lankau et al., 2005; Weinberg & Lankau, 2011, etc.). The findings from these studies suggest that mentor and mentee similarity (demographic and personality) positively impact the mentoring relationship outcomes (such as receipt or provision of more psycho-social support; Lankau et al., 2005; Menges, 2016; Wanberg et al., 2006). Moreover, mentoring relationships were reportedly beneficial when mentors and mentees were more emotionally intelligent and proactive (Chun et al., 2010; Wanberg et al., 2006). However, studies did not explore if or how mentoring programs can prepare mentors and mentees to develop similar perceptions or comparable skills, nor did studies provide strategies for mentor–mentee pairs who were demographically dissimilar to build deeper connections over time.

Next, several articles focused on the structural aspects of the formal mentoring program as independent variables. These included the features of the mentoring program (program design, frequency of interaction, length of mentoring relationship, and matching process), mentoring activities (career development, psycho-social support, and role modeling), sources of support for the mentoring process (such as managerial support and amount of facilitation), evaluation of the program, and simply participation in formal mentoring (e.g., Allen et al., 1997; Allen et al., 2006b; Bean et al., 2014; Carter & Youssef-Morgan, 2019, etc.). Overall, findings from these articles were primarily positive: the program design, the various types of support (career and psycho-social support), and participation in a mentoring program positively predict work outcomes of mentors and mentees (e.g., Allen et al., 1997; Allen et al., 2006b; Bean et al., 2014; Carter & Youssef-Morgan, 2019, etc.). For instance, mentoring programs that facilitated the mentoring experience (provided a trained program coordinator as a third party to guide the mentoring process for the mentors and the mentees; Egan & Song, 2008) and allowed for the establishment of clearly defined goals (Barrera et al., 2010) contributed to the success of the relationship. Moreover, participation in a mentoring program led to reports of subjective and objective benefits, such as increases in psychological capital (Carter & Youssef-Morgan, 2019) and promotions (Morrison et al., 2014). Despite these positive findings, studies did not provide much clarity in regard to which program features (such as duration or frequency of interaction) would yield the most effective mentoring relationships.

Dependent variables

Individual outcomes centered on life domain variables (i.e., variables applicable to one's personal and professional domains in life; self-esteem and trust; Chun et al., 2010; Seibert, 1999; Waters et al., 2002) and career driven variables (i.e., variables applicable to one's professional domain in life; promotion, profit, perceived success, etc.; Morrison et al., 2014; Waters et al., 2002). Findings supported the use of mentoring to positively impact both life and career domain outcomes. However, the life domain variables were not the focus of articles included in the review (i.e., few measured life domain outcomes and when researchers collected responses, life domain variables were one or two of many). This suggests that research on formal mentoring programs lacks a holistic approach. The study of life domain outcomes is important as high-quality mentoring relationships address both personal and professional developmental needs to promote a healthy sense of self (Ragins, 2011). Given this, psychological capital was included as an outcome variable in the recent study conducted by the lead author (Ghosh et al., 2019b).

Next, dyadic level outcomes included psychological constructs for which responses were collected from both mentors and mentees. These included mentor/mentee's perceptions of mentoring relationship quality (satisfaction and effectiveness; e.g., Allen et al., 2006a; Allen et al., 2006b; Chao, 2009, etc.), mentoring support received or given (e.g., Allen et al., 2006a; Lankau et al., 2005; Wanberg et al., 2006 etc.), program quality (frequency of interaction and effectiveness; Allen et al., 2006a; Barrera et al., 2010; Bean et al., 2014), information shared in the dyad (Solansky, 2010), as well as affective well-being (Chun et al., 2012). Overall findings demonstrate that participation in a formal mentoring program had a positive impact on both mentors and mentees' perceptions of the formal mentoring program effectiveness, mentoring relationship satisfaction, as well as affective well-being.

The final category of dependent variables include organizational outcomes that can impact an organization's bottom-line through changes in performance and productivity. These include self-report data collected from mentors and mentees on job satisfaction, retention/turnover intentions, work/job performance, organizational/career commitment, work stress, and person–organization fit (see Table 6.1 for full list; e.g., Egan & Song, 2008; Ragins et al., 2000; Seibert, 1999, etc.). In general, researchers found that participation in a formal mentoring program leads to increased reports of job performance, job satisfaction, goal clarity, and organizational commitment (Carter & Youssef-Morgan, 2019; Chun et al., 2012; Egan & Song, 2008; Wanberg et al., 2006). These findings support the rationale for the majority of Fortune 500 companies engaged in mentoring activities (Bergelson, 2014). However, there were some conflicting findings in regard to organizational outcomes. A few studies (Ragins et al., 2000; Raabe & Beehr, 2003; Seibert, 1999) found that participation in a formal mentoring program did not necessarily lead to positive outcomes across the different groups sampled. Specifically, mentoring alone did not have a significant impact on work satisfaction, commitment, and turnover intentions (Raabe & Beehr, 2003). When mentoring did have a positive influence, the impact was not as large (Ragins et al., 2000), or consistent (Seibert, 1999). These findings suggest that other work-related factors could impact the effectiveness of mentoring. For instance, female mentees who had a mentor in the same department did not report positive outcomes compared to their male counterparts (Ragins et al., 2000). Conversely, Raabe and Beehr (2003) suggested that supervisors and co-workers may be the best sources of mentoring. Thus, future researchers should examine the impact of department engagement on formal mentoring program outcomes.

Overall, there were very few studies that incorporated moderators or mediators. The studies that did include mediators investigated program-related variables (liking of mentor/mentee, interaction frequency, mentor commitment, and program understanding; Allen et al., 2006a; Allen et al., 2006b; Lankau et al., 2005). Only two articles examined life-domain variables (variables that are not necessarily confined to the workplace, but span the boundaries between work and life, such as psychological capital and trust; Carter & Youssef-Morgan, 2019; Chun et al., 2010). Moreover, the studies reviewed did not examine moderating conditions for their hypotheses, barring a handful of studies that examined perceived mentor responsiveness, internal locus of control, and gender (Allen & Eby, 2008; Wanberg et al., 2007; Wang et al., 2010) as moderators.

Mentoring Program Goals and Features

Goals and features of a mentoring program are just as important to the quality and success of developmental relationships as the commitment and motivation of the mentor and mentee. In the sections below, we summarize formal mentoring program goals and features reported by the studies we reviewed.

Goals of the formal mentoring program

Organizations in all industries create formal mentoring programs for various reasons. From our review, there were only 12 empirical articles that included a clear purpose or goal of the formal mentoring program under investigation. The purpose/goals included in the review centered on (1) career development ($n = 6$); (2) support for specific populations ($n = 5$); (3) work-related outcomes ($n = 3$); and (4) socialization ($n = 2$). For career development, goals included training new hires (Wilson et al., 2010b; White et al., 2010; Egan & Song, 2008); career development in general (Raabe & Beehr, 2003; Wang et al., 2010); and leadership development (Eby & Lockwood, 2005; Muir, 2014). For supporting specific populations in their career, articles covered support for early career professionals, entrepreneurs, and diverse individuals (Bisk, 2002; Chao, 2009; Parise & Forret, 2008; Raabe & Beehr, 2003; Waters et al., 2002). With regards to positive impact on organizational members' work-related outcomes, goals included decrease in attrition rates, as well as increases in performance and satisfaction (Egan & Song, 2008; Raabe & Beehr, 2003; Wilson et al., 2010a). Finally, goals of mentoring programs also included socialization of new hires into the organization (Bosch et al., 2010; Wang et al., 2010). It is evident from this review that formal mentoring program goals are geared towards the mentees. Although mentors are typically individuals who hold senior positions in organizations, they too have learning goals or developmental needs. Thus, the impact of mentoring programs could be maximized if program goals focused on mentors as well. In that spirit, our recent study was based on a mentoring program with goals focused on both mentors and mentees in terms of promoting mutual learning and growth (Ghosh et al., 2019a).

Mentoring program features
A mentoring program feature is a design element of the formal mentoring program (Dawson, 2014). The articles included in the review reported several program features: professions or occupational positions of mentors/mentees ($n = 14$), voluntary participation ($n = 13$), matching ($n = 10$), duration of program ($n = 10$), ratio ($n = 10$), and frequency of interactions ($n = 7$). In terms of *mentor and mentee professions or occupational positions*, mentors were senior in expertise or positional status (nursing faculty, librarians, senior executives, business mentors, psychologists, and other senior level organizations) and mentees were more junior in expertise, position, or time within the organization (new hires, early career professionals, underrepresented populations, and high-potentials for leadership positions (Bisk, 2002; Bosch et al., 2010; Carter & Youssef-Morgan, 2019; Chao, 2009; Eby & Lockwood, 2005; Egan & Song, 2008; Muir, 2014; Parise & Forret, 2008; Raabe & Beehr, 2003; Wang et al., 2010; Waters et al., 2002; White et al., 2010; Wilson et al., 2010a; Wilson et al. 2010b).

With regards to *voluntary participation*, most of the formal mentoring programs were voluntary for mentors and mentees (Bisk, 2002; Carter & Youssef-Morgan, 2019; Eby & Lockwood, 2005; Egan & Song, 2008; Muir, 2014; Raabe & Beehr, 2003; Wanberg et al., 2006; White et al., 2010; Wilson et al., 2010a; Wilson et al., 2010b). A few programs required participation from mentors, mentees, or both parties (Parise & Forret, 2008; Wang et al., 2010; Waters et al., 2002). However, it is uncertain whether mandatory participation yields similar positive results as voluntary participation because there is simply not enough information.

The *matching process* can influence the success and quality of a mentoring relationship (Dawson, 2014). As per our review, formal mentoring programs followed several matching processes/criteria in their assignment of mentors to mentees. Most formal mentoring programs included in the review matched mentors and mentees based on the career goals, developmental concerns, and/or needs indicated by the mentee ($n = 5$; Carter & Youssef-Morgan, 2019; Chao, 2009; Wanberg et al., 2006; Wang et al., 2010; Waters et al., 2002). To a lesser extent, program coordinators matched based on preference or requests of participants as a primary consideration (Parise & Forret, 2008; Wang et al., 2010; White et al., 2010; Wilson et al., 2010b). Other programs attempted to match based on the mentors' strengths and skills foremost (Chao, 2009; Raabe & Beehr, 2003). One program matched based on shared interests as a consideration (Carter & Youssef-Morgan, 2019) and another matched randomly (Egan & Song, 2008). No matter what the matching scheme is, it can be problematic because of the program coordinator's inability to match based on all of the previously considered criteria, while pleasing everyone (Chao, 2009; Parise & Forret, 2008). Nevertheless, it is important to align the matching criteria and process with the mentoring program's goal. For instance, as mutual learning and growth was an intended goal of the program we recently studied (Ghosh et al., 2019b), the matching process included collecting input on complimentary expertise and learning needs from all participants and using that information to guide the assignment of mentoring partners.

On a similar note to matching, the extant literature does not have a uniform set-up of how many mentees should be assigned to a mentor. We found that formal mentoring programs tended to assign one mentee to one mentor (Bisk, 2002; Eby & Lockwood, 2005; Raabe & Beehr, 2003; Wanberg et al., 2006; Waters et al., 2002). Three programs assigned more than one mentee to a mentor, but no more than three (Chao, 2009; White et al., 2010; Wilson et al., 2010a; Wilson et al., 2010b). On the other hand, only one study explored the configuration of multiple mentors to one mentee (Bosch et al., 2010). The individuals in this group mentorship shared the responsibilities of a mentor and the mentee and instantly established a network. Thus, more studies should explore group mentoring compositions in formal mentoring programs.

In terms of *duration*, most of the formal mentoring programs in the review lasted from six months (Bosch et al., 2010; Egan & Song, 2008) to approximately one year (Carter & Youssef-Morgan, 2019; Chao, 2009; Eby & Lockwood, 2005; Wanberg et al., 2006; Waters et al., 2002; Wilson et al., 2010a). Only two programs lasted more than one year (Muir, 2014; Wang et al., 2010). Similarly, *frequency of interaction* during the program varied across studies. Suggested intervals were weekly (Wang et al., 2010; Wilson et al., 2010a), bi-weekly (White et al., 2010; Wilson et al., 2010b), or monthly (Egan & Song, 2008; Carter & Youssef-Morgan, 2019; Wanberg et al., 2006) with suggested length of meetings ranging from 30 minutes (Wang et al., 2010) to 90 minutes (Wanberg et al., 2006). Given the findings, the extant literature has not yet identified the appropriate length of time ideal to develop a sustainable development relationship.

IMPLICATIONS AND CONCLUSION

In this chapter, we attempted to summarize and critique how mentoring programs have been studied and designed. Our findings point to several opportunities to advance both the research and practice of formal mentoring programs. Overall, the empirical findings suggest that formal mentoring programs do exert influence on individuals' career outcomes, as well as perceptions of program-related features. Therefore, organizations are seemingly obtaining tangible benefits (i.e., immediate return on investment into the creation of a formal mentoring program through the development of their employees) and can bolster continued investment into formal mentoring programs guided by the literature. On the other hand, more work needs to be done on unpacking *how* formal mentoring programs impact employees. For instance, there were very few studies that incorporated moderators or mediators to shed light on the internal process of how mentoring impacted the psychological constructs examined by the review to lead to the work outcomes (or vice versa – how psychological constructs ultimately impacted mentoring).

With regards to the goals and features of mentoring programs, the findings demonstrate that formal mentoring programs are versatile as organizations design them to meet a variety of employee and organizational needs, as well as meet organizational timelines and fit their budgets. However, the goals primarily focus on influencing mentee behavior, values, and career development as motivated by the traditional mentoring perspective. As a result, senior organizational members serving as mentors bear most of the responsibility in providing their mentees with opportunities to demonstrate their skills, while advocating and/or sponsoring within the organization to push their mentees up the proverbial ladder (Eby & Lockwood, 2005; Ehrich et al., 2004). This may result in the perception that mentoring, although important, is burdensome; especially since most studies in the review reported that there were generally more mentees than mentors (e.g., Chao, 2009; Wilson et al., 2010a; White et al., 2010). Thus, organizations should employ the relational mentoring perspective that emphasizes mutual learning and growth for both mentor and mentee as mutuality can disperse responsibility and provide an incentive to the mentors (i.e., mutual development) (Ragins, 2011).

Furthermore, as alternatives to the traditional mentoring perspective, organizations should explore how to apply the developmental networks perspective (Higgins & Kram, 2001) to designing and studying formal mentoring programs. Given that individuals are increasingly adopting protean and boundaryless careers (Wiernik & Kostal, 2019), knowing how to cultivate developmental networks that include developers from different domains of life and beyond the bounds of one's workplace can be critical for building a successful career. Also, if the formal mentoring program has a goal of supporting women or minority employees or leaders, organizations can borrow from feminist mentoring perspectives to design formal mentoring programs to counter the power inequalities in the traditional mentoring model. Mentees adopting the feminist mentoring approach, tend to work with their mentors collaboratively to challenge the status quo, as their mentors teach them to be social change agents (Fassinger, 1997), and in doing so, experience increases in self-confidence and self-esteem. Future studies employing diverse research methodologies (quantitative, qualitative, and mixed methods) should explore how different theoretical models of mentoring (e.g., traditional, relational, developmental network, feminist mentoring) can inform how formal mentoring programs can support careers in different organizational contexts.

REFERENCES

Allen, T. D., & Eby, L. T. (2008). Mentor commitment in formal mentoring relationships. *Journal of Vocational Behavior, 72*(3), 309–316.

Allen, T. D., Eby, L. T., & Lentz, E. (2006a). The relationship between formal mentoring program characteristics and perceived program effectiveness. *Personnel Psychology, 59*(1), 125–153.

Allen, T. D., Eby, L. T., & Lentz, E. (2006b). Mentorship behaviors and mentorship quality associated with formal mentoring programs: Closing the gap between research and practice. *Journal of Applied Psychology, 91*(3), 567–578.

Allen, T. D., Russell, J. E., & Maetzke, S. B. (1997). Formal peer mentoring: Factors related to protégés' satisfaction and willingness to mentor others. *Group and Organization Management, 22*(4), 488–507.

Barrera, A., Braley, R. T., & Slate, J. R. (2010). Beginning teacher success: An investigation into the feedback from mentors of formal mentoring programs. *Mentoring & Tutoring: Partnership in Learning, 18*(1), 61–74.

Bean, N. M., Lucas, L., & Hyers, L. L. (2014). Mentoring in higher education should be the norm to assure success: Lessons learned from the faculty mentoring program, West Chester University, 2008–2011. *Mentoring & Tutoring: Partnership in Learning, 22*(1), 56–73.

Bell, A., & Treleaven, L. (2011). Looking for professor right: Mentee selection of mentors in a formal mentoring program. *Higher Education, 61*(5), 545–561.

Bergelson, M. (2014). Developing tomorrow's leaders: Innovative approaches to mentorship. *People and Strategy, 37*(2), 18–22.

Bisk, L. (2002). Formal entrepreneurial mentoring: The efficacy of third party managed programs. *Career Development International, 7*(5), 262–270.

Bosch, E. K., Ramachandran, H., Luévano, S., & Wakiji, E. (2010). The resource team model: An innovative mentoring program for academic librarians. *New Review of Academic Librarianship, 16*(1), 57–74.

Carter, J. W., & Youssef-Morgan, C. M. (2019). The positive psychology of mentoring: A longitudinal analysis of psychological capital development and performance in a formal mentoring program. *Human Resource Development Quarterly, 38*(3), 383–405. doi: 10.1002/hrdq.21348.

Chao, G. T. (2009). Formal mentoring: Lessons learned from past practice. *Professional Psychology: Research and Practice, 40*(3), 314–320.

Chun, J. U., Litzky, B. E., Sosik, J. J., Bechtold, D. C., & Godshalk, V. M. (2010). Emotional intelligence and trust in formal mentoring programs. *Group & Organization Management, 35*(4), 421–455.

Chun, J. U., Sosik, J. J., & Yun, N. Y. (2012). A longitudinal study of mentor and protégé outcomes in formal mentoring relationships. *Journal of Organizational Behavior, 33*(8), 1071–1094.

Dawson, P. (2014). Beyond a definition: Toward a framework for designing and specifying mentoring models. *Educational Researcher, 43*(3), 137–145.

Eby, L., Allen, T. D., Hoffman, B. J., Baranik, L. E., Sauer, J. B., Baldwin, S., ... & Evans, S. C. (2013). An interdisciplinary meta-analysis of the potential antecedents, correlates, and consequences of protégé perceptions of mentoring. *Psychological Bulletin, 139*(2), 441–476.

Eby, L. T., & Lockwood, A. (2005). Protégés' and mentors' reactions to participating in formal mentoring programs: A qualitative investigation. *Journal of Vocational Behavior, 67*(3), 441–458.

Egan, T. M., & Song, Z. (2008). Are facilitated mentoring programs beneficial? A randomized experimental field study. *Journal of Vocational Behavior, 72*, 351–362.

Ehrich, L. C., Hansford, B., & Tennent, L. (2004). Formal mentoring programs in education and other professions: A review of the literature. *Educational Administration Quarterly*, *40*(4), 518–540.

Fassinger, R. (1997). *Dangerous Liaisons: Reflections on Feminist Mentoring* [Paper presentation]. Annual Meeting of the American Psychological Association: Chicago, IL.

Ghosh, R., Hutchins, H., Rose, K., & Manongsong, A. M. (2019a). *Unpacking the nuances of mutuality in formal mentoring: Lived experiences of faculty in diverse mentoring partnerships*. Manuscript submitted for publication.

Ghosh, R., & Reio, T. Jr. (2013). Career benefits associated with mentoring for mentors: A meta-analysis. *Journal of Vocational Behavior*, *83*(1), 106–116.

Ghosh, R., Shuck, B., Cumberland, D., & D'Mello, J. (2019b). Building psychological capital and employee engagement: Is formal mentoring a useful strategic human resource development intervention? *Performance Improvement Quarterly*, *32*(1), 37–54.

Gibb, S. (1999). The usefulness of theory: A case study in evaluating formal mentoring schemes. *Human Relations*, *52*(8), 1055–1075.

Higgins, M. C., & Kram, K. E. (2001). Reconceptualizing mentoring at work: A developmental network perspective. *Academy of Management Review*, *26*(2), 264–288.

Kram, K. (1983). Phase of a mentor relationship. *Academy of Management Journal*, *26*(4), 608–625.

Kram, K. (1985). *Mentoring at Work* (1st edn.). London: University Press of America.

Lankau, M. J., Riordan, C. M., & Thomas, C. H. (2005). The effects of similarity and liking in formal relationships between mentors and protégés. *Journal of Vocational Behavior*, *67*(2), 252–265.

Menges, C. (2016). Toward improving the effectiveness of formal mentoring programs: Matching by personality matters. *Group & Organization Management*, *41*(1), 98–129.

Morrison, L. J., Lorens, E., Bandiera, G., Liles, W. C., Lee, L., Hyland, R., … & Levinson, W. (2014). Impact of a formal mentoring program on academic promotion of Department of Medicine faculty: A comparative study. *Medical Teacher*, *36*(7), 608–614.

Muir, D. (2014). Mentoring and leader identity development: A case study. *Human Resource Development Quarterly*, *25*(3), 349–379.

Parise, M. R., & Forret, M. L. (2008). Formal mentoring programs: The relationship of program design and support to mentors' perceptions of benefits and costs. *Journal of Vocational Behavior*, *72*(2), 225–240.

Raabe, B., & Beehr, T. A. (2003). Formal mentoring versus supervisor and coworker relationships: Differences in perceptions and impact. *Journal of Organizational Behavior*, *24*(3), 271–293.

Ragins, B. R. (2011). Relational mentoring: A positive approach to mentoring at work. In K. Cameron & G. Spreitzer (Eds.), *The Handbook of Positive Organizational Scholarship* (pp. 519–536). New York: Oxford University Press.

Ragins, B. R., Cotton, J. L., & Miller, J. S. (2000). Marginal mentoring: The effects of type of mentor, quality of relationship, and program design on work and career attitudes. *Academy of Management Journal*, *43*(6), 1177–1194.

Seibert, S. (1999). The effectiveness of facilitated mentoring: A longitudinal quasi-experiment. *Journal of Vocational Behavior*, *54*(3), 483–502.

Smith, W. J., Howard, J. T., & Harrington, K. V. (2005). Essential formal mentor characteristics and functions in governmental and non-governmental organizations from the program administrator's and the mentor's perspective. *Public Personnel Management*, *34*(1), 31–58.

Solansky, S. T. (2010). The evaluation of two key leadership development program components: Leadership skills assessment and leadership mentoring. *The Leadership Quarterly*, *21*(4), 675–681.

Srivastava, S. B. (2015). Network intervention: Assessing the effects of formal mentoring on workplace networks. *Social Forces*, *94*(1), 427–452.

Underhill, C. M. (2006). The effectiveness of mentoring programs in corporate settings: A meta-analytical review of the literature. *Journal of Vocational Behavior, 68*(2), 292–307.

Wanberg, C. R., Kammeyer-Mueller, J., & Marchese, M. (2006). Mentor and protégé predictors and outcomes of mentoring in a formal mentoring program. *Journal of Vocational Behavior, 69*(3), 410–423.

Wanberg, C. R., Welsh, E. T., & Kammeyer-Mueller, J. (2007). Protégé and mentor self-disclosure: Levels and outcomes within formal mentoring dyads in a corporate context. *Journal of Vocational Behavior, 70*(2), 398–412.

Wang, S., Tomlinson, E. C., & Noe, R. A. (2010). The role of mentor trust and protégé internal locus of control in formal mentoring relationships. *Journal of Applied Psychology, 95*(2), 358–367.

Waters, L., McCabe, M., Kiellerup, D., & Kiellerup, S. (2002). The role of formal mentoring on business success and self-esteem in participants of a new business start-up program. *Journal of Business and Psychology, 17*(1), 107–121.

Weinberg, F. J., & Lankau, M. J. (2011). Formal mentoring programs: A mentor-centric and longitudinal analysis. *Journal of Management, 37*(6), 1527–1557.

White, A., Brannan, J., & Wilson, C. B. (2010). A mentor–protégé program for new faculty, part I: Stories of protégés. *Journal of Nursing Education, 49*(11), 601–607.

Wiernik, B. M., & Kostal, J. W. (2019). Protean and boundaryless career orientations: A critical review and meta-analysis. *Journal of Counseling Psychology, 66*(3), 280–307.

Wilson, A. H., Sanner, S., & McAllister, L. E. (2010a). An evaluation study of a mentoring program to increase the diversity of the nursing workforce. *Journal of Cultural Diversity, 17*(4), 144–150.

Wilson, C. B., Brannan, J., & White, A. (2010b). A mentor–protégé program for new faculty, part II: Stories of mentors. *Journal of Nursing Education, 49*(12), 665–671.

Zhang, Y., Qian, Y., Wu, J., Wen, F., & Zhang, Y. (2016). The effectiveness and implementation of mentoring program for newly graduated nurses: A systematic review. *Nurse Education Today, 37*, 136–144.

PART II

QUANTITATIVE METHODS

7. Text mining in career studies: generating insights from unstructured textual data[1]

Vladimer B. Kobayashi[2], Stefan T. Mol, Jarno Vrolijk, and Gábor Kismihók

Text data pertaining to peoples' careers have proliferated in the past few decades. Due to the digitization of job search, recruitment, and the development of HR systems, it is relatively easy to access and obtain large datasets containing information about jobs or other work-related information at the micro (individual), meso (institutional), and macro (regional, national and global) levels, or some combination thereof. Examples of text data that may be used to study careers include (auto)biographies, résumés, posts in professional social networking sites, online job boards, public surveys, interview transcripts, personal diary entries, and even academic publications. Of particular interest are job vacancies, as aside from education and job experience, they also contain information about individuals' roles, responsibilities, knowledge, skills, and abilities, which comes with the promise of adding specificity and context to the career domain, which has come to be dominated by reductionist and generalist approaches to operationalizing key constructs. Online forums and social media also provide data relevant to the study of careers since employees use these platforms to voice their ongoing opinions and sentiments about their past and present employers.

As a way to characterize big text data we can use the framework of the four "V"s of Big Data: Volume, Velocity, Variety, and Veracity (De Mauro, Greco, & Grimaldi, 2015). The sheer *Volume* of the available text data on careers is unprecedented, and far beyond the traditional qualitative and quantitative datasets in careers research. It is oftentimes not possible to store these data locally on a single computer (e.g. a desktop) and to use traditional analytical software and methods for their analysis. Furthermore, the rate at which data about work and careers is generated (*Velocity*) is also growing. One should simply think about the number of public status or CV updates on popular professional/social networking sites such as LinkedIn or Facebook, or the number of vacancy announcements posted to the Internet on a daily basis. Data also comes in many different guises (*Variety*), and are hardly ever produced with the primary aim of facilitating the conduct of research. Therefore, substantial effort must be invested to process different data types and forms in order to make the data suitable for analysis. A final challenge lies in the question of data and data-source integrity (*Veracity*), which also needs to be carefully considered when one wants to generate valid insights from textual data.

The abundance of "big" text data containing information about careers also offers new avenues for careers research and paves the way for the development of bespoke text analysis methods and applications. Gone are the days when text analysis was limited to the mere counting of words, as contemporary sophisticated methods allow researchers to extract and organize textual content into topics, themes, and semantics, opening the door to theory generation and theory-testing (Kobayashi et al., 2018b). The current chapter was written to illuminate some of these possible avenues and to provide initial guidance to careers researchers who might be interested in working with "big" text data.

Most of the aforementioned types of text data are relatively easy to collect, as they can be simply scraped from the Internet. However, in some cases researchers may need to consult with website owners, and ask for direct access (for instance through an Application Programming Interface or API). It comes without saying that there are privacy and possibly copyright issues associated with the use of such data. Privacy and copyright considerations should be negotiated prior to data collection and analysis (van Wel & Royakkers, 2004).

In an effort to familiarize careers researchers with text mining practices, this chapter provides an overview of the text mining process, from data preprocessing, the application of text mining operations, validation, to post-hoc analysis of the resulting models. Various text mining operations, such as dimensionality reduction, text clustering, topic modeling, text classification, and neural word embeddings are discussed. Finally, to demonstrate the capability of novel text mining methods in the area of careers research, an example use case is provided.

TEXT MINING

The primary aim of text mining (TM) is to generate (exploratory) insights from and/or test hypotheses using free unstructured big text (Kao & Poteet, 2007). Hence, text mining is viewed as an objective-driven, systematic process that is generally performed through the following three steps: (1) text data collection and preprocessing, (2) application of text mining techniques, and (3) postprocessing (Zhang, Chen, & Liu, 2015). Figure 7.1 shows an overview of the different steps in the TM process. The organization of this chapter follows this figure.

Text preprocessing may be further subdivided into *text data cleaning* and *text data transformation* (e.g. converting unstructured text into intermediate forms which are used as input to the actual TM operations). TM operations refer to the application of algorithms with the goal of extracting hidden patterns and characteristics from text. Finally, postprocessing involves interpreting and validating knowledge obtained from TM operations. The focus of this chapter is on the different text mining operations. The readers are referred to other open source papers (Kobayashi et al., 2018b, 2018a) for a more comprehensive treatment of the other steps. Hereafter, all mentions of "data" refer to text data. Moreover, "document" and "text" are used interchangeably and corpus refers to the collection of text.

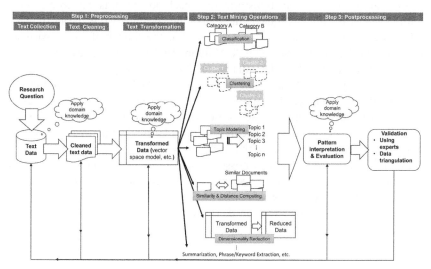

Source: Reprinted from Kobayashi et al. (2018b). Retrieved from https://doi.org/10.1177/
1094428117722619. Licensed under a Creative Commons Attribution-NonCommercial 4.0 License.

Figure 7.1   Flowchart of the text mining process

Text Transformation: From Unstructured to Structured Data

Text mining techniques require that the input data be in a specific format. Before
applying TM techniques, unstructured text data is first transformed so that TM
techniques can be applied (Weiss, Indurkhya, & Zhang, 2015). Unlike common
approaches to analyzing quantitative data, in which data cleaning, data transformation, and data analysis are sequential and separate stages, the specific TM operation
determines the text transformation because oftentimes a TM operation accepts only
a particular text data format. In fact, when subsequent results are unsatisfactory, one
can try different combinations of representations (Lewis, 1992; Scott & Matwin,
1999), different transformation methods, or TM operations. Usually different combinations of data transformation and analytical techniques are tested and evaluated.
In essence, text transformation is a representation strategy in which free text is
converted into structured format (or formally mathematical objects). Most analytical
techniques accept a matrix structure, where the columns are the variables (more commonly referred to as *features*) and the rows are the documents (for instance résumés,
vacancies, or biographies). A straightforward approach is to construct this matrix by
simply using the words (or *terms* as they are more commonly known) as variables.
The resulting matrix is called a "document-by-term matrix" in which the entries
of the matrix are raw frequencies of terms occurring in the documents. In many
applications, this is an obvious choice since words are the basic linguistic units that

express meaning. Thus, in this transformation, each document is transformed into a "vector," the size of which is equal to the size of the vocabulary (i.e. the set of unique words in the corpus), with each element representing the number of times a particular term occurs in that document (Scott & Matwin, 1999). By using raw frequencies, commonly occurring words in documents are given more weight.

Term frequency, in itself, may not be useful if the task is to make groupings or categories of documents (Kobayashi et al., 2018a). Consider the word "study" in a corpus consisting of abstracts of scientific articles. If the objective is to categorize the articles into topics or research themes then this term is not particularly informative in this particular context since many abstracts will contain this word. A way to prevent the inclusion of terms that possess little discriminatory power is to assign weights to each term that reflect its specificity to particular documents in a corpus (Lan et al., 2009). The most commonly used weighting procedure is the Inverse Document Frequency" (*IDF*) (Salton & Buckley, 1988). It is computed using the following formula:

$$\text{IDF}(\text{term i}) = \log \frac{N}{n}$$

where N is the corpus size and n is the number of documents containing term i.

A term with an *IDF* of zero is useless in the discrimination process because that term is present in every document (i.e. $N=n$). In fact, *IDF* can also be used as a criterion to filter out common terms, that is, terms that have a low *IDF* have little discriminatory power and hence can be disregarded. When the raw[3] term frequency (*TF*) and *IDF* are multiplied together it yields the popular *TF-IDF*, which in principle simultaneously accounts for both the word's frequency and specificity (Frakes & Baeza-Yates, 1992) with higher values being more desirable.

One disadvantage of representing texts as a document-by-term matrix, is that it ignores word order information. This can be especially problematic when the goal is to extract semantics in text (Harish, Guru, & Manjunath, 2010). However, it turns out that despite ignoring word order information, this representation seems to work well for many text classification applications, such as in email spam detection, document authorship identification, and topic classification of news articles (Song, Liu, & Yang, 2005; Zhang, Yoshida, & Tang, 2008). Another disadvantage of the document-by-term matrix representation is the resulting high dimensionality, that is, size of the vocabulary. One can use different data dimensionality reduction methods to reduce the number of variables (e.g. variable selection and variable projection techniques) or employ specific techniques suited for data with high dimensionality. These techniques will be discussed in the Text Mining Operations section.

There are other ways to represent text such as using the *n*-gram approach which uses *n* consecutive words or letters (including spaces) as features. Another is one-hot encoding which represents each word as a vector consisting of 1 in the position of the word and 0 in the other positions. The vector has the same size as the vocabulary. For example, suppose that the vocabulary only has these words {"the", "covid-19", "pandemic", "killed", "thousands", "of", "people"} then the vector representation for "pandemic" is (0,0,1,0,0,0,0). This type of representation stands at the basis of neural word embedding (more on this later).

Once text is transformed, techniques such as classification or cluster analyses can be applied. Concatenating noncontiguous words can also tackle substantive questions about the text. For instance, in résumés of job applicants the proximity of the words "experience" and "year" together with a number are used to deduce applicants' length of work experience.

Text Mining Operations

In the following sections, those TM operations which we find most applicable to careers research are discussed. This is followed by a discussion of methods that may be used to assess the credibility and validity of TM outcomes. Most of the techniques covered here accept the document-by-term matrix as input, otherwise we shall explicitly mention the format of the input data.

Dimensionality reduction

Document-by-term matrices tend to have many variables and subsequent analyses may suffer from what is called the *curse of dimensionality* (Aggarwal & Zhai, 2012; Alpaydin, 2014). It is usually desirable to reduce the size of these matrices by applying dimensionality reduction techniques. Benefits of reducing dimensionality include more tractable analysis, greater interpretability of results (e.g. it is easier to interpret variable relationships when there are few of them), and more efficient representation. Compared to working with the initial document-by-term matrices, dimensionality reduction may also reveal latent dimensions (e.g. higher level concepts) (Yarkoni, 2010) and may result in improved performance (Bingham & Mannila, 2001).

Two general approaches are commonly used to reduce dimensionality. One is to construct new latent variables and the second is to eliminate seemingly irrelevant variables. New variables are modeled as a (non)linear combination of the original variables and may be interpreted as latent constructs. For example, the words "flexible", "willingness", and "abroad" may be merged to express the concept of a "willingness to travel" in a corpus of job vacancies. An added advantage of dimensionality reduction techniques is that they may be used to eliminate variable multicollinearity.

Singular Value Decomposition (SVD) is a classic tool which underlies techniques such as Latent Semantic Analysis (Landauer, Foltz, & Laham, 1998) and Principal Components Analysis (PCA) (Jolliffe, 2005). Reducing the number of dimensions is accomplished by retaining only the first few largest singular values. Usually, this implies choosing latent dimensions and recovering the right dimensionality of the data because at times, true dimensionality is obscured by random noise.

Latent Semantic Analysis (LSA) is commonly used when synonymy (i.e. different words that have the same meaning) and polysemy (i.e. one word used in different yet related senses) are present in the data. PCA is effective for data reduction as it preserves the variance in the data. Parallel analysis (Ford, MacCallum, & Tait, 1986;

Hayton, Allen, & Scarpello, 2004; Montanelli Jr & Humphreys, 1976) is the recommended strategy to choose how many dimensions to retain in PCA. A disadvantage of both LSA and PCA is that it may be difficult to interpret the derived dimensions. Another technique is Random Projection (RP) where data points are projected to a lower dimension while maintaining the distances among points (Vempala, 2005). Compared to PCA, RP is computationally less demanding and its results are comparable to those of PCA (Bingham & Mannila, 2001).

An alternative approach to reduce dimensionality is to eliminate variables by using variable selection methods (Guyon & Elisseeff, 2003). In contrast to projection methods, variable selection methods do not create new variables but rather select from the existing variables by eliminating those that are uninformative or redundant (e.g. words that occur in too many documents such as "the", "to", "and", "of"). Three types of methods are available: filters, wrappers, and embedded methods. Filters assign scores to variables and apply a cut-off score in order to select relevant variables. Popular filters are TF-IDF thresholding, Information Gain, and the Chi-squared statistic (Forman, 2003; Yang & Pedersen, 1997). Wrappers select the best subset of variables depending on the particular analytical method that is to be applied. Searching for the best subset of variables using embedded methods is accomplished by minimizing an objective function that simultaneously takes into account model performance and complexity. Model performance can be measured, for example, by prediction error (in the case of classification), and complexity is operationalized in terms of the number of variables in the model. In line with Ockham's razor, the preferred subset is the one that achieves the best balance between the number of variables (fewer is better) and prediction error (lower is better). In practice, the model prediction error is computed using a separate test set. That is, the model is developed on training data and validated on a separate sample of testing data.

Text Clustering

Many tasks in TM involve grouping documents such that documents belonging to the same group are similar and documents from different groups are dissimilar (Jain, Murty, & Flynn, 1999; Steinbach, Karypis, & Kumar, 2000). The process of grouping is called *clustering*. The main uses of text clustering are to organize documents to facilitate efficient search and retrieval and to impose an automatic categorization of documents. For example, text clustering has been used to create topical groupings in a collection of legal documents (Conrad et al., 2005) and automatic grouping of search query results (Osinski & Weiss, 2005). In many clustering procedures the researcher needs to define a measure of distance between texts. Commonly used measures that operate on vector representations are the Euclidean and Hamming distances.

Most clustering algorithms are categorized as either hierarchical or partitional (Steinbach et al., 2000). Hierarchical clustering algorithms are classified into either agglomerative or divisive. In agglomerative clustering, initially there are as many clusters as there are documents and then gradually clusters are merged until all objects belong to a single cluster. Conversely, the divisive approach entails first assigning all documents to a single big cluster and recursively splitting clusters until each document is in its own cluster. The merging (or splitting) of clusters is often-times depicted using a tree or dendrogram.

For partitional clustering the user has to specify the number of clusters beforehand and clusters are formed by optimizing an objective function that is usually based on the distances of the objects to the centers of the clusters to which they have been assigned. The popular k-means algorithm is an example of partitional clustering (Derpanis, 2006). One key challenge in clustering is the determination of how many clusters to form. Since clustering is an exploratory and inductive technique, a common strategy is to try out different numbers of clusters (k) and use cluster evaluation metrics (e.g. Dunn index, Silhouette coefficient, or an external evaluation criterion) to decide upon the most suitable number of clusters (Jain et al., 1999).

Topic Modeling

Topic modeling can be applied to automatically extract topics from documents, where extracted topics represent latent constructs or themes. For example, in a corpus of exit interviews, one could set out to extract the various reasons that people have mentioned for quitting their current job. In machine learning and natural language processing, topic models are probabilistic models that are used to discover topics by examining the pattern of term frequencies (Blei, Ng, & Jordan, 2003). Its mathematical formulation has two premises: a topic is characterized by a distribution of terms and each document contains a mixture of different topics. The most likely topic of a document is therefore determined by its terms. For example, when an exit interview contains words such as "pay", "compensation", "salary", and "incentive", one of its candidate topics is "rewards or compensation".

Perhaps the most popular topic models are the Latent Dirichlet Allocation (LDA) (Blei et al., 2003) model and the Correlated Topic Model (CTM) (Blei & Lafferty, 2007). LDA and CTM both operate on the document-by-term matrix (Porteous et al., 2008). CTM will yield almost the same topics as LDA. The main difference between the two is that in LDA, topics are assumed to be uncorrelated (i.e. orthogonal), whereas in CTM topics can be correlated. In comparing LSA with LDA, the latter has been found to be particularly suitable for documents containing multiple topics (Lee et al., 2010). Supervised Topic Modeling is an extension of LDA (McAuliffe & Blei, 2008). The modeling assumptions remain the same as in LDA except that it is possible to incorporate an outcome variable. For example, one could use Supervised LDA to extract those career shocks from interview transcripts that are related to a quantitative measure of career sustainability.

Classification

Classification is the assignment of objects to predefined classes or categories, which unlike clustering are known a priori. Logistic regression is perhaps the best-known classification method. The goal is to construct a model that can predict the category of a given document. Example applications of text classification are spam or ham classification of emails (Youn & McLeod, 2007), authorship identification (Houvardas & Stamatatos, 2006), thematic categorization (Phan, Nguyen, & Horiguchi, 2008), and identification of sentiments in product reviews (Dave, Lawrence, & Pennock, 2003; Hu & Liu, 2004; Pang & Lee, 2008; Popescu & Etzioni, 2007). In the career domain, one could consider using written performance appraisals to predict dichotomously coded promotion decisions for a particular time period. For a fuller discussion and tutorial on text classification we refer the reader to Kobayashi et al. (2018a).

Neural Word Embeddings

Word embedding involves the mapping of a vocabulary of words to vectors of real numbers, this with the purpose of looking at the similarity and dissimilarity of the word vectors. Similarity and/or dissimilarity between vector representations can help gain intuition in the relation between words, for example "What are the top 5 most similar words to career satisfaction." Furthermore, vector representations allow us to perform certain arithmetic operations with an equal linguistic meaning, for example "Job" – "Pay" might result in a vector representation closest to "Voluntary work" (note that this is but an example).

A central paradigm for deriving these word vector representations is the distributional assumption on which it is based. First proposed by Harris in 1970, the distributional assumption states that words in similar contexts have similar meaning. For example, we could derive the meaning of the knowledge, skill, and abilities (KSAs) from certain occupations by looking at the context in which the KSAs occur. Thus, occupations related to "Computer Science," will then be describing a context containing KSAs such as; "data structures and algorithms," "optimization," "discrete mathematics," and so on. However, in order to fully capture the semantics of, for example, "Computer Science," domain-specific documents fully capturing the terminology describing the phenomenon "Computer Science" has to be eminent.

There are a variety of different methods to derive the word representations. Levy, Goldberg, and Dagan (2015) compared matrix-based algorithms, such as positive pointwise mutual information (PPMI) and singular value decomposition (SVD) to neural methods such as skip-gram with negative sampling (SGNS) and GloVe. Results found mostly local or insignificant performance differences between the methods, with no global advantage to any single approach over the others (Levy et al., 2015). For a more comprehensive overview and practical recommendations towards the implementation of the right method we refer the reader to Levy et al. (2015).

Validation and Postprocessing

The postprocessing step may involve domain experts to assist in determining how the output of the models can be used to improve existing processes, theory, and/or frameworks. Two major issues are usually addressed here. The first is to find out whether the extracted patterns are real and not just random occurrences due to the sheer size of the data (e.g. by applying Bonferroni's principle). The second is, as with all empirical research, whether data and results are valid. Establishing validity (e.g. content, construct, internal, and external validity), and (therewith) the credibility of the output of TM models is particularly important for TM to gain legitimacy in careers research. It is important to note here that it is not the TM procedures that need to be validated but the output (in the same manner that we do not validate Factor Analysis), for example, the predictions of a TM based classifier.

Prior to being applied to support decision making and knowledge generation, the validity of TM based findings will need to be established. When TM is used to identify and operationalize key careers constructs, using different forms of data triangulation will help generate content and construct validity evidence. For example, in our job analysis example of TM application, which follows below, we enlisted the help of job analysts and subject matter experts in evaluating the output of the TM of vacancy texts. In other cases, TM outcomes could be compared to survey data, as was the case in the study on the role of personality in language use (Yarkoni, 2010). More generally, TM based models will require a comparative evaluation in which (part of) the TM output is correlated with independent or external data sources or other "standards" (such as the aforementioned survey or expert data). Though it is easy to view TM as a mechanistic means of extracting information from data, the input of domain/subject matter experts is critically important.

A straightforward practice for content validation is to have independent experts validate TM output. For example, in text classification, subject matter experts (SMEs) may be consulted from time to time to assess whether the resulting classifications of text are correct or not. A high agreement between the experts and the model provides an indication of the content-related validity of the model. The agreement is usually quantified using measures such as the Cohen's kappa or intra-class correlation coefficient.

Another way to validate TM output is through replication, data triangulation, and/ or through an indirect inferential routing (Binning & Barrett, 1989). The standard can be established by obtaining external data using accepted measures or instruments that may provide theory based operationalizations that should or should not be correlated to the model. Such correlations give an indication of construct validity. For example, to validate experience requirements extracted from job vacancies, one can administer questionnaires to job incumbents asking them about their experience. Validity is then ascertained through the correlation between both operationalizations. This can be replicated on various types of text to assess if the TM model consistently generates valid experience requirements for a particular occupation. In theory, one could even compute full multi-trait multi-method correlation matrices (Campbell & Fiske, 1959) to compare the measurements obtained from TM with established instruments, although in practice it may be difficult to obtain the fully crossed dataset that it requires.

As with the statistical analyses that are (more) commonly applied in career research, text mining procedures in and of themselves cannot support causal inference (i.e. internal validity) unless the study design is such that, next to association, temporal precedence and isolation are also established. Given that many text mining applications rely on "data exhaust" (i.e. data that were not purposively collected for investigating the research questions at hand) and between-subjects designs, this is often difficult if not impossible to achieve. Despite these constraints, inferences pertaining to internal validity may be strengthened by collecting multiple waves of data and seeking to establish that changes in (a set of) TM based independent variable(s) are predictably related to changes in some hypothesized dependent variable(s) over time. Furthermore, although the ideal of randomized allocation of subjects to (pseudo-)experimental conditions may not always be viable, the sheer size of the data may likely yield sufficient statistical power to include a large number of theory based (Bernerth & Aguinis, 2016) control variables and/or to leverage a propensity score matching approach. Finally, as to external validity researchers need to be cognizant of the fact that although a given textual dataset may be qualified as being "big" it may still represent a non-randomly selected sample from a (much) larger population to which one wishes to generalize. The fact that Amazon ceased its résumé screening program, could be argued to have resulted from the fact that the (what turned out to be a gender biased) algorithm, was trained on an unrepresentative sample of data that was dominated by successful males. In our own work on vacancy mining we have also struggled with defining what our population is comprised of in the first place. Should the unit of analysis be vacancy, job, job candidate, or task? Clearly, whatever is decided upon has an important bearing on inferences pertaining to external validity. In sum, it is critical that the evaluation metrics developed and accepted within the data science tradition, must be augmented with the aforementioned validity types so as to facilitate adequate and accurate knowledge generation and decision making.

TEXT MINING EXAMPLE: SALARY PREDICTION FROM JOB VACANCIES

The purpose of this section is to illustrate how text mining may be applied in practice. The example uses job vacancies as a data source. The objective is to create a model that can be used to predict the salary associated with a particular occupation from job descriptions in job vacancies. The results could be used to shed light on the pay dynamics across jobs and may answer the question of what makes a particular job pay more as compared with other jobs. Although, there are many factors that affect pay (e.g. discrimination, geographic immobility, supply and demand of labor, etc.), here we examined how text mining could identify those antecedents that derive from the nature of the job. Also, based on the results we briefly discussed the issue of how skill requirements influence pay.

Salary Prediction from Job Vacancies

Every day, thousands of vacancies are posted to job boards and employment web-sites across the world. These vacancies are rapidly becoming a valuable source of job information. Most vacancies contain both worker-oriented (e.g. abilities, skills, knowledge, etc.) and job-oriented (e.g. work activities) information (cf. Peterson et al., 2001). Job analysts and labor organizations are looking for ways on how to use this abundant source of data to answer questions about jobs including evolution of skill demand, emergence of new jobs, and job task analysis. From the career research perspective, TM of vacancies can be to support career counseling and educational choices of students (Messum et al., 2017) and for quantifying the readiness of employees with respect to new work paradigms (Fareri et al., 2020).

A crucial step in using these vacancies is to be able to analyze their textual contents. For example, jobs may be grouped according to skill requirements or activities performed in the job. Also, job categories may reflect differences in salary. Classifying vacancies would give us better understanding of the job demand in each industry and may form the basis of further analysis such as the investigation of which skills are better compensated in the labor market.

Although there are already existing taxonomies of jobs and their associated pay systems, salary differences are still present even within the same job category and likely to change over time. Some researchers ascribe these differences to gender and/ or salary negotiation skill (Säve-Söderbergh, 2019; Voigt & Ruppert, 2019). While other researchers point out other factors including artificial barriers (e.g. union and government restraints) and investment in human capital. In our small example, we will try to elucidate such salary differences just by analyzing job vacancies. Guided by the expansive literature on wage differentials, we attempt to identify some under-lying factors influencing salary differences solely from analyzing vacancies. This approach applies a TM technique, specifically supervised LDA, to automatically extract topics from these vacancies and use these topics to create a predictive model of salary. The approach here is exploratory in nature but can be used as a basis for subsequent hypothesis testing. The following steps, which are explained in greater detail below, were followed: (1) Preprocess and transform the textual content of job vacancies, (2) extract topical patterns and build the model for salary prediction, and lastly, (3) evaluate the performance of the resulting model. This evaluation will be done by running the model on test data (i.e. data not used in building the model). Once we have determined that the model yields a reliable (consistent) prediction of salary, we can then develop strategies to establish evidence for content, construct, internal, and external validity, along the ways that were outlined earlier, although clearly some outcome and design would need to be defined for the establishment of internal validity. Although this process is unwieldy, and perhaps even beyond the scope of a single empirical study, ultimately, the insights we derive from examining how predictions are obtained and how they relate to other constructs may improve our understanding regarding pay differences in jobs and may form the basis for succeeding analyses.

Table 7.1   An example job vacancy text prior to and after text preprocessing

Original text	Resulting cleaned text
Apply now Castles Solicitors are looking for a part / full time Legal Secretary / Admin Assistant to join their team in Hurstpierpoint, working across multiple departments (flexible working hours available ideally 20+ hours a week) Essential skills: Microsoft and excel competentAbility to communicate with clients via email and telephoneOrganisation / good time managementAbility to work independently and as part of a teamGCSE Maths and English C or above Desirable but not essential as full training will be given: Legal background / qualificationsPrevious office experienceExperience with case management systems Role: Communicating with clients and creating appointments / general diary managementOpening and closing fileGeneral correspondence with clients and third partiesDrafting legal documentsTyping from dictationGeneral admin roles	apply now castle solicitor look part full time legal secretary admin assistant join team hurstpierpoint work across multiple department flexible work hour available ideally hour week essential skill microsoft excel competent ability communicate client via email telephone organisation good time management ability work independently part team gcse math english desirable essential full train will give legal background qualification previous office experience experience case management system role communicate client create appointment general diary management open close file general correspondence client 3 party draft legal document type dictation general admin role

Data

The data consisted of 50,000 job vacancies posted to various job boards in the United Kingdom. The automatic prediction of salary from job vacancy descriptions is expected to shed light on how salary differs across job groups. Furthermore, by analyzing the content of vacancies it should be possible to provide career options on jobs that pay better and a more detailed quantification of the skill–salary relationship, that is, how each skill is valued in the labor market.

Preprocessing

The first step in the process is text preprocessing. First, we extracted relevant content from text. Each vacancy is in HTML format, hence, HTML and other formatting tags (e.g. tabs, new line, and long whitespaces) were removed. Moreover, numbers, punctuation marks and stop words (Dolamic & Savoy, 2010; Fox, 1989) for the English language were deleted. Upper case letters were converted to lower case and finally all terms containing only two characters were removed. Extra whitespace and whitespaces at the beginning and end of the description were trimmed out. The extra whitespaces were the result of removing characters. An example job description and the resulting text after applying the preceding text cleaning procedures is shown in Table 7.1.

After text preprocessing, each text is then transformed into a vector resulting in a document-by-term matrix (DTM) representing the entire corpus. The columns of the DTM are the distinct terms occurring in the corpus and the entries are raw term frequencies. Since we want to run a supervised topic model, we need an outcome variable, in this case the outcome variable is annual salary, mentioned in the vacancies. For this, we developed a parser that automatically extracts the salaries. There are a few nuances that we needed to deal with in order to extract the salaries, one is some salaries are provided on an hourly and monthly rate. Another is, some vacancies provide a range rather than a single figure for the salary. In order to harmonize the different salary rates, we converted all hourly and monthly salaries to annual salaries. For the hourly salary, we multiplied the hourly rate by 1538 which is the average hours per year that a full-time employee in the UK will spend working. In the same manner, we multiplied reported monthly salary by 12. For salary ranges, we computed mean salary or the middle of the range as an estimate of the salary and multiplied by an appropriate number to convert them to annual salaries. We put all extracted and calculated salaries in a column vector. Finally, we merged the column containing the salary of each job with the DTM.

Supervised LDA

For the supervised LDA part, we extracted one hundred topics. The choice of 100 topics is default in many other studies (Airoldi & Bischof, 2016; Wallach et al., 2009). However, the choice for the number of topics to retain can be evidenced by examining the prediction accuracy of models with varying numbers of topics. Since the purpose here is to illustrate rather than to optimize accuracy, the choice for 100 topics suffices in this case. The outcome of our supervised LDA here is a predictive model that is used for predicting salary (similar to a linear regression model). Aside from predicting salary, we can also examine the topics that were created. For purposes of illustration, we show nine topics in Table 7.2. The rest of the topics can be obtained upon request from the first author. In principal components analysis (PCA) in quantitative research, factor loadings are examined to interpret PC dimensions, in topic modeling, a topic can be interpreted by inspecting the top words, that is words that have the highest probabilities of belonging to the topic. The content of the vacancies is summarized by the topics such as shown in Table 7.2. Some topics are indicative of the job requirements written in vacancies. Finally, Table 7.3 shows the salary ranges and sample job titles associated to topics 3, 9, 32, 33, and 76.

Predictive performance is measured using the mean squared errors which is computed by the following formula:

$$\text{mean squared error} = \frac{1}{n} \sum_{i=1}^{n} \left(observed_i - predicted_i \right)^2$$

where n is the size of the corpus. The performance was evaluated using 10-fold cross validation Kohavi (1995).

Table 7.2   Sample topics constructed using supervised topic model

Topic 8	Topic 19	Topic 20
food	member	software
chef	ability	developer
restaurant	relevant	technology
kitchen	communicate	test
hotel	effectively	web
hospitality	communication	java
guest	check	net
cater	write	sql
head	responsibility	script
fresh	clear	end
Topic 25	**Topic 27**	**Topic 29**
digital	maintenance	safety
medium	machine	health
campaign	installation	energy
social	system	requirement
content	carry	responsibility
brand	equipment	legislation
channel	tool	environmental
agency	gas	assessment
online	repair	current
strategy	test	qualification
Topic 40	**Topic 61**	**Topic 86**
datum	care	engineer
analyst	people	manufacture
analysis	worker	maintenance
report	social	production
insight	child	mechanical
analyse	young	electrical
model	health	equipment
analytic	home	technical
analytics	community	plant
use	life	electronic

Results

The 10-fold cross validation yielded an average mean squared error of 0.16 which denotes good performance. For the postprocessing, and to establish construct validity, the model is applied to predict the salary in the vacancies in the test data and it yielded a mean squared error of 0.23. We also used the output of the model to examine which topics are associated with high and low salaries. Figure 7.2 shows the highest five topics and lowest five topics as they relate to salary. The figure shows that jobs about strategy planning, banking jobs, and jobs located in big cities (e.g. London and Birmingham) tend to pay more than cleaning and call center jobs. Figure 7.3 shows the ordering of skills and knowledge as they relate to salaries. As can be

Table 7.3   *Job titles, salary ranges associated with topics 3, 9, 32, and 76*

Topics	Terms	Average salary	Top job titles
3	organisation partner strategy develop key stakeholder strategic plan influence relationship	50,000–115,000	"Head of Communications and Engagement," "Head of Internal Communications & Engagement," "Head of Partnerships and Performance," "Stakeholder Engagement Strategy Manager Commercial Excellence," "Chief Product Officer"
9	risk bank programme function operational investment asset knowledge financial senior	90,000–132,000	"Operational Risk Manager," "Senior Investment Risk Manager," "Financial Intelligence Specialist," "Treasury Analyst, Liquidity Management, ALM, Banking," "Brexit Risk Manager – Insurance Delegated Authority Background," "Chief Operation Officer, FX trading"
32	clean area facility duty use keep general part equipment site	16,800–26,000	"School Cleaner," "Housekeeping Assistant/Laundry Assistant," "Cleaning Operatives/Cleaners Night – Gatwick Airport," "Refuse/Recycling Loader," "Aircraft Cleaning Operatives- Heathrow Airport," "Night Cleaning Manager"
33	detail ability attention communication deadline pressure write organisational verbal able	25,000–50,000	"Litigation Support Specialist – Northampton," "Trade and Transaction Reporting Officer," "Recruitment Resourcer – Admin," "Sales Administrator," "Marketing CRM Assistant," "Desktop Publishing Specialist," "IT Project Support Analyst," "Administrator," "Temporary Sales Administrator," "Sales Order Processor," "Immigration Solicitor," "Costs Draftsman"
76	call centre free park yorkshire advisor contact inbound outbound position	22,500–78,000	"Call Centre Advisor," "Your 1st Call Centre Customer Service Advisor Job," "Receptionist," "Assistant Buyer/Purchasing Assistant," "Retail/Shop Supervisor," "Digital Marketing Executive," "Customer Services Adviser – Investment and Financial Services," "Telesales Executive," "Collections Advisor"

Figure 7.2   Top five topics associated to higher pay (first five) and topics associated to least pay (last five)

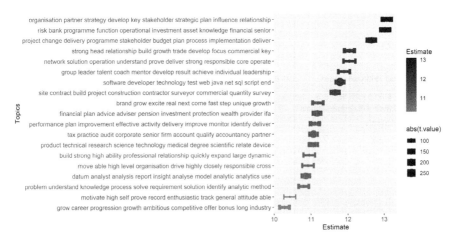

Note: The x-axis represents the coefficients of the predictive model; the higher the coefficients the higher the contribution to salary. The error bars represent the standard errors of the coefficients.

Figure 7.3   Knowledge and skills associated with higher pay

seen, knowledge on finance, software development and data analysis command high salaries in the labor market. Moreover, organizing, leadership, and problem-solving skills are also highly valued. Other employee characteristics that also appear to incur higher pay are being motivated and ambitious. It is surprising to see that communication skills does not figure in the list of high paying skills. One explanation is this skill is commonly required and that it is usually stated in low paying jobs such as in

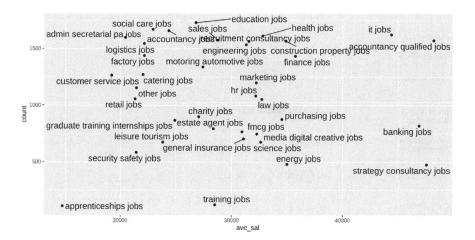

Figure 7.4a   Job categories according to salary and availability

call centers or administrative support. We investigated further by analyzing which job categories tend to pay higher, Figure 7.4a shows a scatter plot of jobs according to average salary and availability. It is obvious that some high paying jobs are not necessarily in high demand, this can be explained by the fact that these jobs require higher ability and more experience (more investment in human capital). Another explanation is that the productivity of workers in these job categories contribute more to the revenue of the companies (banking, strategy, and consultancy jobs). Two job categories seem to offer very good opportunity/outlook because of their high demand and pay, these are IT and accountancy qualified jobs. Professional jobs lie some-where above the median salary and jobs in retail, admin, social care, customer service or related to leisure are the least paying jobs, with the exception of apprenticeship jobs which usually are unpaid jobs. We compared our results with the data from the National Statistics Office of UK (Smith, 2019) (Figure 7.4b) and we find similarity in terms of the ranking of job categories with respect to salary. The similarity provides an evidence of the content validity of the information extracted from job vacancies.

This example showed the feasibility of developing a prediction model for the automatic prediction of salary from text. The resulting classifier is scalable as it can predict salaries on thousands of vacancies which would be laborious and time consuming when done manually. Moreover, the model also sheds light on what determines salaries in jobs which can be difficult to determine especially in the case of new jobs.

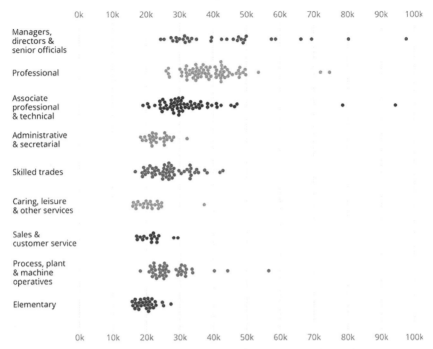

Source: Reprinted from Smith (2019). Public sector information licensed under the Open Government Licence v3.0.

Figure 7.4b   *Plot of salaries according to job categories*

Other Potential Applications

In the preceding section we applied a text mining technique (e.g. supervised topic modeling) on a problem not only of potential interest to career researchers but also to labor economists, and education researchers. Here we explore other potential avenues for future research at the interface between text mining and careers research by suggesting some ideas how existing problems in career research can be reconceptualized as a text mining problem. Our recommendations are purely speculative at the moment and are aimed to excite and provide inspiration to career researchers to incorporate text in their analysis as well as to encourage them to collaborate with text mining experts.

Studies that attempt to analyze how individual attributes relate to career outcomes may benefit from text mining. Specifically TM may provide highly scalable and unobtrusive means of assessing those psychological constructs that careers researchers often hypothesize to predict career outcomes. Not only would this approach prevent burdening respondents with lengthy surveys, it also has the potential to generate data for much larger samples than we are typically accustomed to. One may build a simple score-based system that measures how each word is related to a certain a career concept or dimension using frequency analysis or word-embedding approaches (Shen, Brdiczka, & Liu, 2013; Yarkoni, 2010). Indeed, results from TM can be compared to Likert-scale questionnaires and when the results are properly validated, they may even be used in situations where it is not feasible to gather participants to complete survey measures, for example in observational studies or in the use of secondary text (web blogs, speeches, essays, etc.).

Another potential application is in helping students shape career interests and paths that may lead to satisfaction/well-being. For example, in conceptualizing personal goals, students may be encouraged to write about their career goals in narrative form. By running topic modeling, we may be able to surmise pivotal goal components that relate to career satisfaction. Also, we may build classification models to automatically sort goals into choice or performance goals. The classification is trained by preparing a training data where subject matter experts (SMEs) annotate the goal narratives by manually classifying the mentioned goals into the two categories. Using the annotated narratives, a classification model can be trained and subsequently applied to other goal narratives.

Text mining can also be used in the analysis of mentoring relationships such as in coaching evaluation. Analyzing the written evaluation of or testimonials about career development coaches may be used to analyze which criteria are important for training and development. By analyzing coaches' evaluation using latent semantic analysis (LSA) we may be able to untangle how coaches differ in their evaluation based on length of experience and expertise (Theeboom et al., 2017). This can be done by relating the results of LSA to training outcomes.

Perhaps, one big advantage of text mining in today's research landscape is its ability to analyze big text data that transcend organization and geographical boundaries. Nowadays, online text data about almost anything are readily available and can be collected via an application programing interface (API) or web crawling. Also, these text data can be routinely analyzed even in the absence of a solid theoretical model. A newer approach is to run text analysis on a specific corpus, evaluate whether the patterns extracted are of practical/theoretical significance, before digging deeper in the hope that the extracted information can be used as a basis for building conceptual models (i.e. as is done in grounded theory approach). This approach is particularly useful to study new phenomena in careers research. For example, in the study of new forms of organizing problems, Karanović, Berends, and Engel (2020) applied structural topic modeling to analyze how workers in the platform economy engage with novel forms of organizing across regulatory structures. By analyzing posts in fora set up by the workers themselves, the authors found that workers respond differently to organizing solutions imposed by these platforms. Hence, this may reveal a new dimension of worker–employer relationship in platforms where this relationship is fuzzy. Note that using traditional methods in careers research to investigate this phenomenon may be challenging because it involves non-traditional workers who are dispersed across the globe.

Table 7.4   *Potential applications of text mining in career research*

Career topics	Text source	Text mining methods	Validation	Sample studies
Study of psychological constructs as they relate to career outcomes	Responses in open-ended questions	Frequency analysis, word embedding	Matched to validated Likert-style questionnaires	Shen et al. (2013); Yarkoni (2010)
Training and development	Coaching/trainer evaluation	Latent semantic analysis	Validate through subject matter experts and data triangulation. Also through predictive validity	Theeboom et al. (2017)
New employment relationships	Posts in online forum, web blogs, and twitter data	Structured topic modeling	Subject matter experts	Karanović et al. (2020)
Job turnover intention	Articles and exit interview transcripts	Text classification and frequency analysis	Matched to turnover decisions; convergent validity by investigating its relationship to organizational commitment, job satisfaction, and organizational justice	Barrick & Zimmerman (2005); Frederiksen (2017); Lee, Kim, & Mun (2019)
Work/non-work conflict	Diary; interview transcript; self-evaluation	Longitudinal topic modeling (e.g. dynamic topic models)	Convergent validity as well as predictive validity by relating it to family, physical and psychological health outcomes	Dettmers (2017); Judge, Van Vianen, & De Pater (2004)
Expatriate assignments	Expatriates narratives from semi-structured interviews	Topic modeling and text classification	Subject matter experts (e.g. expatriates coaches)	Salomaa & Makela (2017); Wechtler et al. (2018)

Finally, text mining is not limited to the above-mentioned topics or applications, it can be used to study well-established career topics such as job turnover (Frederiksen, 2017), job burnout (Lizano & Barak, 2015; Reid, Short, & McKenny, 2017), work/non-work conflict (Dettmers, 2017), and expatriation (Wechtler, Koveshnikov, & Tienari, 2018). As long as there are free texts one can get hold of, the limits of investigation lie on the researchers' creativity and imagination. In order to proceed with the analysis, our recommendation is to first investigate whether existing conceptual models are available to guide the text mining process. A model can be used to judge the validity of the extracted patterns. However, the models should not limit the inquiry as potentially interesting patterns may emerge. New interesting patterns may be used to improve or even to refute the model. The researcher may subject the patterns to both data triangulation and validation (e.g. use of subject matter experts, convergent validity and predictive validity) as this will enhance the credibility of the newly discovered concept. Table 7.4 summarizes how existing and new career concepts can be analyzed through text mining.

CONCLUSION

The proliferation of text data about peoples' career and the development of text analytical techniques hold great promise in accelerating and augmenting career research. However, up to this time, most career studies seldom utilize unstructured text as data, and if used, text analysis is usually limited to counting word frequencies. Text mining enables career researchers to augment their text analytical toolkit with powerful analytical techniques from machine learning and statistics. As illustrated in this chapter, text mining is a process that broadly consists of three iterative phases: text preprocessing, the application of TM operations, and finally postprocessing. We hope to have provided readers with: (i) a general understanding of how text is transformed to a form amenable to the application of analytical techniques, (ii) the ability to identify appropriate TM operations to address a research problem, and (iii) tactics to validate the results. Finally, TM derived insights may be further investigated through hypothesis testing in order to inform theory. This perhaps is the real crux why career researchers may be interested in using text mining in their investigations. Although, this chapter is largely written to instruct, it is our hope that through this chapter more career researchers will augment their analytical toolkit with TM, and that this in turn will lead to a better understanding of how careers develop.

NOTES

1. This is an open access work distributed under the Creative Commons Attributio n-NonCommercial-NoDerivatives 4.0 Unported (https://creativecommons.org/licenses/ by-nc-nd/4.0/). Users can redistribute the work for non-commercial purposes, as long as it is passed along unchanged and in whole, as detailed in the License. Edward Elgar Publishing Ltd must be clearly credited as the Publisher of the original work. Any translation or adaptation of the original content requires the written authorization of Edward Elgar Publishing Ltd.
2. This work was supported in part by the European Commission through the Marie-Curie Initial Training Network EDUWORKS (Grant PITN-GA-2013-608311).
   Parts of this chapter were adopted with permission from: Kobayashi et al. (2018a), licenced under CC-BY-NC 4.0 and Kobayashi et al. (2018b), licenced under CC-BY-NC 4.0.
   Correspondence concerning this chapter should be addressed to Stefan T. Mol, Leadership and Management Section, Amsterdam Business School, University of Amsterdam, Valckenierstraat 59, 1018 XE, Amsterdam, the Netherlands; email: s.t.mol@uva.nl; Tel.: +31-(0)20-525 5490.
3. Raw TF refers to the actual frequency of the word in a document.

REFERENCES

Aggarwal, C. C., & Zhai, C. (2012). A survey of text classification algorithms. In C. C. Aggarwal & C. Zhai (Eds.), *Mining Text Data* (pp. 163–222). Springer US. https://doi.org/10.1007/978-1-4614-3223-4_6

Airoldi, E. M., & Bischof, J. M. (2016). Improving and evaluating topic models and other models of text. *Journal of the American Statistical Association, 111*(516), 1381–1403. https://doi.org/10.1080/01621459.2015.1051182

Alpaydin, E. (2014). *Introduction to Machine Learning.* MIT Press.

Barrick, M. R., & Zimmerman, R. D. (2005). Reducing voluntary, avoidable turnover through selection. *Journal of Applied Psychology, 90*(1), 159–166. https://doi.org/10.1037/0021-9010.90.1.159

Bernerth, J. B., & Aguinis, H. (2016). A critical review and best-practice recommendations for control variable usage. *Personnel Psychology, 69*(1), 229–283. https://doi.org/10.1111/peps.12103

Bingham, E., & Mannila, H. (2001). Random projection in dimensionality reduction: Applications to image and text data. *Proceedings of the Seventh ACM SIGKDD International Conference on Knowledge Discovery and Data Mining*, 245–250. http://dl.acm.org/citation.cfm?id=502546

Binning, J. F., & Barrett, G. V. (1989). Validity of personnel decisions: A conceptual analysis of the inferential and evidential bases. *Journal of Applied Psychology, 74*(3), 478–494. https://doi.org/10.1037/0021-9010.74.3.478

Blei, D. M., & Lafferty, J. D. (2007). A correlated topic model of science. *The Annals of Applied Statistics, 1*(1), 17–35.

Blei, D. M., Ng, A. Y., & Jordan, M. I. (2003). Latent dirichlet allocation. *The Journal of Machine Learning Research, 3*, 993–1022.

Campbell, D. T., & Fiske, D. W. (1959). Convergent and discriminant validation by the multitrait-multimethod matrix. *Psychological Bulletin, 56*(2), 81–105. https://doi.org/10.1037/h0046016

Conrad, J. G., Al-Kofahi, K., Zhao, Y., & Karypis, G. (2005). Effective document clustering for large heterogeneous law firm collections. *Proceedings of the 10th International Conference on Artificial Intelligence and Law*, 177–187. https://doi.org/10.1145/1165485.1165513

Dave, K., Lawrence, S., & Pennock, D. M. (2003). Mining the peanut gallery: Opinion extraction and semantic classification of product reviews. *Proceedings of the 12th International Conference on World Wide Web*, 519–528. https://doi.org/10.1145/775152.775226

De Mauro, A., Greco, M., & Grimaldi, M. (2015). What is big data? A consensual definition and a review of key research topics. *AIP Conference Proceedings, 1644*(1), 97–104. https://doi.org/10.1063/1.4907823

Derpanis, K. G. (2006). *K-Means Clustering.* http://citeseerx.ist.psu.edu/viewdoc/summary?doi=10.1.1.217.5155

Dettmers, J. (2017). How extended work availability affects well-being: The mediating roles of psychological detachment and work-family-conflict. *Work & Stress, 31*(1), 24–41. https://doi.org/10.1080/02678373.2017.1298164

Dolamic, L., & Savoy, J. (2010). When stopword lists make the difference. *Journal of the American Society for Information Science and Technology, 61*(1), 200–203. https://doi.org/10.1002/asi.21186

Fareri, S., Fantoni, G., Chiarello, F., Coli, E., & Binda, A. (2020). Estimating Industry 4.0 impact on job profiles and skills using text mining. *Computers in Industry, 118*, 103222. https://doi.org/10.1016/j.compind.2020.103222

Ford, J. K., MacCallum, R. C., & Tait, M. (1986). The application of exploratory factor analysis in applied psychology: A critical review and analysis. *Personnel Psychology, 39*(2), 291–314.

Forman, G. (2003). An extensive empirical study of feature selection metrics for text classification. *Journal of Machine Learning Research, 3*, 1289–1305.

Fox, C. (1989). A stop list for general text. *SIGIR Forum, 24*(1–2), 19–21. https://doi.org/10.1145/378881.378888

Frakes, W. B., & Baeza-Yates, R. (Eds.) (1992). *Information Retrieval: Data Structures and Algorithms*. Prentice Hall.

Frederiksen, A. (2017). Job satisfaction and employee turnover: A firm-level perspective. *German Journal of Human Resource Management, 31*(2), 132–161.

Guyon, I., & Elisseeff, A. (2003). An introduction to variable and feature selection. *The Journal of Machine Learning Research, 3*, 1157–1182.

Harish, B. S., Guru, D. S., & Manjunath, S. (2010). Representation and classification of text documents: A brief review. *International Journal of Computer Applications IJCA, RTIPPR*(2), 110–119.

Hayton, J. C., Allen, D. G., & Scarpello, V. (2004). Factor retention decisions in exploratory factor analysis: A tutorial on parallel analysis. *Organizational Research Methods, 7*(2), 191–205.

Houvardas, J., & Stamatatos, E. (2006). N-gram feature selection for authorship identification. In J. Euzenat & J. Domingue (Eds.), *Artificial Intelligence: Methodology, Systems, and Applications* (Vol. 4183, pp. 77–86). Springer. https://doi.org/10.1007/11861461_10

Hu, M., & Liu, B. (2004). Mining and summarizing customer reviews. *Proceedings of the Tenth ACM SIGKDD International Conference on Knowledge Discovery and Data Mining,* 168–177. http://dl.acm.org/citation.cfm?id=1014073

Jain, A. K., Murty, M. N., & Flynn, P. J. (1999). Data clustering: A review. *ACM Computing Surveys (CSUR), 31*(3), 264–323.

Jolliffe, I. (2005). *Principal Component Analysis*. Wiley Online Library. http://onlinelibrary.wiley.com/doi/10.1002/0470013192.bsa501/full

Judge, T. A., Van Vianen, A. E. M., & De Pater, I. E. (2004). Emotional stability, core self-evaluations, and job outcomes: A review of the evidence and an agenda for future research. *Human Performance, 17*(3), 325–346.

Kao, A., & Poteet, S. R. (2007). *Natural Language Processing and Text Mining*. Springer Science & Business Media.

Karanović, J., Berends, H., & Engel, Y. (2020). Regulated dependence: Platform workers' responses to new forms of organizing. *Journal of Management Studies*, in press. https://doi.org/10.1111/joms.12577

Kobayashi, V. B., Mol, S. T., Berkers, H. A., Kismihók, G., & Den Hartog, D. N. (2018a). Text classification for organizational researchers: A tutorial. *Organizational Research Methods, 21*(3), 766–799. https://doi.org/10.1177/1094428117719322

Kobayashi, V. B., Mol, S. T., Berkers, H. A., Kismihók, G., & Den Hartog, D. N. (2018b). Text mining in organizational research. *Organizational Research Methods, 21*(3), 733–765. https://doi.org/10.1177/1094428117722619

Kohavi, R. (1995). A study of cross-validation and bootstrap for accuracy estimation and model selection. In Ijcai (Vol. 14, pp. 1137–1145). Retrieved from http://frostiebek.free.fr/docs/Machine%20Learning/validation-1.pdf

Lan, M., Tan, C. L., Su, J., & Lu, Y. (2009). Supervised and traditional term weighting methods for automatic text categorization. *IEEE Transactions on Pattern Analysis and Machine Intelligence, 31*(4), 721–735. https://doi.org/10.1109/TPAMI.2008.110

Landauer, T. K., Foltz, P. W., & Laham, D. (1998). An introduction to latent semantic analysis. *Discourse Processes, 25*(2–3), 259–284. https://doi.org/10.1080/01638539809545028

Lee, N., Kim, J.-H., & Mun, H.-J. (2019). Exploration of Emotional Labor Research Trends in Korea through Keyword Network Analysis. *Journal of Convergence for Information Technology*, 9(3), 68–74. https://doi.org/10.22156/CS4SMB.2019.9.3.068

Lee, S., Baker, J., Song, J., & Wetherbe, J. C. (2010). An empirical comparison of four text mining methods. *2010 43rd Hawaii International Conference on System Sciences (HICSS)*, 1–10. https://doi.org/10.1109/HICSS.2010.48

Levy, O., Goldberg, Y., & Dagan, I. (2015). Improving distributional similarity with lessons learned from word embeddings. *Transactions of the Association for Computational Linguistics*, 3, 211–225. https://doi.org/10.1162/tacl_a_00134

Lewis, D. D. (1992). *Representation and learning in information retrieval* [University of Massachusetts]. http://ciir.cs.umass.edu/pubfiles/UM-CS-1991-093.pdf

Lizano, E. L., & Barak, M. M. (2015). Job burnout and affective wellbeing: A longitudinal study of burnout and job satisfaction among public child welfare workers. *Children and Youth Services Review*, 55, 18–28.

McAuliffe, J. D., & Blei, D. M. (2008). Supervised topic models. *Advances in Neural Information Processing Systems*, 121–128.

Messum, D., Wilkes, L., Peters, K., & Jackson, D. (2017). Content analysis of vacancy advertisements for employability skills: Challenges and opportunities for informing curriculum development. *Journal of Teaching and Learning for Graduate Employability*, 7(1), 72–86. https://doi.org/10.21153/jtlge2016vol7no1art582

Montanelli Jr, R. G., & Humphreys, L. G. (1976). Latent roots of random data correlation matrices with squared multiple correlations on the diagonal: A Monte Carlo study. *Psychometrika*, 41(3), 341–348.

Osinski, S., & Weiss, D. (2005). A concept-driven algorithm for clustering search results. *IEEE Intelligent Systems*, 20(3), 48–54. https://doi.org/10.1109/MIS.2005.38

Pang, B., & Lee, L. (2008). Opinion mining and sentiment analysis. *Foundations and Trends® in Information Retrieval*, 2(1–2), 1–135. https://doi.org/10.1561/1500000011

Peterson, N. G., Mumford, M. D., Borman, W. C., Jeanneret, P. R., Fleishman, E. A., Levin, K. Y., Campion, M. A., Mayfield, M. S., Morgeson, F. P., Pearlman, K., Gowing, M. K., Lancaster, A. R., Silver, M. B., & Dye, D. M. (2001). Understanding work using the occupational information network (o*net): Implications for practice and research. *Personnel Psychology*, 54(2), 451–492. https://doi.org/10.1111/j.1744-570.2001.tb00100.x

Phan, X.-H., Nguyen, L.-M., & Horiguchi, S. (2008). Learning to classify short and sparse text & web with hidden topics from large-scale data collections. *Proceedings of the 17th International Conference on World Wide Web*, 91–100. https://doi.org/10.1145/1367497.1367510

Popescu, A.-M., & Etzioni, O. (2007). Extracting product features and opinions from reviews. In A. Kao & S. R. Poteet (Eds.), *Natural Language Processing and Text Mining* (pp. 9–28). Springer London. https://doi.org/10.1007/978-1-84628-754-1_2

Porteous, I., Newman, D., Ihler, A., Asuncion, A., Smyth, P., & Welling, M. (2008). Fast collapsed gibbs sampling for latent dirichlet allocation. *Proceedings of the 14th ACM SIGKDD International Conference on Knowledge Discovery and Data Mining*, 569–577. http://dl.acm.org/citation.cfm?id=1401960

Reid, S., Short, J. C., & McKenny, A. (2017). Tell me how you feel: A content analytic approach to measuring burnout. *Academy of Management Proceedings*, 2017, 14641.

Salomaa, R., & Makela, L. (2017). Coaching for career capital development: A study of expatriates' narratives. *International Journal of Evidence Based Coaching and Mentoring*, 15(1), 114–132.

Salton, G., & Buckley, C. (1988). Term-weighting approaches in automatic text retrieval. *Information Processing & Management*, 24(5), 513–523.

Säve-Söderbergh, J. (2019). Gender gaps in salary negotiations: Salary requests and starting salaries in the field. *Journal of Economic Behavior & Organization*, 161, 35–51.

Scott, S., & Matwin, S. (1999). Feature engineering for text classification. *Proceedings of the Sixteenth International Conference on Machine Learning*, 379–388. http://dl.acm.org/citation.cfm?id=645528.657484

Shen, J., Brdiczka, O., & Liu, J. (2013). Understanding email writers: Personality prediction from email messages. *User Modeling, Adaptation, and Personalization*, 318–330. https://doi.org/10.1007/978-3-642-38844-6_29

Smith, R. (2019). *Employee Earnings in the UK: 2019*. Office for National Statistics. https://www.ons.gov.uk/employmentandlabourmarket/peopleinwork/earningsandworkinghours/bulletins/annualsurveyofhoursandearnings/2019#employee-earnings-data

Song, F., Liu, S., & Yang, J. (2005). A comparative study on text representation schemes in text categorization. *Pattern Analysis and Applications*, *8*(1–2), 199–209. https://doi.org/10.1007/s10044-005-0256-3

Steinbach, M., Karypis, G., & Kumar, V. (2000). A comparison of document clustering techniques. *KDD Workshop on Text Mining*, *400*, 525–526. https://wwws.cs.umn.edu/tech_reports_upload/tr2000/00-034.ps

Theeboom, T., Van Vianen, A. E. M., Beersma, B., Zwitser, R., & Kobayashi, V. (2017). A practitioner's perspective on coaching effectiveness. In L. Nota & S. Soresi (Eds.), *Counseling and Coaching in Times of Crisis and Transitions: From Research to Practice* (pp. 61–78). Routledge.

van Wel, L., & Royakkers, L. (2004). Ethical issues in web data mining. *Ethics and Information Technology*, *6*(2), 129–140. https://doi.org/10.1023/B:ETIN.0000047476.05912.3d

Vempala, S. S. (2005). *The Random Projection Method* (Vol. 65). American Mathematical Society.

Voigt, M., & Ruppert, A. (2019). Salary negotiations: highlights and surprises from 10 years of research. *International Conference on Gender Research*, 639–645.

Wallach, H. M., Murray, I., Salakhutdinov, R., & Mimno, D. (2009). Evaluation methods for topic models. *Proceedings of the 26th Annual International Conference on Machine Learning*, 1105–1112. http://dl.acm.org/citation.cfm?id=1553515

Wechtler, H., Koveshnikov, A., & Tienari, J. (2018). The spouse as "the forgotten other": A qualitative content analysis of expatriation literature. *Academy of Management Proceedings*, *2018*(1), 18361. https://doi.org/10.5465/AMBPP.2018.18361abstract

Weiss, S. M., Indurkhya, N., & Zhang, T. (2015). *Fundamentals of Predictive Text Mining* (2nd ed.). Springer-Verlag London. https://doi.org/10.1007/978-0-387-34555-0_2

Yang, Y., & Pedersen, J. O. (1997). A comparative study on feature selection in text categorization. *Proceedings of the Fourteenth International Conference on Machine Learning*, 412–420. http://dl.acm.org/citation.cfm?id=645526.657137

Yarkoni, T. (2010). Personality in 100,000 words: A large-scale analysis of personality and word use among bloggers. *Journal of Research in Personality*, *44*(3), 363–373. https://doi.org/10.1016/j.jrp.2010.04.001

Youn, S., & McLeod, D. (2007). A comparative study for email classification. In K. Elleithy (Ed.), *Advances and Innovations in Systems, Computing Sciences and Software Engineering* (pp. 387–391). Springer. http://link.springer.com/chapter/10.1007/978-1-4020-6264-3_67

Zhang, W., Yoshida, T., & Tang, X. (2008). Text classification based on multi-word with support vector machine. *Knowledge-Based Systems*, *21*(8), 879–886. https://doi.org/10.1016/j.knosys.2008.03.044

Zhang, Y., Chen, M., & Liu, L. (2015). A review on text mining. *2015 6th IEEE International Conference on Software Engineering and Service Science (ICSESS)*, 681–685. https://doi.org/10.1109/ICSESS.2015.7339149

8.   Only time will tell: conducting longitudinal research on careers

Shoshana R. Dobrow and Hannah Weisman

Careers—defined as the individually perceived sequence of attitudes and behaviors associated with work-related experiences and activities over the span of a person's life (Hall, 2002)—inherently and inextricably involve the role of *time*. At the individual level, time—and particularly change over time—is essential for understanding adults' lives and careers, as noted by both traditional adult development theories (e.g., Erikson, 1963; Ginzberg, 1951; Levinson, Darrow, Klein, Levinson, & McKee, 1978; Super, 1992) and more recent career and identity development theories (e.g., Hall, 2002; Ibarra, 1999; Kroger, 2007; Pratt, 2000; Taylor, Marienau, & Fiddler, 2000). Indeed, research has consistently shown that time can shape work attitudes and experiences ranging from job satisfaction (Ng & Feldman, 2010; Rhodes, 1983) to callings (Dobrow, 2013) to professional identity (Pratt, Rockmann, & Kaufmann, 2006). Nonetheless, the nature of the relationships between important career constructs and time has often been understudied or, when studied, yielded inconsistent patterns of results across different timeframes or across studies. As a result, careers scholars regularly conclude their papers—almost to the point of cliché—by noting the lack of longitudinal research, either as a limitation of their own work or the research area in general, and then by calling for more longitudinal research in the future.

The bottom line here: Time is profoundly important for understanding careers. And yet, even though "everyone" says to do longitudinal research, scholars rarely do it—not only in careers research, but in organizational behavior research more broadly (e.g., George & Jones, 2000; Mitchell & James, 2001; Sonnentag, 2012; Wright, 1997; Zaheer, Albert, & Zaheer, 1999). Why? Put simply, conducting longitudinal research is really hard and takes a long time. It is also amazingly worthwhile.

In this chapter, we draw on our experiences as longitudinal researchers to discuss the realities and challenges of conducting and publishing rigorous longitudinal research. We begin by defining what longitudinal research is, and is not. We then describe five key contributions that longitudinal research can make, above and beyond other research designs like cross-sectional studies. We conclude by offering a "Top 10" list of specific practical tips for conducting and publishing longitudinal research on careers. Throughout this chapter, we are mindful of noting many of the legitimate challenges in conducting and publishing longitudinal research—often drawing on "favorite" comments that we have received from journal reviewers— along with some suggestions for how to deal with them. We have learned a lot about how to do both quantitative and qualitative longitudinal research from actually doing it (as suggested in Pettigrew, 1990), and our hope is to share some of this acquired knowledge with other scholars who may be considering embarking on this type of ambitious data collection or who are already doing so. As an end goal, we hope this chapter will inspire you to conduct longitudinal research—with the benefit of having a realistic "research" preview (cf. Wanous, 1992) to help you weather its challenges and truly enjoy the upsides.

WHAT LONGITUDINAL RESEARCH IS—AND IS *NOT*

A longitudinal study is a type of research design involving repeated observations over time. When conducted on individuals, as would be the case for most careers research, this means repeated observations of individual people. However, longitudinal research can also focus on repeated observations at other levels of analysis, such as groups and organizations. There is considerable variety within this methodology: these observations can be quantitative, such as via surveys, or qualitative, such as via interviews. Sample sizes can be small or large or anywhere in between, while the timespan of data collection can range from short to long. What all longitudinal studies have in common is a quest to understand phenomena over time—often to understand change over time (e.g., Singer & Willett, 2003).

Longitudinal studies fit careers research particularly well, because, by definition, careers and career development occur over time (Hall, 2002). Yet, in spite of this obvious fit between careers research and longitudinal methods, careers scholars have long bemoaned the predominance of cross-sectional (i.e., one wave) studies and have advocated for researchers to instead undertake longitudinal studies (e.g., Barley, 1989; Hall, 2002; Ployhart & Vandenberg, 2010). In recent years, journals have joined this effort by increasingly requesting or even requiring data that go beyond being "merely" cross-sectional. Nevertheless, longitudinal careers research is still all too rare.

Some scholars have responded to the growing requirement for non-cross-sectional research by conducting two-wave studies, often with a very short time lag between waves (e.g., a few weeks)—which they then label as "longitudinal." However, longitudinal research, which by definition allows for examining change over time, requires three or more waves of data (Singer & Willett, 2003; Willett, 1989). So, if cross-sectional studies have one wave of data collection and longitudinal studies require three, what does this mean for *two*-wave studies? In some ways, two-wave studies are in a sort of methodological purgatory. Although using a two-wave design has some advantages over a cross-sectional design—namely, it can begin to mitigate journal and reviewer concerns over common method bias (Podsakoff, MacKenzie, Lee, & Podsakoff, 2003)—we note that these studies are not, in fact, longitudinal. They can only examine change from Time 1 to Time 2 as "merely an increment of difference between two times" (Ployhart & Vandenberg, 2010, p. 97). They cannot shed light on the nature of this change, as longitudinal research can. Further, two-wave studies confound true change and measurement error, such that it is impossible to discern whether a measured difference between timepoints represents true change over time or instead measurement error that makes it look like there is a difference when there is not (Singer & Willett, 2003). Thus, although there are appropriate occasions for using two-wave data collections, such as in quasi-experimental studies with before (Time 1) and after (Time 2) designs (for a review, see Grant & Wall, 2009), we caution against using two-wave designs to investigate most careers research questions, which often involve matters of causality or change. It is worth noting that in our own experience reviewing, two-wave studies are increasingly being rejected from journals, particularly when explicitly labeled as "longitudinal," both because of the methodological shortcomings discussed above, as well as the problematic signaling issue that arises from the inaccurate assertion that a two-wave design is "longitudinal." We hope that by calling attention to these issues with two-wave designs, scholars can avoid falling prey to the false assumption that these types of studies are true longitudinal studies and instead prioritize the careful match of research design to research question, whether longitudinal or not (Bono & McNamara, 2011).

The key value of longitudinal research is that it allows for the examination of many types of research questions that could not otherwise be studied—or at least could not be studied rigorously—by alternative research designs. In the next section, we outline key contributions that longitudinal research can make, above and beyond other research methodologies. To illustrate these contributions richly, and so provide a "behind-the-scenes" view of longitudinal research, we discuss some of the questions that we have examined in our own longitudinal research on topics such as calling, job satisfaction, and developmental mentoring networks. We also make suggestions for future longitudinal research. To aid you in developing your own longitudinal research questions, we organize all research questions mentioned in this chapter in Table 8.1.

CONTRIBUTIONS OF LONGITUDINAL RESEARCH

Contribution #1: Understanding the Nature of Change Itself

Research that primarily considers a construct from a cross-sectional perspective is, by definition, unable to examine the dynamics of this construct. Even though adult and career development theorists have long suggested that careers are dynamic (e.g., Hall, 2002; Ibarra, 1999; Levinson et al., 1978; Schein, 1978; Super, 1992), the predominant use of cross-sectional study designs means that, at a fundamental level, scholars may simply not have empirical evidence about whether constructs change or are stable over time. Understanding these dynamics of career constructs is critical for helping researchers gain greater insight into how career trajectories unfold. To address this

Table 8.1   Sample research questions for longitudinal research on careers

Research Aim	Sample Research Questions
Understanding the nature of change itself	• "How do developmental network characteristics change over a substantial period of time?" (Dobrow Riza & Higgins, 2019) • "Does calling change?" (Dobrow, 2013) • "How do two time metrics, age and tenure, relate to job satisfaction above and beyond the other metric? That is, what is the fundamental picture of how job satisfaction changes over time?" (Dobrow Riza et al., 2018) • "How do the change trends of developmental network characteristics covary with one another?" (Dobrow Riza & Higgins, 2019)
Understanding antecedents	• "What factors predict the change trends of developmental network characteristics over time?" (Dobrow Riza & Higgins, 2019) • "Are higher ability, behavioral involvement, and social comfort in the calling domain related to a subsequent increase or decrease in calling over time?" (Dobrow, 2013)

Understanding consequences	• "To what extent does the degree of calling toward a domain experienced early in life positively predict career pursuit in this domain many years later—above and beyond the effects of other early predictors?" (Dobrow Riza & Heller, 2015)
	• "How are developmental network characteristics related to professional identity over time?" (Dobrow & Higgins, 2005)
	• "How does support received from one's developmental network during early career relate to career outcomes?" (Higgins et al., 2008)
	• "Do people make early career choices based on passions and interests (i.e., their early callings) versus talent (i.e., their early perceived or actual abilities)?" (Dobrow Riza & Heller, 2015)
	• "To what extent is calling related to ignoring negative career advice in the (a) short term, (b) medium term, and (c) long term?" (Dobrow & Tosti-Kharas, 2012)
	• Relationship between developmental network characteristics and optimism from different time perspectives (Higgins et al., 2010):
	  • Cross-sectional perspective: "To what extent is the amount of support provided by one's developmental network (career or psychosocial) related to one's optimism?"
	  • Intercept perspective: "To what extent is the amount of support provided early on in one's career by one's developmental network (career or psychosocial) related to one's current optimism?"
	  • Rate of change perspective: "To what extent is the rate of change of amount of support provided by one's developmental network (career or psychosocial) related to one's current optimism?"

Understanding temporal sequences	• "To what extent is job rewards, as exemplified by pay, a mediator in the relationship between time, both age and tenure, and job satisfaction?" (Dobrow Riza et al., 2018) • "To what extent is the relationship between degree of calling toward a domain experienced early in life and career pursuit in this domain many years later mediated by perceived (or actual) ability—*above and beyond* the effects of other early and contemporaneous actual predictors?" (Dobrow Riza & Heller, 2015)? • "What is the relationship between early callings (in adolescence) and later career pursuit (in adulthood)?" (Dobrow Riza & Heller, 2015) • "Does calling lead to perceived ability or, alternatively, does perceived ability lead to calling?" (Dobrow Riza & Heller, 2015)
Understanding career processes	• "How do people make career transitions to pursue their callings?" (Weisman, 2019) • "How do people craft the self-narrative of a career transition to pursue a calling?" (Weisman, 2019)

gap in knowledge, we, along with our collaborators, have asked longitudinal research questions specifically aimed at understanding the nature of change itself, such as:

- "How do developmental network characteristics change over a substantial period of time?" (Dobrow Riza & Higgins, 2019)
- "Does calling change?" (Dobrow, 2013).

The above types of questions may become more elaborate, or nuanced, by aiming to understand how multiple characteristics—of time or of the construct itself—may change over time, for example:

- "How do two time metrics, age and tenure, relate to job satisfaction above and beyond the other metric? That is, what is the fundamental picture of how job satisfaction changes over time?" (Dobrow Riza, Ganzach, & Liu, 2018)
- "How do the change trends of developmental network characteristics covary with one another?" (Dobrow Riza & Higgins, 2019).

We note that, in spite of the important descriptive information provided by addressing research questions such as these, they are generally not "enough" to be standalone papers. Typically, this type of research question may be the first of several in a given paper, followed by some of the types of research questions described below.

Contribution #2: Understanding Antecedents

After establishing a basic understanding of a construct's dynamics, as above, a next logical step is often to explore whether and which antecedent factors—that is, precursors of the construct—may shape its initial development and subsequent evolution. Given that careers unfold over time, often across multiple organizations in an increasingly "boundaryless" environment (Arthur & Rousseau, 1996), there should be tremendous utility in examining career-related constructs over time to understand what factors predict their development, sustainment, or even loss (e.g., in the area of calling research, see the following examples: Creed, Kjoelaas, & Hood, 2016; Dobrow, 2013; Dobrow & Tosti-Kharas, 2011; O'Keefe, Dweck, & Walton, 2018). However, this type of research has been highly lacking in careers research to date, perhaps because it requires a longitudinal approach, and cannot be adequately addressed using cross-sectional designs. This methodological concern also creates conceptual concerns: antecedents are conceptually distinct from correlates or control variables, yet when studied in cross-sectional designs, antecedents and correlates cannot be distinguished from one another (see Dobrow Riza, Weisman, Heller, & Tosti-Kharas, 2019). Additionally, over the course of time, scholars may come to view, or at least assume, that certain constructs are stable and unchanging, due in part to an over-reliance on cross-sectional research that can only provide a snapshot view of a construct. Indeed, scholars may end up not examining antecedents of a construct at all, instead focusing solely on the outcomes of that construct. As a result, scholars have noted the need for longitudinal research to disentangle questions along these lines, such as Bunderson and Thompson's (2009) exhortation to look at the calling construct as both a cause and as a consequence of various career and life outcomes (p. 53).

In sum, longitudinal research is able to address questions about antecedent factors and their role in shaping career constructs over time, as shown in the following examples. Note that when the focus is on antecedents of a focal construct, in statistical terms the antecedents are the independent variables and the focal construct is the dependent variable:

- "What factors predict the change trends of developmental network characteristics over time?" (Dobrow Riza & Higgins, 2019)
- "Are higher ability, behavioral involvement, and social comfort in the calling domain related to a subsequent increase or decrease in calling over time?" (Dobrow, 2013).

Contribution #3: Understanding Consequences

While careers research often aims to understand the consequences of particular career-related phenomena, such as linking attitudes or intentions to career behaviors, cross-sectional research simply cannot discern whether the career construct actually leads to the outcome or not. Instead, we encourage researchers to shift away from cross-sectionally worded research questions—"What is the relationship between people's satisfaction and performance in their jobs?"—to specify the role of time more precisely. For example, this question could evolve to include time even in a relatively generic way, "What is the relationship between people's satisfaction and *subsequent* performance in their jobs?," or could include time in a more specific way, depending on the research focus, "What is the relationship between newcomers' satisfaction and subsequent performance in their jobs two years later?" Here are some sample research questions from our work that examine consequences of the focal construct:

- "To what extent does the degree of calling toward a domain experienced early in life positively predict career pursuit in this domain many years later—above and beyond the effects of other early predictors?" (Dobrow Riza & Heller, 2015)
- "How are developmental network characteristics related to professional identity over time?" (Dobrow & Higgins, 2005)
- "How does support received from one's developmental network during early career relate to career outcomes?" (Higgins, Dobrow, & Chandler, 2008).

A twist on the above research questions is to examine a focal construct in conjunction with another construct as predictors of consequences over time. This type of research question often positions the two predictors as rivals, and, so, if done well, can make a significant theoretical contribution. An example of this type of question, which sets up calling and two types of ability as rivals, is:

- "Do people make early career choices based on passions and interests (i.e., their early callings) versus talent (i.e., their early perceived or actual abilities)?" (Dobrow Riza & Heller, 2015).

Research questions about the consequences of constructs from a longitudinal perspective often involve specifying time periods, which is usually not relevant for cross-sectional research. This leads to research questions that specifically aim to examine relationships over different amounts of time, such as:

- "To what extent is calling related to ignoring negative career advice in the (a) short term, (b) medium term, and (c) long term?" (Dobrow & Tosti-Kharas, 2012).

Another approach to understanding consequences is to investigate time flexibly, such as by examining levels of a construct at a specific point in time (e.g., at the beginning of people's careers), how this construct changes over time (e.g., the rate of change, or slope, of this construct over time)—and, ironically, even conducting cross-sectional analyses for comparison—all of which can provide further insight into when and how constructs relate to consequences. For instance, the following set of research questions first examines the cross-sectional relationship between two constructs, developmental network characteristics and optimism; then how the intercept of developmental network characteristics relates to optimism at a later point in time; and, then, finally, how the rate of change in developmental network characteristics relates to optimism at a later point in time (Higgins, Dobrow, & Roloff, 2010):

- Cross-sectional perspective: "To what extent is the amount of support provided by one's developmental network (career or psychosocial) related to one's optimism?"
- Intercept perspective: "To what extent is the amount of support provided early on in one's career by one's developmental network (career or psychosocial) related to one's current optimism?"
- Rate of change perspective: "To what extent is the rate of change of amount of support provided by one's developmental network (career or psychosocial) related to one's current optimism?"

Contribution #4: Understanding Temporal Sequences

As careers unfold over time by definition (Hall, 2002), it is almost a truism that understanding how careers unfold over time is important. Put differently, if our goal as careers researchers is to truly understand careers, then we must consider the role of time. This may often mean identifying, explaining, and understanding the sequences in which things occur over the span of our careers. For instance, considerable careers research has examined how people rebound from career set-backs, make career transitions, and choose their careers (e.g., Haynie & Shepherd, 2011; Holland, 1997; Ibarra & Barbulescu, 2010; Vough & Caza, 2017). Yet, if people are studied cross-sectionally (e.g., asked to report their attitudes and career circumstances simultaneously) or retrospectively (e.g., asked to reflect back on their reactions, transitions, or choices), the study cannot conclude that the reported attitudes or intentions led to the current circumstances—or whether the reverse is the case, namely that the current circumstances may actually lead to the attitude or intention via such mechanisms as reducing cognitive dissonance (Vroom, 1966), fostering retrospective rationalization (London, 1983), or rewriting one's career self-narratives over time (Ibarra & Barbulescu, 2010).

Thus, cross-sectional research can, at best, be agnostic about explaining questions fundamental to careers research, like why people choose their line of work, or, at worst, may erroneously draw causal inferences based on data that simply cannot shed light on causality. The challenge with cross-sectional research in this regard, and even some two-wave or short-term longitudinal designs (i.e., a few days, weeks, or months, depending on the research question; for exceptions see diary studies that can rigorously address research questions over many days, e.g., Yang & Diefendorff, 2009), is that it can yield confusing results, in terms of unknown or even jumbled sequences of how careers actually play out. Moreover, by not temporally separating the measurement of constructs, cross-sectional research may be subject to common method bias—systematic measurement error that can inflate, or deflate, the relationship between constructs due to their being measured via the same method or source (Podsakoff et al., 2003).

One key approach to understanding temporal sequences is to begin investigating mediators, or mechanisms, linking a career construct to its outcomes. It is important to note that for these types of research questions to be addressed rigorously, they need to draw on longitudinal data that allow for the measurement of the independent variable, mediator, and dependent variable on temporally separate occasions (i.e., measured at different times than one another) and ideally measured in order (i.e., independent variable first, mediator second, and dependent variable third), as in the following examples:

- "To what extent is job rewards, as exemplified by pay, a mediator in the relationship between time, both age and tenure, and job satisfaction?" (Dobrow Riza et al., 2018).

If possible, longitudinal studies that include repeated measures of the mediator allow for controlling for this variable as measured during an earlier time period, as follows:

- "To what extent is the relationship between degree of calling toward a domain experienced early in life and career pursuit in this domain many years later mediated by perceived (or actual) ability—*above and beyond* the effects of other early (perceived ability, actual ability, and external pressure to pursue this career) and contemporaneous actual (or perceived) predictors?" (Dobrow Riza & Heller, 2015).

Longitudinal research can also enable a second approach to understanding temporal sequences: exploring causality. Although most longitudinal studies, such as multi-wave survey studies, cannot definitively address causality—which can only be accomplished by experimental methods—they can speak to causality. As a start, they can temporally separate constructs, as in the examples of mediators above. More directly, they can use cross-lagged panel analyses to untangle the direction of causality (see methods described in Salamon & Robinson, 2008; Shingles, 1985). Questions involving the direction of causality can be substantive enough to be a paper's primary focus:

- "What is the relationship between early callings (in adolescence) and later career pursuit (in adulthood)?" (Dobrow Riza & Heller, 2015).

Or, these types of questions can be used in support of a newly proposed theoretical model, where it can be helpful to empirically demonstrate that the causal sequence goes in the direction from independent variable to mediator, for example, and not from mediator to independent variable:

- "Does calling lead to perceived ability or, alternatively, does perceived ability lead to calling?" (Dobrow Riza & Heller, 2015).

Contribution #5: Understanding Phenomena over the Long Term

Another contribution of longitudinal research is that it can speak to the long-term nature of careers in ways that other research designs are unable to do. Most importantly, longitudinal research needs to cover an appropriately long research timeframe to capture meaningful change. Indeed, a key limitation of cross-sectional research versus longitudinal research is that cross-sectional research captures only a snapshot in time whereas longitudinal research can capture phenomena over time, to the extent that the two types of study designs can sometimes yield opposite results (Ployhart & Vandenberg, 2010). Even across longitudinal studies, *longer-term* longitudinal research can yield substantively different results than shorter-term longitudinal study designs. For instance, in our own work we found:

- Over the span of two years, on average, developmental network density *increased* (Dobrow & Higgins, 2005).
- Over the span of ten years, developmental network density initially increased for a few years, but then *declined* in a curvilinear fashion in subsequent years (Dobrow Riza & Higgins, 2019).

It is important to note that the above two papers came from the same longitudinal study. The first paper was published when the study included three waves of data spanning five years (1996–2001), whereas the second was published after another wave of data collection had occurred, such that there were four waves of data spanning 10 years (1996–2006). These results highlight the different types of conclusions that might be drawn about the nature of change, in this case of developmental network density, depending on the timeframe used for data collection as well as the analytical approach used. The two years included in the first study represent a legitimately long amount of time by the standards of most careers research. We modeled change in density as the difference between Time 1 and Time 2, which led us to conclude that developmental network density increased over a two-year timeframe and predicted certain Time 3 outcomes.[1] Yet, when we examined developmental network density over a much longer amount of time, where the four waves of data spanning 10 years allowed for a more sophisticated analytical approach, multilevel modeling, we found that a very different picture emerged after the first two years.

In separate research on job satisfaction (Dobrow Riza et al., 2018), we explored whether the job satisfaction "hangover" effect documented in the literature—reflecting that job satisfaction is typically higher at the start of a new job compared to the previous job ("honeymoon") but subsequently tapers off ("hangover") as novelty wears off and normalization sets in (Boswell, Boudreau, & Tichy, 2005; Boswell, Shipp, Payne, & Culbertson, 2009)—continued beyond the one-year timeframe documented in the literature. Drawing on two long-term nationally representative datasets spanning 29 and 11 years, we found that job satisfaction continued to decrease beyond the first year of employment. In fact, we discovered that job satisfaction displayed a cyclical effect, such that it continued to decrease throughout people's tenure in a given organization until they changed organizations, at which point their job satisfaction experienced a boost (i.e., the "honeymoon")—and then started to decline again (i.e., the "hangover"). Thus, a key benefit of longer-term longitudinal studies like this was our ability to extend intriguing results about the honeymoon-hangover effect (Boswell et al., 2005; Boswell et al., 2009). We were able to demonstrate the long-term nature of the relationship between time and job satisfaction, which could not be explored with cross-sectional or shorter-term longitudinal designs.

We suggest that the contrasting findings above do not reflect methodological weaknesses in the shorter-term studies; rather, they reflect that the time perspective researchers select, as well as the selection of statistical techniques, can significantly impact the nature of the findings. Given this, we suggest that for most careers research, the longer the timeframe of data included, the better. That said, as much as we would like our research to be guided by purely conceptual goals, the pragmatic reality in longitudinal research—especially in labor-intensive, long-term research that spans many years—is that scholars need to draw the line somewhere to publish from their longitudinal datasets at different points along the way of data collection, as exemplified by the two different studies of developmental network density mentioned above.

The choice about how many waves of data to include in a given manuscript can even evolve during the review process. In our experience, we once submitted a manuscript with three waves of longitudinal data, with a fourth wave of data collection occurring separately and in parallel to the review process. By the time we received the invitation to revise and resubmit, this fourth wave of data was available for inclusion in the manuscript—and it ultimately contributed to our manuscript's acceptance by allowing us to address specific reviewer concerns (Dobrow Riza & Heller, 2015). Thus, the passage of time, even when it comes to waiting for reviews to come back from journals, can actually be beneficial to longitudinal research. These examples also highlight that often in longitudinal research there is simply no right answer about how many waves of data are "best" or how many waves "should" be included in any given manuscript. Rather, this is a judgment call on the part of researchers, ideally guided by the research question, as well as other theoretical and practical considerations. Longitudinal researchers therefore need to become comfortable with thinking flexibly about their own data collection strategies as well as their choices about how much of their data belong in any given paper.

Contribution #6: Understanding Career Processes

Another major advantage of longitudinal research, particularly longitudinal *qualitative* research, concerns its ability to shed light on career processes (Langley, 1999). While research into processes remains relatively limited in the careers literature, existing research indicates that longitudinal, qualitative methods provide researchers with unique opportunities to build and elaborate theory in this area (Lee, Mitchell, & Sablynski, 1999). For instance, Pratt, Rockmann, and Kaufmann's (2006) qualitative study employed a six-year longitudinal design to develop new theory on the process by which medical residents, and professionals more broadly, constructed their professional identities as they transitioned from medical school graduates to independent medical practitioners. Drawing on multiple sources of qualitative data (e.g., archival documents, observation, short surveys, and four rounds of interviews spanning the duration of the residency program), the researchers elucidated an important, but undertheorized, career and role transition process whose discovery was only possible through the use of longitudinal data (Pratt et al., 2006).

Longitudinal qualitative data can also be useful for delineating processes that connect the dots, so to speak, between career constructs whose relationships have been demonstrated quantitatively. For instance, the benefits of callings have been well-documented in the literature (see Dobrow Riza et al., 2019 for a meta-analytic review), but this research cannot explain the *process* by which people transition from unfulfilling lines of work to pursue their callings, as in the following research questions (Weisman, 2019):

- "How do people make career transitions to pursue their callings?"
- "How do people craft the self-narrative of a career transition to pursue a calling?"

Thus, a qualitative longitudinal design—here, three rounds of semi-structured interviews with participants, spaced roughly evenly over the course of 18 months—is well-suited for investigating these questions because occupational transitions are dynamic phenomena that unfold over time. Examining these same research questions cross-sectionally (i.e., with one round of interviews) would simply not allow for an understanding of the focal process of interest, nor would it allow for insight into the implications of this process. Indeed, as Langley, Smallman, Tsoukas, and Van de Ven (2013) noted, "Longitudinal data (whether obtained with archival, historical, or real-time field observations) are necessary to observe how processes unfold over time" (p. 6).

TOP 10 PRACTICAL TIPS FOR CONDUCTING AND PUBLISHING LONGITUDINAL RESEARCH ON CAREERS

In the previous section, we discussed the key contributions—as well as many of the very real challenges—of conducting longitudinal research. Here, we want to build on these points to offer a "Top 10" list of practical suggestions about conducting and publishing longitudinal research on careers. To the extent possible, we draw on specific comments we have received from reviewers as well as our own anecdotal experiences doing longitudinal research to highlight that these issues do come up in the review process and in our research activities—and offer advice on how to handle them. We include a tip specifically oriented toward qualitative longitudinal research to complement the other more quantitatively-oriented tips. We summarize these "Top 10" tips in Table 8.2.

Tip 1: Get Your Measures "Right"—Or as Right as Possible

"You'd better get this right," Richard Hackman, my (Shoshana's) dissertation chair, said to me, at the time a first-year doctoral student, somewhat ominously. We were meeting to discuss the finishing touches on the survey that was meant to be the first in a multi-wave longitudinal study of calling in the context of young musicians—to which I responded by bursting into tears. The need to repeat measures over several data collections, which is necessary for measuring change over time, felt—and can still feel—like a weighty research choice. In the case of my study, at the time of its launch, there was exactly one existing empirical study on calling in the field of organizational psychology (Wrzesniewski, McCauley,

Table 8.2   Summary of "Top 10" practical tips for conducting and publishing longitudinal research on careers

Practical Tip	Key points
Tip 1: Get your measures "right"—or as right as possible	• For quantitative research: Recognize that you are effectively "stuck" with whatever measures you choose to include in the initial wave of data collection. Therefore, you need to do your homework about the different measurement options available before embarking on any (quantitative) longitudinal data collection. Nonetheless, we encourage you to add measures in subsequent waves of data collection, as applicable. • For qualitative research: You should feel free to go where the research takes you, and to update your interview protocol flexibly over time to explore emerging themes. Your data will dictate the area of careers research that you ultimately contribute to.
Tip 2: Get your sample "right"—or as right as possible	• Your research question should guide which sample you recruit. Think about what type of individual would be ideal for examining your particular research question (e.g., is it someone in a particular life stage or career transition?). • If conducting a qualitative study of individuals going through a particular career process, consider recruiting participants who can provide both retrospective and real-time accounts of that process.
Tip 3: Choose your study length and time intervals carefully	• The length of your study, and the embedded measurement periods, should be informed by the process or phenomena under consideration. • Reviewers will expect you to provide a rationale for the length of your study and measurement intervals. Provide this rationale in your manuscript, or be prepared to add it (when reviewers will likely ask for it) during the review process.
Tip 4: Leverage the passage of time	• With the passage of time comes the opportunity to collect more data. Take advantage of this opportunity! • Consider following up with a sample you have studied in the past (regardless of whether or not you have already published a paper drawing on that sample). • You may also look into collecting data that was sensitive or restricted in the past. Sometimes, data become more accessible with the passage of time.
Tip 5: Be flexible with your data analyses	• Keep in mind that you do not always have to use the data you have collected in its entirety (i.e., use all waves of data in a single paper). • Seek opportunities to learn new ways of analyzing longitudinal data, so that you can be flexible in your approach to data analysis. • Recognize that tools for analyzing longitudinal data are constantly evolving. Developing an openness to ongoing learning will be important for your success as a longitudinal researcher.
Tip 6: Publish multiple papers from longitudinal datasets	• Longitudinal research is arduous for you to conduct and valuable for careers scholarship. Thus, it is of benefit to both your career and the field that you publish multiple papers from a longitudinal dataset. • When attempting to publish multiple papers from a single dataset, be prepared to provide journals with a detailed and transparent overview of the data that have appeared in prior publications.
Tip 7: Leverage and embrace technological change	• Social media and other technology provide new and exciting opportunities for conducting longitudinal research, such as for keeping in touch with your participants and recruiting new participant samples. Think about how you can take advantage of these opportunities.
Tip 8: Organize, analyze, and memo as you go—a specific tip for qualitative research	• Longitudinal qualitative research often generates enormous amounts of data in the form of interview transcripts, observations, and archival documents. It is important to stay on top of these data from the outset, and to analyze and organize continuously throughout the research process, to avoid data overload. • Write memos as you conduct your interviews to summarize key ideas and make note of surprising findings. • Participants in longitudinal qualitative studies want to know that you value and respect their time. After an initial interview with a participant, you should enter every subsequent interview with the ability to demonstrate your knowledge of the previous interview. You can do this by reviewing your memo from the previous interview, or, even better, by re-reading the transcript.
Tip 9: Be resilient	• Given the extra time and effort involved in conducting longitudinal research, any journal rejection can feel particularly painful. Stay positive! If you have collected rigorous longitudinal data to investigate an interesting research question, you will almost certainly find a home for your research!
Conclusion and Tip 10: Do longitudinal research!	• Longitudinal research is fundamental to advancing knowledge of careers. • There are major opportunities for you to shape the field by harnessing this ambitious and rigorous type of data collection.

Rozin, & Schwartz, 1997), so there was a tremendous amount about this construct that was unknown. As a result, I included Wrzesniewski and colleagues' scale in my data collections, and also made what felt like a bet to develop and use my own scale for the study's focal construct, calling, which would ultimately be published only many years later (Dobrow & Tosti-Kharas, 2011). My dissertation ended up including four waves of data spanning as many years. At my defense, I could not have been prouder when my dissertation chair told me I was his first doctoral student who had done a longitudinal dissertation—which highlights both the merits as well as, perhaps, the riskiness of conducting longitudinal research at the doctoral career stage.

Longitudinal researchers also have to be comfortable with the fact that new constructs, as well as new measures for existing constructs, will enter the literature after your study's first data collection. You may also get ideas for new constructs or measures to include after your study has launched. As an example, an informal conversation I (Shoshana) had with a professional musician that occurred between Times 1 and 2 of my longitudinal study of musicians led to the inclusion of new social encouragement measures at Time 2, which turned out to be theoretically and empirically important in my study (Dobrow, 2013). The practical reality of conducting surveys is a need to balance the inclusion of a variety of measures with concern for length and time to complete the survey, both of which affect respondent fatigue. This can lead you to opt not to include measures in a given data collection that, in retrospect, you wish you had (e.g., I did not include my scale to measure calling on the Time 3 survey, as this data collection centered on other aspects of my participants' lives, but I wish I had collected it). Thus, in a sense, longitudinal studies can seem like time capsules of where the literature—or where the researcher's thinking—stood at a particular point in time.

To address these types of concerns when conducting quantitative longitudinal research, you should accept that you are effectively "stuck" with the measures you select at the launch of your study. This point applies not only to primary data collection, but also to quantitative longitudinal research that draws on archival data. In these cases, you may be limited by measures that are not exactly what you would have chosen (e.g., a single-item, global measure of the focal construct, job satisfaction, rather than a multi-item scale, as in Dobrow Riza et al., 2018) or changes in how the constructs were measured at different waves of the data collection (e.g., shortening scale lengths, such as by dropping items, over time). In contrast, when conducting qualitative longitudinal research, particularly using a grounded theory approach, it is often a best practice to modify your interview protocol as needed, stay true to your data, and let emerging findings direct your subsequent data collections, rather than allowing your early thinking to dictate the direction of your research—even if that means drawing on new literatures or new constructs.

As your work progresses through the publication process, you may very well need to defend your choice—or, in the case of archival data, the choices made by the parties that collected the data—to reviewers, even many years later. These points can be somewhat awkward to respond to, as the following reviewer comment shows. I (Shoshana) submitted a paper based on my longitudinal study of musicians, which included the core measure of calling dating back to the study's launch in 2001, even though this scale was published only later:

> You mention that you used the Dobrow and Tosti-Kharas (2011) 12-item calling scale to measure calling. I had a few issues with this … you say that you "collected this measure five times over 11 years (Times 1 through 5)," yet Time 1–4 periods all occurred prior to 2011 when the Dobrow & Tosti-Kharas measure was published. Can you explain this discrepancy?

This comment was difficult to respond to without violating the norms of the double-blind review process. This type of sequencing issue leads us to strongly encourage reviewers to be aware of and compassionate to similar issues that may come up in quantitative longitudinal research. All this said, if and when you encounter new ideas and/or new measures during the course of your longitudinal study, as we have, we strongly suggest you include them in your subsequent data collection. As we discuss in Tip 5 below, you should be flexible in how you analyze your data and there may very well be approaches you can use to rigorously include measures that were not collected at all previous timepoints.

Tip 2: Get Your Sample "Right"—Or as Right as Possible

You also need to make a bet about the sample you focus on in longitudinal research, as again, you are effectively "stuck" with it. Even the most brilliant longitudinal researchers do not have crystal balls. They cannot possibly know how participants' careers will unfold over time—nor can they foresee the external shocks that may impact participants' careers, such as in the case of the COVID-19 pandemic. This uncertainty is both one of the joys and one of the challenges of being a longitudinal researcher. Ultimately, as with other research designs, you need to select a sample that is the best possible fit for your research question at the time. For instance, my (Shoshana's) longitudinal study of young musicians progressing from high school into adulthood, an "unconventional" sample for organizational behavior or management research (Bamberger & Pratt, 2010), spans the specific, critical life stages relevant to addressing research questions about early career choices in a challenging labor market context, where the core construct being studied—calling—is highly salient. With longitudinal research, you especially need to be mindful of your participants' likelihood of continuing to participate over the years. Whether you are conducting quantitative or qualitative longitudinal research, your participants' involvement in multiple, time-consuming rounds of surveys or interviews is truly generous. We thus encourage longitudinal researchers to acknowledge participants' contributions through various means, which may include offering research incentives, expressing thanks verbally or in writing, and providing follow-up information about your research findings.

Tip 3: Choose Your Study Length and Time Intervals Carefully

To be effective, longitudinal study designs should include the "right" time periods, such that they span the specific and/or critical life stages relevant for addressing your research question in your particular type of context. For instance, in my (Hannah's) three-wave qualitative longitudinal study of the process by which people transition from unfulfilling lines of work to pursue their callings, I needed a timeframe that would allow me to observe turnover behavior in a sample of adults considering career "jumps." This resulted in my choice of an 18-month study design—with the three data collections occurring at the beginning (Time 1), middle (Time 2, roughly 9 months after Time 1), and end (Time 3, roughly 18 months after Time 1)—which prior research has suggested is an appropriate length of time to observe these types of behaviors (Felps et al., 2009).

In the first review I (Shoshana) ever received on a paper from my longitudinal study of musicians, one reviewer asked, "Why were these particular time intervals chosen?" To this day, I am mindful of this question in terms of both being as thoughtful as possible about structuring the spacing of data collections in longitudinal research designs as well as being as clear as possible about this in my manuscripts. However, longitudinal data collections present numerous challenges, and you—as well as your reviewers—should appreciate the need to be both conceptually- and pragmatically-driven with longitudinal data collection timings.

You might be surprised to see how often editors and reviewers of papers that use multi-year, multi-wave longitudinal datasets still, nonetheless, ask the authors for yet more waves of data during the revision process. Granted, this may be justified conceptually, as in the following comment from an action editor in regard to the initial submission of a paper based on my longitudinal study of musicians. At the time, it was a four-wave, seven-year study:

> It also occurs to me that it has been several years since the last data collection on this sample; are there plans for continued collection with them? If such data exist or will in the near future, I think it would be a mistake to hold them out of this paper. I think it will be difficult to reach the standard for contribution if your revised model continues to end with just behavioral intentions as an outcome.

In this case, we were not "holding data out" of the paper; rather, the next data collection was happening at the same time—which fortunately already included the type of behavioral outcomes the editor requested. We were able to add this wave of data, including a new, stronger dependent variable, into our manuscript, such that the version ultimately accepted was based on a five-wave, 11-year study. At a big picture level, we cannot overstate how important it is for your data to address your underlying conceptual questions (Bono & McNamara, 2011)—no matter how much impressive longitudinal data you might have.

Tip 4: Leverage the Passage of Time

Not only does the passage of time offer numerous conceptual and methodological benefits to your study, as already discussed in this chapter, but it can also create another potential benefit: access to more data. Data that are sensitive at one point in time, and thus potentially unavailable to you as a researcher, may become available to you at a later point in time. For instance, if you are studying adolescents progressing into adulthood, as is often relevant to research about initial career choices (e.g., Rogers, Creed, & Glendon, 2008), some topics that are sensitive (e.g., mental health, sexual orientation) or even not applicable (e.g., marital status) for minors during an earlier wave of your data collection may become less sensitive and more relevant and/or appropriate during a later wave of data collection when your participants are adults.

Another example comes from my (Shoshana's) longitudinal study of musicians. From early on in the study, I knew I wanted and needed some measure of objective musical ability. My participants were originally students at two selective summer music programs in 2001 that used auditions to ascertain who would be admitted. These audition ratings, which were consistent across participants within each site, were the best possible indicator of objective ability that I could think of—and I desperately wanted these data for my study. However, not only did the summer programs not inform the participants of their own audition ratings, but they also refused to grant me access to this information because it was too sensitive. Only in 2005, four years after the auditions occurred, did the programs finally grant me access to this information in their archives. In one case, the data were electronic, and so, relatively easy to handle, and in the other case, the data existed only in hard copy in basement archives where I spent considerable time doing manual data entry. The bottom line here is that patience and persistence can pay off when it comes to longitudinal data. And, when there are data you need, be willing to put in the work to get it.

Tip 5: Be Flexible With Your Data Analyses

Once you are at the stage of analyzing your longitudinal data, we strongly encourage you to be flexible with your approach to using your data. You do not always need to use all waves of your data nor do you always need to examine change over time. For instance, I (Shoshana) first learned how to do longitudinal analyses using multilevel modeling, also known as individual growth modeling (Singer & Willett, 2003), in a course during my doctoral program. It took me quite a while afterward to realize that I did not *need* to use this analytical approach—that is, using all available waves of data and/or analyzing change in the focal construct over time—for every analysis of longitudinal data afterwards. Rather, as with all empirical research, it is important to match your analyses and use of data to your research questions. For example, several of my (Shoshana's) own papers that draw on longitudinal data use multiple regression analyses (e.g., Dobrow Riza & Heller, 2015; Dobrow & Tosti-Kharas, 2012; Higgins et al., 2010) while others use more sophisticated multilevel modeling, both two-level (e.g., Dobrow Riza & Higgins, 2019; Dobrow, 2013) and even three-level (Dobrow Riza et al., 2018; see Snijders & Bosker, 2011 for an introduction to multilevel analysis). We discuss tips for analyzing qualitative longitudinal data in Tip 8.

To prepare for these different analytic approaches, you can and should train yourself in analytical methods to the extent possible and always keep your eyes open for new opportunities to gain this type of expertise (e.g., if you're a doctoral student, take any/all courses related to longitudinal analyses, and if you're in a more advanced career stage, you can enroll in training seminars or attend workshops at conferences). It is also typical for virtually every quantitative paper you write to require at least one new type of statistical analysis that you have never done before, so it is important to recognize and even embrace this aspect of continual learning in your research. There are other tactics you can use if you find that your longitudinal study requires analyses beyond your expertise, including recruiting a coauthor who knows these types of statistical approaches or hiring a statistician.

Related to Tip 7, the passage of time can offer statistical advances that benefit longitudinal research. When I (Shoshana) first started trying to publish papers using multilevel modeling, this type of analysis was regarded as highly novel, even unusual and borderline impenetrable, by many editors and reviewers. As such, over the years, as is often the case with leading-edge methodological and statistical approaches, I have had to devote a lot of energy, both in manuscripts and in responses to reviewers, introducing, justifying, explaining, and defending the (appropriate) use of this type of analysis. Indeed, reviewers have even asked us to switch from this type of analysis to more "standard" multiple regression analyses, which would not have been as good a match for our research question or data, likely because they were not familiar with multilevel analyses. Reviewers have also confused our multilevel analyses with similar, but different, approaches like latent growth modeling. Fortunately, as multilevel modeling, as well as other analytical approaches like structural equation modeling, have become more mainstream, the burden on longitudinal researchers to justify even the most basic aspects of their analytical choices has diminished. Yet, we find that we are still routinely asked by editors and reviewers to explain our analyses in such a way that readers who are unfamiliar with these methods can understand.

In sum, we encourage scholars to follow the latest best practices in longitudinal research, in general. While the methods discussed in this chapter and adopted in our previous research may reflect "current" best practices (or best practices at the time when the research was conducted), longitudinal research methods and analytical approaches are rapidly evolving and increasing in sophistication over time. Overall, just as longitudinal research sheds light on the evolution of constructs, the methods for conducting and analyzing longitudinal research are going through an evolution of their own over time.

Tip 6: Publish Multiple Papers from Longitudinal Datasets

Given the investment required to collect longitudinal data, you most likely will want more than one publication out of your dataset. To successfully do this, each paper needs to make novel contributions to the literature in order to "justify" a separate publication. In our experience, the threshold for demonstrating a contribution from the same dataset may be—or at least feel—even higher than for a paper that uses a novel dataset. Thus, it is incumbent upon longitudinal researchers to be extra clear in articulating novel contributions from datasets that have generated previous publications. The following example is from a rejection of a manuscript using the first author's longitudinal study of musicians dataset. Here, a reviewer expressed concern—which was very frustrating to hear—about the potential for contribution based on this longitudinal dataset that had already generated prior publications: "However, given the previous research on the topic, including several papers based on this data, I struggled to see how this study significantly increases our understanding of the phenomenon."

The rise in calls for transparency in research—including pre-registering studies and making datasets publicly available—poses unique challenges for longitudinal research. First, when submitting a paper based on data that has been used in prior publications, the current norm at most journals is that authors must provide information about data transparency (often in the form of a table), describing variables included in those prior publications as well as in the current manuscript. This is relatively straightforward to do, but comes with some risks of unblinding the review process as well as potentially unintentionally raising the bar for contribution by highlighting prior work from the same dataset. We have found in our experience that sometimes this information is shared with not just the editor considering the manuscript but with reviewers as well. Second, if you began collecting longitudinal data in the past, practices like pre-registration, which are now strongly encouraged, were not at all common (Center for Open Science, 2017). Some psychology scholars have suggested that in cases such as this, where pre-registration is no longer possible, it is still possible to share study protocols, data, and other materials on the Open Science Framework (OSF) (e.g., Tackett, Brandes, & Reardon, 2019). Even for longitudinal studies starting now in the current era of transparency, practically speaking, it would be impossible for most longitudinal researchers to accurately predict, and, so pre-register, studies that will continue long into the future. Third, some scholars may right-fully feel less comfortable making their longitudinal datasets, which require such high levels of investment, public relative to other types of datasets that are considerably easier to obtain.

Given these particular issues, we encourage scholars, including the OSF, to push for methods of transparency tailored to diverse research methodologies.

In the case of newly launched quantitative longitudinal research, transparency may include pre-registering variables and research questions prior to each data collection, as well as sharing survey materials. However, for ongoing or already-completed longitudinal studies, journals and reviewers should be mindful that requirements to pre-register may be applied moving forward, but are impossible to apply retrospectively.

Tip 7: Leverage and Embrace Technological Change

Significant amounts of time pass over the course of conducting long-term longitudinal research on careers, and so we must expect that the technology we use in conducting this research will evolve. For instance, my (Shoshana's) initial involvement in longitudinal studies in the early 2000s saw a shift from drawing on paper-based surveys in the early waves of data collection to online surveys, which were considered quite technologically advanced at the time, in later waves. If you fast forward to studies launched more recently, current technologies like online communities can enable both data collection and access to samples. For example, I (Hannah) recruited participants for my qualitative longitudinal study from an online community comprised primarily of individuals who made or were deliberating making a "jump" to pursue a calling in their careers. This context was thus an ideal, "extreme" context for finding participants who could shed light on the career phenomenon of interest (Eisenhardt, 1989), but would have been difficult to pinpoint without this type of online community even as recently as several years ago.

Technology is also critical for a key task of longitudinal research: the ongoing ability to track and contact your participants over time. For instance, in the early stages of my (Shoshana's) longitudinal study of musicians, around 2001–2003, I collected—and used—mailing addresses and phone numbers to stay in contact with participants. As my data collection shifted to online surveys, I needed a different type of contact information—email addresses. This information was not stable for participants like mine, who were graduating from high school, entering college, and then entering the workforce, with each transition often yielding a new email address. Thus, be prepared to put in a lot of effort—and creativity—to track participants over the long term if you want to achieve high response rates.

During its first few years of existence, roughly 2004–2006, Facebook was a social networking platform for university students only—and as such, it seemed like a perfect means to reach out to my primarily university-aged study participants for whom I did not have current contact information. For my data collections occurring during these years, I did successfully reconnect with many participants this way. Nonetheless, a word of caution: unlike email or other direct means of communication, platforms like Facebook have their own standards of use that may limit your ability to use the platform for your research purposes. For instance, I apparently sent enough similar-looking emails via Facebook to my study participants that, in spite of these messages being for legitimate academic research purposes, Facebook classified the emails as spam and shut down my account. Platforms like LinkedIn can also be extremely useful for longitudinal research—with the same caution that each platform has its own standards for use. We are highly aware that the rapid rate of technology change makes even these relatively recent examples almost immediately sound outdated, thus reinforcing this tip to be ready to leverage and embrace technological change!

Tip 8: Organize, Analyze, and Memo as You Go—a Specific Tip for Qualitative Research

Based on our experience, we offer two main suggestions for conducting qualitative longitudinal research on career processes. First, use highly organized practices for managing your data because qualitative longitudinal studies involve extraordinary amounts of data. For instance, a 45-minute interview can yield a typed transcript of 10 or more pages. Thus, if your study involves 50 participants interviewed at three points in time, you can expect to conclude your study with over 1,500 pages of interview transcripts. Moreover, if you attempt to triangulate your interview findings with other qualitative sources (e.g., archival or observational data), as we often do in our own qualitative research, you will likely end up with hundreds of additional pages in archival documents, observational notes, and memos. It is thus not surprising that scholars often mention the sheer magnitude or "immense amount of data" (Lifshitz-Assaf, 2018, p. 752) generated by their longitudinal qualitative studies.

In order to avoid "death by data asphyxiation" (Pettigrew, 1990, p. 281), it is important to develop systematic procedures for naming and storing files, keeping track of future contact dates for each participant, and conducting timely analyses of interview transcripts. This last point is particularly important, as promptly analyzing the interview transcripts one-by-one (or even in small batches) allows researchers to stay on top of emerging findings that can be explored in subsequent rounds of data collection (Spradley, 1979). Indeed, as a result of this process, your interviews can even become "progressively more focused to capitalize on emerging themes" (Petriglieri, Petriglieri, & Wood, 2018, p. 485) across your rounds of data collection. In sum, it is crucial to begin data analysis early on. If not, you may become overwhelmed by your data, and you may discover unexpected findings that you are unable to explore further. Analyzing your data along the way enables you to approach the data in manageable chunks, and to modify your interview protocol alongside your emerging theory (Glaser & Strauss, 1967).

Our second suggestion concerns writing memos, a hallmark of the grounded theory method of data analysis (Glaser & Strauss, 1967). Memo-writing is important for qualitative research in general, and we would argue that it is especially important for longitudinal research involving successive rounds of semi-structured interviews. Weeks, months, or even years pass between interview rounds, making it difficult for qualitative researchers to remember with accuracy the precise content of their previous interviews. Researchers who enter interviews unable to remember their previous conversations may have to spend time clarifying technical points (e.g., about participants' job roles or career histories) covered in those prior conversations. Not only does this use up valuable time in the interview, but such clarifications may also inadvertently annoy participants by violating participants' expectation that the researcher would enter the conversation with some level of baseline knowledge based on prior conversations and, further, may signal that the researcher places little value on participants' time. Thus, unless it is appropriate for your research—for example, your research focuses on sense-making (e.g., Maitlis, 2009; Vough & Caza, 2017) or the evolution of people's self-narratives (Weisman, 2019), which specifically require understanding how answers to the same questions change over time—it is important to demonstrate this baseline knowledge. Try to avoid repetitive questions and be prepared to answer participants' questions, such as "Can you remind me what I said last time?" One technique we recommend for being prepared in this way is by writing memos after each interview, and by reviewing these memos before each subsequent interview. If you have time, you can also re-read the prior transcripts on the interview day.

Tip 9: Be Resilient

Weathering the ups and downs—and risks—of conducting long-term research, where the payoff in terms of results and publications may take years, requires resilience. The first paper I (Shoshana) submitted to a journal from my longitudinal dissertation initially received a revise and resubmit—and was then rejected in the next round of review. One of the reviewers boldly proclaimed: "I appreciate how hard it is to give up on a project in which so much time has been invested in data collection and in manuscript preparation." Well, in spite of the fact that this reviewer's comment is permanently seared in my memory, I certainly did not "give up" on this study—five years into collecting data, at that point—and I not only collected subsequent waves of data but also successfully published papers from this dataset. Thus, when the going gets tough, remind yourself why it matters to you—and our field more broadly—to study your research questions in the first place.

Conclusion and Tip 10: Do Longitudinal Research!

We hope this chapter has highlighted the legitimate benefits—and challenges—of conducting rigorous longitudinal research to better understand careers, along with tips on how to address some of these challenges. Although hearing cautionary advice from your dissertation chair like, "You'd better get this right," could make you burst into tears (as it did for Shoshana!), we nonetheless encourage you to undertake the amazing journey of conducting longitudinal research, even for your dissertation. Both of us have done it, and so, too, can you. We fully acknowledge that doing longitudinal research, especially over the long term, can sometimes seem, to put it bluntly, crazy, but it is also completely worth doing. The caveat here is when you make the decision to launch a longitudinal study, it should be for a real research purpose, not simply because you think you need this type of data to get published. Longitudinal research can offer insights into career phenomena in a way no other research methodology can. It can also be very powerful in your own career for helping you establish a clear research identity.

An exciting aspect of longitudinal research on careers is that no matter what career stage you choose to focus on in your study, your participants will likely be facing significant questions about what the next steps in their careers—and lives—will be. As a result, any given data collection is truly a journey into the lives of your participants. At the end of each data collection, you, as a researcher, are left with a cliffhanger about what will happen next. This is the blessing and curse of longitudinal research: each new answer or insight leads to numerous new questions. This sets the stage for an ongoing research program, where, ultimately, only time will tell.

NOTE

1. We add a cautionary note that our use of a difference score to model change in this paper reflected guidance at that point in time (early to mid 2000s), where readers were not assumed to have been exposed to analytical approaches (e.g., multilevel analyses) appropriate for analyzing three or more waves of data, as they are currently. We *do not encourage* future research to use difference scores (Edwards, 2001).

REFERENCES

Arthur, M. B., & Rousseau, D. M. (1996). Introduction: The boundaryless career as a new employment principle. In M. B. Arthur & D. M. Rousseau (Eds.), *The Boundaryless Career: A New Employment Principle for a New Organizational Era* (pp. 3–20). New York, NY: Oxford University Press.
Bamberger, P. A., & Pratt, M. G. (2010). Moving forward by looking back: Reclaiming unconventional research contexts and samples in organizational scholarship. *Academy of Management Journal, 53*(4), 665–671.
Barley, S. R. (1989). Careers, identities, and institutions: The legacy of the Chicago School of Sociology. In M. B. Arthur, D. T. Hall & B. S. Lawrence (Eds.), *Handbook of Career Theory* (pp. 41–65). New York, NY: Cambridge University Press.
Bono, J. E., & McNamara, G. (2011). From the editors: Publishing in AMJ—Part 2: Research design. *Academy of Management Journal, 54*(4), 657–660.
Boswell, W. R., Boudreau, J. W., & Tichy, J. (2005). The relationship between employee job change and job satisfaction: The honeymoon-hangover effect. *Journal of Applied Psychology, 90*(5), 882–892.

Boswell, W. R., Shipp, A. J., Payne, S. C., & Culbertson, S. S. (2009). Changes in new-comer job satisfaction over time: Examining the pattern of honeymoons and hangovers. *Journal of Applied Psychology, 94*(4), 844–858.

Bunderson, J. S., & Thompson, J. A. (2009). The call of the wild: Zookeepers, callings, and the double-edged sword of deeply meaningful work. *Administrative Science Quarterly, 54*(1), 32–57. doi: 10.2189/asqu.2009.54.1.32

Center for Open Science. (2017). A brief history of COS, from https://cos.io/about/briefhistory-cos-2013-2017/

Creed, P. A., Kjoelaas, S., & Hood, M. (2016). Testing a goal-orientation model of antecedents to career calling. *Journal of Career Development, 43*(5), 398–412. doi: 10.1177/0894845315603822

Dobrow Riza, S., Ganzach, Y., & Liu, Y. (2018). Job satisfaction over time: A longitudinal study of the differential roles of age and tenure. *Journal of Management, 44*(7), 2558–2579.

Dobrow Riza, S., & Heller, D. (2015). Follow your heart or your head? A longitudinal study of calling and ability in the pursuit of a challenging career. *Journal of Applied Psychology, 100*(3), 695–712. doi: dx.doi.org/10.1037/a0038011

Dobrow Riza, S., & Higgins, M. C. (2019). The dynamics of developmental networks. *Academy of Management Discoveries, 5*(3), 221–250. doi: https://doi.org/10.5465/amd.2013.0029

Dobrow Riza, S., Weisman, H., Heller, D., & Tosti-Kharas, J. (2019). *Calling attention to 20 years of research: A comprehensive meta-analysis of calling.* Best Papers Proceedings of the Academy of Management Conference, Boston, MA.

Dobrow, S. R. (2013). Dynamics of calling: A longitudinal study of musicians. *Journal of Organizational Behavior, 34*(4), 431–452. doi: 10.1002/job.1808

Dobrow, S. R., & Higgins, M. C. (2005). Developmental networks and professional identity: A longitudinal study. *Career Development International, 10*(6/7), 567–583. doi: 10.1108/13620430510620629

Dobrow, S. R., & Tosti-Kharas, J. (2011). Calling: The development of a scale measure. *Personnel Psychology, 64*(4), 1001–1049. doi: 10.1111/j.1744-6570.2011.01234.x

Dobrow, S. R., & Tosti-Kharas, J. (2012). Listen to your heart? Calling and receptivity to career advice. *Journal of Career Assessment, 20*(3), 264–280. doi: 10.1177/1069072711434412

Edwards, J. R. (2001). Ten difference score myths. *Organizational Research Methods, 4*(3), 265–287.

Eisenhardt, K. M. (1989). Building theories from case study research. *Academy of Management Review, 14*, 532–550.

Erikson, E. H. (1963). *Childhood and Society.* New York, NY: Norton.

Felps, W., Mitchell, T. R., Hekman, D. R., Lee, T. W., Holtom, B. C., & Harman, W. S. (2009). Turnover contagion: How coworkers' job embeddedness and job search behaviors influence quitting. *Academy of Management Journal, 52*(3), 545–561.

George, J. M., & Jones, G. R. (2000). The role of time in theory and theory building. *Journal of Management, 26*(4), 657–684.

Ginzberg, E. (1951). *Occupational Choice: An Approach to a General Theory.* New York, NY: Columbia University Press.

Glaser, B. G., & Strauss, A. L. (1967). *The Discovery of Grounded Theory: Strategies for Qualitative Research.* Chicago, IL: Aldine Publishing Company.

Grant, A. M., & Wall, T. D. (2009). The neglected science and art of quasi-experimentation: Why-to, when-to, and how-to advice for organizational researchers. *Organizational Research Methods, 12*(4), 653–686.

Hall, D. T. (2002). *Careers In and Out of Organizations.* Thousand Oaks, CA: Sage Publications.

Haynie, J. M., & Shepherd, D. (2011). Toward a theory of discontinuous career transition: Investigating career transitions necessitated by traumatic life events. *Journal of Applied Psychology*, *96*(3), 501–524. doi: https://doi.org/10.1037/a0021450

Higgins, M. C., Dobrow, S. R., & Chandler, D. E. (2008). Never quite good enough: The paradox of sticky developmental relationships for elite university graduates. *Journal of Vocational Behavior*, *72*(2), 207–224. doi: 10.1016/j.jvb.2007.11.011

Higgins, M. C., Dobrow, S. R., & Roloff, K. S. (2010). Optimism and the boundaryless career: The role of developmental relationships. *Journal of Organizational Behavior*, *31*, 749–769. doi: 10.1002/job.693

Holland, J. L. (1997). *Making Vocational Choices: A Theory of Vocational Personalities and Work Environments* (3rd edn.). Englewood Cliffs, NJ: Prentice Hall.

Ibarra, H. (1999). Provisional selves: Experimenting with image and identity in professional adaptation. *Administrative Science Quarterly*, *44*, 764–791.

Ibarra, H., & Barbulescu, R. (2010). Identity as narrative: Prevalence, effectiveness, and consequences of narrative identity work in macro work role transitions. *Academy of Management Review*, *35*(1), 135–154.

Kroger, J. (2007). *Identity Development: Adolescence Through Adulthood* (2nd edn.). Thousand Oaks, CA: Sage Publications.

Langley, A. (1999). Strategies for theorizing from process data. *Academy of Management Review*, *24*(4), 691–710.

Langley, A., Smallman, C., Tsoukas, H., & Van de Ven, A. H. (2013). Process studies of change in organization and management: Unveiling temporality, activity, and flow. *Academy of Management Journal*, *56*(1), 1–13.

Lee, T. W., Mitchell, T. R., & Sablynski, C. J. (1999). Qualitative research in organizational and vocational psychology, 1979–1999. *Journal of Vocational Behavior*, *55*(2), 161–187.

Levinson, D. J., Darrow, C. N., Klein, E. B., Levinson, M. H., & McKee, B. (1978). *The Seasons of a Man's Life*. New York, NY: Knopf.

Lifshitz-Assaf, H. (2018). Dismantling knowledge boundaries at NASA: The critical role of professional identity in open innovation. *Administrative Science Quarterly*, *63*(4), 746–782.

London, M. (1983). Toward a theory of career motivation. *Academy of Management Review*, *8*(4), 620–630.

Maitlis, S. (2009). Who am I now? Sensemaking and identity in posttraumatic growth. In L. Morgan Roberts & J. Dutton (Eds.), *Exploring Positive Identities and Organizations: Building a Theoretical and Research Foundation* (pp. 47–76). New York, NY: Psychology Press.

Mitchell, T. R., & James, L. R. (2001). Building better theory: Time and the specification of when things happen. *Academy of Management Review*, *26*, 530–547.

Ng, T. W. H., & Feldman, D. C. (2010). The relationships of age with job attitudes: A meta-analysis. *Personnel Psychology*, *63*(3), 677–718. doi: 10.1111/j.1744-6570.2010.01184.x

O'Keefe, P. A., Dweck, C. S., & Walton, G. M. (2018). Implicit theories of interest: Finding your passion or developing it? *Psychological Science*, *29*(10), 1653–1664.

Petriglieri, G., Petriglieri, J. L., & Wood, J. D. (2018). Fast tracks and inner journeys: Crafting portable selves for contemporary careers. *Administrative Science Quarterly*, *63*(3), 479–525.

Pettigrew, A. M. (1990). Longitudinal field research on change: Theory and practice. *Organization Science*, *1*(3), 267–292.

Ployhart, R. E., & Vandenberg, R. J. (2010). Longitudinal research: The theory, design, and analysis of change. *Journal of Management*, *36*(1), 94–120.

Podsakoff, P. M., MacKenzie, S. B., Lee, J. Y., & Podsakoff, N. P. (2003). Common method biases in behavioral research: A critical review of the literature and recommended remedies. *Journal of Applied Psychology*, *88*(5), 879–903. doi: 10.1037/0021-9010.88.5.879

Pratt, M. G. (2000). The good, the bad, and the ambivalent: Managing identification among Amway distributors. *Administrative Science Quarterly*, *45*(3), 456–493.

Pratt, M. G., Rockmann, K., & Kaufmann, J. (2006). Constructing professional identity: The role of work and identity learning cycles in the customization of identity among medical residents. *Academy of Management Journal*, *49*(2), 235–262.

Rhodes, S. R. (1983). Age-related differences in work attitudes and behavior: A review and conceptual analysis. *Psychological Bulletin*, *93*(2), 328–367.

Rogers, M. E., Creed, P. A., & Glendon, A. I. (2008). The role of personality in adolescent career planning and exploration: A social cognitive perspective. *Journal of Vocational Behavior*, *73*(1), 132–142.

Salamon, S. D., & Robinson, S. L. (2008). Trust that binds: The impact of collective felt trust on organizational performance. *Journal of Applied Psychology*, *93*(3), 593–601. doi: 10.1037/0021-9010.93.3.593

Schein, E. H. (1978). *Career Dynamics: Matching Individual and Organizational Needs* (Vol. 24). Reading, MA: Addison-Wesley.

Shingles, R. (1985). Causal inference in cross-lagged panel analysis. In H. M. Blalock (Ed.), *Causal Models in Panel and Experimental Design* (pp. 219–250). New York, NY: Aldine.

Singer, J. D., & Willett, J. B. (2003). *Applied Longitudinal Data Analysis: Modeling Change and Event Occurrence*. New York, NY: Oxford University Press.

Snijders, T. A. B., & Bosker, R. J. (2011). *Multilevel Analysis: An Introduction to Basic and Advanced Multilevel Modeling* (2nd edn.). London: Sage Publications.

Sonnentag, S. (2012). Time in organizational research: Catching up on a long neglected topic in order to improve theory. *Organizational Psychology Review*, *2*(4), 361–368.

Spradley, J. P. (1979). *The Ethnographic Interview*. New York, NY: Holt, Rinehart & Winston.

Super, D. E. (1992). Toward a comprehensive theory of career development. In D. H. Montross & C. J. Shinkman (Eds.), *Career Development: Theory and Practice* (pp. 35–64). Springfield, IL: Charles C. Thomas.

Tackett, J. L., Brandes, C. M., & Reardon, K. W. (2019). Leveraging the Open Science Framework in clinical psychological assessment research. *Psychological Assessment*, *31*(12), 1386–1394.

Taylor, K., Marienau, C., & Fiddler, M. (2000). *Developing Adult Learners: Strategies for Teachers and Trainers*. San Francisco, CA: Jossey-Bass.

Vough, H. C., & Caza, B. B. (2017). Where do I go from here? Sensemaking and the construction of growth-based stories in the wake of denied promotions. *Academy of Management Review*, *42*(1), 103–128. doi: 10.5465/amr.2013.0177

Vroom, V. H. (1966). Organizational choice: A study of pre-and post-decision processes. *Organizational Behavior and Human Performance*, *1*(2), 212–225. doi: 10.1016/0030-5073(66)90013-4

Wanous, J. P. (1992). *Organizational Entry: Recruitment, Selection, and Socialization of Newcomers* (2nd edn.). Reading, MA: Addison-Wesley.

Weisman, H. (2019). *For better or for worse? Changing careers to pursue a calling*. Paper presented at the INFORMS/Organization Science Best Dissertation Proposal Competition, Seattle, WA.

Willett, J. B. (1989). Questions and answers in the measurement of change. *Journal of Research in Education*, *15*, 345–422.

Wright, T. A. (1997). Time revisited in organizational behavior. *Journal of Organizational Behavior*, *18*(3), 201–204.

Wrzesniewski, A., McCauley, C. R., Rozin, P., & Schwartz, B. (1997). Jobs, careers, and callings: People's relations to their work. *Journal of Research in Personality, 31*(1), 21–33. doi: 10.1006/jrpe.1997.2162

Yang, J., & Diefendorff, J. M. (2009). The relations of daily counterproductive workplace behavior with emotions, situational antecedents, and personality moderators: A diary study in Hong Kong. *Personnel Psychology, 62*(2), 259–295.

Zaheer, S., Albert, S., & Zaheer, A. (1999). Time scales and organizational theory. *Academy of Management Review, 24*(4), 725–741. doi: 10.5465/amr.1999.2553250

9. The role of social networks in contemporary careers

Jessica R. Methot and Scott E. Seibert

THE ROLE OF SOCIAL NETWORKS IN CONTEMPORARY CAREERS

Individuals are embedded in networks of personal and professional relationships. These networks create systems of information, contacts, and support; increase employees' visibility and exposure to opportunities; facilitate organizational sensemaking; and enhance skill development and learning capabilities that are crucial for career success (Lankau & Scandura, 2002; Whiting & de Janasz, 2004; Wolff & Moser, 2009). Networks also regulate access to mentorship and jobs, channel the flow of information and referrals, and boost individuals' reputations (Brass, 1984; Higgins & Kram, 2001; Ibarra, 1992). Not surprisingly, then, decades of research have demonstrated that who individuals are connected to, how they are connected, and the quality of those connections affect a range of career outcomes, including perceived potential for advancement, promotion rates, status, income attainment, mobility, and career satisfaction (Burt, 1997; Campbell, Marsden, & Hurlbert, 1986; Granovetter, 1973; Ibarra, 1995; Lin, Ensel, & Vaughn, 1981; Podolny & Baron, 1997; Wolff & Moser, 2009).

Career outcomes can encompass job search, career development, career transitions, and extrinsic or intrinsic career success. The underpinnings of the link between social networks and various career outcomes center on three pivotal theories: weak tie theory (Granovetter, 1973), structural holes theory (Burt, 1992), and social resources theory (Lin, 1999). These theories have laid the foundation for scholars to disentangle how *social capital*—the resources individuals access through their network connections—offers a critical complement to *human capital*—individuals' knowledge, skills, and capabilities—when predicting career outcomes. Importantly, though, the nature of careers is changing. With the rise of boundaryless careers and the gig economy, we are witnessing a dramatic decline in traditional, vertical, stable careers paths and less secure employment contracts. Where our relationships with organizations are becoming more transient, stable and reliable personal and professional relationships become more critical to our success and happiness.

Therefore, our goal for this chapter is to better articulate the role of social networks in the current career context and synthesize new perspectives on the role of social networks in driving career outcomes. We first offer a network primer with fundamentals about social network data and characteristics. Then, we overview the three foundational network theories that are traditionally applied to careers. Next, we introduce a framework of social network constructs that have been linked to career outcomes, including those that emerged as scholars sought to address the changing nature of work. We organize this framework around: (1) three network features—composition, configuration/structure, and content and (2) three network levels of analysis—dyadic, individual, and whole network (cf. Borgatti & Foster, 2003). Last, we identify future directions for scholars interested in exploring careers through a social network lens.

A SOCIAL NETWORK PRIMER

Social networks are comprised of a set of actors and ties connecting them (Borgatti & Foster, 2003). These ties act as conduits through which resources such as information, trust, advice, and support flow. In their typology of ties studied in network analysis, Borgatti, Mehra, Brass, and Labianca (2009) divided ties, or relations, into four types: (1) *similarities* (e.g., shared location, membership, or attribute), (2) *social relations* (e.g., kinship, affective, cognitive, or other roles such as "boss"), (3) *interactions* (e.g., helped or talked to), and (4) *flows* (e.g., information, resources). The pattern of these ties in a network (i.e., how actors are connected) yields a particular structure, and actors occupy positions within this structure.

There is also a distinction between *ego* (i.e., personal) and *whole* (i.e., organizational) networks. Individuals are embedded in ego networks, which index how their local or direct connections to other individuals (or, *alters*) to whom they are directly connected impact outcomes such as their career success. Burt, Kilduff, and Tasselli (2013) explain, "network structure can be studied as a proxy for the distribution of variably sticky information in a population, the network around ego indicates her advantaged or disadvantaged access and control in the distribution, and ego acting on her advantage is rewarded with recognition, compensation, and promotion" (p. 529). Collecting ego network data most often involves a questionnaire known as a name generator, where respondents are asked to indicate the names of alters in their personal or professional lives (e.g., coworkers, mentors, friends) and provide information about the nature of the relationship (e.g., friendship, mentor) and alter attributes (e.g., gender, race). Respondents then indicate whether the alters are connected (e.g., is A friends with B?), which provides the overall ego network structure. In this case, focal individuals are the only source of data about the connections in their network, and information is restricted to the ego's direct (i.e., first order) connections (Everett & Borgatti, 2005).

However, because most individuals are not directly connected to all others in a population (i.e., an organization), it can be useful to go beyond individuals' ego networks—which are subsets of the organizational population—to explore how the extent to which individuals are embedded in more macro-organizational network structures (including their direct and indirect connections) impacts their career outcomes. Whole network data can be collected in a variety of ways. Surveys are quite common, and often involve the use of the roster method where individuals are provided with a list of contacts that exist within the boundaries set by the researchers (e.g., an organization). Respondents will review the list of names and indicate the presence or absence (or strength) of particular types of ties with alters. Whole network data can also be gathered using methods such as wearable electronic sensors (Chaffin, Heidl, Hollenbeck, Howe, Yu, Voorhees, & Calantone, 2017) and what Leonardi and Contractor (2018) label "digital exhaust"—logs, e-trails, and contents of everyday digital activity such as email.

Social network data is frequently presented in the form of a matrix (though numerous other input forms are possible), where the rows represent the source of directed ties and the columns represent the targets (e.g., A nominated B as a friend). These matrices are then input into social network software (e.g., UCINET, R, Pajek), which apply mathematical routines to summarize and find patterns and produce network metrics. Network metrics can identify characteristics of an actor's location in a network (e.g., *centrality*), characteristics of the dyad (the relation between actors A and B, e.g., *homophily*), or characteristics of the overall network (e.g., *density*). We summarize common network metrics and their definitions in Table 9.1. Whereas ego networks offer the benefit of relatively less challenging data collection procedures compared to whole networks, the analytic techniques available are more limited because only local connections are reported. For example, metrics such as *third-party ties* and *transitivity* require information about the indirect connections between network actors. Notably, however, many metrics can be applied to both ego networks and whole networks. Metrics derived from ego networks can be based on individual network location such as *betweenness centrality* (i.e., the extent to which an individual lies on the shortest path between all other actors in a network), dyadic similarity in attributes between ego and their alters (e.g., homophily), and representations of the full ego network such as density (e.g., the degree to which alters are connected; Burt, 1992). In this way, even though ego networks are a reflection of an individual's personal network, it does not mean only individual-level metrics can be applied to their analysis.

NETWORK THEORY AND CAREERS

Network theories refer to the mechanisms and processes through which network structures yield outcomes for individuals and groups (i.e., the consequences of network variables; Borgatti & Halgin, 2011; Brass, 2002). There are three network theories that have consistently been employed to explain why networks generate career outcomes. Weak ties theory (Granovetter, 1973) centers on the notion that individuals' network ties vary in strength, where stronger ties are characterized by greater time, emotional intensity, and reciprocity investments. According to this theory, individuals' strong ties tend to be densely connected (i.e., all of our close contacts know each other because we frequently interact with them), whereas our weak ties act as bridges to diverse, extended networks of people. As a result, our strong ties produce redundant information, whereas our weak ties provide unique,

Table 9.1   Overview of common network metrics

Individual Measures	
In-degree centrality	Number of incoming ties an actor has (i.e., nominations from others; network size)
Out-degree centrality	Number of outgoing ties an actor has (i.e., nominations of others; network size)
Betweenness centrality	Extent to which an actor lies on the shortest path "between" all other actors in a network
Closeness centrality	The average of the shortest path length from the actor to every other actor in the network (i.e., how few links connect the actor to others)
Brokerage	Extent to which the actor bridges a structural hole, connecting otherwise disconnected others
Dyadic Measures	
Homophily	Similarity in attributes (e.g., gender, values) between ego and their alters
Equivalence	Extent to which two actors have similar network profiles (i.e., similar patterns of connections with alters)
Tie strength	Quality of the relationship between two actors; compared to weak ties (e.g., acquaintances), strong ties are characterized by greater emotional intensity, mutual confiding, and reciprocal exchange
Multiplexity	Coexistence of multiple types of relations simultaneously in a tie between two actors (e.g., task information *and* emotional support)
Triadic Measures	
Third-party ties	When two actors A and B are connected through a common third party C, but do not have a direct connection to each other (i.e., the friend of a friend)
Transitivity	Type of balance where, if A directs a tie to B, and B directs a tie to C, then A also directs a tie to C (e.g., a friend of a friend becomes a friend)
Network Measures	
Density	Percentage of ties that exist out of the total possible ties that could exist in a network (i.e., connectedness, or closure, of a network)
Structural holes	Extent to which disconnects between actors exist in the whole network

Note: Although we did not include triad level constructs in our framework, we define examples here to highlight key network tendencies that we reference in the chapter.

non-redundant information that can be beneficial for career outcomes such as mobility. In other words, individuals with more weak ties in their network gain an information advantage with respect to job market opportunities. Recent research has linked networks of weak ties with receipt of diverse and useful knowledge (Levin & Cross, 2004), greater creativity (Baer, 2010), and likelihood of CEO appointment (Wiersema, Nishimura, & Suzuki, 2018).

Weak tie theory focuses on the properties of individual ties (strength) and the number of such ties, but not the patterns of such ties. Focusing more explicitly on this structural aspect of social networks, structural holes theory (Burt, 1992) asserts that it is advantageous for individuals to be positioned as network brokers—or, a bridge—between two disconnected alters in their personal networks. According to this theory, individuals derive benefits from the "holes" in the pattern of their network ties. Specifically, networks rich in structural holes generate three primary benefits: access to timely information from a broad range of sources, greater bargaining power and control by exploiting the lack of connection between their network contacts, and greater visibility and career opportunities.

Social resource theory (or, social capital theory) purports that valuable resources are inherent in, accessible through, and derived from networks of informal relationships (Adler & Kwon, 2002; Leana & Van Buren, 1999). In other words, the value of the network is in the social resources of the alters it is able to reach. Networks serve as conduits of resources, and individuals who invest in social relations will have higher rates of return, often in the form of career advantages such as occupational prestige (Lin, 1999).

THE EVOLVING ROLE OF SOCIAL NETWORKS

The global workforce is increasingly characterized by non-traditional career trajectories (Kleinbaum, 2012), shorter organizational tenure (Twenge, 2010), irregular work schedules (Presser, 2003), and frequent role transitions (Ashforth, 2001; Ashforth & Saks, 1995). As a result, employees are constantly navigating a stream of newly hired coworkers, daily fluctuations in shift-based or contract personnel, and gaining and losing personal and professional contacts. For instance, approximately 30 percent of workers in the U.S. have an alternative work arrangement as their primary job, and more than 36 percent are in the gig economy, which includes independent contractors, online platform workers, on-call workers, and temporary workers (Gallup, 2018). These work arrangements can occur voluntarily (e.g., if an individual wants more flexibility, or sees limited growth potential in their organization) or involuntarily (e.g., as a function of layoffs). Further, the pressure to remain lean and agile has led organizations to be hesitant to sustain long-term relationships with employees whose skill sets might become outdated, leading to rises in job loss and declines in job stability (Greenhaus, Callanan, & DiRenzo, 2008).

What's more, many organizations, and in turn, traditional employment relationships, are experiencing disruptions as a result of digital transformations—the planning, implementation, and application of information technology for networking and supporting the interaction of at least two individual or collective actors to transform business operations (Marler & Fisher, 2013). This transformative change can be challenging to navigate effectively; as a result, since 2000, 52 percent of Fortune 500 companies have either gone bankrupt, been acquired, or ceased to exist as a result of digital disruption. Importantly, the digital transformation is changing the way individuals work and seek employment. Indeed, job seekers are moving to digital channels to find jobs, employees are using social platforms to express opinions, companies are providing smart technologies and applications through which employees can quickly and seamlessly communicate, and employees are receiving timely, accessible, and crowdsourced feedback through digital tools. Interestingly, scholars and practitioners alike are acknowledging that organizational network analysis (ONA) can help leaders successfully transform their businesses. For instance, more than 50 percent of individuals who are the most influential in an organization—the key opinion leaders (Burt, 1999) who can act as change agents—are unknown to management (Leonardi & Contractor, 2018), and with just 4 percent of influencers identified by ONA, management can reach about 70 percent of employees. From this perspective, individuals can maximize their networks as they navigate digitally mediated careers, and leverage their networks for strategic outcomes.

As the nature of careers evolves, so too does the role of social networks in career development and success. While social networks are generally vital for career outcomes, their value is magnified for individuals who are navigating dynamic and potentially competing social environments (Raider & Burt, 1996). In contexts without clearly defined procedures, or that require coordination with others within and outside an organization, social networks are key drivers of success. Individuals with alternative work arrangements have fewer relationships within their organizations (Gallup, 2018), which puts pressure on their external networks for support. For example, individuals in boundaryless careers are more frequently involved in job searches, which necessitates more frequent contact with network connections regarding career opportunities. People in boundaryless careers will depend on their contacts for accurate information about potential positions and prospective employers. Informal networks of connections help job seekers circumvent formal employment search processes by leveraging referrals, adding to the competitive advantage of individuals with boundary spanning, diverse network connections.

A MULTILEVEL FRAMEWORK OF CAREER-RELATED NETWORK CONSTRUCTS

There is mounting interest in incorporating principles from social network perspectives into the study of employment relationships (Soltis, Brass, & Lepak, 2018), and the development of social network analytic methods (i.e., organizational network analysis; ONA) has accelerated this trend (e.g., Hatala, 2006; Hollenbeck & Jamieson, 2015). Therefore, we see value in providing clarity around the evolving role of social networks in the changing nature of work. To this end, we develop a guiding framework to organize a breadth of network constructs—pointing a spotlight on more contemporary constructs and areas that could benefit from greater attention—to articulate the various ways social networks impact career outcomes.

This framework presents a combination of *relational features* and *relational levels of analysis*. With respect to relational features, the social network paradigm has established categories that define and arrange types of relationships into three groups (cf., Kaše, Paauwe, & Zupan, 2009; Methot, Rosado-Solomon, & Allen, 2018): network *composition*, network *configuration*, and network *content*. Network composition refers to the set of actors in a social network (i.e., *who* an individual is connected to), and includes constructs such as network size and homogeneity. Network configuration refers to the structural arrangement or pattern of relations among actors in a network (i.e., *how* actors are connected), and includes constructs such as structural holes and density. Network content refers to the properties characterizing a relation-

Table 9.2   Multilevel framework of career-related network constructs

	Dyad-level (e.g., n = 9,900 possible dyadic relationships among 100 individuals in a network)	Individual-level (e.g., n = 100 individuals in a network)	Network-level (e.g., n = 1 network)
Composition	(1) Homophily Referrals Dormant ties	(2) Degree centrality Job embeddedness (i.e., links) Networking behaviors	(3) Developmental networks
Configuration	(4) Structural equivalence	(5) Brokerage	(6) Structural holes/closure
Content	(7) Tie strength Multiplexity	(8) Social resources	(9) Social capital

Note: Several of these phenomena are purely network metrics that have been applied to career outcomes, whereas others are career-focused phenomena that are rooted in network methodology.

ship between two actors (i.e., *what* defines the relation), and includes constructs such as tie strength. With respect to levels of analysis, social networks are inherently multilevel (Brass, Galaskiewicz, Greve, & Tsai, 2004), spanning the *dyadic*, *individual*, and *whole network* levels. Importantly, levels of analysis in social networks (dyadic, individual, network) do not necessarily correspond to levels of organizational entities (individual, unit, firm) (cf. Borgatti & Foster, 2003). For instance, the network level can be an organizational unit (team, department) and/or the whole firm. In network analysis, sample size decreases from dyadic to individual to network level; dyad-level values are computed by $n*(n-1)$; individual-level values equal n, and network-level values equal 1 (Wasserman & Faust, 1994). Combining these categories, we present a table with nine cells that provide an organizing scheme for the various dyadic, individual, and network phenomena that impact career outcomes (Table 9.2). In the sections below, we introduce and review prominent network phenomena in each of the nine categories. Some of these phenomena are purely network metrics that have been applied to career outcomes, whereas others are career-focused phenomena that are rooted in network methodology.

Network Composition

Dyad-level

Beginning with network composition constructs that manifest at the dyad level, a salient characteristic is *homophily*—the tendency to interact with others who are similar on attributes such as gender, race, and education (McPherson, Smith-Lovin, & Cook, 2001). The principle underlying homophily is that attitudinal, behavioral, cultural, or material information that flows through networks will be localized, because similar individuals are more likely to interact with one another. Research demonstrates that, in the context of individuals' careers, there are gender differences in homophily. For example, Ibarra (1992) found that men were more likely to have networks characterized by greater homophily (i.e., friendship and instrumental networks that include ties to other men), whereas women have more differentiated (less homophilous) networks (i.e., friendship ties to other women, and instrumental ties to men). In turn, men derived greater returns on their network investments in the form of more valuable and central network positions.

A second dyad-level composition concept is *referrals*—a form of network-based hiring whereby current employees recommend candidates from their personal networks. Traditionally, referrals have been viewed positively in terms of promoting better career outcomes. For example, Fernandez and Weinberg (1997) found that job applicants who were referred by a current employee had more appropriate résumés and better-timed applications, were more likely to be interviewed, and were ultimately more likely to receive a job offer than non-referral-based applicants. They theorized that these effects functioned through the mechanisms of information—such that social ties communicate information that otherwise would not be available—and influence—such that current employees have an impact on the hiring decision. However, recent research suggests these advantages are not isomorphic across demographic groups. Indeed, Merluzzi and Sterling (2017) found that referral-based hiring had unique promotion advantages for minority groups, blacks in particular, compared to their counterparts not hired by referral. The authors suggest this may be because referrals provide vital signals of quality for black employees beginning with their entry into the organization, which can positively influence their evaluations during their tenure, and these signals can counteract potentially harmful biases associated with racial minorities.

A more contemporary network construct that taps who an individual is connected to is termed *dormant ties*. Coined by Levin, Walter, and Murnighan (2011), dormant ties are former ties with individuals to whom one is currently out of touch, but has the option for future reconnection. These authors explain that, while the majority of social networks research suggests that ties must be maintained, and continue to be activated, in order to retain value, losing touch with our connections is incredibly common. They make an important distinction between dormancy and tie strength, noting that tie strength involves the perceived closeness that has accumulated over the life of a relationship, whereas the time that has elapsed since the last interaction determines whether a tie is active or dormant. In other words, "both strong and weak ties can become dormant" (Levin et al., 2011, p. 924). Research has found that rekindling dormant professional relationships can offer tremendous career benefits to executives. For instance, Levin and colleagues (2011) asked employees to choose two people with whom they had not communicated for at least three years, including someone with whom they once had a close or strong relationship and someone with whom they once had a weak or distant relationship, who "might provide information, knowledge, or advice that would help you [on] a major, ongoing work project that has significance for your career." They found that reconnections conferred benefits typically associated with both strong and weak ties, including that they efficiently provided useful information, provided access to novel insights, and retained the foundations of trust and shared perspectives. They also found that weak dormant ties were nearly as valuable as strong dormant ties. Thus, similar to the value of weak ties in providing novel, non-redundant insights, dormant ties can prove valuable for access to information that can benefit individuals' careers (Walter, Levin, & Murnighan, 2016).

Individual-level

A prominent composition concept at the individual level is *embeddedness*. This phenomenon has been approached primarily by two siloed camps. From a social network perspective, Granovetter (1985) coined the term embeddedness to capture the network constraints and opportunities that shape actors' decisions. Along these lines, Uzzi (1996) posited that individuals' degree of embeddedness in a social network impacts performance by facilitating trust, resource pooling, cooperation, and coordinated adaptation. In a separate camp, turnover scholars have developed rich theory around embeddedness, defined as the feeling of being "stuck" or "enmeshed in a web of relationships," and comprises a person's fit, links, and sacrifice (Mitchell, Holtom, Lee, Sablynski, & Erez, 2001). Most relevant to our relational perspective is the "links" dimension, which is characterized as the formal or informal connections (e.g., work and nonwork friends, community groups) between a person and others—in other words, who individuals are connected to. Indeed, research shows that embeddedness mitigates the influence of job search effort (Swider, Boswell, & Zimmerman, 2011) and unsolicited-job-offers (Mitchell & Lee, 2001) on turnover.

A second individual-level composition phenomenon involves networking behaviors (or, the act of social *networking*), which refers to "the building and nurturing of personal and professional relationships to create a system of information, contacts, and support thought to be crucial for career and personal success" (Casciaro, Gino, & Kouchaki, 2014, p. 706). Networking can involve joining prestigious professional associations, connecting with highly visible people in our organizations, or participating in social events (e.g., Forret & Dougherty, 2004). Building, maintaining, and leveraging relationships is a core competency for any professional or job seeker (Kuwabara, Hildebrand, & Zou, 2018). For example, Forret and Dougherty (2004) found that, controlling for human capital factors such as work experience and educational background, networking behaviors that involved engaging in professional activities (e.g., attending conferences, accepting speaking engagements) and increasing internal visibility (e.g., accepting visible work assignments, going to lunch with a current supervisor) were positively associated with number of promotions, total compensation, and perceived career success. Similarly, Wolff and Moser (2009) adopted a dynamic perspective on the effects of networking on career success; specifically, in a longitudinal study, they assessed networking with six subscales: building internal contacts, maintaining internal contacts, using internal contacts, building external contacts, maintaining external contacts, and using external contacts. They found that, over three consecutive years, networking was related to concurrent salary and the growth rate of salary over time.

Network-level

A valuable network-level composition phenomenon is *developmental networks*—a constellation of individuals who take an active interest in and action to advance one's career (Higgins & Kram, 2001). Given the breadth of the developmental networks concept, we will note that it can also arguably fall into other categories in our framework, including individual-level composition (with its focus on the position of an individual in their ego-network), configuration (with its focus on the structure of connections), or content (with its focus on what resources developers are providing). However, we position them here because network-level metrics such as density can be applied, and developmental networks are also comprised of "who" is in the network (i.e., the number of different social systems—such as work, community, or professional organizations—the relationships stem from).

Traditionally, mentoring relationships were considered formal, one-on-one interactions whereby a senior individual conferred coaching, guidance, and visibility to less experienced junior colleagues (e.g., Allen, Eby, Poteet, Lentz, & Lima, 2004; Fagenson, 1989). However, several trends linked to the changing nature of careers have prompted a re-evaluation of formal mentoring. Individuals need to look beyond their employing organization to multiple relationships that can anchor their personal and professional identities (Thomas & Higgins, 1996); boundaryless careers, virtual work, and flatter organizational structures constrain the reliance on a single mentor inside one's organization (Hall, 1996); the rapid pace of change in digital technologies has increased the importance of knowledge workers who can draw from multiple sources for information; and the increasing diversity of organizational members suggests that minorities may be more successful when drawing from multiple people for assistance (Thomas & Gabarro, 1999). The developmental networks literature is informed by the social network paradigm and, thus, these networks are characterized by the strength of the relationships (weak vs. strong) and the diversity of the relationships (spanning few or many different social domains) (Higgins & Kram, 2001). Research shows that developmental networks are vital for achieving a variety of career outcomes, including promotion and career advancement (Singh, Ragins, & Tharenou, 2009) and clarity of one's professional identity (Dobrow & Higgins, 2005). However, we will limit our discussion of developmental networks, as more detail will be provided in Chapter 8 of this book.

Network Configuration

Dyad-level

A relevant network configuration (i.e., how individuals are connected) construct is *structural equivalence*, or the extent to which two individuals have similar network profiles (i.e., that they have similar patterns of connections with alters). There is very little research focusing on the role of equivalence on career outcomes, yet we see promising areas for scholars to explore. First, a key characteristic of equivalent actors is that they can be considered substitutable for one another in the network (Burt, 1976). On one hand, this may send a signal to the equivalent actors that they have redundant skills and are not adding unique value to the organization. In turn, equivalent actors may be motivated to seek alternative employment opportunities. On the other hand, individuals look to equivalent actors for cues about effective behaviors (Ibarra, 1999), which can aid with decision-making, adaptation, organizational learning and, ultimately, career success.

Individual-level

A prominent network construct that represents an individual's location in a network of ties is *brokerage*. Brokerage is the act of coordinating across a structural hole (i.e., two individuals or groups who are disconnected; Burt, 2004); in other words, brokers build bridges between otherwise disconnected parts of a network where it is valuable to do so. Individuals in brokerage positions are advantaged in at least three ways: information breadth, timing, and arbitrage (Burt et al., 2013). First, and consistent with weak ties theory, brokers' networks have greater breadth because they have access to non-redundant information from diverse contacts. Next, brokers are "positioned at a crossroads in the flow of information between groups" (Burt et al., 2013, p. 531) so they will access information early, and be more likely to be a first-mover in diffusing that information to others (i.e., key opinion leaders; Burt, 1999). Last, brokers are in a unique position to know when it would be rewarding to bring disconnected groups together, giving a disproportionate weight to whose interests are served.

Burt and colleagues (2013) provide a comprehensive review of the various metrics that distinguish different brokerage characteristics in a network. For instance, network *density* is the average strength of a connection between an individual's contacts (i.e., the number of existing connections divided by the total possible number of connections); greater network density suggests communication between actors is more frequent and influential, there are more shared norms and trust, and individuals in the network share similar views (Burt, 2005). Another is "non-redundant contacts," a count of ego's contacts discounting those that are redundant with other contacts; this is a measure of accessing unique knowledge in a network. A final example is Freeman's (1977) *betweenness* index, which captures the structural holes to which an individual has sole access, and is a proxy for access to diverse information. All these metrics assess the extent to which an individual's location in the network facilitates decoding and encoding of information to move it between clusters of others. As a result of their network positions, brokers have marked career advantages. Relative to individuals in closed networks, brokers experience greater bonus compensation, industry recognition, higher annual evaluations, and faster rates of promotion (see Burt, 2005, 2010 for reviews). Similarly, in their meta-analysis of personality, network position and career outcomes, Fang, Landis, Zhang, Anderson, Shaw, and Kilduff (2015) found that controlling for indegree centrality (i.e., the number of nominations by alters), brokerage in an instrumental, or workflow, network was a significant predictor of overall career success, defined as the achievement of objectively observable outcomes such as promotion and compensation. However, the pitfalls of bridging ties are that they are difficult to maintain and susceptible to decay, because they are subject to short-term cost–benefit analysis and are not protected by mutuality found in close, trusting relationships (Burt, 2010).

Network-level

At the network level, *structural holes* confer the same benefits to individuals as the phenomena of brokerage and weak ties. People on either side of the hole circulate in different flows of information. Significant differences in understanding are more likely to occur between people in separate clusters than between people in the same cluster. As such, the value-potential of structural holes is that they define non-redundant sources of information, sources that are more additive than overlapping. However, there is also value in networks characterized by closure. For example, Rousseau, Sitkin, Burt, and Camerer (1998) argued for the value of closure and trust, and being within a network of trust presumably helps one advance in organizations.

Network Content

Dyad-level
As we noted earlier, *tie strength*—specifically, weak tie theory (Granovetter, 1973)—is one of the foundational theories linking social networks and career outcomes. Tie strength captures the nature of the relationship between two individuals, where strong ties are characterized by a greater amount of time, emotional intensity, mutual confiding, and reciprocal services (Granovetter, 1973). Strong ties typically involve positive interpersonal interactions and emotions and a genuine sense of relatedness and mutuality, where both parties improve and enrich each other's experiences (Dutton & Heaphy, 2003). They are considered more intimate, flexible, and resilient (Eby & Allen, 2012), are marked by heightened vitality (Dutton & Heaphy, 2003), are free of calculative or instrumental norms (Silver, 1990), and can withstand strain even when faced with demanding circumstances (Dutton & Heaphy, 2003). Despite these clear benefits, research has adopted the view that weak ties are more valuable for career outcomes related to job search success and mobility for at least two reasons (Granovetter, 1973). Specifically, first, strong ties have a tendency toward *transitivity*, whereby individuals are more likely to interact with others to whom their alters have strong ties (e.g., a social preference to become friends with your friends' friends). As a result, strong ties tend to exist in densely connected networks, where individuals share commonly held information. In contrast, weak ties act as bridges across clusters of densely connected groups, allowing for access to non-redundant information. Second, because parties in strong relationships spend continued time together, information in the group becomes "sticky," or difficult to transmit to other groups (Von Hippel, 1994). Given that the foundational theoretical

explanations are similar, the career benefits of weak ties are comparable to those for brokerage we discussed earlier.

Additionally, *mentoring relationships* are primarily defined by the types of resources or support mentors provide to protégés, situating them as a network content phenomenon at the dyad level. Specifically, mentoring relationships can provide career support (e.g., sponsorship, protection, visibility) and/or psychosocial support (e.g., acceptance and confirmation, friendship, personal feedback) (Dobrow, Chandler, Murphy, & Kram, 2012; Janssen, van Vuuren, & de Jong, 2013; Kram & Isabella, 1985). For instance, Higgins (2007) developed a framework of developer types that are categorized by the extent to which they provide low to high levels of career support, and low to high levels of psychosocial support. This provides a distinction between "true mentors" (those who provide high amounts of both career and psychosocial support), "sponsors" (those who provide high levels of career but low levels of psychosocial support), "friends" (those who provide high levels of psychosocial but low levels of career support), and "allies" (those who provide low levels of each).

Mentoring and developmental relationships characterized by *multiplexity*—the coexistence of both career and psychosocial support—are of particular interest in the context of contemporary careers because professional development occurs within a dynamic, relational context (Dobrow Riza & Higgins, 2019). Multiplex relationships providing both career and psychosocial support are "more indispensable, more critical to development" than other relationships (Kram, 1985, p. 24) and may have unique effects on career success beyond relations involving either independently (Shapiro, Hom, Shen, & Agarwal, 2016). Cotton, Shen, and Livne-Tarandach (2011) conceptualized three forms of multiplexity between mentors and mentees: relationships containing more than one type of career support, more than one type of psychosocial support, and both career support and psychosocial support (or, "hybrid multiplexity," p. 19). In their study of baseball hall of famers, they found that the most successful athletes had large networks with both single-function and multiplex relationships.

Individual-level

In a seminal integration of the weak ties, structural holes, and social resources perspectives, Seibert, Kraimer, and Liden (2001) developed a social capital theory of career success in which they position two network constructs—weak ties and structural holes—as related forms of social resources. Specifically, they assessed the extent to which individuals were connected to developmental alters who, "have acted to help your career by speaking on your behalf, providing you with information, career opportunities, advice or psychological support or with whom you have regularly spoken regarding difficulties at work, alternative job opportunities, or long-term career goals" (p. 227). They found that weak ties and structural holes in individuals' networks predicted salary, promotions over one's career, and career satisfaction through their effects on access to information, access to resources, and career sponsorship.

Network-level

The guiding tenet of the social capital perspective is that patterns of interactions and goodwill mobilize the transmission of resources such as information, influence, and solidarity that drive individual and organizational effectiveness (Adler & Kwon, 2002; Nahapiet & Ghoshal, 1998). In other words, social capital refers to the value individuals derive from their personal connections. Social capital can be internal (resources from relationships with coworkers) or external (the information benefits from ties employees have with those outside their organization, e.g., friends, family members, nonwork acquaintances; see Adler & Kwon, 2002 for a review).

AVENUES FOR FUTURE RESEARCH

Taken together, it becomes clear that some areas have been more heavily studied, whereas others are ripe for future research development. For example, while there is ample research focusing on phenomena at the dyadic- and individual-levels of analysis, less attention has been paid to applying traditional network level metrics, such as density and centralization, to career-related outcomes. Below, we highlight some potential avenues for scholars interested in applying network analytic techniques to contemporary careers.

For example, embeddedness is particularly relevant in contemporary careers because individuals need to remain employable in volatile economies by engaging in ongoing cycles of job search activities. For individuals in boundaryless careers, job search is a cyclical, self-regulatory process; they access information from others during the job search process that enables them to sharpen their understanding of the labor market and refine their perceptions of their employability over time (Steel, 2002). However, those who are more embedded in their organizations are less likely to quit, which can compromise their continued development of career competencies and, ultimately, their mobility (Direnzo & Greenhaus, 2011).

Interestingly, Kleinbaum (2012) examined the precursors to brokerage positions in the context of non-traditional career trajectories. Traditional perspectives on career trajectories involve a simple sequence of jobs held over time, typically with upward movement. Contemporary, or non-traditional, career trajectories involve more diverse career histories where mobility is not necessarily upward, including lateral or industry shifts that are seen as career-enhancing because it broadens and deepens one's human capital (Wexley & Latham, 2002). In his study of career history data for 30,000 employees in a large technology firm over six years, Kleinbaum (2012) found that individuals following more diverse, atypical career paths are more likely to ultimately occupy advantageous brokerage positions that benefit their careers because they connect parts of the organization that are rarely linked.

As a final example, recent research challenges the well-established notion that weak ties are the key to job mobility. Driven by the increased use of mobile, web-based, and social media platforms to find jobs, individuals are no longer relying on weak ties—in fact, in a recent study, Gershon (2017) found that of 141 job seekers who reported that networking helped them find a job, only 17 percent indicated that weak ties were the reason (compared to 83.4 percent in Granovetter's (1973) study). With a steady and accessible stream of information about job opportunities, research can shift toward examining how the digital transformation is impacting how individuals utilize their networks to achieve successful job search outcomes.

CONCLUSION

While social networks are generally vital for career outcomes, their value is magnified for individuals navigating boundaryless careers, alternative work arrangements, and dynamic and potentially competing social environments. In this chapter, we present a framework that combines relational features and relational levels of analysis to clarify the evolving role of social networks, and social network analysis, in the changing nature of work. We organize a breadth of network metrics to synthesize the existing literature, and spotlight contemporary constructs and areas that could benefit from greater attention. Taken together, social network analysis provides a rich methodological and theoretical toolbox for advancing the link between personal and professional networks and career outcomes.

REFERENCES

Adler, P. S., & Kwon, S. (2002). Social capital: Prospects for a new concept. *Academy of Management Review, 27*(1), 17–40. doi: 10.5465/AMR.2002.5922314

Allen, T. D., Eby, L. T., Poteet, M. L., Lentz, E., & Lima, L. (2004). Career benefits associated with mentoring for protégés: A meta-analysis. *Journal of Applied Psychology, 89*(1), 127–136. doi: 10.1037/0021-9010.89.1.127

Ashforth, B. E. (2001). *Role transitions in organizational life: An identity-based perspective.* Mahwah, NJ: Routledge.

Ashforth, B. E., & Saks, A. M. (1995). Work-role transitions: A longitudinal examination of the Nicholson model. *Journal of Occupational and Organizational Psychology, 68*(2), 157–175. doi: 10.1111/j.2044-8325.1995.tb00579.x

Baer, M. (2010). The strength-of-weak-ties perspective on creativity: A comprehensive examination and extension. *Journal of Applied Psychology, 95*(3), 592–601. doi: 10.1037/a0018761

Borgatti, S. P., & Foster, P. C. (2003). The network paradigm in organizational research: A review and typology. *Journal of Management, 29*(6), 991–1013. doi: 10.1016/S0149-2063(03)00087-4

Borgatti, S. P., & Halgin, D. S. (2011). On network theory. *Organization Science, 22*(5), 1168–1181. doi: 10.1287/orsc.1100.0641

Borgatti, S. P., Mehra, A., Brass, D. J., & Labianca, G. (2009). Network analysis in the social sciences. *Science, 323*(5916), 892–895. doi: 10.1126/science.1165821

Brass, D. J. (1984). Being in the right place: A structural analysis of individual influence in an organization. *Administrative Science Quarterly, 29*(4), 518–539. doi: 10.2307/2392937

Brass, D. J. (2002). Social networks in organizations: Antecedents and consequences. *Unpublished manuscript: University of Kentucky.*

Brass, D. J., Galaskiewicz, J., Greve, H., & Tsai, W. (2004). Taking stock of networks and organizations: A multilevel perspective. *Academy of Management Journal, 47*(6), 795–817. doi: 10.2307/20159624

Burt, R. S. (1976). Positions in networks. *Social Forces, 55*(1), 93–122. doi: 10.1093/sf/55.1.93

Burt, R. S. (1992). *Structural holes: The social structure of competition.* Cambridge, MA: Harvard University Press.

Burt, R. S. (1997). Contingent value of social capital. *Administrative Science Quarterly, 42*(2), 339–365. doi: 10.1037/0011646

Burt, R. S. (1999). Entrepreneurs, distrust, and third parties. In L. Thompson, J. Levine, & D. Messick (Eds.), *Shared cognition in organizations: The management of knowledge* (pp. 213–243). Mahwah, NJ: Lawrence Erlbaum Associates.

Burt, R. S. (2004). Structural holes and good ideas. *American Journal of Sociology, 110*(2), 349–399. doi: 10.1086/421787

Burt, R. S. (2005). *Brokerage and closure: An introduction to social capital.* New York: Oxford University Press.

Burt, R. S. (2010). *Neighbor networks: Competitive advantage local and personal.* New York: Oxford University Press.

Burt, R. S., Kilduff, M., & Tasselli, S. (2013). Social network analysis: Foundations and frontiers on advantage. *Annual Review of Psychology, 64,* 527–547. doi: 10.1146/annurev-psych-113011-143828

Campbell, K. E., Marsden, P. V., & Hurlbert, J. S. (1986). Social resources and socioeconomic status. *Social Networks, 8*(1), 97–117. doi: 10.1016/S0378-8733(86)80017-X

Casciaro, T., Gino, F., & Kouchaki, M. (2014). The contaminating effects of building instrumental ties: How networking can make us feel dirty. *Administrative Science Quarterly, 59*(4), 705–735. doi: 10.1177/0001839214554990

Chaffin, D., Heidl, R., Hollenbeck, J. R., Howe, M., Yu, A., Voorhees, C., & Calantone, R. (2017). The promise and perils of wearable sensors in organizational research. *Organizational Research Methods, 20*(1), 3–31. doi: 10.1177/1094428115617004

Cotton, R. D., Shen, Y., & Livne-Tarandach, R. (2011). On becoming extraordinary: The content and structure of the developmental networks of major league baseball hall of famers. *Academy of Management Journal, 54*(1), 15–46. doi: 10.5465/amj.2011.59215081

Direnzo, M. S., & Greenhaus, J. H. (2011). Job search and voluntary turnover in a boundaryless world: A control theory perspective. *Academy of Management Review, 36*(3), 567–589. doi: 10.5465/amr.2009.0333

Dobrow, S. R., Chandler, D. E., Murphy, W. M., & Kram, K. E. (2012). A review of developmental networks: Incorporating a mutuality perspective. *Journal of Management, 38*(1), 210–242. doi: 10.1177/0149206311415858

Dobrow, S. R., & Higgins, M. C. (2005). Developmental networks and professional identity: A longitudinal study. *Career Development International, 10*(6/7), 567–583. doi: 10.1108/13620430510620629

Dobrow Riza, S., & Higgins, M. C. (2019). The dynamics of developmental networks. *Academy of Management Discoveries, 5*(3), 221–250. https://doi.org/10.5465/amd.2013.0029

Dutton, J. E., & Heaphy, E. D. (2003). The power of high-quality connections. In J. E. Dutton, R. E. Quinn, & K. S. Cameron (Eds.), *Positive organizational scholarship: Foundations of a new discipline* (pp. 263–278). San Francisco, CA: Berrett-Koehler Publishers.

Eby, L. T., & Allen, T. D. (2012). *Personal relationships: The effect on employee attitudes, behavior, and well-being.* New York: Taylor & Francis.

Everett, M., & Borgatti, S. P. (2005). Ego network betweenness. *Social Networks, 27,* 31–38.

Fagenson, E. A. (1989). The mentor advantage: Perceived career/job experiences of protégés versus non-protégés. *Journal of Organizational Behavior, 10*(4), 309–320. doi: 10.1002/job.4030100403

Fang, R., Landis, B., Zhang, Z., Anderson, M. H., Shaw, J. D., & Kilduff, M. (2015). Integrating personality and social networks: A meta-analysis of personality, network position, and work outcomes in organizations. *Organization Science, 26*(4), 1243–1260. doi: 10.1287/orsc.2015.0972

Fernandez, R. M., & Weinberg, N. (1997). Sifting and sorting: Personal contacts and hiring in a retail bank. *American Sociological Review, 62*(6), 883–902. doi: 10.2307/2657345

Forret, M. L., & Dougherty, T. W. (2004). Networking behaviors and career outcomes: Differences for men and women? *Journal of Organizational Behavior, 25*(3), 419–437. doi: 10.1002/job.253

Freeman, L. C. (1977). A set of measures of centrality based on betweenness. *Sociometry, 40*(1), 35–41. doi: 10.2307/3033543

Gallup (2018). The gig economy and alternative work arrangements. https://www.gallup.com/file/workplace/240878/Gig_Economy_Paper_2018.pdf. Accessed May 12, 2019.

Gershon, I. (2017). *Down and out in the new economy: How people find (or don't find) work today.* Chicago, IL: University of Chicago Press.

Granovetter, M. (1973). The strength of weak ties. *American Journal of Sociology, 78*(6), 1360–1380.

Granovetter, M. (1985). Economic action and social structure: The problem of embeddedness. *American Journal of Sociology, 91*(3), 481–510. doi: 10.1086/228311

Greenhaus, J. H., Callanan, G. A., & DiRenzo, M. (2008). A boundaryless perspective on careers. In J. Barling & C. L. Cooper (Eds.), *The Sage handbook of organizational behavior: Volume I micro approaches* (pp. 277–299). Thousand Oaks, CA: Sage Publications.

Hall, D. T. (1996). Protean careers of the 21st century. *Academy of Management Perspectives, 10*(4), 8–16.

Hatala, J.-P. (2006). Social network analysis in human resource development: A new methodology. *Human Resource Development Review, 5*(1), 45–71. doi: 10.1177/1534484305284318

Higgins, M. C. (2007). A contingency perspective on developmental networks. In J. E. Dutton & B. R. Ragins (Eds.), *Exploring positive relationships at work: Building a theoretical and research foundation* (pp. 207–224). Mahwah, NJ: Lawrence Erlbaum Associates Publishers.

Higgins, M. C., & Kram, K. E. (2001). Reconceptualizing mentoring at work: A developmental network perspective. *Academy of Management Review, 26*(2), 264–288. doi: 10.5465/amr.2001.4378023

Hollenbeck, J. R., & Jamieson, B. B. (2015). Human capital, social capital, and social network analysis: Implications for strategic human resource management. *Academy of Management Perspectives, 29*(3), 370–385. doi: 10.5465/amp.2014.0140

Ibarra, H. (1992). Homophily and differential returns: Sex differences in network structure and access in an advertising firm. *Administrative Science Quarterly, 37*(3), 422–447. doi: 10.2307/2393451

Ibarra, H. (1995). Race, opportunity, and diversity of social circles in managerial networks. *Academy of Management Journal, 38*(3), 673–703. doi: 10.5465/256742

Ibarra, H. (1999). Provisional selves: Experimenting with image and identity in professional adaptation. *Administrative Science Quarterly, 44*(4), 764–791. doi: 10.2307/2667055

Janssen, S., van Vuuren, M., & de Jong, M. D. (2013). Identifying support functions in developmental relationships: A self-determination perspective. *Journal of Vocational Behavior, 82*(1), 20–29. doi: 10.1016/j.jvb.2012.09.005

Kaše, R., Paauwe, J., & Zupan, N. (2009). HR practices, interpersonal relations, and intrafirm knowledge transfer in knowledge-intensive firms: A social network perspective. *Human Resource Management, 48*(4), 615–639. doi: 10.1002/hrm

Kleinbaum, A. M. (2012). Organizational misfits and the origins of brokerage in intrafirm networks. *Administrative Science Quarterly, 57*(3), 407–452. doi: 10.1177/0001839212461141

Kram, K. E. (1985). *Mentoring at work: Developmental relationships in organizational life*. Glenview, IL: University Press of America.

Kram, K. E., & Isabella, L. A. (1985). Mentoring alternatives: The role of peer relationships in career development. *Academy of Management Journal*, *28*(1), 119–132. doi: 10.5465/256064

Kuwabara, K., Hildebrand, C. A., & Zou, X. (2018). Lay theories of networking: How laypeople's beliefs about networks affect their attitudes toward and engagement in instrumental networking. *Academy of Management Review*, *43*(1), 50–64. doi: 10.5465/amr.2015.0076

Lankau, M. J., & Scandura, T. A. (2002). An investigation of personal learning in mentoring relationships: Content, antecedents, and consequences. *Academy of Management Journal*, *45*(4), 779–790. doi: 10.5465/3069311

Leana, C. R., & Van Buren, H. J. (1999). Organizational social capital and employment practices. *Academy of Management Review*, *24*(3), 538–555. doi: 10.5465/amr.1999.2202136

Leonardi, P. M., & Contractor, N. S. (2018). Better people analytics measure who they know, not just who they are. *Harvard Business Review*, *96*(6), 70–81.

Levin, D. Z., & Cross, R. (2004). The strength of weak ties you can trust: The mediating role of trust in effective knowledge transfer. *Management Science*, *50*(11), 1477–1490. doi: 10.1287/mnsc.1030.0136

Levin, D. Z., Walter, J., & Murnighan, J. K. (2011). Dormant ties: The value of reconnecting. *Organization Science*, *22*(4), 923–939. doi: 10.1287/orsc.1100.0576

Lin, N. (1999). Social networks and status attainment. *Annual Review of Sociology*, *25*(1), 467–487. doi: 10.1146/annurev.soc.25.1.467

Lin, N., Ensel, W., & Vaughn, W. (1981). Social resources and strength of ties: Structural factors in occupational status attainment. *American Sociological Review*, *46*(4), 393–405. doi: 10.2307/2095260

Marler, J. H., & Fisher, S. L. (2013). An evidence-based review of e-HRM and strategic human resource management. *Human Resource Management Review*, *23*(1), 18–36. doi: 10.1016/j.hrmr.2012.06.002

McPherson, M., Smith-Lovin, L., & Cook, J. M. (2001). Birds of a feather: Homophily in social networks. *Annual Review of Sociology*, *27*(1), 415–444. doi: 10.1146/annurev.soc.27.1.415

Merluzzi, J., & Sterling, A. (2017). Lasting effects? Referrals and career mobility of demographic groups in organizations. *ILR Review*, *70*(1), 105–131. doi: 10.1177/0019793916669507

Methot, J. R., Rosado-Solomon, E. H., & Allen, D. G. (2018). Network architecture of human capital: A relational identity perspective. *Academy of Management Review*, *43*(4), 723–748. doi: 10.5465/amr.2016.0338

Mitchell, T. R., Holtom, B. C., Lee, T. W., Sablynski, C. J., & Erez, M. (2001). Why people stay: Using job embeddedness to predict voluntary turnover. *Academy of Management Journal*, *44*(6), 1102–1121. doi: 10.5465/3069391

Mitchell, T. R., & Lee, T. W. (2001). The unfolding model of voluntary turnover and job embeddedness: Foundations for a comprehensive theory of attachment. *Research in Organizational Behavior*, *23*(1), 189–246. doi: 10.1016/S0191-3085(01)23006-8

Nahapiet, J., & Ghoshal, S. (1998). Social capital, intellectual capital and the organizational advantage. *Academy of Management Review*, *23*(2), 242–266. doi: 10.5465/amr.1998.533225

Podolny, J. M., & Baron, J. N. (1997). Resources and relationships: Social networks and mobility in the workplace. *American Sociological Review*, *62*(5), 673–693. doi: 10.2307/2657354

Presser, H. B. (2003). *Working in a 24/7 economy: Challenges for American families*. New York: Russell Sage Foundation.

Raider, H. J., & Burt, R. S. (1996). Boundaryless careers and social capital. In M. B. Arthur & D. M. Rousseau (Eds.), *Boundaryless careers* (pp. 187–201). New York: Oxford University Press.

Rousseau, D. M., Sitkin, S. B., Burt, R. S., & Camerer, C. (1998). Not so different after all: A cross-discipline view of trust. *Academy of Management Review, 23*(3), 393–404. doi: 10.5465/amr.1998.926617

Seibert, S. E., Kraimer, M. L., & Liden, R. C. (2001). A social capital theory of career success. *Academy of Management Journal, 44*(2), 219–237. doi: 10.2307/3069452

Shapiro, D. L., Hom, P., Shen, W., & Agarwal, R. (2016). How do leader departures affect subordinates' organizational attachment? A 360-degree relational perspective. *Academy of Management Review, 41*(3), 479–502.

Silver, A. (1990). Friendship in commercial society: Eighteenth-century social theory and modern sociology. *American Journal of Sociology, 95*(6), 1474–1504.

Singh, R., Ragins, B. R., & Tharenou, P. (2009). What matters most? The relative role of mentoring and career capital in career success. *Journal of Vocational Behavior, 75*(1), 56–67. doi: 10.1016/j.jvb.2009.03.003

Soltis, S. M., Brass, D. J., & Lepak, D. P. (2018). Social resource management: Integrating social network theory and human resource management. *Academy of Management Annals, 12*(2), 537–573. doi: 10.5465/annals.2016.0094

Steel, R. P. (2002). Turnover theory at the empirical interface: Problems of fit and function. *Academy of Management Review, 27*(3), 346–360. doi: 10.5465/amr.2002.7389900

Swider, B. W., Boswell, W. R., & Zimmerman, R. D. (2011). Examining the job search–turnover relationship: The role of embeddedness, job satisfaction, and available alternatives. *Journal of Applied Psychology, 96*(2), 432–441. doi: 10.1037/a0021676

Thomas, D. A., & Gabarro, J. J. (1999). *Breaking through: The making of minority executives in corporate America*. Boston, MA: Harvard Business School Press.

Thomas, D. A., & Higgins, M. C. (1996). Mentoring and the boundaryless career: Lessons from the minority experience. In M. B. Arthur & D. M. Rousseau (Eds.), *The boundaryless career: A new employment principle for a new organizational era* (pp. 268–281). New York: Oxford University Press.

Twenge, J. M. (2010). A review of the empirical evidence on generational differences in work attitudes. *Journal of Business and Psychology, 25*(2), 201–210. doi: 10.1007/s10869-010-9165-6

Uzzi, B. (1996). The sources and consequences of embeddedness for the economic performance of organizations: The network effect. *American Sociological Review, 61*(4), 674–698. doi: 10.2307/2096399

Von Hippel, E. (1994). "Sticky information" and the locus of problem solving: Implications for innovation. *Management Science, 40*(4), 429–439. doi: 10.1287/mnsc.40.4.429

Walter, J., Levin, D. Z., & Murnighan, J. K. (2016). How to reconnect for maximum impact. *MIT Sloan Management Review, 57*(3), 18–20.

Wasserman, S., & Faust, K. (1994). *Social network analysis: Methods and applications*. Cambridge, UK: Cambridge University Press.

Wexley, K. N., & Latham, G. P. (2002). *Developing and training human resources in organizations*, 3rd edn. Upper Saddle River, NJ: Pearson/Prentice Hall.

Whiting, V. R., & de Janasz, S. C. (2004). Mentoring in the 21st century: Using the internet to build skills and networks. *Journal of Management Education, 28*(3), 275–293. doi: 10.1177/1052562903252639

Wiersema, M. F., Nishimura, Y., & Suzuki, K. (2018). Executive succession: The importance of social capital in CEO appointments. *Strategic Management Journal, 39*(5), 1473–1495. doi: 10.1002/smj.2766

Wolff, H. G., & Moser, K. (2009). Effects of networking on career success: A longitudinal study. *Journal of Applied Psychology, 94*(1), 196–206. doi: 10.1037/a0013350

10. Multilevel modeling for careers research
Bert Schreurs, Joeri Hofmans, and Bart Wille

INTRODUCTION

In this chapter, we argue that our understanding of careers can be improved by adopting a multilevel perspective. We first provide a rationale for using multilevel analyses by describing the "multileveled" nature of contemporary careers, with individuals nested within organizations, individuals and organizations nested within geographical boundaries, and time nested within individuals. Next, we describe the basic structure of multilevel (regression) analyses: the nature of the models and the type of parameters they can estimate, and how to conduct multilevel analyses, including different aspects of analyses such as centering, proportion of variance accounted for, statistical power, and software packages for testing multilevel models. We conclude by highlighting two "forgotten" types of nesting that hold particular promise for careers research: individuals nested within occupations, and romantic partners nested within dyads.

THE MULTILEVEL NATURE OF CAREER STUDIES

The term "career" has been defined in a number of ways in the literature. The most influential and commonly used definition is arguably the one by Arthur and colleagues, who define career as "an evolving sequence of a person's work experiences over time" (Arthur, Hall, & Lawrence, 1989, p. 8). A more recent, but equally comprehensive, definition is offered by Gunz and Mayrhofer (2018), for whom a career is "a pattern of a career actor's positions and conditions within a bounded social and geographical space over their life to date" (p. 70). Upon close inspection of these (and other contemporary) definitions of career (see Arnold, 1997; Greenhaus, Callanan, & Godshalk, 2010; Hall, 2002; De Vos & Van der Heijden, 2015), it is apparent that careers span multiple levels of analysis. The term "levels of analysis" refers to the entities, units or objects of observation, such as working days, individuals, work teams, and organizations (Yammarino & Gooty, 2017). The direct implication of the statement that careers "span multiple levels of analysis" is that data about careers are oftentimes hierarchical in nature, with some units of analysis *nested* within other, higher-level units. More specifically, and drawing on the abovementioned definitions, at least three types of nesting can be distinguished: (1) individuals nested within organizations, (2) individuals (and organizations) nested within geographical boundaries, and (3) time nested within individuals.

Individuals Nested Within Organizations[1]

Faced with uncertainty and change, 21st-century employees are forced to take charge of their own careers (Strauss, Griffin, & Parker, 2012), which oftentimes entails looking for employment beyond the boundaries of a single employment setting (Arthur, 1994; DeFillippi & Arthur, 1994). Despite the increased importance of agency and career self-management, today's organizations continue to employ a wide range of career management techniques, such as mentoring, succession planning, and retirement planning. Organizations, uncertain about the level of career support they should offer to their employees (Nelissen, Forrier, & Verbruggen, 2017; Van der Heijde & Van der Heijden, 2006) differ greatly in their policies and systems that affect career outcomes (Baruch & Peiperl, 2000; Sonnenfeld & Peiperl, 1988; Wiernik & Wille, 2018). Individuals working for the same organization are exposed to similar career (and HR) management practices. Accordingly, organizational membership, the clustering of individuals within organizations, is expected to explain part of the variance in career outcomes. Even career outcomes that are typically considered to be individual-level constructs, such as turnover intentions and work-to-family conflict, are—because they are influenced by management practices—likely to be influenced by organizational membership (e.g., El Akremi, Colaianni, Portoghese, Galletta, & Battistelli, 2014; Major, Fletcher, Davis, & Germano, 2008).

An example of how organizational membership influences individual career outcomes is provided by Chang, Wang, and Huang (2013). Using a sample of 1,149 employees clustered within 144 stores, they investigated the extent to which employee-turnover intention could be explained by job-related (e.g., autonomy, skill variety, task identity) and store-related factors (e.g., training and development, leadership, communication). Their results showed that 16 percent of the variance in employee-turnover intention resided between stores. Employees felt less inclined to leave the organization when store colleagues were of similar age and tenure, when the store manager showed transformational leadership, and when the store maintained an open-communication policy.

Another example comes from a study by Van Vianen, Rosenauer, Homan, Horstmeier, and Voelpel (2018). Using a sample of vocational job starters (*N* ranged from 230 to 290) nested within teams (*N* ranged from 56 to 68), they investigated the effect of career mentoring by the team supervisor on two career outcomes: employee turnover intention (the authors use the term intention-to-stay) and promotability. Eleven percent of the variance in turnover intention, and 10 percent of the variance in promotability resided at the team level. The results showed that career mentoring climate – team members' average mentoring perceptions – was a significant predictor of both turnover intention and promotability.

These examples illustrate that differences at the organizational – company, department, store or team – level can explain a significant portion of the variance in individual-level career outcomes. Moreover, the association between individual-level predictors and career outcomes may vary across organizations. This means that the explanatory variable may have a different effect on the criterion for each organization, which in a multilevel regression framework means that each organization has its own organization-specific slope. Organizational-level variables can then be used to explain differences between slopes. For example, Sawyer, Young, Thoroughgood, and Dominguez (2020), using archival data from an all-female sample of 3,015 active military personnel nested in 321 teams, investigated the relationship between perceptions of gender discrimination and job satisfaction. They found that up to 10 percent of the variance in job satisfaction was due to team membership, and that the relationship between perceived gender discrimination and job satisfaction differed across teams. The between-slope variance was partly explained by the extent to which teams were male dominated, such that the negative relationship was more pronounced in teams that were less male dominated versus teams that were more male dominated.

Individuals Nested Within Geographical Boundaries

Much of the careers literature since the 1990s has focused on career mobility, especially with the rise of the boundaryless career paradigm (Arthur, 1994; DeFillippi & Arthur, 1994). Today, not only do employees transition more easily than ever before from one organization into another, they are also more likely to cross national boundaries, as is evidenced by the growing number of expatriates and migrant workers (Al Ariss & Crowley-Henry, 2013; Finaccord, 2018; International Labour Organization, 2015). With international mobility on the rise, career scholars became increasingly aware that career trajectories are heavily conditioned by national labor regulations, public policies, labor market and national cultures. Institutional pressures place limitations on variation in career patterns within nations and magnify between-country differences in careers (DiMaggio & Powell, 1983; Ituma & Simpson, 2009). Several studies have shown that our understanding of individual careers can be increased by accounting for the fact that individuals are nested within geographical boundaries.

For example, Sjöberg (2004), using data from the International Social Survey Programme, found that individual attitudes towards female labor force participation differed across countries, with 10 percent of the variance residing at the country level. Variations in national family policy models accounted for part of the cross-national variation, providing evidence for the importance of institutional forces. Similarly, Erlinghagen (2007), in a sample of 13,207 individuals nested in 17 European countries, found significant cross-country differences in individual perceptions of job insecurity, that is, "the subjectively experienced anticipation of a fundamental and involuntary event related to job loss" (Sverke, Hellgren, & Näswall, 2002, p. 243), which could be largely explained by differences in social-structural, institutional and cultural factors.

Other work by Debus, Probst, König and Kleinmann (2012) looked at country-level differences in individuals' appraisals of job insecurity. More specifically, in a sample of 15,200 employees from 24 countries they investigated whether country-level variables (i.e. uncertainty avoidance and social safety net) affected the relations between job insecurity and job attitudes such as satisfaction and affective organizational commitment. The results first demonstrated that between-country differences accounted for 5.7 percent and 10.5 percent of the variance in job satisfaction and affective commitment, respectively. Moreover, consistent with their expectations, country-level enacted uncertainty avoidance and the social safety net act as cross-level buffer variables for the effects of job insecurity on the two job attitudes.

As a final example, research has also considered the effects of geographical context on pathways to career success. Boudreau, Boswell, and Judge (2001) for instance looked at the effects of personality on career success in large European and U.S. samples of executives. Differences emerged between the two regional contexts in that neuroticism associated with lower levels of extrinsic success for the U.S. executives but not the Europeans, and extraversion associated with higher levels of extrinsic success for the European executives but not the U.S. executives. Along a similar line, Smale and colleagues (2019) demonstrated how pathways to career success may differ across countries. They investigated the relationship between career proactivity and two aspects of subjective career success – financial success and work–life balance – in a sample of 11,892 employees nested in 22 countries. Eleven percent of the variance in financial success and 5 percent of the variance in work–life balance resided at the country-level. They further found that the relationship between career proactivity and career success differed across countries and that national culture partly explained these cross-national variations. Together, findings such as these suggest that certain individual characteristics or traits are either more effective or perceived as more important in various cultures or national contexts, but more work is definitely needed to capture the unobserved factors that correlate with geographical differences.

Time Nested Within Individuals

In spite of the many definitions of career, there is general agreement among career scholars about the importance of time in studying careers. Individual careers play out over time as is evidenced by references made in career definitions to terms such as "sequence," "moving perspective," "patterns of experiences spanning a life," "continuity," and "life's work" (Gunz & Mayrhofer, 2018). Throughout their life span, people make countless big and small career-related decisions, varying from accepting a job offer to taking a training course. Career trajectories reflect the accumulation of such decisions over time. Each of these decisions, in turn, is influenced by myriad factors, some of which are person-related (e.g., values, personality), others context-related (e.g., work pressure, leadership). Most of these factors vary not only between, but also within persons. For example, there is now growing consensus that stable dispositional variables such as work values (Barnes-Farrell & Matthews, 2012), but also personality traits (e.g., Wille, Hofmans, Feys, & De Fruyt, 2014; Woods, Lievens, De Fruyt, & Wille, 2013), continue to develop as workers mature. Capturing these within-person differences contributes to our understanding of the unfolding of individual careers, as is evidenced by the recent upsurge of within-person studies in the career field.

Various studies have demonstrated that within-person variation in motivation explains why people's effort expenditure on exploring career opportunities or seeking employment varies over time. For example, Lee, Porfeli and Hirschi (2016) examined the relationship between motivation (i.e., work valences and agency beliefs) and career exploration in a sample of 201 high school students during three consecutive years. The results showed that more than half of the variance in career exploration was located at the within-person level, and that these within-person variations could be partly explained by within-person fluctuations in motivation: students tended to engage more in career exploration the moment they were more motivated than normally. In a similar vein, Da Motta Veiga and Turban (2018) showed a within-person association between motivation (i.e., employment self-efficacy) and job search intensity. Fifty-eight percent of the variance in job search intensity was within-person. Interestingly, they found that job search intensity *decreased* the moment job seekers felt more efficacious. This study is important as it shows that findings at the between-person level (i.e. job search intensity is higher among more efficacious job seekers) do not automatically apply at the within-person level.

Another category of studies considers the role of time in long-term longitudinal research on career development. To give one example, Wille and colleagues (2014) repeatedly assessed a cohort of college alumni across the first fifteen years of their professional career. They demonstrated that over the entire time interval, between the ages of 22 and 37 years, people's standings on big five personality traits significantly shifted in the direction of greater functional maturity (i.e., increases in conscientiousness, agreeableness and emotional stability). Moreover, these changes in trait scores over time were also related to concurrent changes in relevant job attitudes such as job satisfaction and work involvement. For instance, as individuals became more emotionally stable over time, they also increased in job satisfaction, a mechanism which was described as maturation of work attitudes. Finally, in addition to empirical work describing long-term within-person changes, theoretical frameworks have now also been developed that provide an explanation of mechanisms through which dispositional factors such as values and personality traits develop over time and how this interacts with experiences at work. For example, the Demands-Affordances TrAnsactional model (Woods, Wille, Wu, Lievens, & De Fruyt, 2019) explains how work demands at different levels (i.e., occupation, job, organization, and group or team) trigger the activation of certain affordances (e.g., personality states) which may, over time, lead to longlasting personality trait development. These newly designed models shed a new light on the way in which time is nested within individuals as they gradually develop their careers.

The examples given above are meant to illustrate that phenomena studied by career scholars are often hierarchical, with some variables clustered within other variables, and that the presence of such variables necessitates the use of multilevel analysis. This is not to say that the three types of nesting – individuals within organizations, individuals within geographical boundaries, time within individuals – are the only forms of nesting relevant to career studies (for example, careers may differ within and between occupations, sectors, etc.). At the end of this chapter we describe other types of nesting that might offer interesting avenues for future research. But first we introduce some notation to explain the basic principles of multilevel regression analysis.

ANALYZING MULTILEVEL DATA

The Basic Two-Level Regression Model for Clustered Data

Assume we have (clustered) data from J organizations, each with a different number of employees n_j. In each organization, we measured for each employee an outcome variable Y and a predictor variable X. The multilevel regression model relating X to Y then looks like this:

$$Y_{ij} = \beta_{0j} + \beta_{1j}X_{ij} + e_{ij} \tag{10.1}$$

In this Equation, Y_{ij} is the outcome, β_{0j} represents the intercept, β_{1j} is the slope or regression coefficient relating our predictor X_{ij} to the outcome variable, and e_{ij} is the residual error term. Because of the multilevel—and more specifically the two-level—nature of the data, the coefficients in our model have two subscripts. Subscript j is for the organizations ($j = 1, 2, …, J$) while subscript i is for the employees ($i = 1, 2, …, I$). Thus, unlike in traditional regression analysis, the parameters of the regression model have an organization-specific subscript j, meaning that they can be different for the different organizations in our sample. In other words, each organization has a different intercept and slope, which is why the intercept and slope in Equation 10.1 are referred to as random coefficients. More formally, this idea can be expressed using the following set of separate equations (Bryk & Raudenbush, 1992):

$$\beta_{0j} = \gamma_{00} + \mu_{0j} \tag{10.2}$$
$$\beta_{1j} = \gamma_{10} + \mu_{1j} \tag{10.3}$$

In Equations 10.2 and 10.3, γ_{00} and γ_{10} represent the overall intercept and slope, respectively. The fact that these coefficients do not vary across organizations can be seen from the fact that the regression coefficients γ have no subscript j. μ_{0j} and μ_{1j} are (random) residual error terms at the organization-level. That is, they capture the difference between the overall intercept (respectively slope) and the organization-specific intercept (respectively slope). Similar to the residual error term e_{ij} in Equation 10.1, μ_{0j} and μ_{1j} are assumed to be normally distributed with a mean of zero. Moreover, the residual errors at the organization-level are assumed to be independent from the residual errors at the employee-level and the residual error terms e_{ij} are assumed to be independent from each other.

Combining Equation 10.1 and Equations 10.2 and 10.3 into a single-model regression equation, yields:

$$Y_{ij} = \left(\gamma_{00} + \mu_{0j} \right) + \left(\gamma_{10} + \mu_{1j} \right) X_{ij} + e_{ij} \tag{10.4}$$

or when rearranging terms:

$$Y_{ij} = \gamma_{00} + \gamma_{10} X_{ij} + \mu_{0j} + \mu_{1j} X_{ij} + e_{ij} \tag{10.5}$$

The segment $\left[\gamma_{00} + \gamma_{10} X_{ij} \right]$ in Equation 10.5 contains the fixed coefficients and is therefore referred to as the fixed part of the model. The segment $\left[\mu_{0j} + \mu_{1j} X_{ij} + e_{ij} \right]$ contains the random coefficients and is therefore called the random part of the model.

In case one also has organization-level data, an organization-level predictor Z can be introduced in Equation 10.2 and/or Equation 10.3:

$$\beta_{0j} = \gamma_{00} + \gamma_{01} Z_j + \mu_{0j} \tag{10.6}$$
$$\beta_{1j} = \gamma_{10} + \gamma_{11} Z_j + \mu_{1j} \tag{10.7}$$

In this case, the organization-specific intercept β_{0j} (respectively slope β_{1j}) is predicted by an overall intercept γ_{00} (respectively slope γ_{10}), a covariate Z_j, and a residual error term μ_{0j} (respectively μ_{1j}). In Equations 10.6 and 10.7, γ_{01} and γ_{11} represent the regression coefficients relating covariate Z_j to the organization-specific intercept β_{0j} and slope β_{1j}, respectively. Again, Equations 10.1, 10.6 and 10.7 can be written as a single regression equation:

$$Y_{ij} = \left(\gamma_{00} + \gamma_{01} Z_j + \mu_{0j} \right) + \left(\gamma_{10} + \gamma_{11} Z_j + \mu_{1j} \right) X_{ij} + e_{ij} \tag{10.8}$$

or when rearranging terms:

$$Y_{ij} = \gamma_{00} + \gamma_{01} Z_j + \gamma_{10} X_{ij} + \gamma_{11} Z_j X_{ij} + \mu_{1j} X_{ij} + \mu_{0j} + e_{ij} \tag{10.9}$$

As before, the segment $\left[\gamma_{00} + \gamma_{01} Z_j + \gamma_{10} X_{ij} + \gamma_{11} Z_j X_{ij} \right]$ pertains to the fixed part of the model, while the segment $\left[\mu_{1j} X_{ij} + \mu_{0j} + e_{ij} \right]$ concerns the random part. In the fixed part, the term $\gamma_{11} Z_j X_{ij}$ is an interaction term resulting from the fact that we predicted β_{1j}, or the relationship between X_{ij} and Y_{ij}, using Z_j. In other words, we test the moderating effect of the organization-level covariate Z_j on the employee-level relationship between X_{ij} and Y_{ij}, which is why $\gamma_{11} Z_j X_{ij}$ is referred to as a cross-level interaction. The other interaction term in Equation 10.9 is $\mu_{1j} X_{ij}$, and is part of the random part of the model. This term allows the error to covary with the predictor variable X_{ij}, thereby allowing for heteroscedasticity in the data.

The Basic Two-Level Regression Model for Repeated Data

In case of repeated data, or data on *J* individuals, each measured across a number of days or situations, slight changes to the model are needed. First of all, in case of repeated data, subscript *j* no longer refers to organizations, but to individuals. Subscript *i*, in turn, indicates different measurement moments. Thus, Y_{11} no longer refers to the level of the outcome variable for Person 1 in Organization 1, but the level of the outcome of Person 1 on Measurement moment 1.

A second important difference—and one that goes beyond a mere relabeling of the subscripts—is that in repeated data, the assumption of independence of the error terms e_{ij} tends to be violated. That is, in repeated measures data, measurements can be considerably correlated when they are collected at occasions that are close together, a phenomenon that is referred to as autocorrelation (or the correlation of a variable with itself at a previous point in time). Note that this is often the case in high-density repeated measures designs, such as daily diary studies, or even more so in Experience Sampling (ESM) Research (see Hofmans, De Clercq, Kuppens, Verbeke, & Widiger, 2019). Because autocorrelation in the data violates the assumption of independence of the error terms e_{ij}, such effects should ideally be included in the model, and this can be done in either of two ways.

A first way to deal with autocorrelation in the data is to include the lagged outcome variable as a predictor into the model (West & Hepworth, 1991). West and Hepworth (1991) argue that one should investigate the correlations between the current observations and lagged prior observations, after which one should include the lags that are significantly related with the current observations. In general, this approach works well when the repeated data are equally spaced (i.e., when the lags between consecutive measurements are the same), but this is often not the case in ESM research. In response to this issue, Beal and Weiss (2003) suggest to slightly modify the approach of West and Hepworth (1991) by also accounting for the interval between measurements. That is, in case of unequally spaced measurements, one can include the lagged outcome variable, the interval between the current and the previous observation and the interaction between both in the model.

A second way to deal with autocorrelation in the data is to explicitly model correlated error terms in the multilevel regression model. The most complicated model is one with an unrestricted residual error covariance matrix. In this model, and in case of *k* measurement moments, $k(k-1)/2$ unique elements are estimated since each variance and covariance in the residual error covariance matrix is unique. In most cases, such an unrestricted residual error covariance matrix is unnecessarily complex and more parsimonious models can fit the data equally well. On the other side of the spectrum, we have the compound symmetry model. This model is quite restrictive because it assumes that the residual correlations between the measurement occasions are all the same (thus only requiring one value for the off-diagonal elements of the residual error covariance matrix). In between the unrestricted residual error covariance matrix and the compound symmetry model, there are several other options, such as a simplex or a Toeplitz model. It is beyond the reach of this chapter to discuss all of these models, but the interested reader can consult Hox, Moerbeek, and van de Schoot (2017, Chapter 5) for more information on different residual error covariance structures. In terms of selecting the most appropriate residual error covariance structure, it should be noted that, generally speaking, researchers will have little or no theoretical reasons to favor a particular type of residual error covariance structure over another. What can be done in this case is to fit a wide range of models, each with a different residual error covariance structure, to the data and see which model fits the data best. To decide which model to select, one can make use of the Akaike Information Criterion (AIC) or the Bayesian Information Critarion (BIC).

Testing a Multilevel Regression Model: A Stepwise Approach

Having explained the differences and similarities between models for clustered and repeated data, our next goal is to present the reader with a stepwise plan (s)he can use when testing multilevel regression models. To make the discussion more concrete, we apply the different steps to a hypothetical research model that examines the relationship between newcomers' career-related mentoring and career satisfaction. For the clustered data, we assume that newcomers are nested within organizations. For the repeated data, we assume that the independent and dependent variable are measured every week over a period of six months.

In case one has a strong theoretical expectation concerning the specification of one's model, immediately testing it might be the way to go. However, multilevel regression analysis implies testing complicated models that often result in computational problems. Therefore, and in line with others' recommendations (e.g., Bliese, 2016; Hox et al., 2017; Nezlek, 2008; Snijders & Bosker, 1999), we propose to build one's model using an upward or "bottom-up" approach. In this approach, one starts with the simplest model and adds parameters that are tested for significance once they have been added. Using this procedure, Hox and colleagues (2017) distinguish five steps (see Bliese, 2002 for a similar approach).

1.   Testing the intercept-only model
Typically, the first step of a multilevel regression analysis involves testing an intercept-only model, which is also referred to as an empty model (because the model contains no predictors). In this model, the outcome is predicted by a random intercept only:

$$Y_{ij} = \beta_{0j} + e_{ij} \tag{10.10}$$

$$\beta_{0j} = \gamma_{00} + \mu_{0j} \tag{10.11}$$

or when rearranging terms:

$$Y_{ij} = \gamma_{00} + \mu_{0j} + e_{ij} \tag{10.12}$$

Recall that γ_{00} in Equation 10.12 represents the overall intercept, while μ_{0j} captures group-specific deviations from this intercept. In case of clustered data, this can be the difference between the overall intercept (across organizations) and the organization-specific intercept. In case of repeated data, μ_{0j} might represent the difference between the overall intercept (across individuals) and the person-specific intercept. In other words, μ_{0j} captures differences in intercept *between* organizations/individuals. e_{ij}, in turn, represents the difference between the group-specific intercept and the actual score (Y_{ij}). As such, it captures differences *within* organizations/individuals.

Taking these two pieces of information (i.e., differences *between* organizations/individuals and differences *within* organizations/individuals) allows testing to what extent the scores in Y_{ij} are due to differences between or within organizations/individuals. This question is answered by calculating the intraclass correlation ρ:

$$\rho = \frac{\sigma^2_{\mu_0}}{\sigma^2_{\mu_0} + \sigma^2_e} \tag{10.13}$$

In the intraclass correlation, the variance in Y_{ij} is decomposed into two orthogonal components: the within-variance, or the variance of the lowest-level errors (e_{ij}), and the between-variance, or the variance of the higher-level errors (μ_{0j}). The intraclass correlation then indicates the proportion of variation in Y_{ij} that is due to between-organization (in case of clustered data) or between-person differences (in case of repeated data).

In our clustered data example, we might observe that the lion share of the variance in career satisfaction resides at the individual level, but that organizational membership also explains part of the differences in career satisfaction. In our repeated data example, we may find that career satisfaction varies equally within and between individuals.

2.   Adding predictors at the lowest level

In the second step, one adds the lowest-level predictors to the model. In case of clustered data with people at the first and organizations at the second level, these predictors are person-specific predictors. In our example, the person-specific predictor refers to newcomers' views of their supervisor's career-related mentoring behaviors after x weeks on the job (Gentry, Weber, & Sadri, 2008). In case of repeated data, with measurement occasions at the first and people at the second level, these predictors vary across the measurement moments. In our example, with newcomers being surveyed every week over a period of six months, if no missing data, we would have 24 reports on supervisors' career-related mentoring behavior for each newcomer.

In this stage of the analysis, we do not yet include random effects for the slopes. In other words, the slopes are specified to be the same across organizations/persons. This can be seen in Equation 10.14, where the slope coefficient β_1 has no subscript j.

$$Y_{ij} = \beta_{0j} + \beta_1 X_{ij} + e_{ij} \tag{10.14}$$

3.   Adding higher-level predictors

In the third step, higher-level predictors are added to the model (see Z_j in Equation 10.15). In case of clustered data with people at the first and organizations at the second level, these predictors are organization-level variables. In our example, we may be interested in accounting for the impact of the organization's structure on newcomers' career satisfaction. Information about the organization's structure can be obtained from company records, from interviews with the top management team, or from aggregating employees' perceptions about the organic-mechanistic orientation of the business (Hegstad & Wentling, 2005; Naman & Slevin, 1993). In case of repeated data, with measurement occasions at the first and people at the second level, these predictors are people-specific variables. Here, one can think of investigating the influence of newcomers' proactive personality (Wang, Hu, Hurst, & Yang, 2014), measured once, at the beginning or at the end of the six-month data collection.

$$Y_{ij} = \beta_{0j} + \beta_1 X_{ij} + \beta_2 Z_j + e_{ij} \tag{10.15}$$

4.   Adding random slopes

In the fourth step, one tests whether the effect of the lower-level variables on the outcome – or the slopes in Equation 10.15 – differ as a function of the higher-level groups (see Equation 10.16). In case of clustered data, this implies testing whether the effect of employee-level variables on the outcome differs as a function of the organization the employee is working in. When applied to our example, this means testing whether the relationship between career-related mentoring and career satisfaction differs across organizations, as the relationship may be more positive in some organizations than in others. In case of repeated data, one tests whether the effect of time-varying variables on the outcome differs as a function of the person under consideration. In our example, this means testing whether the relationship between weekly career-related mentoring and weekly career satisfaction differs across individuals, as mentoring may benefit some individuals more than others.

$$Y_{ij} = \beta_{0j} + \beta_{1j} X_{ij} + \beta_2 Z_j + e_{ij} \tag{10.16}$$

Following Hox and colleagues (2017), we argue that testing for random slopes is best done for each explanatory variable separately. The reason is that including all random effects at once might lead to computational issues and model nonconvergence. After having tested the random effects associated with each slope, statistically significant random effects are included in the model whereas non-significant random slopes are trimmed (e.g., Sieracki, Leon, Miller, & Lyons, 2008).

5. Adding cross-level interactions

In the final step, predictors of the random slopes (i.e., cross-level interactions) are added to the model (see Equation 10.17). In the clustered data example, we may want to test whether the effect of career-related mentoring on career satisfaction varies as a function of organizational structure. More specifically, we may want to test the possibility that career-related mentoring is more satisfactory, because it is more instrumental, in organizations with several levels in the corporate hierarchy than in organizations with flattened hierarchies (Hegstad & Wentling, 2005). In the repeated data example, we may want to examine the possibility that the within-person association between career-related mentoring and career satisfaction is stronger for newcomers with high (versus low) levels of proactive personality, because proactive individuals are more likely to put the advice received into action (Bateman & Crant, 1993).

$$Y_{ij} = \beta_{0j} + \beta_{1j}X_{ij} + \beta_2 Z_j + \beta_3 X_{ij}Z_j + e_{ij} \tag{10.17}$$

A relevant question concerning these cross-level interactions is whether significant random slope variation is a prerequisite for testing a cross-level interaction. Logically it would make sense since cross-level interactions are used to explain between-group differences in slopes, and this might be challenging in case there are no such differences. However, there is a statistical issue that complicates matters. Because tests of random effects are less powerful (in a statistical sense) than tests of fixed effects, the test of a specific cross-level interaction will have more statistical power than the test of the associated random effect. Because of this reason, one might still test for cross-level interactions, even if the random effect was non-significant.

In case a significant cross-level interaction is found, one might want to inspect the exact nature of this interaction. Recall in this respect that a cross-level interaction is simply a moderation effect with one term of the moderation being a lower-level term and the other being a higher-level term. Thus, very much like the probing of interaction effects in typical regression analysis, cross-level interactions can and should be probed. However, in case of a cross-level interaction, probing is a complex, tedious and error-prone task (Preacher, Curran, & Bauer, 2006). To address this concern, Preacher and colleagues (2006) have developed a freely available online resource that can be used to obtain significance tests for simple slopes, to compute regions of significance, and to obtain confidence bands for simple slopes (see http://www .quantpsy.org/interact/hlm2.htm).

Important Issues When Testing a Multilevel Model (For an Overview, see Table 10.1)

In what follows, we review a number of important issues career researchers should attend to when testing multilevel models. Specifically, we will discuss different types of centering the data, computing the proportion of variance accounted for in multilevel models, statistical power in multilevel regression analysis, and software to test multilevel regression models.

1.   Centering

As is true for ordinary least squares regression, in multilevel analysis, centering is important for the interpretation of the intercept and for the interpretation of the regression coefficients when there are interactions in the model. That is, in regression the intercept represents the predicted value of the outcome when all predictor variables equal zero. In case zero is not a meaningful value, the intercept becomes meaningless, which might be resolved by centering the data. For example, when age is the predictor, zero is absurd as a predictor value because this means that the intercept is the predicted value for a newborn. By centering the data, the value of zero becomes meaningful as it now means that the predictor is at the average of the sample (in case of grand-mean centering) or organization/person (in case of group-mean centering). Similarly, when there is an interaction in the model, the coefficients of the main effects represent the effect of one predictor on the outcome when the other predictor is zero (because when one of the predictors is zero, the interaction drops from the equation). Again, when zero is not a meaningful value, the interpretation of the main effects is compromised, which can be resolved by centering the predictors.

In multilevel modeling, centering is arguably way more important than it is in ordinary least squares regression (Enders & Tofighi, 2007). Moreover, it is more complicated because there are different ways of centering the data in multilevel regression analysis: centering the data at the grand mean (i.e., grand-mean centering) and centering the data at the group mean (i.e., group-mean centering or centering within cluster). Because of its importance for multilevel modeling, and because of the complexities involved, we discuss both types of centering below in more detail.

a.   Grand-mean centering

With grand-mean centering, one centers the data relative to the grand mean. In case of clustered data, the grand mean is the mean across employees and organizations. In case of repeated data, the grand mean is computed across moments and people. More formally, grand-mean centering can be expressed as:

$$X_{ij}^* = X_{ij} - \frac{\sum_{i=1}^{I}\sum_{j=1}^{J} X_{ij}}{n} \tag{10.18}$$

with n being the total number of observations.

Centering the data using the grand-mean implies performing a linear transformation of the raw data. The consequence of such linear transformation is that the regression coefficients and their associated standard errors are also linearly transformed. Moreover, the proportion of unexplained variance remains unaffected. All of this means that the model is invariant to grand-mean centering of the predictor variables. One just obtains a reparameterization of the same model (i.e., exactly the same fit to the data but different parameter estimates).

b.   Group-mean centering
In case of group-mean centering, the data are centered relative to the mean of the group (being the organization in case of clustered data or the person in case of repeated data). This type of centering can formally be expressed as follows:

$$X_{ij}^* = X_{ij} - \frac{\sum_{i=1}^{I} X_{ij}}{I} \tag{10.19}$$

What happens with group-mean centering is that all between-group differences are removed from the data. That is, because the data are centered relative to the group's average, only within-group fluctuations remain. Thus, by group-mean centering the data, one filters out between-group variation, while retaining within-group variation in the predictor (Nezlek, 2001).

Unlike grand-mean centering, group-mean centering implies a complex, non-linear way of transforming the data (Enders & Tofighi, 2007). The consequence is that group-mean centering changes the meaning of the regression model in complicated ways (i.e., it is not just a reparameterization of the same model, but a totally different model). Because of this reason, novel users are recommended to be cautious when using group-mean centering (Hox et al., 2017). Our take on this is that group-mean centering offers many possibilities, and not in the least the ability to test pure, unconfounded within-organization (in case of clustered data) or within-person relationships (in case of repeated data). Often, our multilevel studies are designed for studying particularly those within-organization or within-person relationships, and in such cases group-mean centering is indispensable (Hofmans et al., 2019). Moreover, group-mean centering is also valuable when the model includes cross-level interactions, because it then allows testing whether a pure level 1 relationship (e.g., a within-person or within-organization relationship) is moderated by a level 2 predictor (e.g., a person-level or an organization-level variable) (Enders & Tofighi, 2007).

2.   Proportion of variance accounted for
In multilevel regression analysis, one has regression equations (with residual error terms) at multiple levels. Hence, there is unobserved variance at multiple levels. For example, in a two-level model (see Equation 10.12), one has an error term at the first level (i.e., e_{ij}) and at least one at the second level (i.e., μ_{0j}). This implies that in a multilevel model, the proportion of variance accounted for by the predictors can be

different for different levels of the model (LaHuis, Hartman, Hakoyama, & Clark, 2014).

One straightforward way of testing the proportion of variance accounted for consists of testing a series of models and examining to what extent the residual error variances of these models are affected (LaHuis et al., 2014). For example, to test to what extent including a level 1 predictor in the model matters in the prediction of our outcome variable, one can test the empty model (see Equation 10.20) and compare this model to a model including the level 1 predictor (and possibly a random slope; see Equation 10.21).

$$Y_{ij} = \gamma_{00} + \mu_{0j} + e_{ij} \tag{10.20}$$

$$Y_{ij} = \gamma_{00} + \gamma_{10}X_{ij} + \mu_{0j} + \mu_{1j}X_{ij} + e_{ij} \tag{10.21}$$

Using these models, the percentage of variance explained at the first level can be calculated as follows:

$$R^2_{level1} = \frac{\sigma^2_{e_{Formula18}} - \sigma^2_{e_{Formula19}}}{\sigma^2_{e_{Formula18}}} \tag{10.22}$$

While the percentage of variance explained at the second level is obtained by:

$$R^2_{level2} = \frac{\sigma^2_{\mu_{0Formula18}} - \sigma^2_{\mu_{0Formula19}}}{\sigma^2_{\mu_{0Formula18}}} \tag{10.23}$$

Using this procedure, one tests a series of models and each time test the R^2 or the change in R^2 across the different levels of the model. Whereas this procedure seems straightforward, an important caveat is that, in some cases, it might lead to a negative R^2 (see Snijders & Bosker, 1994 for an explanation of this phenomenon).

3.   Statistical power in multilevel models

In the multilevel regression model, power—or the probability of rejecting the null hypothesis when the null hypothesis is false—is a complicated matter. In general, power increases when (1) the population effect is larger, (2) the sample size is larger, (3) the Type 1 error rate is higher, (4) the variables (criterion and predictors) are measured more reliably, (5) the distributions of the variables are not restricted, and (6) the assumptions of the statistical test are not violated (Mathieu, Aguinis, Culpepper, & Chen, 2012). Although these general ideas are—particularly for single-level data—well understood, the issue for multilevel regression analysis is that "statistical power in multilevel designs is a complex combination of the number of higher level units and lower level units under investigation, the co-variances within and between units, and a slew of other factors that are still being investigated" (Mathieu & Chen, 2011, p. 631). Moreover, the factors contributing to power in the multilevel framework differ depending on whether one considers lower-level effects, cross-level effects, or cross-level interactions (Mathieu et al., 2012).

In general terms, the power of lower-level effects (i.e., the effect of a level 1 variable on the outcome) is more affected by the number of lower-level units than the number of upper-level units, while for cross-level effects (e.g., the effect of a level 2 variable on the outcome) the number of upper-level units matters more. In case of cross-level interactions, both the number of lower-level and upper-level units matter (Mathieu et al., 2012).

Because of the many elements affecting power in the multilevel regression framework, providing guidelines that are generally applicable is not feasible. Instead, several authors have proposed to use Monte Carlo simulation research to test power in multilevel models (e.g., Bosker, Snijders, & Guldemond, 2003; Mathieu et al., 2012). In power simulations, the researcher specifies the parameters of the data that he/she expects and then generates a series of datasets from the resulting model using a pseudo random number generator. Because the resulting datasets have been generated from a model for which the underlying parameters are known, power represents the percentage of datasets that return a significant effect when the effect exists (Lang, Bliese, & Runge, in press). Two useful tools adopting a simulation-based approach are Power IN Two-level designs (PINT; Bosker et al., 2003) and the Monte Carlo tool by Mathieu and colleagues (2012). PINT is a program that allows determining optimal sample sizes in two-level designs. The program also calculates approximate standard errors for estimates of fixed effect parameters. The Monte Carlo tool by Mathieu and colleagues (2012) is specifically designed to test the power to detect cross-level interaction effects. Provided a long list of model specifications (including the samples sizes at both levels, the intra-class correlation coefficient, the regression coefficients, variance components, and the alpha level), the tool computes the statistical power to detect a specific cross-level interaction.

4.   Software packages for testing multilevel models

Multilevel regression models can be tested in most statistical software packages, including SPSS, SAS, STATA, MPLUS, and R. Moreover, there are programs that are specifically designed for testing multilevel regression models, such as HLM. This latter program differs from the former ones in the sense that it allows for the specification of the equations per level, rather than requiring a single model equation. Moreover, for some of the programs the specification of error covariance structures is rather straightforward (e.g., SPSS), while for others this is hard or impossible to do (e.g., the lme4 package in R). An exhaustive overview and comparison of software for testing multilevel regression models is beyond the scope of this chapter, but interested readers can consult the website of the Center for Multilevel Modelling of the University of Bristol, which provides an extensive list of reviews of multilevel modeling software (http://www.bristol.ac.uk/cmm/learning/mmsoftware/).

Table 10.1   *Important issues to consider when testing a multilevel model*

Centering	The decision regarding how (or if) to center a variable should be made on conceptual grounds (Raudenbush & Bryk, 2002). Group-mean centering assumes that one's *relative* standing on an independent variable (either within a group or within the individual) is the important factor, whereas grand-mean centering assumes that one's *overall* standing matters. Although it is challenging to give blank recommendations, according to Enders and Tofighi (2007), group-mean centering is most useful when the research question primarily concerns (a) relations among level 1 variables, (b) interactions among level 1 variables, or (c) interactions between level 1 and level 2 variables. Grand-mean centering is most useful when the research question primarily concerns (a) a level 2 predictor but includes level 1 covariates or (b) interactions specified at level 2 (Enders & Tofighi, 2007). Note that there is no need to center dependent variables.
Proportion of variance accounted for	In ordinary least squares (OLS) regression, it is common practice to compute and report the proportion of variance accounted for. In multilevel regression analysis, however, this is more complicated because there is variation at different levels. One way to tackle this issue is to test the reduction in unexplained (error) variance at the different levels of analysis when adding predictors. However, this approach can result in negative variance estimates. Addressing this issue, one approach is to neglect the hierarchical nature of the data and use OLS regression to obtain explained variance estimates, while Nakagawa and Schielzeth (2013) propose to ignore random slope variance and base the calculations on the random intercept model only. LaHuis and colleagues (2014) compared these approaches using a simulation study, demonstrating that they all perform relatively well.
Statistical power	Statistical power refers to the long-term probability of detecting a statistically significant effect when the effect is present (Cohen, 1992). Power questions are important because they relate to a fundamental consideration when designing a multilevel study: How many observations are needed at each level of analysis? Unfortunately, estimating power for multilevel designs is considerably more complicated than estimating power for single-level analyses. In a multilevel design, power depends on the number of observations at each level of analysis, the variance distributions of measures, the type of effect being examined (e.g., within levels or cross-levels), to mention a few. Such complexity makes it impossible to provide hard and fast rules. Nevertheless, some guidance is available, and one relevant source of information is Maas and Hox (2005).
Software	Perhaps the most popular program dedicated specifically for multilevel analyses is HLM (Raudenbush, Bryk, Cheong, Congdon, & Du Toit, 2011). HLM data files are created by importing either raw data or system files from software programs such as SPSS and SAS. Users specify the level 1 and level 2 data files, and HLM creates a "multivariate data matrix" file that is used for further analysis. Models are specified by creating separate level 1 and level 2 equations using a simple point-and-click interface. MLM analyses can also be conducted in software designed to test latent variable models (e.g., Mplus and LISREL) as well as general statistical software such as SPSS and SAS. In SPSS, multilevel analyses are conducted with the MIXED MODELS procedure. In SAS, this is done using PROC MIXED (among other procedures). Finally, various packages have been developed for R, such as *multilevel* and *nlme*. One good source of information for conducting multilevel analyses using R can be found here: http://rsync .udc.es/CRAN/doc/contrib/Bliese_Multilevel.pdf. In general, software choice can be a function of the user's comfort with different approaches to statistical software.

FUTURE RESEARCH AND CONCLUDING COMMENTS

We started this chapter by outlining three types of nesting relevant to career research: (1) individuals nested within organizations, (2) individuals (and organizations) nested within geographical boundaries, and (3) time nested within individuals. However, needless to say that there are many other types of nesting that – although currently less elaborately explored in the literature – might also offer interesting avenues for future research aimed at a better understanding of the multilevel nature of careers. We start this concluding section by outlining two such potentially promising types of nesting, that is, (a) individuals nested within occupations and (b) romantic partners nested within dyads.

Individuals Nested Within Occupations

The term occupation derives from the verb occupy, which logically implies that an occupation is an entity within which individuals are situated (or "nested"). Occupations reflect divisions of labor that are socially constructed, and they develop from negotiated consensus around distinctive sets of tasks as well as knowing how to perform these tasks (Trice, 1993). Occupations are a meaningful level to consider because people performing the same type of job oftentimes have similar educational backgrounds, perform similar tasks, have similar working conditions, types of customer/clients, and so on. Occupations thus create both objective boundaries (i.e., work performed) and subjective boundaries (e.g., professional identity), which offer a variety of possible demarcations of context that span social or interpersonal elements, physical demands, values, norms, regulations, interests, and so on. Accordingly, occupation and occupational-level variables are likely to explain variance in individual career-related outcomes, such as career satisfaction, career success, employability, and so on over and beyond variance explained by individual-level predictors.

Dierdorff (2019) identified several reasons for revitalizing an occupational focus in work and organizational psychology, and these also give substance to our call for incorporating this type of nesting in career research. First, occupations have their own cultural features that are as potent as those attributed to organizational cultures. The uniqueness of occupational cultures thus provides a lens through which individuals make sense of individual (or organizational) events (Van Maanen & Barley, 1984). Aronsson and colleagues (Aronsson, Gustafsson, & Dallner, 2000), for example, examined the extent to which ill health resulted in presenteeism at work (i.e., attending work while sick). Across 42 occupational groups, results showed significant variability in sickness presenteeism. More specifically, high levels of sickness presenteeism were shown for occupations such as nursing home aides, welfare workers, primary school teachers, and cashiers, whereas low levels of sickness presenteeism were shown for occupations such as engineers, computer programmers and technicians, and physical and occupational therapists. Results such as these indicate how the same phenomena (ill health and work presence) can result in substantially different saliences depending on the occupation in which they occur. A second argument for considering the occupation-level in career research refers to changes in today's world of work. More specifically, sociologists have pointed out a reality of increased fluidity with which human capital and intellectual capital passes industries, economic sectors, and organizations (e.g., Hollister, 2011). In other words, for most individuals, long gone are the days of working at one organization (or even two) over the span of an individual's entire career, and it may well be that occupation is the more stable unit of analysis for many workers today. Third and finally, existing evidence from organizational psychology is convincing that occupations exert meaningful influences on a host of organizational behavior variables which may, in turn, have important effects for career-relevant behaviors and variables. To give one example, previous research has demonstrated that occupational commitment is empirically distinct from organizational commitment (Meyer, Allen, & Smith, 1993), and occupational commitment has in some cases also been shown to be even a stronger predictor of intention's to quit one's organization than organizational commitment (Lee, Carswell, & Allen, 2000). This suggests that considering occupations can reveal additional antecedents to attitudes linked to a variety of mobility or other career-relevant behaviors.

Partners Nested Within Dyads: Dual-Earner Couples

Dual-earner couples, that is, couples in which both romantic partners participate in the labor market, are the new normal in the world of work. Conceptually, the one-to-one linkages between the two romantic partners are defined as dyadic relationships. These dyadic relationships transcend a single level of conceptualization and analysis and are in the realm of multilevel research and theory testing (Gooty & Yammarino, 2011; Hofmans, Dóci, Solinger, Choi, & Judge, 2019; Tse & Ashkanasy, 2015).

The study of dual-earner dyadic relationships has gained traction in recent years, especially amongst researchers studying the work–family interface (e.g., Ho, Chen, Cheung, Liu, & Worthington, 2013; Matthews, Del Priore, Acitelli, & Barnes-Farrell, 2006; van Steenbergen, Kluwer, & Karney, 2014). Studies in this field consistently show that each member of the dual earner dyad affects and is affected by his/her partner's work and family experiences. For example, Schooreel and Verbruggen (2016), in a sample of 186 dual-earner couples, found that employees whose partner made use of family-friendly work arrangements experienced less home demands. Interestingly, employees whose partner made use of reduced work time arrangements (i.e., part-time work regime) worked on average more hours a week, and, as a result, experienced more work-to-family conflict.

We suggest that the use of dual-earner dyads has a much broader potential application that extends beyond the traditional study of work–family conflict and enrichment. For example, one could investigate the extent to which (female) employees are constrained in their careers because of their partner's gender stereotypes or attitudes toward career progression (see Martínez & Paterna, 2019, for a rare example). More generally, the use of dyadic designs may help in answering the question of how "boundaryless" contemporary careers really are. After all, it is plausible to assume that individuals' physical and psychological room for maneuver is at least partly constrained by the other member of the dyadic relationship. In a similar vein, the dyadic approach allows testing the extent to which romantic partners mutually influence each other's objective and/or subjective career success, thereby challenging popular phrases such as "behind every great man there's a(n) (even) great(er) woman." As a final example, dyadic designs may be relevant to career scholars studying employees' reactions to career shocks, defined as "any event that triggers deliberation involving the prospect of change in an important career-related behavior such as seeking further education, changing occupations, or changing employment status" (Seibert, Kraimer, Holtom, & Pierotti, 2013, p. 172). The (positive or negative) impact of such career shocks may cross over to the other member of the relationship dyad. Also, partners may mutually influence each other's coping process. This was demonstrated by Debus and Unger (2017) who examined job insecurity in the context of dual-earner couples, showing interactive effects of partners' insecurity levels, and highlighting the relevance of "family" as a context factor that influences individual career-related affect and behavior. Importantly, when studying partners nested within dyads—and particularly when testing crossover mechanisms between the dyad members—an extension of the multilevel regression framework is needed. Such extension is referred to as the Actor–Partner Interdependence Model (APIM) and is described in Cook and Kenny (2005).

In conclusion, we believe that adopting a multilevel perspective can enhance our understanding of contemporary careers. New questions can be expected to emerge as career researchers recognize the multilevel features of the data they have collected, and old questions may be reinterpreted. As noted by Kreft and de Leeuw (1998), "Once you know that hierarchies exist you see them everywhere" (p. 1). We hope that this chapter will serve as a valuable resource, both for multilevel disciples and novices, that it will spur new thinking, and add a unique perspective to the study of careers.

NOTE

1. The term "organization" broadly refers to a group of deliberately organized people who collaborate toward a shared goal or purpose (Daft, Murphy, & Willmott, 2017). Therefore, other business units, such as departments and work teams also fit the definition of organization.

REFERENCES

Al Ariss, A., & Crowley-Henry, M. (2013). Self-initiated expatriation and migration in the management literature: Present theorizations and future research directions. *Career Development International*, *18*(1), 78–96.
Arnold, J. (1997). *Managing careers into the 21st century*. London, UK: Sage.

Aronsson, G., Gustafsson, K., & Dallner, M. (2000). Sick but yet at work: An empirical study of sickness presenteeism. *Journal of Epidemiology and Community Health, 54*, 502–509.

Arthur, M. B. (1994). The boundaryless career: A new perspective for organizational inquiry. *Journal of Organizational Behavior, 15*, 295–306.

Arthur, M. B., Hall, D. T., & Lawrence, B. S. (Eds.). (1989). *The handbook of career theory*. New York: Cambridge University Press.

Barnes-Farrell, J., & Matthews, R. A. (2012). Age and work attitudes. In K. S. Shultz & G. A. Adams (Eds.), *Aging and work in the 21st century* (pp. 139–162). Mahwah, NJ: Lawrence Erlbaum Associates.

Baruch, Y., & Peiperl, M. (2000). Career management practices: An empirical survey and implications. *Human Resource Management, 39*(4), 347–366.

Bateman, T. S., & Crant, J. M. (1993). The proactive component of organizational behavior: A measure and correlates. *Journal of Organizational Behavior, 14*(2), 103–118.

Beal, D. J., & Weiss, H. M. (2003). Methods of ecological momentary assessment in organizational research. *Organizational Research Methods, 6*(4), 440–464.

Bliese, P. D. (2002). Using multilevel random coefficient modeling in organizational research. In F. Drasgow & N. Schmitt (Eds.), *Advances in measurement and data analysis* (pp. 401–445). San Francisco: Jossey-Bass.

Bliese, P. (2016). Multilevel modeling in R (2.6). http://cran.r-project.org/doc/contrib/Bliese _Multilevel.pdf

Bosker, R. J., Snijders, T. A. B., & Guldemond, H. (2003). PINT (Power in Two-level designs). Estimating standard errors of regression coefficients in hierarchical linear models for power calculations. User's manual version 2.1. Groningen: University of Groningen. https://www.stats.ox.ac.uk/~snijders/multilevel.htm#progPINT

Boudreau, J. W., Boswell, W. R., & Judge, T. A. (2001). Effects of personality on executive career success in the United States and Europe. *Journal of Vocational Behavior, 58*, 53–81.

Bryk, A. S., & Raudenbush, S. W. (1992). *Hierarchical linear models: Applications and data analysis methods*. New York: Sage.

Chang, W.-J. A., Wang, Y.-S., & Huang, T.-C. (2013). Work design-related antecedents of turnover intention: A multilevel approach. *Human Resource Management, 52*(1), 1–26.

Cohen, J. (1992). A power primer. *Psychological Bulletin, 112*, 155–159.

Cook, W. L., & Kenny, D. A. (2005). The actor-partner interdependence model: A model of bidirectional effects in developmental studies. *International Journal of Behavioral Development, 29*, 101–109.

Daft, R. L., Murphy, J., & Willmott, H. (2017). *Organization theory and design: An international perspective*. Andover, UK: Cengage Learning.

Da Motta Veiga, S. P., & Turban, D. B. (2018). Insight into job search self-regulation: Effects of employment self-efficacy and perceived progress on job search intensity. *Journal of Vocational Behavior, 108*, 57–66.

Debus, M. E., Probst, T. M., König, C. J., & Kleinmann, M. (2012). Catch me if I fall! Enacted uncertainty avoidance and the social safety net as country-level moderators in the job insecurity-job attitudes link. *Journal of Applied Psychology, 97*(3), 690–698.

Debus, M. E., & Unger, D. (2017). The interactive effects of dual-earner couples' job insecurity: Linking conservation of resources theory with crossover research. *Journal of Occupational and Organizational Psychology, 90*, 225–247.

DeFillippi, R. J., & Arthur, M. B. (1994). The boundaryless career: A competency-based perspective. *Journal of Organizational Behavior, 15*, 307–324.

De Vos, A., & Van der Heijden, B. I. J. M. (2015). *Handbook of research on sustainable careers*. Cheltenham, UK and Northampton, MA, USA: Edward Elgar Publishing.

Dierdorff, E. C. (2019). Toward reviving an occupation with occupations. *Annual Review of Organizational Psychology and Organizational Behavior, 6*, 397–419.

DiMaggio, P. J., & Powell, W. W. (1983). The iron cage revisited: Institutional isomorphism and collective rationality in organizational fields. *American Sociological Review, 48*(2), 147–160.

El Akremi, A., Colaianni, G., Portoghese, I., Galletta, M., & Battistelli, A. (2014). How organizational support impacts affective commitment and turnover among Italian nurses: A multilevel mediation model. *International Journal of Human Resource Management, 25*(9), 1185–1207.

Enders, C. K., & Tofighi, D. (2007). Centering predictor variables in cross-sectional multilevel models: A new look at an old issue. *Psychological Methods, 12*(2), 121–138.

Erlinghagen, M. (2007). Self-perceived job insecurity and social context: A multi-level analysis of 17 European countries. *European Sociological Review, 24*(2), 183–197.

Finaccord (2018). Global expatriates: Size, segmentation and forecasts for the worldwide market. https://www.finaccord.com/home/reports/Global-Expatriates-Size,-Segmentation -and-Forecas

Gentry, W. A., Weber, T. J., & Sadri, G. (2008). Examining career-related mentoring and managerial performance across cultures: A multilevel analysis. *Journal of Vocational Behavior, 72*(2), 241–253.

Gooty, J., & Yammarino, F. J. (2011). Dyads in organizational research: Conceptual issues and multilevel analyses. *Organizational Research Methods, 14*(3), 456–483.

Greenhaus, J. H., Callanan, G. A., & Godshalk, V. M. (2010). *Career management.* Thousand Oaks, CA: Sage.

Gunz, H., & Mayrhofer, W. (2018). *Rethinking career studies: Facilitating conversation across boundaries with the social chronology framework.* Cambridge, UK: Cambridge University Press.

Hall, D. T. (2002). *Careers in and out of organizations.* Thousand Oaks, CA: Sage.

Hegstad, C. D., & Wentling, R. M. (2005). Organizational antecedents and moderators that impact on the effectiveness of exemplary formal mentoring programs in Fortune 500 companies in the United States. *Human Resource Development International, 8*(4), 467–487.

Ho, M. Y., Chen, X., Cheung, F. M., Liu, H., & Worthington Jr, E. L. (2013). A dyadic model of the work–family interface: A study of dual-earner couples in China. *Journal of Occupational Health Psychology, 18*(1), 53–63.

Hofmans, J., De Clercq, B., Kuppens, P., Verbeke, L., & Widiger, T. A. (2019). Testing the structure and process of personality using ambulatory assessment data: An overview of within-person and person-specific techniques. *Psychological Assessment.* doi: 10.1037/ pas0000562

Hofmans, J., Dóci, E., Solinger, O. N., Choi, W., & Judge, T. A. (2019). Capturing the dynamics of leader–follower interactions: Stalemates and future theoretical progress. *Journal of Organizational Behavior, 40*, 382–385.

Hollister, M. (2011). Employment stability in the U.S. labor market: Rhetoric versus reality. *Annual Review of Sociology,* 37, 305–324.

Hox, J. J., Moerbeek, M., & van de Schoot, J. (2017). *Multilevel analysis: Techniques and applications.* New York, NY: Routledge.

International Labour Organization (2015). ILO global estimates on migrant workers. https:// www.ilo.org/wcmsp5/groups/public/---dgreports/---dcomm/documents/publication/wcms _436343.pdf

Ituma, A., & Simpson, R. (2009). The boundaryless' career and career boundaries: Applying an institutionalist perspective to ICT workers in the context of Nigeria. *Human Relations, 62*(5), 727–761.

Kreft, I., & de Leeuw, J. (1998). *Introducing multilevel modeling.* London, UK: Sage.

LaHuis, D. M., Hartman, M. J., Hakoyama, S., & Clark, P. C. (2014). Explained variance measures for multilevel models. *Organizational Research Methods, 17*, 433–451.

Lang, J. W. B., Bliese, P. D., & Runge, J. M. (in press). Detecting consensus emergence in organizational multilevel data: Power simulations. *Organizational Research Methods*. https://doi.org/10.1177/1094428119873950

Lee, B., Porfeli, E. J., & Hirschi, A. (2016). Between- and within-person level motivational precursors associated with career exploration. *Journal of Vocational Behavior*, *92*, 125–134.

Lee, K., Carswell, J. J., & Allen, N. J. (2000). A meta-analytic review of occupational commitment: Relations with person- and work-related variables. *Journal of Applied Psychology*, *85*, 799–811.

Maas, C. J. M., & Hox, J. J. (2005). Sufficient sample sizes for multilevel modeling. *Methodology*, *1*, 86–92.

Major, D. A., Fletcher, T. D., Davis, D. D., & Germano, L. M. (2008). The influence of work–family culture and workplace relationships on work interference with family: A multilevel model. *Journal of Organizational Behavior*, *29*(7), 881–897.

Martínez, C., & Paterna, C. (2019). Attitude towards career progression in Spanish dual-earner couples: A dyadic approach. *The Social Science Journal*, *56*(1), 60–68.

Mathieu, J. E., Aguinis, H., Culpepper, S. A., & Chen, G. (2012). Understanding and estimating the power to detect cross-level interaction effects in multilevel modeling. *Journal of Applied Psychology*, *97*(5), 951–966.

Mathieu, J. E., & Chen, G. (2011). The etiology of the multilevel paradigm in management research. *Journal of Management*, *37*(2), 610–641.

Matthews, R. A., Del Priore, R. E., Acitelli, L. K., & Barnes-Farrell, J. L. (2006). Work-to-relationship conflict: Crossover effects in dual-earner couples. *Journal of Occupational Health Psychology*, *11*(3), 228–240.

Meyer, J. P., Allen, N. J., & Smith, C. A. (1993). Commitment to organizations and occupations: Extension and test of a 3-component conceptualization. *Journal of Applied Psychology*, *78*(4), 538–551.

Nakagawa, S., & Schielzeth, H. (2013). A general and simple method for obtaining R^2 from generalized linear mixed-effects models. *Methods in Ecology and Evolution*, *4*(2), 133–142.

Naman, J. L., & Slevin, D. P. (1993). Entrepreneurship and the concept of fit: A model and empirical tests. *Strategic Management Journal*, *14*(2), 137–153.

Nelissen, J., Forrier, A., & Verbruggen, M. (2017). Employee development and voluntary turnover: Testing the employability paradox. *Human Resource Management Journal*, *27*(1), 152–168.

Nezlek, J. B. (2001). Multilevel random coefficient analyses of event and interval contingent data in social and personality psychology research. *Personality & Social Psychology Bulletin*, *27*, 771–785.

Nezlek, J. B. (2008). An introduction to multilevel modeling for social and personality psychology. *Social and Personality Psychology Compass*, *2*, 842–860.

Preacher, K. J., Curran, P. J., & Bauer, D. J. (2006). Computational tools for probing interactions in multiple linear regression, multilevel modeling, and latent curve analysis. *Journal of Educational and Behavioral Statistics*, *31*(4), 437–448.

Raudenbush, S. W., & Bryk, A. S. (2002). *Hierarchical linear models: Applications and data analysis methods*. Thousand Oaks, CA: Sage Publications.

Raudenbush, S. W., Bryk, A. S., Cheong, Y. F., Congdon, R. T., & Du Toit, M. (2011). *HLM 7: hierarchical linear and nonlinear modeling*. Skokie, IL: Scientific Software International.

Sawyer, K., Young, S. F., Thoroughgood, C., & Dominguez, K. M. (2020). Does reducing male domination in teams attenuate or intensify the harmful effects of perceived discrimination on women's job satisfaction? A test of competing hypotheses. *Applied Psychology: An International Review*, *69*(2), 557–577.

Schooreel, T., & Verbruggen, M. (2016). Use of family-friendly work arrangements and work–family conflict: Crossover effects in dual-earner couples. *Journal of Occupational Health Psychology*, *21*(1), 119–132.

Seibert, S. E., Kraimer, M. L., Holtom, B. C., & Pierotti, A. J. (2013). Even the best laid plans sometimes go askew: Career self-management processes, career shocks, and the decision to pursue graduate education. *Journal of Applied Psychology*, *98*(1), 169–182.

Sieracki, J. H., Leon, S. C., Miller, S. A., & Lyons, J. S. (2008). Individual and provider effects on mental health outcomes in child welfare: A three level growth curve approach. *Children and Youth Services Review*, *30*(7), 800–808.

Sjöberg, O. (2004). The role of family policy institutions in explaining gender-role attitudes: A comparative multilevel analysis of thirteen industrialized countries. *Journal of European Social Policy*, *14*(2), 107–123.

Smale, A., Bagdadli, S., Cotton, R., Dello Russo, S., Dickmann, M., Dysvik, A., ... & Rozo, P. (2019). Proactive career behaviors and subjective career success: The moderating role of national culture. *Journal of Organizational Behavior*, *40,* 105–122.

Snijders, T. A. B., & Bosker, R. J. (1994). Modeled variance in two-level models. *Sociological Methods & Research*, *22*(3), 342–363.

Snijders, T. A. B., & Bosker, R. J. (1999). *Multilevel analysis: An introduction to basic and advanced multilevel modeling.* London, UK: Sage.

Sonnenfeld, J. A., & Peiperl, M. A. (1988). Staffing policy as a strategic response: A typology of career systems. *Academy of Management Review*, *13*(4), 588–600.

Strauss, K., Griffin, M. A., & Parker, S. K. (2012). Future work selves: How salient hoped-for identities motivate proactive career behaviors. *Journal of Applied Psychology*, *97*(3), 580–598.

Sverke, M., Hellgren, J., & Näswall, K. (2002). No security: A meta-analysis and review of job insecurity and its consequences. *Journal of Occupational Health Psychology*, *7*(3), 242–264.

Trice, H. M. (1993). *Occupational subcultures in the workplace.* Ithaca, NY: Cornell University Press.

Tse, H. H., & Ashkanasy, N. M. (2015). The dyadic level of conceptualization and analysis: A missing link in multilevel OB research? *Journal of Organizational Behavior*, *36*(8), 1176–1180.

Van der Heijde, C. M., & Van der Heijden, B. I. J. M. (2006). A competence-based and multidimensional operationalization and measurement of employability. *Human Resources Management*, *45*(3), 449–476.

Van Maanen, J., & Barley, S. R. (1984). Occupational communities: Culture and control in organizations. *Research in Organizational Behavior*, *6*, 287–365.

van Steenbergen, E. F., Kluwer, E. S., & Karney, B. R. (2014). Work–family enrichment, work–family conflict, and marital satisfaction: A dyadic analysis. *Journal of Occupational Health Psychology*, *19*(2), 182–194.

Van Vianen, A. E. M., Rosenauer, D., Homan, A. C., Horstmeier, C. A. L., & Voelpel, S. C. (2018). Career mentoring in context: A multilevel study on differentiated career mentoring and career mentoring climate. *Human Resource Management*, *57*, 583–599.

Wang, Y. H., Hu, C., Hurst, C. S., & Yang, C. C. (2014). Antecedents and outcomes of career plateaus: The roles of mentoring others and proactive personality. *Journal of Vocational Behavior*, *85*(3), 319–328.

West, S. G., & Hepworth, J. T. (1991). Statistical issues in the study of temporal data: Daily experiences. *Journal of Personality*, *59*(3), 609–662.

Wiernik, B. M., & Wille, B. (2018). Careers, career development and career management. In D. S. Ones, N. Anderson, C. Viswesvaran, & H. K. Sinangil (Eds.), *The Sage handbook of industrial, work and organizational psychology* (2nd ed., Vol. 3, pp. 547–585). Thousand Oaks, CA: Sage.

Wille, B., Hofmans, J., Feys, M., & De Fruyt, F. (2014). Maturation of work attitudes: Correlated change with big five personality traits and reciprocal effects over 15 years. *Journal of Organizational Behavior*, *35*(4), 507–529.

Woods, S. A., Lievens, F., De Fruyt, F., & Wille, B. (2013). Personality across working life: The longitudinal and reciprocal influences of personality on work. *Journal of Organizational Behavior, 34*(S1), S7–S25.

Woods, S. A., Wille, B., Wu, C. H., Lievens, F., & De Fruyt, F. (2019). The influence of work on personality trait development: The Demands-Affordances TrAnsactional (DATA) Model, an integrative review, and research agenda. *Journal of Vocational Behavior, 110*, 258–271. https://doi.org/10.1016/j.jvb.2018.11.010

Yammarino, F. J., & Gooty, J. (2017). Multi-level issues and dyads in leadership research. In B. Schyns, R. J. Hall, & P. Neves (Eds.), *Handbook of methods in leadership research* (pp. 229–255). Cheltenham, UK and Northampton, MA, USA: Edward Elgar Publishing.

PART III

QUALITATIVE AND MIXED METHODS

11. Engaging grounded theory to study careers: attending to the relational tensions

Kerry Roberts Gibson and Danna Greenberg[1]

Among organizational and management researchers there has been growing acceptance and embracement of inductive research which is theory-building rather than theory testing. Once an under-legitimized methodological approach, an ever-increasing number of rigorous studies are being published in top management journals with editorial boards being expanded to include editors with expertise in qualitative methodology. Corley (2015) recently suggested that grounded theory research, a particular type of qualitative methodology, might be one of the most powerful forms of inquiry for understanding the rapidly shifting world of work and organizations. Because grounded theory enables a scholar to stay connected to the lived experience of the individuals who are involved with a particular phenomenon, it is a valuable paradigm for ensuring that theory remains tightly connected to practice – a growing concern among management scholars (e.g. Aguinis, Shapiro, Antonacopoulou, & Cummings, 2014; Haley, Page, Pitsis, Rivas, & Yu, 2017).

While organizational scholars in general may be engaging qualitative methodology, and specifically grounded theory, with increased frequency, the same does not appear to be true for careers scholars. In a review of human resources (HR) research, which is aligned and in some cases overlapping with careers research, Murphy, Klotz, and Kreiner (2017) reviewed close to 200 articles published in *Academy of Management Journal* which utilized some elements of grounded theory and found that only 10 emphasized HR-related topics. They also found HR research utilizing grounded theory to be rare if non-existent in *Personnel Psychology* and the *Journal of Applied Psychology*. Out of curiosity regarding the domain of careers research, we conducted a key word search within the *Journal of Vocational Behavior* – a, or the, most respected and impactful careers-focused management journal. Utilizing Web of Science and searching for "grounded theory," we found only 11 articles with publication dates ranging from 2001 to 2020. While not all grounded theory papers in the journal used the methodology as a key word, the publication dates of those that did are surprising given that grounded theory was introduced as a methodology more than 50 years ago. While there are some notable exceptions of high-quality grounded theory-based careers scholarship of late (e.g. Modestino, Sugiyama, & Ladge, 2019; Nigam & Dokko, 2019; Petriglieri, Ashford, & Wrzesniewski, 2019; Schabram & Maitlis, 2017), in general careers scholars appear to be slow to adopt this methodology.

We argue that there is reason now, more than ever, for careers scholars to embrace grounded theory. In modern organizations, globalization, technology, world crises, and ever-changing economic realities mean the relationships between individuals, their careers, and organizations are increasingly complex. The traditional employment model has been replaced with more diverse, shifting work arrangements, all of which have implications for individuals' understanding and construction of their careers and career identity, which drives career behavior (Shepherd & Williams, 2018). Grounded theory is well suited for exploring these issues as it enables a researcher to build theory in response to new, previously unexplored research questions and organizational experiences (Bansal & Corley, 2011). Grounded theory may be vital for ensuring that careers theory remains connected to the continual shifts of the modern-day work world, particularly in a post Covid-19 world where career uncertainty is expected to grow exponentially.

In this chapter, we encourage careers scholars who are interested in engaging grounded theory approaches to consider the relational aspects of the process of conducting this kind of research, particularly within the study of careers. Moving beyond a brief introduction to grounded theory, we focus on three important relationships a researcher must attend to when engaging grounded theory. These relationships are one's relationship with the phenomenon under investigation, one's relationship to the participants, and one's relationship with their research audience. We draw upon our own research experiences along with that of seminal careers scholars who engaged grounded theory to expand upon these relational tensions and to provide researchers with insights on how to effectively manage these struggles as they arise in their own work. We argue that managing these tensions is essential for rigorous application of grounded theory. Finally, while we are focused primarily on these relational tensions when conducting careers research, we believe these insights are applicable to many scholars who are engaged in other areas of grounded theory research.

A BRIEF INTRODUCTION TO GROUNDED THEORY

Broadly defined, grounded theory is a method for conducting research in which one is focused on building theory based on the realities of individuals who experience a particular phenomenon. The underlying tenets of grounded theory were first introduced over 50 years ago by Glaser and Strauss (1967) in their seminal book, *The Discovery of Grounded Theory*. Grounded theory centers on investigating a phenomenon from the perspective of those who are or have experience with it and building theoretical insights that are grounded in the data (Murphy et al., 2017). This methodology is built upon inductive reasoning, meaning that the researcher allows the answers to the research question to emerge from the data, remaining open to any possible answer as well as new questions versus testing a pre-developed hypothesis as demonstrated through traditional quantitative research. Ideally, what emerges from grounded theory is an underlying theoretical explanation for the why and/or how of the phenomenon that goes beyond a descriptive explanation of the what (Corley, 2015). In so doing, grounded theory provides an important middle ground between empiricism and relativism as theoretical insights are developed that remain attached to the realities of the individuals who are experiencing the phenomenon which underlies the theory (Suddaby, 2006). This research method can be applied through a variety of data collection techniques including interviews, observations, and even archival data. While scholars have extended and adapted grounded theory as they apply this methodology to different contexts (Walsh et al., 2015), there are two central elements to this approach, which distinguish it from other qualitative methods – constant comparison and theoretical sampling and saturation. As the relational aspects of grounded theory emerge from these elements, we briefly review them here.

A core building block of grounded theory is "*constant comparison.*" In contrast to more positivist traditions in which there is a clear separation between data collection and data analysis, grounded theory requires the researcher to iterate between data collection, data analysis, and theorizing. A researcher enters the field with a broad research question that is well suited for a grounded theory approach. Throughout data collection, the researcher will hit the pause button in order to analyze the data, return to extant theory, and make adjustments to the data collection process based on the patterns that are emerging from the data. It is expected that the research methods, the research protocol, even the research questions will shift as the research team moves back and forth between data collection and analysis. One mistake many novice scholars make with constant comparison is to assume this iterative process means the researcher refrains from reviewing existing theory before developing a research question and entering the field (Suddaby, 2010). Rather, existing theory, referred to as substantive theory, provides the basis for developing a preliminary research question and for conceptualizing the emerging patterns in the data (Glaser & Strauss, 1967). Existing theory is also essential for guiding future decisions regarding both data collection and analysis.

Constant comparison means grounded theory is a messy, ambiguous, reciprocal process (Corley, 2015). The cyclical nature of this methodology is crucial for developing the creative, unexpected insights that are essential for exemplary theoretical contributions. Researchers who are newer to grounded theory may struggle to understand this iterative process, as all too often the methods sections of published work do not articulate fully how this cyclical process is the basis for the rigor of grounded theory. In most grounded theory studies the authors have conducted, they have cycled between data and theorizing so much that they cannot begin to say how many iterations they engaged to develop rigorous theorizing entrenched in the data. Furthermore, this iterative process is intellectually and time intensive. For those newer to this method, we encourage you to read Harrison and Rouse (2014), who provide an excellent model for showing the rigor of "constant comparison" without reducing it to a staged methodological description.

Grounded theory is also defined by the linked techniques of "*theoretical sampling and theoretical saturation.*" With theoretical sampling, data collection decisions are made based on the phenomenon under investigation. A researcher may choose to target a particular data source in order to be immersed in the phenomenon under investigation. Rather than gathering data from a diverse, representative sample, in grounded theory one centers on finding data sources that are most relevant to the research question being asked (Murphy et al., 2017). Furthermore, there is an expectation that as new insights emerge as one iterates between data collection, analysis, and theorizing, the researcher will adjust the sampling. For instance, as one of the authors gathered data on a study of careers of early stage academics, she and her colleagues noticed a distinct difference in the perspective of individuals who had received a PhD from the most elite research institutions. To explore further this perspective, the authors refocused their sampling to interview more individuals who had gone to elite research institutions. This approach is in direct contrast to quantitative research wherein samples are pre-determined and hypotheses are pre-registered preventing any changes to the data collection plan once the research begins. Theoretical saturation refers to how a researcher knows they have gathered enough data points to produce rigorous, impactful, innovative theoretical insights. Furthermore, with grounded theory there are not specific rules about what makes a dataset large enough to argue for the robustness of one's theory development. There is no rule that says 25–30 interviews are needed to achieve saturation even though scholars sometimes make that claim (Suddaby, 2010). With theoretical sampling, the researcher relies on data analysis and the emerging theory to determine when saturation has occurred. The researcher continues data collection until no new patterns and insights are emerging from the data that need to be added to the emerging theoretical model (Charmaz, 2014). Drawing more explicit attention to this process when writing the methods section may help circumvent editors and reviewers who may be tempted to rely on pre-determined expectations for interview quantities as opposed to relying on the technique of theoretical saturation.

The freedom provided by theoretical sampling and theoretical saturation is both unnerving and empowering for the researcher. It is also essential for developing deep theoretical insights. The researcher must pay close attention to determine the best match between research site, phenomenon and core research question and use this insight to identify whom to collect data from to answer their primary research question. As the researcher engages in a constant comparison process, they may either make decisions to shift whom they are collecting data from or choose to add additional sources of data to triangulate their findings. Alternatively, a researcher may decide that a matched or paired approach will generate the most insights with a particular phenomenon. The freedom of theoretical sampling and theoretical saturation is essential for generating the creative insights from which rigorous theoretical insights will emerge.

These principles of grounded theory highlight the necessity for the researcher to be immersed in the phenomenon under investigation. Rigorous grounded theory research requires the researcher to establish an intimate, enduring relationship between themselves and their research site (Suddaby, 2010). We would also argue this deep, enduring relationship extends to one's commitment to the phenomenon under investigation, to one's research participants, and to the field. It is only by remaining deeply connected to all aspects of the research that the researcher can be open and attentive to potential new theoretical insights while ensuring these insights are linked to individuals' experiences and understanding. As such, grounded theory is inherently a relational methodology. In fact, Corley (2015, p. 602) describes grounded theory as fundamentally seeking out a "whole new relational externality." Yet, rarely have we considered the basis of these relationships and how they affect the research process.

RELATIONAL TENSIONS WITHIN GROUNDED THEORY METHODOLOGY

Understanding how the relationships present within grounded theory methodology affect the research process requires consideration of relational theory – or the research regarding how work relationships affect outcomes within organizations. We define work relationships as the dyadic, interpersonal connections that exist in conjunction with an individual's role in a given organization (Dutton & Heaphy, 2003; Dutton & Ragins, 2007; Ferris et al., 2009; Sluss & Ashforth, 2007). As this burgeoning research field suggests, work relationships affect how and why job tasks are completed within organizations (Dutton & Ragins, 2007; Ferris et al., 2009). While scholars have attended to how work relationships affect individual and organizational life, this research also has interesting implications for our own work as researchers. That is to say, we can think beyond grounded theory as only a methodological research process to see the "work" embedded within the course of completing research projects (i.e. obtain IRB approval, recruit participants, schedule interviews, conduct interviews, analyze interviews, present findings, etc.). Therefore, we argue attention needs to be paid to the presence of *relational* work that is implicitly and explicitly embedded within the grounded theory research process. By unpacking the relational work within the methodological process, we create a broader, more holistic understanding of the impact of choosing grounded theory to study a research question.

Given this, we bring attention to how the research on relational theory undergirds the process and methodology within grounded theory. That is to say, these often-unexplored work relationships implicit and explicit within grounded theory influence the insights or discoveries that result. The paradox that relationships at work are both central to work while also often dismissed or even erased from organizational attention was first highlighted by the work of Fletcher (1998). As Fletcher so aptly argues: "There was a dynamic process in operation in which relational practice got disappeared as work and got constructed as something other than work" (Fletcher, 1998, p. 178). Grounded theory research is no exception to this paradox or reality. The problem with ignoring this work or the relational component of grounded theory is that it negates our ability to acknowledge how this dimension affects both the research process and research outcomes. While it is true that relationships are messy, ignoring their presence does not remove them or their influence on our work as researchers.

For clarity, we are using the word *relational* to reference the multiple levels of connections researchers have within the grounded theory process. Rather than limiting this question exclusively to dyadic, interpersonal connections, we broaden the conceptualization of work relationships to include a variety of relationships that surface throughout the research process. This relational element, while arguably present in all grounded theory research, is potentially most prominent within careers research given the inherent complexity of studying the careers of others through a process that is central to the researcher's own career.

To explore the relational element of grounded theory research, we focus on three specific relationships the researcher has when invoking this methodology. First, there is the scholar's relationship with the research question they are asking. This relationship explains why the scholar wants to study the given research topic and illuminates any personal or implicit connections the scholar has to the topic being studied. Second, a scholar typically has a myriad of dyadic relationships that can affect the process of grounded theory research, of which we focus on the interpersonal relationship between scholar and research participant. This particular dyadic interpersonal relationship is foundational to the discovery process when conducting grounded theory research (cf. Locke, Golden-Biddle, & Feldman, 2008). Finally, there is the collective relationship between scholar and reader, or more broadly the audience for one's scholarship, which is (ideally) a collective group of many. Therefore, we use the word "relational" to reference these specific types of relationships scholars must navigate when they participate in grounded theory research.

Below, we explore each of these relationships and highlight the tensions embedded within. By exploring one intrapersonal relational tension (between scholar and research question), one dyadic interpersonal relational tension (between scholar and interview participant), and one collective relational tension (between scholar and audience), we draw attention to three separate "levels" at which relational tensions can surface. In explaining the tension, we also suggest strategies researchers can engage to manage the risks inherent within each relational tension and to mitigate its impact on the rigor of one's research. Table 11.1 provides an overview of each relational tension, its level, and proposed strategies for navigating that tension.

RELATIONAL TENSION IN SEEING THE TOPIC

When engaged with grounded theory, the first relationship the scholar needs to be attentive to is their personal relationship to the phenomenon being studied. Traditionally, organizational scholars are advised to study topics to which they have little to no personal connection. Having a strong emotional connection or opinion about the phenomenon being investigated is assumed to hinder a scholar's ability to remain objective and maintain their professional distance during the research process (Rudestam & Newton, 2014). This in turn may obstruct the rigor of one's methodology. Yet, for careers scholars maintaining a detached relationship to one's research is likely to be the exception rather than the rule. As working adults, every

Table 11.1 *Navigating the relational tensions when conducting grounded*
theory research

Relational Tension	Seeing the Topic	Hearing the Participants	Sharing the Findings
Level	Intrapersonal	Interpersonal	Collective
Key Tension	Personally-relevant research topic/phenomenon can bias the researcher	Relationship paradigm used can influence data collection and analysis	Transparent disclosure (or lack thereof) regarding research process impacts colleagues' interpretation of findings and implications for future research
Strategies for Responding	• Self-assessment of underlying interests, motives, and desired findings • Relational memoing • Maintain an insider–outsider research collaboration	• Determine emotional and relational response • Communicate this to participants • Disclose your stance when communicating findings	• Consider the impact of your research if you withhold disclosure • Consider the impact on the field if we maintain the implicit assumption of "objective distance" • Consider the impact of disclosing to your own career • Maintain an insider–outsider research collaboration
	• Enlist a grounded-theory research mentor		

researcher is on their own career path and thereby may have experiences with the topic under investigation. Scholars interact daily with students, peers, friends and family members each of whom are on their own career journey with their own stories, struggles, and successes. These interactions can spark a scholar's interest in new careers research questions. As such, we believe careers scholars need to be attentive to their personal relationship with the phenomenon they are researching.

This type of research is defined by Jones and Bartunek (in press) as personally-relevant research, which references "research that addresses questions in which scholars are personally invested or involve a population to which they belong or in which they hold a personal interest." This type of connection can be found in Ladge and Greenberg's (2015) research where they already had experienced becoming working mothers and returning to work when they embarked on research of women's experiences of returning to work after maternity leave. We see a similar relationship between researcher and phenomenon in Amabile and Hall's (in press) research on how individuals conceptualize and experience retirement as the researchers themselves were either in the process of retiring or had recently retired when they embarked upon this study. Both of these studies are a distinct form of personally relevant research categorized as self-relevant research (Amabile & Hall, in press). With self-relevant research, the relationship between the researcher and research study is embedded in the researchers' own personal experience with the phenomenon under investigation. As such, the researcher has a deeply personal relationship with the topic under investigation. We argue that careers research is at a minimum personally-relevant research, if not inherently self-relevant research. Given this, careers researchers need to attend to this relationship between themselves and the phenomenon under investigation as it affects how they "see" the topic.

More specifically, there are two components of the relationship between the researcher and the research study that can influence what the researcher "sees" through the grounded theory process. First, for all researchers there is an emotional component of this relationship. Researchers typically have deep emotional involvement when research emanates from one's membership in a group (MacLean, Anteby, Hudson, & Rudolph, 2006), or when one has a personal interest in vulnerable people (e.g. Sawyer, in press), or when the research question is relevant to one's own life (Ladge, Clair, & Greenberg, 2012). One is likely to have both positive and negative emotional responses that will shift over the course of the research process. Researchers may find it difficult, if not impossible, to separate out these emotional responses from their intellectual interpretations of the data as they iterate between data collection and analysis. Furthermore, if the research is also self-relevant, there will be an experiential aspect of the relationship between researcher and research study. As one is engaged in the grounded theory process and deeply immersed in the lived experience and understanding of one's research participant, it is difficult to separate out this data from one's own experiences with that phenomenon. As the researcher iterates between data collection and analysis as is advised by the tenets of constant comparison, they are likely to find their analysis will be influenced by their experiences as these emotional and experiential connections affect what the researcher sees or recognizes within the data. Said another way, the researcher's experience and viewpoint may challenge the researchers' ability to highlight and attend to data that contradicts their own experiences, resulting in the researcher unconsciously prioritizing their experience over that of participants, which can introduce biases in the theorizing.

Managing the Tension

Because management and organizational scholars have historically emphasized the importance of the detached, objective researcher, researchers often feel pressure to hide any connections they may have to the phenomenon under investigation. This tendency is particularly true with qualitative research where scholars have been warned about engaging in research that involves "being native" even if it does not involve "going native" (Kanuha, 2000).[2] Only more recently have management and organizational scholars begun to acknowledge, and embrace, the personal relationship researchers may have to their area of study. According to this emerging school of thought, the recommendation is for these personal relationships to be managed and leveraged, rather than minimized, to improve the rigor of personally-relevant research (Jones & Bartunek, in press; Greenberg, Clair, & Ladge, in press).

When engaged in grounded theory research, there are a number of tactics careers scholars may want to employ to manage the personally relevant nature of their scholarship. First, when conducting grounded theory research, the researcher needs to attend to their own assumptions and motivations for studying this particular phenomenon. Careers researchers will want to consider why they are interested in a particular careers topic, illuminating any assumptions or personal interests about what they are hoping to uncover, and what pre-existing ideas they have based on their own emotional or experiential connection to this phenomenon. Building this internal assessment requires a significant level of honesty with oneself when starting a new research project. A suitable self-assessment requires reflection regarding all the ways in which your own experiences and life journey have been impacted by or interacted with the phenomenon you are studying. This step is key to unearthing any implicit motivations that may be guiding your interest in the research project, any emotional responses that your work generates for you, and any conclusions you may be secretly hoping the research uncovers. Skipping this step can result in decreased objectivity and decreased transparency, which can negatively affect the rigor of the research process. Before you can be honest with your participants and the consumers of your research, you have to be honest with yourself. While this is a necessary component of grounded theory research regardless of the topic, for careers research specifically this step cannot be omitted. By definition as a researcher, you have a career, which means all careers research is in some way connected to your own experiences.

One way to maintain the ongoing necessity of self-assessment is through the process of memoing, a key component of grounded theory. Traditionally, grounded theory researchers are encouraged to write theoretical memos from the beginning of the project through the writing phase because the researcher may have trouble keeping track of categories, generative questions, and emerging theory during the research process. These theoretical memos help the scholar maintain a firm connection between emerging theory and data and ensure the analysis has theoretical depth (Corbin & Strauss, 1990). The concept of theoretical memos can be adapted to help the researcher address these relational tensions by becoming more aware of what they are seeing during idea generation, data collection, and analysis. Early in the research formulation process, the researcher may find it helpful to memo on what they know about the careers phenomenon based on their own relationship to the topic. As the research process evolves, the researcher can use these memos to consider how their own perspective may be affecting their ability to see their data and theorize from the data. Similar to theoretical memoing, relational memoing helps the researcher keep track of and manage the connection they have to their research and the analysis they are conducting. While it is undoubtedly challenging to highlight one's own potential for bias, raising your own awareness to potential conflicts of perspective can be the first step to ensuring preconceived notions and experiences do not cloud your interpretation of the data collected. Developing this relational clarity continues throughout the research process and is critical to managing the relational tension regarding what you as a researcher see within the data.

Once the hard work of self-assessment is complete, utilizing a *relational insider–outsider* researcher collaboration can be an additional strategy to ensure an adequate level of objectivity is present, thereby further improving the rigor of grounded theory.

An insider–outsider collaboration is one where the insider has a close personal connection with the topic under investigation or the research site and the outsider does not maintain the same connection (Louis & Bartunek, 1992). With an insider–outsider researcher team, the outsider provides a check or an alternative perspective on the insider's deep relationship with the topic. While the insider–outsider paradigm (Louis & Bartunek, 1992) is usually applied to research where the "objective" researcher partners with an organizational insider, the same frame can be applied to manage relational connections. The varying perspectives of the relational insider and outsider can be particularly useful for uncovering new insights as one interacts between data analysis and data collection. For instance, the two authors are currently employing such an approach in a study we are conducting on the careers of single individuals in the workplace. One of the authors is single and the other is married. As we conducted a first series of interviews, we found our differing relationships to the phenomenon led us to have different emotional reactions to the interviews we were conducting. Furthermore, our differing experiences also led us to see the data differently. Reconciling these differing emotional and experiential relationships strengthened our initial data analysis and guided the next set of choices we made regarding data collection. Our varied perspectives have enhanced the quality of our grounded theory approach.

RELATIONAL TENSION IN HEARING THE PARTICIPANTS

In addition to managing the relationship between researcher and research topic, grounded theory researchers need to manage the relational tension between themselves and their participants. Within this dyadic, interpersonal relationship, the researcher may vary in the similarities, connection, and emotional response they have to a participant. Thus, to understand how this dyadic relationship affects the process of grounded theory as a methodology, we first must explore the current research concerning work relationship paradigms.

At least two potential paradigms for work relationships exist, based on the research of Clark and Mills (1979). These authors argue for two different types of relationships: exchange relationships and communal relationships. Exchange relationships are based on the norm of reciprocity in which needs are met based on a quid pro quo system of trading (cf. Blau, 1964; Gouldner, 1960). Communal relationships on the other hand are relationships built upon the notion of mutuality and a sense of care giving (Clark & Mills, 1979). These types of relationships are explored in the management literature through the foundational work of Dutton and Heaphy (2003), who explored the concept of high-quality connections. Counter to the social exchange perspective, high-quality connections are based on mutuality, positive regard, and vitality (Dutton & Heaphy, 2003). While at the surface, these different relational paradigms might not seem readily connected to grounded theory as a research methodology, we argue that these paradigms have a distinct impact on how researchers interact with participants, most especially in the case of interviews or participant-observation work. That is, if a scholar believes that relationships are instrumental and function on a quid pro quo basis, then they will interact with interview participants differently than if they believe the foundational purpose of relationships is to engage in mutual care and concern for the other.

More specifically, this implicit belief a scholar holds will impact whether the relational work gets erased from the grounded theory process (Fletcher, 1998). For example, when an interview participant expresses a deep emotional reaction, what are grounded theory researchers supposed to do with the expressed emotion of the participant? How should researchers handle their own resulting emotional experiences? If the researcher utilizes a social exchange perspective, then the researcher may be less likely to "see" the emotion in the first place. That is to say, because the emotional expression does not fit squarely within the "rational" process of grounded theory research, it would be easy to ignore (or not even see) the emotional expression because the researcher may assume there is nothing to be learned from said expression. There is no quid pro quo exchange possible because the emotional expressions offered by the participant have no use for the grounded theory researcher as they do not "fit" within what the researcher has to exchange for and with.

If, on the other hand, the researcher utilizes a communal/mutual care and concern perspective on dyadic interpersonal relationships (Clark & Mills, 1979; Dutton & Heaphy, 2003), then the researcher makes space for the emotional expression because that is the requirement within that perspective. In other words, utilizing this lens requires that an emotional expression of one member of the relationship (even if that member is an interview participant) be seen as a concern to the other member of the relationship such that it cannot be ignored. As Fletcher (1998) highlighted, this work is often forsaken within organizations, and we would argue in the grounded theory research process in general. However, it is a misconception to believe that ignoring this work makes it disappear or negates its importance.

Not responding to an emotional expression by an interview participant will inherently affect how the interviewee participates in the interview moving forward, as will responding to the emotional expression. Sociometer theory tells us that all social interactions are governed by our own internal monitor that seeks cues of acceptance or rejection (Leary, Tambor, Terdal, & Downs, 1995). The cues that our internal sociometers detect influence our subsequent behavior (Anthony, Wood, & Holmes, 2007). Regardless of whether we respond to (and accept) or ignore (and reject) the relational aspects inherent within an interview, our choices as researchers play a role in the insights we are able to discover because our choice impacts the participant's engagement within the ensuing interview. While we acknowledge that grounded theory research does not always include interviewing participants, this example serves to show one frequent way in which relational theory interacts with grounded theory research methodology.[3]

Managing the Tension

To address this relational tension, we recommend considering the emotional display you might demonstrate during the interview prior to beginning your interviews. Will you respond to all answers the participants provide sans emotion? Alternatively, will you engage with the participant based on the emotional response embedded within their answers? For instance, if a research participant starts crying as they answer your questions, will you offer empathy and understanding, communicating support? On the other hand, will you continue with the interview questions as if there are no tears? Furthermore, will you allow yourself to display your own emotions in response? Following this example of tears, will you allow yourself to show your own sadness or communicate empathy in your words? Thinking through your response and how you will handle the emotion expressed by the research participant (as well as your own emotions the participant elicits) will help maintain the integrity of one's data collection process. When a participant expresses emotion, the researcher will not be caught off guard, but rather will be able to respond confidently given your preparation. Deciding in advance how you might handle this situation will also enable you to prepare your participant, which is especially important when the research questions address sensitive or emotional topics. We recommend that you communicate your stance to your participant before you begin asking questions. While conducting research is an ordinary task for a researcher, it can be an intimidating and uncomfortable experience for participants. Given this, preparing the participant for what to expect can minimize the impact of whichever stance you will be enacting. For example, if you prepare the participant in advance that you will be remaining neutral throughout the interview, the participant will be less likely to take your neutral response as a form of judgment or rejection. If, on the other hand, you do not communicate this in advance, a participant could interpret your silence or lack of empathy as a form of rejection (cf. Leary, Haupt, Strausser, & Chokel, 1998). In this case, the participant's willingness to fully disclose throughout the remainder of the interview would likely be diminished (cf. Altman & Taylor, 1973). Additionally, it may be important to remind the participant of your emotional stance, as appropriate, during the interview.

Conversely, if you choose to engage with the participant emotionally, then we recommend also disclosing this choice up front. We encourage you to communicate to your participant before the interview begins that you are going to conduct the interview as a conversation. While this is likely to generate the most forthcoming and transparent answers from the participant, it also might affect your ability to follow the interview guide in a precise and systematic way. Of course, by altering the way in which you ask the questions, the order you ask the questions, and so on, this too will affect the information you obtain.

As in life, research is a series of tradeoffs. The point is that regardless of which tradeoff you choose, there are consequences regarding what you "find" through the grounded theory research process. Therefore, our final suggestion is that in addition to being upfront with your participants about how you will handle the relationship, we encourage you to disclose that choice every time you present or write about your research. Allowing your readers or audience to understand the relational stance you utilized in your participant interviews is the first step to building trust and credibility with that audience and is relevant to their interpretation of your results. Because this new approach may require explanation and buy-in from editors and reviewers, this decision to disclose to your readers the relational stance you adopted highlights the third relational tension within grounded theory research—the researchers' relationship with their audience—which we explore below.

RELATIONAL TENSION IN SHARING THE FINDINGS

The final relational tension embedded within the grounded theory research process is about what researchers choose to share with the audience, or consumers, of their research. When researchers write or present their findings to others, they are faced with decisions regarding the degree of transparency as to the procedural choices enacted in their research study. In other words, the heart of this relational tension concerns the level of self-disclosure required for one's peers regarding the researcher's connection or experience with the phenomenon under investigation. Self-disclosure, or the sharing of personally relevant information (Jourard & Lasakow, 1958), carries a variety of consequences. In an often-referenced meta-analysis, Collins and Miller (1994) found that individuals tend to disclose more to people they like, while simultaneously increasing their liking for those they disclose to, while recipients of disclosure also tend to increase their liking of the disclosers. These findings highlight the reciprocal nature of self-disclosure such that the breadth and depth of self-disclosure typically increase in a matched way, meaning that as one member of a relationship increases self-disclosure, the other member of the relationship is likely to follow (Altman & Taylor, 1973; Worthy, Gary, & Kahn, 1969). In summary, the research on self-disclosure in social relationships generally argues that more disclosure is better for the quality of relationships (Greene, Derlega, & Mathews, 2006). However, the limited research on self-disclosure within the context of work relationships argues that more nuance is necessary to predict how recipients of self-disclosure will respond (Gibson, 2018; Gibson, Harari, & Marr, 2018). In light of this discrepancy, questions abound regarding how researchers can balance their own connections or experience with the phenomenon being studied and how they share that with the audience of their research, including but not limited to reviewers and colleagues. The current norm in the literature on careers research, as well as organizational behavior research more broadly, is to remain silent regarding any connection to the topic being studied based on the premise that anything else would shatter the illusion of scientific distance. This silence, however, does not ensure scientific distance but rather distorts it. Furthermore, it contributes to the continued illusion of objectivity in the scientific process (Anteby, 2013). This leaves the researcher with a final relational tension to wrestle.

Managing the Tension

The first step for managing the relational tension regarding what you share is to consider how self-disclosing your connection to the research will affect those who receive the disclosure. That is, when a researcher chooses to self-disclose, the disclosure will affect those who hear it in unique ways, which cannot always be predicted. Throughout the tensions above, we have argued for transparency in regards to motives and choices. This notion of transparency, however, can be costly to the researcher. Disclosing your own motivations and emotions places you, as researcher, in the path of judgment and, at least within the academic community, a likely target for criticism. However, because grounded theory research requires immersion with the phenomenon being studied, lack of disclosure of the process hampers the objectivity and rigor of the research highlighting the need for researchers to challenge the prevailing norm of silence in this regard. That is to say, not disclosing your connection with the phenomenon also risks judgment and criticism when and if that connection later surfaces given the potential for your connection to have affected the findings and theoretical conclusions.

Realizing that what you choose to disclose to your interview participants will likely need to be disclosed to your academic community will allow you to consider more carefully how much of your connection to the topic you will be sharing. As we have argued earlier, the choice you make regarding the relational stance you adopt when interacting with research participants necessitates communicating your choice to participants in advance. Likewise, the stance you choose should be communicated when writing or presenting your findings. When you choose to engage in a communal relational stance, it is likely that your connection to the research will emerge throughout the conversation/interview you conduct with participants. Because the research on self-disclosure illuminates the reciprocal nature of self-disclosure (Altman & Taylor, 1973; Worthy et al., 1969), your disclosure will likely elicit similar levels of disclosure from the participant. That is, choosing to withhold self-disclosure may adversely affect what your participants are willing to disclose to you. Therefore, academic peers, reviewers, editors, and readers will need to have access to these details to enable an objective consideration of your findings. As such, transparency has the potential to strengthen the rigor with a grounded theory research process (Anteby, 2013; Jones & Bartunek, in press).

Yet, depending on the phenomenon one is studying, this can have varying degrees of potential impact on the scholar's own career. Furthermore, the stage of the researcher's career and publication record will interact with the disclosure to varying degrees. The challenge is that exactly how it will interact is difficult to predict, making the disclosure of personally relevant research feels risky for all researchers, but likely riskier for the more vulnerable researchers (e.g. those without tenure or members of marginal groups). One way of combating this risk is to draw on methodological practices in psychology, sociology, and gender studies where sensitivity and transparency in one's relationship to one's research is seen as enhancing the rigor of the methodology (e.g. Barry, 2015; McCorkel & Myers, 2003: Rice, 2009).

Managing the risks and tradeoffs this vulnerability entails relative to your own toler-ance for such risks will enable you to make more informed decisions regarding your research process and disclosure choices.

One additional way to address this relational tension is through the relational insider–outsider research partnership, which was discussed earlier. Collaborating with someone who does not share the same connection to the research can offer enormous support as you manage this tension. Having a co-author who can offer an objective perspective on how much disclosure is appropriate as well as help you consider how others may judge your disclosure can help you know how much disclosure is too much. Often, we have found within our partnership, that what feels incredibly vulnerable to disclose to the scholar with the closer relationship to a par-ticipant's experience is seen as less of a vulnerability by the more relationally distant researcher. Given this, having an outsider to offer perspective can mitigate potential risks to both under-sharing and over-sharing throughout the research process.

CONCLUDING THOUGHTS

For careers researchers, grounded theory is a methodological approach that has the potential to uncover new theoretical and practical insights into the rapidly evolving world of careers. This inductive approach provides a valuable complement to more deductive, positivist methodological approaches as it ensures that our evolving theoretical understanding of careers keeps pace with the shifting realities of careers in the world today. Better integration of deductive and inductive methodologies is one-way scholars can expand existing theories of management and organizations in such a way that they remain relevant to the work and career experiences of today's workforce (Hoffman, 2016). In focusing specifically on the application of grounded theory to the study of careers, we become attentive to how relational this method-ology is within the careers context. We suggest it is difficult, if not illogical, for researchers to try to detach themselves from the complications inherent in a relational research methodology. This perspective is consistent with other scholars who have challenged traditional epistemological principles, which suggest researcher objectiv-ity and detachment are foundational to rigorous "scientific" organizational research (e.g. Anteby, 2013; Jones & Bartunek, in press; Sawyer, in press). Relationships are embedded in the research process, particularly grounded theory. By remaining attentive to one's relationship to one's research questions, participants and academic audience and how these relationships affect what one sees, hears, and shares about the phenomenon under investigation, a scholar can ultimately enhance the rigor of their research.

Throughout this chapter, we have discussed many of the strategies that are relevant to navigating the relationships inherent to careers grounded theory research. In addi-tion to these strategies, we draw attention to one additional strategy that transcends all three relationship tensions – mentorship. To learn about grounded theory, novice researchers can take a grounded theory course and should read some of the foundational books (e.g. Charmaz, 2014; Glaser & Strauss, 1967; Corbin & Strauss, 1990). However, the only way to learn to do grounded theory is to embark on a project. When embarking on a grounded theory research project, we believe novice researchers will benefit from intentionally seeking a mentor with experience in grounded theory research to serve as a guide for the project to provide the novice with both task and social-emotional support (Murphy & Kram, 2014). A grounded theory research mentor – in the form of an advisor, a co-author, or a friend – can provide specific, immediate guidance as the research process unfolds. A novice researcher who is immersed in a grounded theory project may not have the distance or experience to recognize when a relational tension is affecting the research process. A mentor can help the novice researcher see and respond to these tensions in order to improve the quality of the methodology. Beyond task support, a mentor can also provide a newer researcher with social-emotional support as they navigate these relational tensions. As we have previously noted, engaging in grounded theory research on careers can surface a strong emotional response from the researcher. The researcher may struggle with how to manage these feelings on both a personal and project level. A mentor can be particularly helpful here in validating both these feelings and helping the researcher know how to be aware of, but not constrained by, their emotions as they continue the iterative process of engaging in grounded theory. A mentor becomes important to helping the novice researcher develop their skills with both the art and science of grounded theory.

Finally, it is worth noting that while this chapter has centered on a specific area of management research, careers, and a specific methodology, grounded theory, we believe this issue of relational tensions goes beyond a single area of study or a single methodological approach. For careers researchers, we have a hard time imagining the study of any phenomenon to which one does not have a relationship. The Academy of Management Careers Division supports scholarship, which addresses "people's lifelong succession of work experiences, the structure of opportunity to work, and the relationship between careers and other aspects of life."[4] As researchers, we have our own careers to manage, making the study of careers topics inherently personal. This means that, regardless of the methodology being employed, the careers scholar will have a relationship with the phenomenon being studied. As a result, we encourage careers researchers who are engaged with other methodological approaches to be more open to considering how their relationship to their research affects how and what they see, hear, and share during the research process. Consequently, being more aware and responsive to these relational tensions has the potential to become another mechanism for improving the quality and rigor of all methodological practices.

NOTES

1.   Authors contributed equally and are listed alphabetically.

2. We acknowledge the inherent cultural insensitivity of these phrases which refer to one's research participants as natives. We do not intend to endorse their use, rather are referencing earlier research in which this was the phrase used by the scholar.
3. In the interest of brevity, we have tackled this challenge for qualitative interviews with initial participants – meaning that there is no prior relationship with the participant being interviewed. In the case of participant-observer or other data collection techniques wherein the relationship between researcher and participant exists outside the qualitative interview (e.g. a multiplex relationship), the challenge presented here is likely more nuanced and more complex regarding the effect of the relational paradigm used within interviews.
4. From the career's division domain statement: https://car.aom.org/about-us/new-item2 retrieved February 13, 2021.

REFERENCES

Aguinis, H., Shapiro, D. L., Antonacopoulou, E. P., & Cummings, T. G. (2014). Scholarly impact: A pluralist conceptualization. *Academy of Management Learning & Education*, *13*(4), 623–639.

Altman, I., & Taylor, D. A. (1973). *Social penetration: The development of interpersonal relationships*. New York: Holt, Rinehart and Winston.

Amabile, T. M., & Hall, D. T. (in press). The undervalued power of self-relevant research: The case of researching retirement while retiring. *Academy of Management Perspectives*.

Anteby, M. (2013). Relaxing the taboo on telling our own stories: Upholding professional distance and personal involvement. *Organization Science*, *24*(4), 1277–1290.

Anthony, D. B., Wood, J. V., & Holmes, J. G. (2007). Testing sociometer theory: Self-esteem and the importance of acceptance for social decision-making. *Journal of Experimental Social Psychology*, *43*(3), 425–432.

Bansal, P., & Corley, K. (2011). The coming of age for qualitative research: Embracing the diversity of qualitative methods. *Academy of Management Journal*, *54*(2), 233–237.

Barry, B. (2015). The toxic lining of men's fashion consumption: The omnipresent force of hegemonic masculinity. *Critical Studies in Men's Fashion*, *2*(2&3), 143–161.

Blau, P. M. (1964). *Exchange and power in social life*. New York: John Wiley & Sons.

Charmaz, K. (2014). *Constructing grounded theory*. Los Angeles, CA: Sage Publications.

Clark, M. S., & Mills, J. (1979). Interpersonal attraction in exchange and communal relationships. *Journal of Personality and Social Psychology*, *37*(1), 12–24.

Collins, N. L., & Miller, L. C. (1994). Self-disclosure and liking: A meta-analytic review. *Psychological Bulletin*, *116*(3), 457–475.

Corbin, J. M., & Strauss, A. (1990). Grounded theory research: Procedures, canons, and evaluative criteria. *Qualitative Sociology*, *13*(1), 3–21.

Corley, K. G. (2015). A commentary on "what grounded theory is..." engaging a phenomenon from the perspective of those living it. *Organizational Research Methods*, *18*(4), 600–605.

Dutton, J. E., & Heaphy, E. D. (2003). The power of high-quality connections. In K. S. Cameron, J. E. Dutton, & R. E. Quinn (Eds.), *Positive organizational scholarship: Foundations of a new discipline*: 263–278. San Francisco, CA: Berrett-Koehler.

Dutton, J. E., & Ragins, B. R. (Eds.) (2007). *Exploring positive relationships at work: Building a theoretical and research foundation*. Mahwah, NJ: Lawrence Erlbaum Associates.

Ferris, G. R., Liden, R. C., Munyon, T. P., Summers, J. K., Basik, K. J., & Buckley, M. R. (2009). Relationships at work: Toward a multidimensional conceptualization of dyadic work relationships. *Journal of Management*, *35*, 1379–1403.

Fletcher, J. K. (1998). Relational practice: A feminist reconstruction of work. *Journal of Management Inquiry*, *7*(2), 163–186.

Gibson, K. R. (2018). Can I tell you something? How disruptive self-disclosure changes who "we" are. *Academy of Management Review, 43*(4), 570–589.

Gibson, K. R., Harari, D., & Marr, J. C. (2018). When sharing hurts: How and why self-disclosing weakness undermines the task-oriented relationships of higher status disclosers. *Organizational Behavior and Human Decision Processes, 144*, 25–43.

Glaser, B. G., & Strauss, A. L. (1967). *The discovery of grounded theory: Strategies for qualitative research.* Mill Valley, CA: Sociology Press.

Gouldner, A. W. (1960). The norm of reciprocity: A preliminary statement. *American Sociological Review, 25*(2), 161–178.

Greenberg, D., Clair, J., & Ladge, J. J. (in press). A feminist perspective on conducting personally relevant research: Working mothers studying pregnancy and motherhood at work. *Academy of Management Perspectives.*

Greene, K., Derlega, V. J., & Mathews, A. (2006). Self-disclosure in personal relationships. In A. L. Vangelisti & D. Perlman (Eds.), *The Cambridge handbook of personal relationships*: 409–427. New York: Cambridge University Press.

Haley, U. C. V., Page, M. C., Pitsis, T. S., Rivas, J. L., & Yu, K. F. (2017). Measuring and achieving scholarly impact: A report from the *Academy of Management's Practice Theme Committee*, Academy of Management, Briar Cliff, New York. http://aom.org/About-AOM/ StrategicPlan/Scholarly-Impact-Report.aspx?terms=measuring%20and%20achieving %20scholarly%20impact.

Harrison, S. H., & Rouse, E. D. (2014). Let's dance! Elastic coordination in creative group work: A qualitative study of modern dancers. *Academy of Management Journal, 57*(5), 1256–1283.

Hoffman, A. (2016). Academia's emerging crisis of relevance and the consequent role of the engaged scholar, *Journal of Change Management, 16*(2), 77–96.

Jones, E. B., & Bartunek, J. M. (in press). Too close or optimally positioned? The value of personally relevant research. *Academy of Management Perspectives.*

Jourard, S. M., & Lasakow, P. (1958). Some factors in self-disclosure. *The Journal of Abnormal and Social Psychology, 56*(1), 91–98.

Kanuha, V. K. (2000). "Being" native versus "going native": Conducting social work research as an insider. *Social Work, 45*(5), 439–447.

Ladge, J. J., Clair, J. A., & Greenberg, D. (2012). Cross-domain identity transition during liminal periods: Constructing multiple selves as professional and mother during pregnancy. *Academy of Management Journal, 55*(6), 1449–1471.

Ladge, J. J., & Greenberg, D. N. (2015). Becoming a working mother: Managing identity and efficacy uncertainties during resocialization. *Human Resource Management, 54*(6), 977–998.

Leary, M. R., Haupt, A. L., Strausser, K. S., & Chokel, J. T. (1998). Calibrating the sociometer: The relationship between interpersonal appraisals and state self-esteem. *Journal of Personality and Social Psychology, 74*(5), 1290–1299.

Leary, M. R., Tambor, E. S., Terdal, S. K., & Downs, D. L. (1995). Self-esteem as an interpersonal monitor: The sociometer hypothesis. *Journal of Personality and Social Psychology, 68*(3), 518–530.

Locke, K., Golden-Biddle, K., & Feldman, M. S. (2008). Perspective – making doubt generative: Rethinking the role of doubt in the research process. *Organization Science, 19*(6), 907–918.

Louis, M. R., & Bartunek, J. M. (1992). Insider/outsider research teams: Collaboration across diverse perspectives. *Journal of Management Inquiry, 1*(2), 101–110.

MacLean, T., Anteby, M., Hudson, B., & Rudolph, J. W. (2006). Talking tainted topics: Insights and ideas on researching socially disapproved organizational behavior. *Journal of Management Inquiry, 15*(1), 59–68.

McCorkel, J., & Myers, K. (2003). What difference does difference make? Position and privilege in the field. *Qualitative Sociology*, *26*(2), 199–231.

Modestino, A. S., Sugiyama, K., & Ladge, J. (2019). Careers in construction: An examination of the career narratives of young professionals and their emerging career self-concepts. *Journal of Vocational Behavior*, *115*, 103306.

Murphy, C., Klotz, A. C., & Kreiner, G. E. (2017). Blue skies and black boxes: The promise (and practice) of grounded theory in human resource management research. *Human Resource Management Review*, *27*(2), 291–305.

Murphy, W. M., & Kram, K. E. (2014). *Strategic relationships at work: Creating your circle of mentors, sponsors, and peers for success in business and life*. New York: McGraw-Hill.

Nigam, A., & Dokko, G. (2019). Career resourcing and the process of professional emergence. Academy of Management Journal, *62*(4), 1052–1084.

Petriglieri, G., Ashford, S. J., & Wrzesniewski, A. (2019). Agony and ecstasy in the gig economy: Cultivating holding environments for precarious and personalized work identities. *Administrative Science Quarterly*, *64*(1), 124–170.

Rice, C. (2009). Imaging the other? Ethical challenges of researching and writing women's embodied lives. *Feminism & Psychology*, *19*(2), 245–266.

Rudestam, K. E., & Newton, R. R. (2014). *Surviving your dissertation: A comprehensive guide to content and process*. Thousand Oaks, CA: Sage Publications.

Sawyer, K. (in press). When objectivity is out of reach: Learnings from conducting research with commercially sexually exploited women. *Academy of Management Perspectives*.

Schabram, K., & Maitlis, S. (2017). Negotiating the challenges of a calling: Emotion and enacted sensemaking in animal shelter work. *Academy of Management Journal*, *60*(2), 584–609.

Shepherd, D. A., & Williams, T. A. (2018). Hitting rock bottom after job loss: Bouncing back to create a new positive work identity. *Academy of Management Review*, *43*(1), 28–49.

Sluss, D. M., & Ashforth, B. E. (2007). Relational identity and identification: Defining ourselves through work relationships. *Academy of Management Review*, *32*(1), 9–32.

Suddaby, R. (2006). From the editors: What grounded theory is not. *Academy of Management Journal*, *49*(4), 633–642.

Suddaby, R. (2010). Editor's comments: Construct clarity in theories of management and organization [Editorial]. The Academy of Management Review, *35*(3), 346–357.

Walsh, I., Holton, J. A., Bailyn, L., Fernandez, W., Levina, N., & Glaser, B. (2015). What grounded theory is … a critically reflective conversation among scholars. *Organizational Research Methods*, *18*(4), 581–599.

Worthy, M., Gary, A. L., & Kahn, G. M. (1969). Self-disclosure as an exchange process. *Journal of Personality and Social Psychology*, *13*(1), 59–63.

12. Using in-depth interviews in careers research

Suzanne C. de Janasz and A. Julie Katz

OVERVIEW

Research on careers attempts to explain and predict the impact of individual differences (e.g., personality, values), decisions (e.g., vocational choice), experiences (e.g., jobs held, layoffs experienced), interactions with others (e.g., mentoring, learning), and interaction with the environment (e.g., person–environment fit, work–family conflict) on the unfolding occupational choices and development throughout the vocational cycle. Quantitative methods of data collection and analysis are powerful means for exploring relationships among variables collected at a point in time (cross-sectional), and over a bracketed period (longitudinal). However, qualitative, in-depth interviews offer significant advantages in allowing researchers to discover and explain phenomena from an inside out perspective—enabling those interviewed to explain choices, non-choices, and unplanned events, as well as the beliefs (motivation, fears, and expectations) that preceded and resulted from these choices and events.

This chapter focuses on the importance and advantages of utilizing in-depth interviews for careers research, developing and executing interview protocols, collecting and analyzing the data, challenges inherent in utilizing this method, and strategies for overcoming them. We build on existing literature and offer insights that facilitate increased knowledge and application of in-depth interviews to gather the kind of multi-faceted and nuanced data needed in the study of careers.

IMPORTANCE AND ADVANTAGES OF IN-DEPTH INTERVIEWS IN CAREERS RESEARCH

The nature of careers research reflects how the individual makes sense of his or her passage through life and in a broader sense, how this contributes to a societal construction of *work* (Gunz & Peiperl, 2007). Of course, society's view of and need for the collective "work" of individuals is dynamic, reflecting economic, demographic, and technological trends. Not surprisingly, scholars in fields as diverse as psychology, sociology, anthropology, economics, history, politics, and of course, business, draw on the concept of careers. How we make sense of careers—as snapshots in time (past, present, and a predicted future), in response to intended and unintended events or jolts, and over the course of decades—is complex and necessitates an array of methodological approaches to capture, analyze, and interpret the relevant data. The in-depth interview, in which a trained researcher engages a respondent in a structured conversation that enables them "to explore their perspectives on a particular idea, program, or situation" (Boyce & Neale, 2006), can follow along with the twists and turns of a career path and produce rich data that reflect the complexity of that person's experience and narrative. Rather than fit subjects' answers to their pre-selected variables, careers researchers can use interviews to "understand the world from the subjects' points of view and to unfold the meaning of their lived world" (Kvale, 2006).

In-depth interviews allow the researcher to gain a holistic view of careers because they allow space for participants to "speak in their own voice and express their own thoughts and feelings" (Berg, 2007, p. 96); in so doing, researchers can uncover the beliefs, attitudes, worldview, and experiences that influence a participant's decisions and sense of self. In recounting career-related dilemmas and decisions, interviewees have an opportunity to reflect not only on what actions they have taken (or not), but also why they took them. This degree of agency they believe they have (or have had) in decision-making processes encountered along their career, in the context of concurrent issues, becomes part of the narrative of the in-depth interview, enabling the dyad to discover (retrospectively) connections and insights that might also shed light on current and planned career pathways. This discovery, aided by well-constructed open-ended questions and well-timed probes, underscores the single most defining characteristic of the method: "asking questions that are based on the interviewee's responses and simultaneously linked to the research objectives" (Guest, Namey, & Mitchell, 2013, p. 114). Flexible and adaptable, the in-depth interview reflects the interest in individuals and their stories (Seidman, 2013), and it provides the kind of rich, qualitative data that provides important "meanings, insights and causal chains" in the study of careers (Guest et al., 2013, p. 114).

Compared to other qualitative methods such as a focus group, an interview's one-on-one format allows a participant to share ideas freely, without the constraints of pre-formed answer categories and without the influence or judgment of others. Moreover, the privacy this kind of setting offers is critical for the formation of trust and safety that facilitates the sharing of sensitive or confidential information. Focus groups are public forums that may have the opposite effect: amplify outspoken individuals, suppress shy or introverted individuals, and heighten the discomfort or fear of feeling vulnerable about information or views they share. In addition, a more public setting could jeopardize the confidentiality and safety of any party.

Compared to quantitative methods such as surveys containing multiple fixed questions with multiple fixed (e.g., five- or seven-point Likert Scale) responses, the process of interviewing is iterative, and allows the dyad to address ambiguities and misunderstandings within the interview. This flexibility provides confidence that a participant interpreted a question correctly (increasing study validity and reliability) and also enables the interviewee to reinforce, emphasize, or prioritize issues or events and their impacts—something nearly impossible to do using surveys.

APPROACHES TO IN-DEPTH INTERVIEWS

Careers researchers can employ structured, semi-structured, and unstructured interviews. The variations characterize the degree to which questions asked are prescribed in content and in sequence. Structured interviews have a fairly rigid format. They are designed to elicit responses to phenomena that are well-defined, and are comprised of fixed questions that are asked of each interviewee, and in a stipulated sequence. Structured interviews are often used in job interviews, as they are less susceptible to bias (every candidate is asked the same questions and in the same order). Semi-structured interviews tend to use open-ended questions that follow a pattern; however, the process allows the interviewer to delve into an area of interest that arises during the discussion. For example, in their study of CEO mentoring, following a series of questions about the interviewee's current mentoring relationship, de Janasz and Peiperl (2015) asked how this relationship compared to previous mentoring relationships. Many responded that they "had never had a mentor before." Realizing that the term "mentor" was likely being interpreted in a formal sense (e.g., someone assigned to them by Human Resources), the researchers then asked interviewees about people in their past who had been sounding boards, advisors, or sponsors. In nearly every case, the participant recalled more than one individual who had fit this description, and with prompting, proceeded to elaborate on how this person facilitated their career development.

Finally, there are unstructured interviews, wherein the interviewer has the freedom and responsibility to ask questions that he or she thinks will elicit responses that deepen understanding about the area of study. In the previous example, the researchers were examining the role of mentoring on CEO career development and overall effectiveness. However, the research objective and related line of questioning assumes that mentoring plays an important role in the development and success of CEOs. What if that were not the case? There are many mechanisms by which CEOs learn skills, acquire knowledge, and make choices that affect their career and success. What if, instead, the researchers asked, "Reflecting on your career, what has had the greatest impact on your success?" Answers might point to early education, cultural impacts, family influence, travels, books, or incidental conversations, and so on. Such an open-ended and non-directive question, followed by prompts like "please say more" and, "what about that made it important for you?" does not assume a particular theory or direct a response. As this example illustrates, unstructured interviewing can be an effective approach when less is known about a topic and a greater level of exploration is needed.

THE WHAT, WHY, AND HOW OF IN-DEPTH INTERVIEWS: BEFORE, DURING, AND AFTER

Before: Developing the Interview Protocol

The first step in conducting an in-depth interview is the development, testing, and revising of the interview protocol. After choosing the appropriate level of structure for the interview consistent with the novelty of the research question/s, questions are developed that align with the focus of the study. In general, the more exploratory the research, the more unstructured the interview should be. For example, while current estimates suggest that more than a third of the US and European workforce engages in the gig economy (either full- or part-time) (McCue, 2018), very little is known about the employees who are drawn to this kind of work, their personality profiles, the path that led them to this work, and the implications this kind of employment will have on outcomes such as income, well-being, satisfaction, and future employment. In the absence of well-established theoretical concepts, testable variables, and reliable findings, careers scholars interested in studying gig work and gig workers might first consult the literature on part-time and temporary employment, clarify the research question/s of interest, and then develop an unstructured in-depth interview protocol to explore this emerging field.

Similar to developing questions for a quantitative survey instrument, researchers designing an in-depth interview protocol should follow basic rules of survey design. Easier and less personal questions should be asked first, to allow respondents to "warm up" to the process. Jargon and abbreviations are to be avoided, as is overly scientific language especially if respondents are less sophisticated or their native language differs from the language used in the protocol. The structure and wording of questions is important too. For example, the question "Do you find gig work to be financially and emotionally satisfying?" is double-barreled and confusing for a respondent who might want to answer "yes" and "no" simultaneously. Any findings related to this kind of question would be in doubt and should be thrown out. Even if the question were simplified to "Do you find gig work to be emotionally satisfying," such a question is "closed" and limits the subject's responses (yes, no, or don't know) and the researcher's opportunity to learn more about why gig work is or isn't emotionally satisfying. Transforming this question to an open-ended one, for example, "in what ways has your employment in the gig economy been positive?" provides greater clarity. Probing further, questions that encourage an interviewee to "think back" to a specific event or time provide opportunity for a response that connects their experience and beliefs with actions and promotes further conversation. For example, "can you share an example about a time or incident that made you realize that this kind of work was satisfying?" Note that not all open-ended questions have the same effect. While the question, "how did you arrive at that position?" allows for an interpretive response, a question such as "why did you make that choice?" could be perceived as interrogative and elicit a defensive response.

Augmenting primary open-ended questions with probes and prompts can clarify a response or elicit more information during the interview. With a probe like, "please say more…" or, "…and then what happened?" or, "what about her comment triggered your emotional response?" an interviewer encourages a more reflective and analytical response. A prompt is a cueing technique that can be used to direct or redirect conversation back to an earlier point. Prompts can be verbal (e.g., "Remember when you started to talk about what was important to you in a mentor relationship…" or "I really liked how your example highlighted the way both you and your mentor benefitted from the relationship") or non-verbal gestures (e.g., approving nods, a smile, leaning in) which coupled with a pause can encourage an interviewee to continue. Waiting a few seconds lessens the chance of interrupting as respondents often take a moment to think before continuing.

Once the protocol is developed, it should be tested, among several respondents and researchers. If the target population is small or difficult to access, testing can be done using the research team or graduate students. The researchers should conduct the interview and note how well the sequencing of questions proceeds logically from respondents' point of view. Do some questions bring about the answers to later questions, which if also asked, can reduce the interviewer's credibility ("didn't I answer that a few minutes ago?")? Do the probes elicit the depth of response sought? Does the interview take about as long to conduct as estimated? Did unplanned data emerge that was interesting enough to warrant adding a specific question or prompt to the protocol? The team piloting the interview protocol should discuss their findings and make the necessary revisions.

Before: Sampling Strategy

In this phase, the researchers must decide whom to interview, how many to target, and how to engage or incentivize their participation. The first question is driven primarily by the research question and secondarily by the difficulty in accessing the target population. While some careers research prioritizes generalizability, which is aided by a diversity of respondents, other careers research prioritizes the deep (and accurate) exploration of a particular phenomenon or group, for example gig work, caregiving, accounting professionals, health care workers, or CEOs. Students, while an "easy" population from which to gather data, may be too heterogeneous to enable a focused inquiry of the phenomenon of interest and may require a larger sample in order to identify meaningful themes (Guest, Bunce, & Johnson, 2006). While gig workers might be more homogeneous, they may be harder to target, and require creative means to access.[1] These examples help the researcher(s) determine the approximate number of in-depth interviews that need to be conducted. In general, the expectation is that each participant will provide a large amount of quality data, reducing the need for large sampling. More specifically, in a study involving 60 interview participants (when purposive sampling was used), "saturation" of themes (i.e., the maximum number of distinct themes) occurred within the first twelve interviews and meta-themes (i.e., recurring) emerged in the first six (Guest et al., 2006).

How researchers access and engage interview respondents will vary according to the population targeted. Professionals who dedicate themselves to advancing their careers are by definition, busy individuals. While it may be relatively easy to convince a recent college graduate to talk for 30–60 minutes about career-related phenomena (e.g., choice of major, impact of internships on job choice, impact of a mentor), it is quite difficult to convince a CEO of a major company to spend even 15 minutes talking about his or her career. Some elements that facilitate a positive response to the request include the interviewer's credibility and reputation, a compelling research question, "a subjective interest" in the topic (Clark, 2010), promise of confidentiality, ease of fitting it in (time, schedule, location), and a trusted intermediary. In the CEO mentoring study (de Janasz & Peiperl, 2015), the interviewers were part of a world-class executive education institution and were sought out to assess and validate a firm's approach to matching CEOs and near-CEOs with more senior board chairpersons in formally arranged, year-long, exclusive[2] mentoring relationships. Once the researchers and firm decided to collaborate (and sign a Non-Disclosure Agreement), a plan was developed and access to the mentors and mentees was not only granted but also scheduling was done by the firm's administrative staff who communicated the purpose of the interviews, obtained consent, and confirmed the interview time, date, and mode. Given the stature of these interviews and respect demonstrated to the CEOs, most of the interviews were conducted face-to-face, with a few conducted using audio or videoconferencing. Because of this well-orchestrated process, and the fact that the mentors and mentees were formally committed to this prestigious mentoring program, there was little difficulty conducting the interviews, and only a few had to be rescheduled.

In research on the effects of layoff on educated career professionals, the structured, written interview process used by de Janasz and Kenworthy (2015) was different, partly deriving from the fact that the two researchers were on opposite sides of the world (US and Australia). An email invitation explaining the purpose and expected value of the research was sent to individuals in the researchers' networks—who were encouraged to respond to the mostly open-ended questions, and then forward the email to others in their networks. While the use of snowball sampling can produce a reasonably large and diverse sample, it is not possible to compute a response rate, and it is difficult to target and ensure a representative sample.

During: Conducting the Interview

Perhaps the most important minutes of the interview are the first few. Aside from the obvious—showing up a few minutes early, dressing appropriately, and using a culturally appropriate greeting—the interviewer should begin by thanking the interviewee for agreeing to meet, establishing credibility ("As a Professor of x, I've been doing research on y for n years"), clarifying the purpose of the research ("As you know, my colleague(s) and I are studying the role of mentoring in the careers of CEOs"), and managing expectations ("During this 30 minute interview, I'll be asking questions about x and y and taking notes simultaneously. All of the data you share will be confidential and only reported in the aggregate as common themes. If we would like to quote you specifically in any future publication, we will come back to you and explicitly seek your permission. Do you have any questions before we begin?"). In these examples, we have described a face-to-face interview, but that is not always the case. While face-to-face interaction is the most personal and allows an interviewer to observe non-verbal cues, videoconferencing produces similar benefits while using fewer resources (such as travel and space for discussion). Voice-only telephone interviews do allow for some non-verbal feedback (tone, inflection) and can work well particularly when other options are cost-prohibitive or in situations where a participant needs to keep all or part of their identity confidential (Trier-Bieniek, 2012).

During: Collecting Data

Capturing the data during the interview can take multiple forms. Notetaking (by hand or by typing on a laptop) in-session may help create a comfortable setting for the interview, and a good interviewer can capture key ideas, highlight interest in what is being said, and use paraphrasing and questions to ensure accuracy. Audio recording the interview can reduce the need for detailed notetaking, ensure accuracy, and enable the interviewer to focus more intently on the conversation—both the verbal and non-verbal communication. However, even when the interviewer obtains consent to record the interview, it is important to note that recording the interview may make an interviewee uncomfortable, and it creates the need for transcription which can be time-consuming or expensive.

After: Debriefing Participants

At the end of the interview, the researcher should thank the interviewee and remind him/her/them of the next steps, including a follow-up contact to clarify the data collected, request permission to use an attributed quote, and communicate the expected date that the completed report will be available. Interviewees typically like to know not only how their data will be used but also how their data compared to the aggregate. Within a few days, the researcher can read through the notes and make any corrections to errors or abbreviations that might be difficult to clarify weeks or months later; and back up the file[3] (or image the notes).

After: Data Analysis

The next step is to analyze the interview data. Content analysis is a method that enables researchers to systematically analyze text to make valid inferences from interview data (e.g., Krippendorff, 2004; Holsti, 1969). There are both quantitative and qualitative approaches, however, since a thorough review of the choices and the steps involved are beyond the scope of this chapter, see Flick (2014) for an overview of a variety of qualitative methods. The level of formality of the option employed depends on the nature of the research (exploratory versus established area), the size of the sample, and the expected reliability of the findings. For example, in their exploratory study of post-layoff career moves, de Janasz and Kenworthy (2015) received 12 emailed completed structured, written interviews. Following Krippendorff (2004), each author independently read through the responses to the open-ended questions and identified phrases that seemed to represent distinct themes. Employing this "emergent" approach to identifying themes (cf. Haney, Russell, Gulek, & Fierros, 1998), the authors exchanged their lists of preliminary themes, and found that while one author had four themes and the other had five, three of the themes were nearly identical, and one author's fourth theme was the other author's fourth and fifth, that is, split into two themes. Differences were equitably resolved through open and frank discussion.

In a more formal approach, trained coders are employed to identify themes and then the researchers (or different coders) analyze the data to determine the prevalence and commonality of the themes. An interrater reliability score (similarity between the independent coders) can be computed; it implies, for example, that all coders have consistently and repeatedly coded material the same way, regardless of which texts they examined. Reliability provides an empirical grounding for the confidence that the interpretation of the data will mean the same to anyone who analyzes it, and that as much bias as possible has been removed from the interpretation. It is important to mention that there are computer programs (e.g., Nudist, CATA) that can perform content analysis using typed or transcribed interview data. Recent research by Ward (2012) suggests that despite the availability of these computer-based content analysis programs, human coding is more common. However, with large datasets, human coding is labor intensive, and therefore costly, making software-aided content analysis desirable. It is yet unknown which method is more reliable (Ward, 2012); some researchers use a combination of methods to increase the validity and reliability of content analysis.

USING IN-DEPTH INTERVIEWS IN CAREERS RESEARCH: CHALLENGES AND POTENTIAL RESOLUTIONS

Using interviews in careers research can be advantageous for a variety of reasons; there are also a number of challenges which the following strategies and suggestions may help to address. The first set of challenges concerns the interviewing skill of the researcher. Compared with the construction of a survey, which after multiple iterations and tests to ensure the validity of the instrument's measures and response categories, can be presumed to be a reliable mechanism to collect data from respondents, a well-constructed interview protocol can fail at collecting data if it is administered by an untrained or ineffective interviewer. While the open-ended and inductive framework of an in-depth interview provides a flexible mechanism for the deep exploration of a research question, the process can falter if an interviewer fails to remember key points or steps (e.g., thanking the participant, presenting informed consent), put an interviewee at ease, or manage the breadth and depth of a discussion so it remains on-point. Preparing a session guide (separate from the protocol) can assist with these challenges. This session guide can range from something as simple as a checklist of key points to a guide that annotates, in detail, the interview protocol from start to finish. The guide might also include something specific about a participant's education, experience, or accomplishment that is relevant to the interview and that the researcher can communicate to demonstrate his or her preparation and ability to highlight commonalities between them. Doing so serves to increase the credibility and trustworthiness of the interviewer (Conger, 2008), which helps affirm an interviewee's decision to participate, expectation for a positive, empowering experience, and sense of purpose in which to share their narrative with an interested audience (Hutchinson, Wilson, & Wilson, 1994; Kvale, 1983), ultimately improving the quality of the data collected in the process.

This approach embodies what preeminent careers scholar Edgar H. Schein has termed "humble inquiry" (2013)—a way of facilitating conversation, through one's approach, tone, and body language, that creates a sense of equality, mutual interdependence, and partnership in a truly balanced discovery process. This philosophy—which focuses on *asking* (rather than assuming)—demonstrates an inquisitiveness that stems from curiosity and interest, and supports a more open, honest, and deeper conversation which enables the interviewer to learn more about the complexity of ideas embodied in the respondent's perspective. Humble inquirers allow respondents to speak uninterrupted, focus on what is being said, and query an unclear idea or non-verbal response. If for example, the conversation takes an unexpected path which the interviewer wishes to explore, and it is something that will require additional time, the interviewer (checking his or her protocol) might then ask to extend the originally agreed upon time, or failing that, whether an additional shorter session may be possible. Asking for permission increases the interviewer's credibility, demonstrates his or her commitment to the schedule, and the value he or she places on the respondent's time. Another helpful technique is to build in a few minutes of time at the end to transition out of the more intense interview discussion and into follow-up remarks. This can be done by stating that you do not have any other questions, asking if the participant does, clarifying next steps in the process, and sharing appreciation for their time and contribution (Corbin & Morse, 2003). Allowing ten additional minutes after each interview to reflect on what is learned can improve practice skills (Kvale, 2007). Scheduling time between multiple interviews can help the interviewer "reset," and consider process learnings (assessment of what went right, and what can be improved) and then apply them in upcoming interviews. Longer periods of reflection and, if appropriate, asking for feedback, can enhance interviewers' self-awareness, skills, and "artistry" (Argyris & Schön, 1974; Schön, 1987)—which includes practice flexibility—because "interviews often do not proceed as planned," and "researchers must continuously deal with challenges as they arise" (Roulston, 2011).

Another set of challenges concerns the (perceived) validity of the data. Organizational studies in general, and careers research in particular, rely heavily on quantitative approaches, and the trend is self-fulfilling: only a minority of researchers use qualitative methods because it is more difficult to complete and publish the study; therefore there are fewer qualitative studies published, and fewer editors and reviewers who might be favorably predisposed to qualitative research (or said differently, more confident in critiquing quantitative research). Absent F-scores, fit statistics, and r^2 computations, reviewers may feel less certain about the validity of the data and thus findings of interview-based research, particularly when viewing the research through a quantitative lens. Clarke (2009) provides a good example of an inductive and qualitative careers research study where the validity is strong and is based on in-depth interviews. Topics chosen by Clarke (2009) for discussion (age, experience, interview experiences, networks, support, etc.) connected to the study's focus on experienced, mid-level managers, and career transition; the many quotes from participants' narratives provide clear evidence of her findings. Two quotes,[4] procured from "well-qualified and highly experienced managers," reflect the persistence, frustration, and disappointment in many of the narratives and demonstrate that barriers to career transition are not limited to unskilled individuals in low-paying jobs. This clear conclusion is facilitated by the quality data obtained through the in-depth interviews. Ameliorating challenges related to validity in using in-depth interviews can be accomplished with a strong, clear, and focused research question, a well-thought out protocol centered on inductive learning rather than deductive proving, quality data collection and analysis, and a strong connection between all of these.

Validity can also be strengthened by using multiple methods. Shah and Corley (2006) explain how integrating multiple methods can broaden the discovery process and triangulate results, particularly in theory-building research. To build theory on identity, career aspirations, and achievement for Aboriginal women in high school in Australia, Gool and Patton's (1999) study participants completed a brief questionnaire (demographic questions) and were then interviewed first in small focus groups, and then in one-on-one interviews. Each subsequent step built on the previous one, and provided a forum for participants to discuss their views of Aboriginality, racism, school, family influences, careers, and employers. Not only did this path help to expand the researchers' cultural awareness and sensitivity (essential for building trust in the one-on-one interviews) but also helped uncover the interplay between Aboriginal cultural identity and the fear of, and experiences with, racism in broader society. The researchers note that their approach enabled more nuanced advice for school counselors and others advocating for Aboriginal students; that it's necessary to look below surface data and recognize the impact of individual and other systemic biases that affect career advising process and outcomes.

CONCLUSION

The narratives contained in individuals' employment recollections reflect the often unexpected, circuitous paths that careers scholars retrospectively refer to as careers. As the nature of careers continues to evolve, careers researchers engaging in in-depth interviews have the capacity to go beyond the "what" and "when" questions and explore the answers to (and interconnections between) questions such as the "why," "how," "in what context," and "why not?" In-depth interviewing provides a process to inquire beneath the surface, build theory, and understand the unique and evolving patterns of work in individuals, groups, and societies.

NOTES

1. In an in-progress study of Airbnb hosts personality, experience, and outcomes of their participation in the gig economy, de Janasz and her colleagues (2019) used posts in multiple Airbnb-related Facebook groups and follow-up emails and private Facebook messages to collect data from 184 respondents over several months.
2. In almost every case, the mentee's company paid for their participation in the program as an investment in the CEO's development.
3. If the interview was recorded, the tapes should be sent to transcription immediately with all copies kept in a secure and confidential location.
4. These two partial quotes are representative of the many included in Clarke's research from male and female participants who ranged from 30 to 60 years old. The first is from a 40-year-old man who describes the way employers and recruiters in the private sector downplay his prior experience in that they "tend to see me as a public servant and try and put me in some form of a box." The second is from a man in his mid 40's: "A recruiter said to me last week, hmm, you're starting to get to that age…"

REFERENCES

Argyris, C., & Schön, D. (1974). *Theory in Practice: Increasing Professional Effectiveness.* San Francisco, CA: Jossey-Bass Publishers.

Berg, B. L. (2007). *Qualitative Research Methods for the Social Sciences* (6th edn.). Boston, MA: Pearson/Allyn and Bacon.

Boyce, P., & Neale, P. (2006). *Conducting In-depth Interviews: A Guide for Designing and Conducting In-Depth Interviews for Evaluation Input.* Pathfinder International. http://www2.pathfinder.org/site/DocServer/m_e_tool_series_indepth_interviews.pdf

Clark, T. (2010). On 'being researched': why do people engage with qualitative research? *Qualitative Research*, 10(4), 399–419. https://doi.org/10.1177/1468794110366796

Clarke, M. (2009). Boundaries and barriers: a study of managers in career transition. *International Journal of Employment Studies*, 17(2), 34–65.

Conger, J. A. (2008). *The Necessary Art of Persuasion.* Boston, MA: Harvard Business School Press.

Corbin, J., & Morse, J. M. (2003). The unstructured Interactive interview: issues of reciprocity and risks when dealing with sensitive topics. *Qualitative Inquiry*, 9, 335–354.

de Janasz, S. C., Beutell, N. J., Kim, S., Schneer, J. A., & Wong, C. (2019, unpublished). Work–family integration and segmentation in the gig economy: a look at work–family strategies of Airbnb hosts. Presented at the 2020 Work Family Researchers Network Annual Conference, New York City, June.

de Janasz, S. C., & Kenworthy, A. L. (2015). Toward authenticity or defeat: the jolting effect of layoff, in Baugh, S. G., & Sullivan, S. E. (eds), *Searching for Authenticity: Research in Careers, Vol. 2* (pp. 67–88). Charlotte, NC: Information Age Publishing.

de Janasz, S. C., & Peiperl, M. (2015). CEOs need mentors too. *Harvard Business Review*, 93(4), 100–103.

Flick, U. (2014). *The Sage Handbook of Qualitative Data Analysis*. Thousand Oaks, CA: Sage Publications.

Gool, S., & Patton, W. (1999). Career aspirations of young Aboriginal women. *Australian Journal of Career Development*, 8(1), 26–31. https://doi.org/10.1177/103841629900800108

Guest, G., Bunce, A., & Johnson, L. (2006). How many interviews are enough? An experiment with data saturation and variability. *Field Methods*, 18(1), 59–82.

Guest, G., Namey, E. E., & Mitchell, M. (2013). In-depth interviews, in *Collecting Qualitative Data: A Field Manual for Applied Research* (pp. 113–171). Thousand Oaks, CA: Sage Publications.

Gunz, H., & Peiperl, M. (2007). Introduction, in Gunz, H., & Peiperl, M. (eds), *Handbook of Career Studies* (pp. 1–10). Thousand Oaks, CA: Sage Publications.

Haney, W., Russell, M., Gulek, C., & Fierros, E. (1998). Drawing on education: using student drawings to promote middle school improvement. *Schools in the Middle*, 7(3), 38–43.

Holsti, O. R. (1969). *Content Analysis for the Social Sciences and Humanities*. Reading, MA: Addison-Wesley.

Hutchinson, S. A., Wilson, M. E., & Wilson, H. S. (1994). Benefits of participating in research interviews. *Image the Journal of Nursing Scholarship*, 26(2), 161–164. doi:10.1111/j.1547-5069.1994.tb00937.x

Krippendorff, K. (2004). *Content Analysis: An Introduction to its Methodology* (2nd edn.). Newbury Park, CA: Sage Publications.

Kvale, S. (1983). The qualitative research interview: a phenomenological and a hermeneutical mode of understanding. *Journal of Phenomenological Psychology*, 14(2), 171–196. https://doi.org/10.1163/156916283X00090

Kvale, S. (2006). Dominance through interviews and dialogues. *Qualitative Inquiry*, 12(3), 480–500. https://doi.org/10.1177/1077800406286235

Kvale, S. (2007). *Qualitative Research Kit: Doing Interviews*. London, UK: Sage Publications.

McCue, T. J. (2018). 57 million U.S. workers are part of the gig economy. *Forbes*, August 31. https://www.forbes.com/sites/tjmccue/2018/08/31/57-million-u-s-workers-are-part-of-the-gig-economy/#7b7332557118

Roulston, K. (2011). Working through challenges in doing interview research. *International Journal of Qualitative Methods*, 10(4), 348–366. https://doi.org/10.1177/160940691101000404

Schein, E. H. (2013). Humble inquiry: The gentle art of asking instead of telling (an excerpt). https://www.bkconnection.com/static/Humble_Inquiry_EXCERPT.pdf

Schön, D. A. (1987). *Educating the Reflective Practitioner* (1st edn.). San Francisco, CA: Jossey-Bass.

Seidman, I. (2013). *Interviewing as Qualitative Research: A Guide for Researchers in Education and the Social Sciences* (4th edn.). New York: Teachers College Press.

Shah, S. K., & Corley, K. G. (2006). Building better theory by bridging the quantitative–qualitative divide. *Journal of Management Studies*, 43(8), 1821–1835. https://doi.org/10.1111/j.1467-6486.2006.00662.x

Trier-Bieniek, A. (2012). Framing the telephone interview as a participant-centered tool for qualitative research: A methodological discussion. *Qualitative Research*, 12(6), 630–644. https://doi.org/10.1177/1468794112439005

Ward, J. H. (2012). *Managing Data: Content Analysis Methodology*. Unpublished manuscript, University of North Carolina at Chapel Hill.

13. Careers, identities and institutions: the promise of narrative analysis
Holly Slay Ferraro

... men and women "make their own history, but not ... under conditions they have chosen for themselves; rather on terms immediately existing, given and handed down to them." How are these lives, their histories, and their meanings to be studied ... How do sociologists, anthropologists, historians and literary critics read, write, and make sense of their lives?
(Denzin, 1989, p. 10)

... narrative frames the insecure nature of contemporary employment as a means through which workers accumulate a varied and valuable portfolio of skills that will ensure their future prosperity ... Amid the insecurity inherent in the fast paced, innovation-fueled world of high tech, workers espouse a worldview modeled after America's origin myth of self-reliant pioneers fending for themselves in a risky environment where job security is something you create yourself rather than something gifted from above ... The unemployed worker is refashioned into a frontierlike, self-sufficient career manager who, in the words of one job seeker, "takes control of [his or her] own destiny." (Lane, 2011, pp. 48–49)

INTRODUCTION

The scholars who birthed career studies saw careers as "a lens for peering at larger social processes known as institutions" (Barley, 1989, p. 49). Careers were not confined to work organizations but were integrated into and encompassed one's entire life. This research examined scripts for enacting various roles (such as worker, parent, and citizen) that defined the self, drove individual action and, consequently, maintained or changed institutions. Goffman (1961) argued career studies could allow one to "move back and forth between the personal and the public, between self and its significant society" (p. 127). Thus, early career investigators forged a broad conception of careers and sought to understand them through investigations of life and work histories (Barley, 1989).

Contemporary researchers have built on early scholars' foundation by increasingly exploring careers through studies of identity as formed inside and outside of work (Cinque, Nyberg, & Starkey, 2020; Demetry, 2017; Galperin, 2017). As the epigraph from Lane's (2011) compelling research on unemployed tech workers illuminates, career narratives reflect what employees believe about themselves, how they should navigate work, and their views about why they should engage in vocational behaviors. Her study reveals that conformity to cultural rules and myths, such as the rugged American pioneer, fuel career narratives and behavior. Tech workers may find a "career entrepreneur" identity compelling because it aligns with a core national mythology. Ibarra and Barbulescu (2010) argue for even greater consideration of identity and contend organizational researchers have not paid adequate attention to narrative forms of identity expression. They introduce the term *narrative identity work* "to refer to social efforts to craft self-narratives that meet a person's identity aims" (p. 137). The potential for insights about identities, institutions, and individuals which may be gained by studying careers through narrative informs this chapter and provides the foundation on which I propose future research directions for the study of careers. This chapter familiarizes readers with narrative methods for studying careers and identity. Specifically, I address these central questions:

- Why should careers researchers use narrative methods to study careers and identity?
- What narrative methods are appropriate for and used by careers researchers?
- How does one conduct high-quality narrative research?

I introduce readers to narrative careers research, highlight exemplars, and challenge researchers to move to more critical examinations of identities and institutions in ways consistent with the vision of early careers scholars. I begin by defining identity and institutions and briefly explicating their relationships to careers. Next, I discuss how narrative methods provide a holistic understanding of people's lives and how people exercise individual agency while under institutional constraints. Finally, I provide narrative methods guidelines for researchers in the study of careers.

INSTITUTIONS, IDENTITY, AND CAREERS

Institutions are defined as, "regulative, normative, and cultural-cognitive elements that together with associated activities and resources, provide stability and meaning to social life" (Scott, 2014, p. 56). North (1991, p. 98) describes institutions as the "rules of the game" devised to shape political, economic, and social interaction. He explains that rules are required to engender cooperation and orderly transactions, to reduce uncertainty, and to indicate how future encounters will be structured. Institutions have "logics" or rationales that convey the appropriate relationship between people, practices, and things (Scott, 2014). For example, capitalism, as an institution, has a central logic (i.e., commodification and individualism) that provides people with a sense of self (i.e., identity), and a language for interacting (Thornton & Ocasio, 2008).

Identity is conceptualized at various levels of analysis, such as individual, relational, and organizational (Ashforth, Rogers, & Corley, 2010). Across levels, identity is commonly defined as the "essence" (p. 1145) of the entity (e.g., person or organization) as characterized by traits or relationships to other entities (e.g., ingroups vs. outgroups) and a key determinant of how people behave in various settings. Recent research on professional identity has sought to articulate and measure the connection between identity and institutions (Barbour & Lammer, 2015) to provide insight into how people make meaning about work, their place in the world, what they should believe, and how they should behave as a result. Professional identity is defined as "the relatively stable and enduring constellation of attributes, beliefs, values, motives, and experiences in terms of which people define themselves in a professional role" (Ibarra, 1999, p. 764). Institutional theorists have argued professions and occupations are institutions governing how people carry out work and interact with other institutions, such as the state. For example, the training of physicians is influenced by accrediting agencies and governing bodies certify the right to practice.

A career is defined as "the evolving sequence of a person's work experiences over time" (Arthur, Hall, & Lawrence, 1989, p. 8). These authors conceptualize work as constituting myriad ways of perceiving and experiencing people, organizations, and society. Savickas (2002) contends careers are best understood by examining patterns of vocational behavior rather than individual actions, such as turnover decisions. Indeed, I contend careers research has contributed much to the field of organizational studies because it examines interactions between individuals and the environment *over time*. For example, scholars have considered careers as status passages, responses to market forces, and as unfolding social roles that maintain or enhance the social order or institutional functioning (Becker, 1975; Glaser & Strauss, 1971; Hughes, 1958; Van Maanen & Barley, 1984). All of this work enables a greater understanding of individuals and institutions (Arthur, Hall, & Lawrence, 1989) as the authors illuminate both how individuals make sense of and enact work and the institutions which structure work and life external to work organizations.

When taken together, careers research has historically provided insight *beyond* how people make career decisions as individuals. Instead, careers are defined in terms of the evolution of individuals as they interact with the social order. Thus, studies of careers need a methodology that allows for inquiry into meaning-making across time, institutions, and organizational boundaries as careers take place over the life course, not solely within organizations. In the next section, I discuss how narrative research provides a better understanding of institutions, identities, and careers.

REASONS FOR CAREER RESEARCHERS TO USE NARRATIVE METHODS

Social sciences and humanities scholars have used narrative analysis because story-telling is essential to how people make sense of their worlds and define themselves (Brinkmann & Kvale, 2015). Narratives are examples of speech or communications used to represent a connected series of events (Lieblich, Tuval-Mashiach, & Zilber, 1998). McAdams (1993) argues people construct narratives or personal myths which he describes as "act[s] of imagination" (p. 12) that integrate past remembrances, perceptions of the present, and future expectations. Personal myths evolve throughout our lives and contain the elements constitutive of identity (Ibarra & Barbulescu, 2010). Important elements of identity include traits such as intelligence or habits (Stryker, 2007) but people also come to know themselves through the "company they keep" or avoid (Stets & Burke, 2000). Further, identities are influenced by others through the internalization of roles and the appraisals of others (Westen & Heim, 2003). Identity is constituted by the roles we take and the expectations attendant on those roles (e.g., I am a mother and, therefore, I should enact my career in particular ways) (Ladge, Clair, & Greenberg, 2012). But it is through storytelling that people put it all together, interpret identity elements, and make sense of relationships, roles, and appraisals of role performances (Murray, 2003). Narrative analysis has proven invaluable in illuminating how stories embody powerful interests and how people must negotiate between personal narratives and dominant societal narratives (Murray, 2003; Snow & Anderson, 1987; Rosen, 2017).

Narrative analysis may be especially valuable for careers researchers seeking to examine how people construct the self, respond to institutional opportunities and constraints, and manage relationships. Ibarra and Barbulescu (2010) urge researchers to develop conceptual frameworks explaining how narrating processes influence identity construction (such as professional identity work). They suggest a stronger focus on story elements that enable people to achieve identity aims and more attention to story evolution, such as the retaining and discarding of stories for future use (Ibarra & Barbulescu, 2010, p. 135). In this work, researchers are encouraged to explore how individuals navigate work role transitions and engage in identity work.

While career narratives provide insight into identities or the meanings people attach to themselves during work role transitions, they also reveal how people manage meanings attached to them by others or by social structures throughout the life course. Identity work and identity construction may be based not only on changes in work and social roles but also by membership in social groups. For example, Slay and Smith's (2011) work examines how African American journalists construct professional identities in the face of racial stigma and institutional racism. Racial oppression presented constraints on professional opportunities but also required black journalists to create new avenues for conceiving the self and the profession. LaPointe (2013) studies the stories of women career changers for insight into how career agency is constrained by gender. Her research questions extant theories that suggest careers are boundaryless (Arthur, 1994) or driven by one's personal values (Hall, 1996). When taken together, these works reintroduce the power of institutions to the study of careers by considering institutional racism and sexism (Martin, 2004). Specifically, the researchers challenge the reduction of gender or race as an individual trait (e.g., biological or psychological) and emphasize "its profound sociality" (Martin, 2004, p. 1259). Career scholars who employ narrative analysis have an opportunity to show how people understand and enact careers through the stories they tell and how race and gender are a part of those stories at various levels (e.g., organizational, societal, or cultural).

Narrative career studies are particularly promising as careers change, become more discontinuous and more likely to be lived through "gigs," defined as short-term independent freelance or contractual work rather than employment at a single organization (Ashford, Caza, & Reid, 2018). Because narrative methods are well-positioned to uncover how people make sense of themselves, career scholars using these methods might contribute to the literature by exploring linkages between role transitions, societal changes, and identity processes. As McAdams (1999) suggests, narrative methods can enable a greater understanding of the kinds of transitions (e.g., marriage) that create significant identity work and the types of transitions that result in tweaks and minor identity work. For example, Obodaru (2017) develops a process model describing how people manage professional identity construction when they forego or sacrifice pursuing career alternatives that express an essential alternative self. By studying the stories people tell, she taps into how sacrificed-selves may play a vital role in self-narratives and the values underlying the importance of these identities. She also finds that sacrificed-selves go beyond what one sacrifices at work (e.g., a managerial role) but also living out familial roles such as son, husband, and father in a less distracted and more devoted way.

Caza, Moss and Vough's (2018) multi-year study of plural careerists or those engaging in multiple jobs for identity reasons rather than financial ones demonstrates the power of narrative methods for comprehending how people manage multiple work identities. Their findings explicate how people enact agency within societal constraints. Specifically, they explore authenticity, an "enduring sense of alignment of one's actions with one's true, actualized self" and one's sense of congruence between self-expression (e.g., actions and words) and experiences (p. 705). Of particular note are the stories plural careerists share of navigating others' expectations that their careers be defined by a single role rather than many. Detaching from relationships with some people while attaching to others (and using various kinds of identity resources and practices), pluralists can harmonize identities in ways they deem authentic. Finally, Nigam and Dokko (2019) explicitly explore the relationship between careers and institutions in a study of the emergence of a new profession using oral history interviews as source material. They uncover a career resourcing process which is a structuration model illuminating the recursive relationship between individual agency and structural change.

The potential of narrative methods to advance career scholarship is considerable. Yet, scholars argue this research does not treat narrative in sufficient depth given its focus on events rather than putting "skin on the bones" by theorizing how events are raw material for narrative identity work designed to meet identity goals (Ibarra & Barbulescu, 2010, p. 149). While the exemplars summarized in this section meet this call, more research is needed to extend knowledge of how careers are enacted, institutions transformed, and professional identities are constructed.

NARRATIVE RESEARCH METHODS

Grounded in hermeneutics, phenomenology, ethnography, and literary analysis, narrative research eschews methodological orthodoxy in favor of doing what is necessary to capture the lived experience of people in terms of their own meaning making and to theorize about it in insightful ways. (Josselson, 2011, p. 225)

What constitutes narrative research? Lieblich, Tuval-Mashiach, and Zilber (1998) state that narrative research refers to any study that uses or analyzes narrative material. This definition suggests that many methods, such as grounded theory, could be used within narrative research. What defines narrative research is not how the data is analyzed, but the narrative form of the data. Stories could be written or spoken during interviews and can be used to study phenomenon at all levels of analysis (from individual to societal). A narrative careers research project aims to collect rich data containing detailed descriptions at the intersection of individual and structure allowing insights into the complexity of individual career decisions in the face of organizational and societal constraints and opportunities. Therefore, in the remainder of this chapter, I do not advocate for specific methods or techniques but consider how various methods may lead to deeper meaning-making, theorizing, and significant contributions to the literature. Specifically, I focus on strategies and techniques frequently used in narrative research, name key issues related to these strategies, and offer recommendations for improving the use of narrative methods.

Sampling

When collecting data for narrative research, one must consider which materials should be studied (e.g., interview responses or written stories) and the source of the material (e.g., people or oral history collections) (Smith, 2000). Narrative research—and qualitative research generally—frequently collects data that is not designed to be representative but instead is chosen for its relevance to theory building through purposive sampling (Mishler, 1999). As stated in this section's epigraph by Josselson, narrative research is based in hermeneutic and other philosophies which stress knowledge as an activity and that gaining knowledge requires an inquiry into the "living, acting, knowing human being" (Brinkmann & Kvale, 2015, p. 56). This ontological assumption requires narrative researchers to conduct investigations into a phenomenon as lived by human beings who construct their reality as they are affected by culture and history. Therefore, narrative research appropriately uses sampling methods that are non-probabilistic and give primacy to the world as it is lived to enable greater contribution to knowledge.

Examples of this form of sampling in careers research can be seen in several narrative research study exemplars. For example, Slay and Smith (2011) explored the stories of stigmatized workers in a single vocation to illuminate how professional identity construction for members of marginalized social identity groups requires a redefinition of occupational rhetoric, stigma, and self. A compilation of narratives by Terry (2007), triangulated with narratives provided by the focal journalists in other fora, provided source material for the study of professional identity construction of black journalists. In their examination of how new professions develop, Nigam and Dokko (2019) used historical archives composed of the oral histories of individuals involved in the emergence of health services research. The study required a longitudinal analysis to understand how professions become institutionalized. Caza, Moss, and Vough (2018) used snowball sampling, a variant of a purposive sample, that involves asking informants with relevant experiences or backgrounds required for theory building to nominate similar others for study participation. Snowball sampling was appropriate because the phenomenon under consideration was authenticity when one has multiple work role identities that are important to them. Study participants needed to be people who engaged in multiple work roles because they enjoyed them—not just to make ends meet—to understand better how identities could be harmonized and coherent to the individual. Each of these studies demonstrates sampling methods for narrative research are focused on finding participants who have a lived experience relevant to theory development.

Issues and limitations in purposive sampling

While purposive sampling aligns with the aim of delving into lived experience and understanding how people make meaning from those experiences, researchers should be aware of potential limitations. First, different researchers studying similar questions are likely to uncover "different sampled elements from the target population in terms of important characteristics and typical elements to be in the sample" (Battaglia, 2008). That is, what we learn about the lived experience of job transition may be influenced by important characteristics of the sample such as race or socio-economic status. This may be especially true in a snowball sample where members of the group recommend those who are like themselves on dimensions other than the phenomenon of interest. As a result, we may oversample majority groups, fail to hear hidden populations' stories, and miss seeing how societal relations are reproduced in the workplace (Nkomo, 1992). Because this is a potential pitfall, it is reasonable for narrative researchers to make their criteria for sampling decision-making fully transparent (Oliver, 2006). For example, Caza, Moss, and Vough's (2018) inclusion criteria were people who had two or more work roles *with which they identified.* Moonlighters, people who chose to work multiple roles out of financial need but do not see the roles are part of their self-concept, were not included because they did not identify with their supplemental work roles and therefore could not contribute to understanding the phenomenon of interest. The inclusion of detailed criteria used by authors offer consumers of research ways to contextualize the findings.

Data Collection

Written narratives

Studying life documents, such as autobiographies, oral histories, diaries, and letters, is used in narrative research and is defined as interpretative biography or the biographical method (Denzin, 1989). Denzin states "a life is a social text, a fictional, narrative production" (p. 9). Therefore, life stories frequently conform to many Western literary conventions which govern how people narrate and write stories. These conventions include (but are not limited to):

1. The existence of others. Texts are written with an audience in mind and the "gaze" of the audience directs the writer suggesting what to conceal, amplify, or omit.

2. The influence and importance of gender, class, and race. Denzin (1989) argues that written texts are, "gendered, class productions reflecting the biases and values of patriarchy and the middle class" (p. 18). Increasingly, scholars in many fields recognize that written texts also reflect the values and biases of whiteness "described as an ongoing and unfinished history, which orientates bodies in specific directions, affecting how they 'take up' space" (Ahmed, 2007, p. 150). The knowledge of this convention can assist researchers in seeing gaps in knowledge as a result of members of minoritized or stigmatized identity groups being discouraged or prohibited from writing their biographies. Moreover, members of dominant identity groups (e.g., whites, men) have not been encouraged or incentivized to write about minoritized careerists or those from subordinated identity groups.

3. Family beginnings. Stories, and perhaps especially career stories, are rooted in family beginnings characterized by the presence or absence of mothers and fathers which also places people within society and patriarchal structures. For example, family beginnings are prominently featured within Slay and Smith's (2011) work on the professional identity construction of black journalists. The researchers theorize that, for stigmatized professionals, the family of origin had a major influence on the repertoire of professional selves available which ultimately influenced how one redefined the self, professional rhetorics, and stigma in ways that permitted one to be a journalist in a society that maligned black people.

4. Objective markers. As people tell their stories, and interviewers attempt to gather narratives, objective markers are used and sought to provide meaning and coherence. For example, Lieblich, Tuval-Mashiach, and Zilber (1998) provided the following instructions for informants:

> Every person's life can be written as a book. I would like you to think about your life now as if you were writing a book. First, think about the chapters of this book. I have here a page to help you in this task. Write down the years on the first column—from zero, from the day you were born. When did the first stage end? Write it here. Then go on to the next chapters, and put down the age that each one begins and ends for you. Go on till you reach your present age. You can use any number of chapters or stages that you find suitable to your own life. (p. 25)

Informants were instructed to title each chapter and asked during an interview to respond to the following questions:

a. "Tell me about a significant episode or a memory that you remember from this stage."

b. "What kind of a person were you during this stage?"

c. "Who were significant people for you during this stage, and why?"

d. "What is your reason for choosing to terminate this stage when you did?"

When stories are structured in this way, researchers can chart informants' lives in ways that give meaning and coherence, allowing for an understanding of the values, people, or experiences that influence observed behavior and may be of theoretical value. It is important to keep in mind, however, that stories are created and recreated as people live, have new experiences, and discover new patterns in their lives and behavior (Denzin, 1989).

5. Turning-point experiences. Career narratives, like other life stories, are shaped by turning points or moments in the narrators' lives that are believed to have shaped their experiences and left permanent marks. Ibarra (2003) details the lives of thirty-nine career changers providing evidence of the use of epiphanies in career stories. One such story is related by Lucy, a tech manager who transitioned to become a coach:

> By this time, it was clear that I wanted to move on to something different. But I needed to build more confidence before taking a bigger chance on reinventing myself. So I decided to stay in the high-tech environment, which I knew well, but also to go back to school. I started a master's program in organizational development, thinking that at least it would make me a better leader and hoping it would be the impetus for a real makeover. Three incidents marked a turning point. (p. 9)

Career epiphanies are often invoked to explain how people are liberated to be more fully themselves by significant events. Attending to conventions used to construct written narratives can help researchers design narrative studies and, specifically, craft data collection through interviews.

Interviews

The goal of an interview is to elicit information related to the phenomenon of interest, to lay the groundwork for the analysis phase of the project, and provoke communications that could lead to theoretical contributions. The design and conduct of narrative inquiry interviewing are influenced by the ontological and epistemological paradigms to which the researcher subscribes (Brinkmann & Kvale, 2015). Collecting stories through interviews is therefore consistent with philosophies which contend meaning is made and expressed through discourse (Mishler, 1986). Researchers in this tradition refrain from presupposing that narratives mirror a "core" self or truth that is unearthed during the interview. Instead, scholars consider themselves "probers" or "participants" who go beyond the reported interview answers to apprehend how reality is constructed and institutions are experienced (Brinkmann & Kvale, 2015). Probers delve deep into the inner world of study informants while participants see their role as engaging in active creation of meaning with study informants. Probers and participants do not consider the opinions of interviewees as sacrosanct and are willing to subject them to critical analysis. This does not mean that researchers are free to ignore the statements of research informants in favor of their own interpretations; however, it does mean that the interview process is designed with the knowledge that narratives are often performed for others or in uncritical adherence to conventions.

There are several types of interview questions and types of interviews that narrative researchers may employ. Brinkmann and Kvale (2015) name nine types of interview questions ranging from introductory questions (e.g., "Can you tell me about...?") to interpreting questions ("Does the expression...cover what you have just expressed?"). The use of a variety of questions is on display in narrative inquiry exemplars. Haynie and Shepherd's (2011) study of the influence of traumatic life events on how career transitions are experienced provides an excellent example of protocol design using multiple question forms. The study informants are soldiers and Marines disabled by wartime combat and enrolled in an entrepreneurship training program. The protocol revolved around four themes: (1) the informant's motivations, aspirations, and goals associated with joining the military; (2) a retelling of the traumatic event that lead to the disability and loss of their military career; (3) a discussion about returning home, coping with trauma, and leaving the military; and (4) a description of the training program and the vision for a future career.

Atkinson (1998) discusses life story interviewing as an interview type. This method takes a holistic look at the life of an individual encompassing but not solely focused on specific incidences such as career transitions. Atkinson (1998) suggests three types of questions—descriptive, structural, and contrast—that are more likely to create thoughtful stories useful for narrative research studies. Descriptive questions provide an overview of one's life or a period within one's life (e.g., "How would you describe your childhood?"). A structural question gets at the organization of knowledge or activities, such as, "What were some of the things you did as a child?" (p. 41). Finally, contrast questions are intended to evoke "dimensions of meaning," such as, "How was your childhood different from your adolescence?"

Wolf's (2019) research on managerial identities takes a life story approach in an exploration of how people construct protean or self-directed career identities. She contends a narrative approach is useful because the focus of analysis is "on the stories people create around their life trajectories" (p. 509). Specifically, the narratives people tell about being self-directed, motivated persons are linked to stories throughout their lives that predate any specific career transition or professional role. Current constructions of the self are shaped across the entire life span and require methods that delve into how people connect different phases of life and various career roles. Wolf conducted 29 interviews with professionals from different career backgrounds and stages but who were all considered protean careerists because of their stories about controlling their career destiny. The interviews were loosely structured but frequently started with a significant career episode that provided a starting point for tracing the evolution of the career. Atkinson's (1998) life story interview questions provided guidance for follow-up questions.

Analysis (Coding, Training, etc.)

The process of analysis is one of piecing together data, making the invisible apparent, deciding what is significant and insignificant, and linking seemingly unrelated facets of experience together. Analysis is a creative process of organizing data so that the analytic scheme will emerge. (Brinkmann & Kvale, 2015, p. 227)

An aim of narrative researchers interested in career phenomena is to evoke informant stories and translate them into analyses that illuminate how individuals make sense of life events and how values, emotions, and interactions with others influence career behavior. To achieve this aim, stories can be analyzed in numerous ways such as evaluations of narrative structure, plot, and genre (Brinkmann & Kvale, 2015). Structural analysis seeks to match spoken phrases to sequences of events and highlights that "what is done" is the core of the narrative (Franzosi, 1998, p. 523). Description, while a part of a narrative, becomes "evaluative commentary" (p. 523) rather than central to analysis. For example, job or organization descriptions become most informative when they are linked to actions people took, identity work engaged in, and subsequent career behavior. Plot analysis examines the way events are arranged and connected. Plot differs from skeletal descriptions of action and the order in which actions occurred (Franzosi, 1998). It binds together events and provides a logic for both events and their reported order. Finally, genre or narrative type analysis, based in literary criticism, considers whether the story is comedy, romance, tragedy or satire (Lieblich, Tuval-Mashiach, & Zilber, 1998). Comedies tell of heroes' use of skill to overcome threats to the social order while romances are stories about the victory of heroes over challenges that would keep them from achieving their goals. In tragedies, heroes suffer defeat and ostracism and satires provide cynical accounts of hegemonic power.

Stories may also be analyzed using propositions advanced by Ibarra and Barbulescu (2010). They assert that narrative identity work is more prevalent when career transitions have certain characteristics (degree of radicalness, institutionalization, and social desirability) and/or episode characteristics (stakes and visibility of interaction, relationship between storyteller and audience). Future researchers could use these characteristics to create research questions or coding structures in examinations of how people use stories as identity work when they engage in normative career change versus when they engage in careers in opposition to an accepted social order. Obodaru's (2017) study of foregone identities extends Ibarra and Barbulescu's (2010) work using narratives to understand identity construction in an investigation of fulfilled and unfulfilled values as well as characteristics of the career transition. This literature can be extended further though examinations of the extent to which narratives are effective in achieving identity aims using concepts such as coherence, legitimacy, and audience participation or acceptance by role set members (Ibarra & Barbulescu, 2010).

A variety of analytical methods are employed in exemplary narrative research studies. Haynie and Shepherd (2011) use the multiple case analysis methodology as they sought to develop an emerging theory about career responses to traumatic life events (Eisenhardt, 1989; Yin, 2003). They focused on ten cases each based on a U.S. military member who sustained career ending injuries as a result of combat trauma. The cases represented individuals experiencing contrasting outcomes, that is, five cases reflect people that transitioned well into new careers and five cases are of those that transitioned "less well" (Haynie & Shepherd, 2011, p. 503). In addition to using the stories told during semi-structured interviews, the researchers gathered supplemental data such as application materials for a training program (e.g., military discharge paperwork, application essays, medical disability determination) and correspondence between staff of the training program and research participants. Using within-case analyses, they emphasized relationships and constructs elucidating the career transitions of single individuals. Finally, they conducted cross-case analysis to compare individual cases and develop propositions for a process model of transition.

In contrast, Wolf (2019) uses constructivist grounded theory approaches in the examination of protean career identities. Theoretical (purposive) sampling is utilized and interviews are loosely structured using a reference guide of life story interview questions based on Atkinson (1998) for follow-up questions. Data collection and analysis were iterative with early analysis informing an evolving data collection process. The first step of analysis involved the creation of initial codes while the second step distinguished between the narrative practices used to describe identity construction and core themes of protean identity. It is especially noteworthy that Wolf highlights narrative practices rather than theoretical constructs emerging from the analysis. For example, questioning is a narrative practice explained as, "becoming aware of and challenging conformity with taken-for-granted assumptions and externally imposed expectations" (p. 513). An exemplar quote for questioning from the data is, "I did have an identity crisis at one point and I was like what am I? I don't fit into this and this" (p. 513).

Finally, Nigam and Dokko (2019) drew data from an oral history project designed to capture the stories of "innovators and leaders in the field of health services research" (p. 1055). Additionally, they obtained data from a variety of archival sources, such as transcripts from a conference panel and published accounts of the health services research profession's history from a variety of organizations. Their analysis iterated between inductive data coding and the creation of narrative career summaries based on the oral histories of 23 people. The summaries captured career motivations and actions over time. The authors constructed several tables illustrating analytical movement from initial coding to theoretical model generation. This article is distinct from many of the other exemplars in its discussion of participant account accuracy as a potential limitation (p. 1059) and details how triangulation was used (e.g., official documents, CVs) to reduce bias and increase objectivity. This treatment is important to the authors' stated research question: "What is the process by which individuals' career actions can lead to the emergence of a new profession?" (p. 1053). However, accuracy will be less germane to narrative researchers adopting a constructionist paradigm as the meaning made by participants and their interpretations of events and actions is frequently the subject of study. In such cases, researchers depend on accounts, even inaccurate ones, to inform rather than thwart study aims. As Atkinson (1998) states, "we are…seeking *the teller's* story" (p. 75).

CONCLUSION

This chapter has sought to answer three central questions. First, why should researchers use narrative methods in the study of careers? I have argued that narrative career studies have great potential to enable the understanding of lived experience but, perhaps more importantly, can help us see how stories told are shaped by broader social discourses. Thus, narrative career research can explain how agentic career behavior is influenced by structural constraints and how structures evolve through individual agency. This lens is especially important for responding to voices within the Academy which state stories that relate to how racial, gendered, or other forms of oppression influence organizational phenomena, such as careers, are frequently neglected (Nkomo, 1992). Narrative inquiry into careers has the potential to amplify stories that are rarely heard and poorly understood because the experiences and stories of the marginalized are infrequently studied. Narrative studies allow scholars to move beyond race, gender, and age as controls in quantitative studies where problems of sample size obscure how career experiences may vary dramatically for members of different social identity groups.

Second, what research methods are appropriate for and used by researchers? I have presented exemplary research using a variety of methodologies such as grounded theory and case study. Further, I have presented perspectives of narrative scholars stating that the objective of narrative inquiry is to hear the authentic voices of storytellers in order to learn how people view their experiences and interactions with others. Finally, I addressed the question "how does one conduct high-quality narrative research?" I have emphasized that narrative research is defined by the collection and analysis of stories rather than specific methods. The guiding principle for narrative research is that identity is developed through the lifelong process of storytelling. My hope is that scholars seeking to extend the literature and provide insights into career behavior will devote more time to studying how people shape stories that shape self, and in turn, shape society.

REFERENCES

Ahmed, S. (2007). A phenomenology of whiteness. *Feminist Theory*, *82*(2), 149–168.

Arthur, M. B. (1994). The boundaryless career: a new perspective for organizational inquiry. *Journal of Organizational Behavior*, *15*(4), 295–306.

Arthur, M. B., Hall, D. T., & Lawrence, B. S. (1989). Generating new directions in career theory: the case for a transdisciplinary approach. In M. B. Arthur, D. T. Hall, & B. S. Lawrence (eds.), *Handbook of Career Theory* (pp. 7–25). Cambridge: Cambridge University Press.

Ashford, S. J., Caza, B. B., & Reid, E. M. (2018). From surviving to thriving in the gig economy: a research agenda for individuals in the new world of work. *Research in Organizational Behavior*, *38*, 23–41.

Ashforth, B. E., Rogers, K. M., & Corley, K. G. (2010). Identity in organizations: exploring cross-level dynamics. *Organization Science*, *22*(5), 1144–1156.

Atkinson, R. (1998). *The Life Story Interview*. Thousand Oaks, CA: Sage Publications.

Barbour, J. B., & Lammer, J. C. (2015). Measuring professional identity: a review of the literature and a multilevel confirmatory factor analysis of professional identity constructs. *Journal of Professions and Organization, 2,* 38–60.

Barley, S. R. (1989). Careers, identities, and institutions: the legacy of the Chicago School of Sociology. In M. B. Arthur, D. T. Hall, & B. S. Lawrence (eds.), *Handbook of Career Theory* (pp. 41–65). Cambridge: Cambridge University Press.

Battaglia, M. P. (2008). Purposive sample. In P. J. Lavrakas (ed.), *Encyclopedia of Survey Research Methods* (pp. 645–647). Thousand Oaks, CA: Sage Publications. doi:10.4135/9781412963947

Becker, G. S. (1975). *Human Capital.* New York: Columbia University Press.

Brinkmann, S., & Kvale, S. (2015). *InterViews: Learning the Craft of Qualitative Research Interviewing.* Thousand Oaks, CA: Sage Publications.

Caza, B. B., Moss, S., & Vough, H. (2018). From synchronizing to harmonizing: the process of authenticating multiple work identities. *Administrative Science Quarterly, 63*(4), 703–745.

Cinque, S., Nyberg, D., & Starkey, K. (2020). "Living at the border of poverty": how theater actors maintain their calling through narrative identity work. *Human Relations,* 1–26. doi: 10.1177/0018726720908663

Demetry, D. (2017). Pop-up to professional: emerging entrepreneurial identity and evolving vocabularies of motive. *Academy of Management Discoveries, 3*(2), 187–207.

Denzin, N. K. (1989). *Interpretive biography.* Newbury Park: Sage Publications.

Eisenhardt, K. M. (1989). Building theories from case study research. *Academy of Management Review, 14*(4), 532–550.

Franzosi, R. (1998). Narrative analysis—or why (and how) sociologists should be interested in narrative. *Annual Review of Sociology, 24,* 517–554.

Galperin, R. V. (2017). Mass-production of professional services and pseudo-professional identity in tax preparation work. *Academy of Management Discoveries, 3*(2), 208–229.

Glaser, B., & Strauss, A. (1971). *Status Passages.* Chicago, IL: Aldine.

Goffman, E. (1961). *Asylums: Essays on the Social Situation Of Mental Patients And Other Inmates.* New York: Doubleday.

Hall, D. T. (1996). Protean careers of the 21st century. *Academy of Management Executive, 10*(4), 8–16.

Haynie, J. M., & Shepherd, D. (2011). Toward a theory of discontinuous career transition: investigating career transitions necessitated by traumatic life events. *Journal of Applied Psychology, 96*(3), 501–524.

Hughes, E. C. (1958). *Men and their Work.* Westport, CT: Greenwood Press.

Ibarra, H. (1999). Provisional selves: experimenting with image and identity in professional adaptation. *Administrative Science Quarterly, 44,* 764–791.

Ibarra, H. (2003). *Working Identity: Unconventional Strategies for Reinventing your Career.* Boston, MA: Harvard Business School Publishing.

Ibarra, H., & Barbulescu, R. (2010). Identity as narrative: prevalence, effectiveness, and consequences of narrative identity work in macro work role transitions. *Academy of Management Review, 35*(1), 135–154.

Josselson, R. (2011). Narrative research: constructing, deconstructing, and reconstructing story. In F. J. Wertz, K. Charmaz, L. M. McMullen, R. Josselson, R. Anderson, & E. McSpadden (eds.), *Five Ways of Doing Qualitative Analysis* (pp. 224–242). New York: Guilford Press.

Ladge, J. J., Clair, J. A., & Greenberg, D. N. (2012). Cross-domain identity transition during liminal periods: constructing multiple selves as professional and mother during pregnancy. *Academy of Management Journal, 55*(6), 1449–1471.

Lane, C. M. (2011). *A Company of One: Insecurity, Independence, and the New World of White-Collar Unemployment.* Ithaca, NY: ILR Press.

LaPointe, K. (2013). Heroic career changers? Gendered identity work in career transitions. *Gender, Work, & Organizations, 20*(2), 133–146.

Lieblich, A., Tuval-Mashiach, R., & Zilber, T. (1998). *Narrative Research: Reading, Analysis, and Interpretation.* Thousand Oaks: Sage Publications.

Martin, P. Y. (2004). Gender as social institution. *Social Forces, 82*(4), 1249–1273.

McAdams, D. P. (1993). *The Stories We Live By: Personal Myths and the Making of the Self.* New York: Guilford Press.

McAdams, D. P. (1999). Personal narratives and the life story. In L. A. Pervin, & O. P. John (eds.), *Handbook of Personality: Theory and Research* (2nd edition, pp. 478–500). London: Guilford Press.

Mishler, E. G. (1986). *Research Interviewing: Context and Narrative.* Cambridge, MA: Harvard University Press.

Mishler, E. G. (1999). *Storylines: Craftartists' Narratives of Identity.* Cambridge, MA: Harvard University Press.

Murray, M. (2003). Narrative psychology and narrative analysis. In P. M. Camic, J. E. Rhodes, & L. Yardley (eds.), *Qualitative Research in Psychology: Expanding Perspectives in Methodology and Design* (pp. 95–112). Washington, DC: American Psychological Association.

Nigam, A., & Dokko, G. (2019). Career resourcing and the process of professional emergence. *Academy of Management Journal, 62*(4), 1052–1084.

Nkomo, S. (1992). The emperor has no clothes: rewriting "race in organizations". *Academy of Management Review, 17*(3), 487–513.

North, D. C. (1991). Institutions. *Journal of Economic Perspectives, 5*(1), 97–112.

Obodaru, O. (2017). Foregone, but not forgotten: toward a theory of forgone professional identities. *Academy of Management Journal, 60*(2), 523–553.

Oliver, P. (2006). Purposive sampling. In V. Jupp (ed.), *The Sage Dictionary of Social Research Methods* (p. 145 ebook). London: Sage Publications. doi:10.4135/9780857020116

Rosen, E. (2017). Horizontal immobility: how narratives of neighborhood violence shape housing decisions. *American Sociological Review, 27*(1), 270–296.

Savickas, M. L. (2002). Reinvigorating the study of careers. *Journal of Vocational Behavior, 61*(3), 381–385.

Scott, R. W. (2014). *Institutions and Organizations: Ideas, Interests, and Identities* (4th edition). Thousand Oaks, CA: Sage Publications.

Slay, H. S., & Smith, D. A. (2011). Professional identity construction: Using narrative to understand the negotiation of professional and stigmatized cultural identities. *Human Relations, 64*(1), 85–107.

Smith, C. P. (2000). Content analysis and narrative analysis. In H. T. Reis, & C. M. Judd (eds.), *Handbook of Research Methods in Social and Personality Psychology* (pp. 313–335). Cambridge: Cambridge University Press.

Snow, D. A., & Anderson, L. (1987). Identity work among the homeless: the verbal construction and avowal of personal identities. *American Journal of Sociology, 92*(6), 1336–1371.

Stets, J. E., & Burke, P. J. (2000). Identity theory and social identity theory. *Social Psychology Quarterly, 63*(3), 224–237.

Stryker, S. (2007). Identity theory and personality theory: mutual relevance. *Journal of Personality, 75*(6), 1083–1102.

Terry, W. (2007). *Missing Pages: Black Journalists of Modern America: An Oral History.* New York: Carroll & Graf.

Thornton, P. H., & Ocasio, W. (2008). Institutional logics. In R. Greenwood, C. Oliver, R. Suddaby, & K. Sahlin-Andersson (eds.), *The Sage Handbook of Organizational Institutionalisms* (pp. 99–129). London: Sage Publications.

Van Maanen, J., & Barley, S. (1984). Occupational communities: culture and control in organizations. *Research in Organizational Behavior, 6*, 287–365.

Westen, D., & Heim, A. K. (2003). Disturbances of self and identity in personality disorders. In M. R. Leary, & J. P. Tangney (eds.), *Handbook of Self and Identity* (pp. 643–664). New York: Guilford Press.

Wolf, C. (2019). Not lost in translation: managerial career narratives and the construction of protean identities. *Human Relations*, *72*(3), 505–533.

Yin, R. K. (2003). *Case Study Research: Design and Methods* (5th edition). Los Angeles: Sage Publications.

14. Qualitative and quantitative examination of metaphorical language use in career-life preparedness

Allison Creed and Susan Nacey

INTRODUCTION

This chapter introduces a procedure for metaphor identification allowing for an integrated qualitative and quantitative approach to investigating career guidance discourse. We offer a step-by-step demonstration of the Metaphor Identification Procedure Vrije Universiteit (henceforth MIPVU; Steen et al., 2010b), applied to metaphorical language used in student testimonials in promotional online videos of an Australian and Norwegian university. Metaphor is a specific form of communicative behavior that may function as an initiator of framing for topics in public discourse (Krippendorff, 2017) as well as a reasoning device that adds conceptual content (Burgers, Kronijn, & Steen, 2016). In these publicly available videos, students talk about their experiences in higher education as well as express their thoughts and feelings about career and future working life. The videos were transcribed, and metaphor identified using the English and Norwegian versions of MIPVU.

Metaphor identification can open a window to deeper understanding of how individuals and organizations make meaning about education and career development over the lifespan. For instance, the interpersonal and social existence of individuals can be surveyed in terms of *career-life preparedness* (Lent, 2013) to stimulate and nourish career adaptability, resilience, and coping. Although metaphors are recognized as fundamental to making meaning in relation to notions of career, workforce, and organizations (Inkson & Amundson, 2002; Inkson, Dries, & Arnold, 2015; Morgan, 2006), metaphor analysis has been reliant on more intuitive methods and has thus far had no robust systematic foundation for metaphor identification. Significantly, metaphor remains underexplored in naturalistic discourse within the field of vocational psychology. MIPVU addresses this gap with a protocol for metaphor identification and affords both linguistic and conceptual analysis.

BACKGROUND

The vocational choices people make about career and working life and their adjustment to occupational situations involves two processes according to Super (1963). The first is the development of a concept of who a person really is and the second is turning that concept into a reality. Metaphor analysis offers a means to explore self and identity (e.g., self-concepts) as well as a framework for theorizing career and working life; such analysis is currently emerging within the field of vocational psychology for the study of career, work, and organizational dynamics. Metaphor is recognized as fundamental figurative language that frames individual and institutional ways of being in the contexts of career development (Inkson, 2004, 2006; Mignot, 2000; Super, 1957, 1980), narratives of self in working life (Inkson, Dries, & Arnold, 2015; Lengelle, Meijiers, & Hughes, 2016; Savickas, 2011), and organizational management (Cornelissen, Oswick, Thøger Christensen, & Phillips, 2008; El Sawad, 2005; Morgan, 2006).

For instance, Super (1957) conceptualized career as a vehicle or lifelong path, Inkson (2004) proposed nine metaphors for framing career including actions, encounters and relationships, a journey, a story, and more recently, boundaryless and protean careers (Inkson, 2006), and El Sawad (2005) provided insight concerning metaphors that graduate level employees drew upon to conceptualize career in blue chip organizations. Their findings reveal dominant ways of thinking in career development literature. More specifically, Whiston, Lindeman, Rahardja, and Reed (2005) performed a retrospective analysis of case materials and found themes within experts' opinion. McIlveen and Creed (2018) extended this line of research and used the structured narratives of case formulation—summarized data from counselor interviews with a client—to highlight metaphors used in clinical vocabulary and conventions. Given metaphors both enhance and constrain meaningfulness in case conceptualization, they suggest metaphor analysis has a pedagogical utility. For example, enabling the exploration of transcripts of audio-visual recordings of counseling sessions or post session reflections to minimize cognitive bias and improve specificity of interventions. With the exception of such publications, the analysis of metaphor in career development literature has been notably absent, something that may be due to the lack of a usable and replicable method for scholars of career and working life.

THEORETICAL FRAMEWORK

Lakoff and Johnson (1980) pioneered the Conceptual Metaphor Theory (CMT) and argued that metaphor is fundamentally significant to individual making of meaning. Conceptual thought and systematic linguistic correspondences are central to CMT, as is a decontextual and universalist focus on conceptual metaphor indicative of socially shared realities. In contrast, discourse analysts and discursive psychologists argue for locally contextualized conventions, choice, and application that reflect the in situ lived experience of people. Nevertheless, it is generally agreed that metaphor facilitates, organizes, and extends understanding, thereby structuring how people understand more abstract concepts such as emotions, ideas and time. In addition to this relational role, metaphor plays a process role in communication: metaphors may create insight and indicate appropriate actions but also "create ways of *not* seeing" (Morgan, 2006, p. 348). Similarly, Mignot (2000) suggested that metaphor analysis offers a means to explore an individual's career construction, along with ways in which they are constrained by it. Therefore, alternate world views reflected by metaphors can veil or reveal features of career concepts and may influence an individual's proactivity in career and work. For instance, the concepts of "school-like surveillance" or "the Wild West" discussed by El Sawad (2005) suggest contrastive, situationally contextualized, meanings of career offered by graduate level employees.

Cognitive linguists maintain that human cognition functions through the asymmetrical mapping of concepts from two different domains of knowledge. An abstract or less tangible concept (i.e., the *target domain*) is mapped onto a more physical or concrete *source domain* through some real or perceived similarity and comparison (Gentner & Markham, 1997; Kövecses, 2010). For instance, primary metaphors include GOOD IS UP and BAD IS DOWN, whereas more socially situated conceptual metaphors include LOVE IS A JOURNEY, ARGUMENT IS WAR, and SOCIAL ORGANIZATIONS ARE PLANTS.[1] Metaphorical expressions in the language we produce (e.g., *I'm feeling down today*) reflect underlying conceptual metaphors. Although many conceptual metaphors are universal, the actual words used in linguistic metaphors to reflect the underlying concepts vary by language and culture.

CMT has made an essential and enduring contribution to metaphor research. However, current literature calls attention to the socially situated notion of understanding (Bowdle & Gentner, 2005; Gibbs Jr., 2008; Kövecses, 2010) and cultural cognitive models (Blount, 2014; Frank, Dirven, Ziemke, & Bernárdez, 2008; Kövecses, 2005). As a "unique cognitive mechanism underlying social thought and attitudes," metaphorical expressions form fuzzy categorical clusters of expectations and associations accessed in culturally and socially situated contexts of discourse (Landau, Meier, & Keefer, 2010, p. 1046). With the focus on the individual and meaning making, particularly in the schools of narrative and critical psychology, metaphor analysis offers a further means to individualize qualitative assessment in career counseling. Text, visual imagery, gesture, and artifact involved in narratives and stories are rich sources detailing human experience and are ripe for an examination of the validity of established career metaphors.

More specifically, conceptual metaphor is relevant to practices of career development that emphasize cognitively embodied construction of the social and psychological worlds through social processes and interaction. This is because metaphor is foregrounded in all aspects of people's lives. As Lakoff and Johnson (1980) argue:

> [W]e define our reality in terms of metaphors and then proceed to act on the basis of the metaphors. We draw inferences, set goals, make commitments, and execute plans, all on the basis of how we in part structure our experience, consciously and unconsciously, by means of metaphor. (p. 158)

Our intention in this chapter is to demonstrate a method of metaphor identification that complements more intuitive and introspective analyses with an explicit, valid, and reliable procedure applicable to contemporary constructivist theories and constructs that emphasize meaning making embodied in personal narratives.

PRIMARY DATA AND METHOD

In this chapter, we maintain that the analysis of metaphor in thought and communication depends upon systematic, transparent, reliable, and replicable means for identification of metaphor in language, that is, linguistic metaphor. MIPVU has been put forward as a suitable method for such purposes (Steen et al., 2010b). Although MIPVU does not identify conceptual metaphor, it does identify words that have the *potential* of reflecting the metaphors in people's minds. In doing so, MIPVU provides a methodological bridge to operationalize metaphor analysis and thereby provides foundational knowledge and understanding to inform and facilitate the analyst's capability to enhance theorizations about career and technical developments.

Our demonstration analyzes publicly accessible online videos where Australian and Norwegian university students and college graduates talk about education and career. The videos were created between 2014 and 2015 to promote career-related benefits of higher education and to attract prospective students. Although the videos therefore clearly represent the institutional voice rather than the spontaneous voices of students, the sentiments expressed in these short messages are certainly intended to be recognizable to potential incoming students. In this way, they illustrate authentic education and career-related discourse and showcase current thinking of and in higher education in the context of the two institutions responsible for the video productions.

We apply MIPVU to the English transcriptions and an adapted Scandinavian version of MIPVU to the Norwegian transcriptions of the videos to illustrate the method for qualitative and quantitative approaches to data analysis of metaphorical expressions. Our demonstration thus provides a means of cross-cultural comparison of metaphors with those previously postulated by scholars of vocational psychology. This work represents an innovative methodological advance to enrich existing methods of research into career and working life.

Metaphor Identification

The analysis of metaphorical language requires a robust foundation, that is, a valid, reliable, and replicable procedure for metaphor identification. MIPVU is a systematic and explicit language-in-use approach to metaphor analysis, developed by Steen et al. (2010b). The procedure involves the manual annotation of lexical units for metaphor identification using corpus-based dictionaries. The aim of MIPVU is the identification of possible linguistic metaphors in discourse, the surface realizations of underlying conceptual metaphors. The procedure consists of six steps, as follows:

(1)   read the text as a whole,

(2)   determine the lexical units,
(3)   determine their contextual meaning,
(4)   determine if there is a more basic meaning (i.e., a more concrete, precise and/ or human-related sense),
(5)   decide if the basic and the contextual meanings can be contrasted and understood by comparison,
(6)   label the lexical unit as metaphorical if yes.

As part of the development of MIPVU, patterns of metaphor in English discourse were explored in four registers: academic discourse from a science discipline, conversation, fiction, and news. Results of these studies, reported in Steen et al. (2010b), indicate the lowest frequency of occurrence of metaphorical language was identified in conversation, and the most in academic discourse. Importantly, interrater reliability tests, where analysts independently applied MIPVU to the same texts and then compared their results, found a high rate of agreement (>90%) for all four registers the group examined. This means that it is possible for the procedure to be applied by different researchers in a reliable way. Since its development, MIPVU has been successfully applied to other types of English texts, including the written production of second language learners (Nacey, 2013) and vocational discourse (Creed & McIlveen, 2017). Moreover, the procedure, originally developed on the basis of and for English, has been adapted for a variety of languages other than English, most recently with a volume about MIPVU in multiple languages containing extensions of the procedure to eleven different language varieties (Nacey, Dorst, Krennmayr, & Reijnierse, 2019). This volume includes the Scandinavian version of MIPVU applied in the present study (Nacey, Greve, & Johansson Falck, 2019).

MIPVU identifies primarily two different types of linguistic metaphor: indirect metaphor and direct metaphor.[2] With indirect metaphors, there is a contrast and comparison between the contextual sense and a more basic sense. The word *down* in *I'm feeling down today* is an example of such an indirect metaphor. The contextual sense is "sad," while a more basic sense is "to/towards a lower place." These two senses differ considerably, and the link between them may be understood through comparison: we understand negative feelings in terms of being in a physically lower location or position. The spatial positioning of sadness is coherent with the conceptual metaphor GOOD IS UP / BAD IN DOWN (Lakoff & Johnson, 1980). By contrast, direct metaphors consist of similes, analogies, and so on where there is no contrast between a contextual and more basic sense, despite a metaphorical comparison being evident; the metaphor is thus expressed through direct language. Steen et al. exemplify this with the word *ferret* in the sentence *he's like a ferret* where the contextual "animal" sense matches also the basic meaning.[3] Given that "he" is a person, there is nevertheless an underlying conceptual metaphor, signaled here by the preposition *like*, a word functioning here as a metaphorical flag.

Empirical studies have found that the bulk of metaphorical language is indirect, prompting Steen et al. (2010a) to call this metaphor type "the classic case of metaphorically used words" (p. 783). Note, however, that indirect metaphors are not necessarily deliberately intended nor perceived as metaphors; rather, they often represent conventional ways of expressing thoughts. This aligns with one of the fundamental claims of the CMT, namely that metaphor pervades our everyday language and our thought, with the former reflecting the latter.

Primary Data

For the purposes of demonstrating MIPVU, thirty publicly available online videos containing individual student testimonials about their university experiences were downloaded and transcribed. In both sets of videos, current or recently graduated students introduce themselves and then briefly discuss their choice of study and why they selected the particular institution featured in the video. They sometimes also talk about the careers they either plan for or have recently embarked upon. Half of the videos were developed to promote an Australian university (the University of Southern Queensland; USQ), while the other half advertise for a Norwegian university (Oslo and Akershus University of Applied Sciences; HiOA, which has since been renamed Oslo Metropolitan University).

Our main criterion for video selection was that they all have a similar format, by being "testimonials" featuring a single student each, as opposed to videos focusing on images or groups of students, or voiceover videos with an anonymous narrator. The only information we have about the featured individuals derives from what we can see and hear in the videos. We can thus say, for example, that the Australian videos feature seven female students and eight male students, whereas the Norwegian videos feature five female students and ten male students. The videos are all quite short, ranging from around half a minute to two minutes at the longest. While word count length in the Australian videos ranges from a low of Kate with 145 words to a high of Eliza with 319 words, the Norwegian videos range from Niosha with 71 words to Amund with 304 words. More specifically we analyzed roughly 400 more words of Australian English text, 3,369 Australian English words versus 2,825 Norwegian words.[4] No information about production conditions is available; as a result, we know nothing about, for example, the degree of spontaneity of the student's testimonials, whether the videos were scripted, or indeed, whether the people portrayed in the videos were actual students rather than actors. Nevertheless, as marketing tools promoting the two universities, the videos are intended to convey similar messages about the value of education, with the ultimate goal of attracting future students.

Procedure

MIPVU was applied to the testimonials collected from online videos that had been transcribed into each country's national language. The video transcriptions were transferred to a custom-made Excel spreadsheet for analysis.

Step 1: Read the whole text
The analyst begins by reading the text in its entirety to gain a thorough understanding. For the purposes of this demonstration, the following sentence taken from the AuE transcript of Stephen, an Indigenous Australian student studying a Bachelor of Arts / Bachelor of Law, in which he compares his personal experiences of high school and university, is the focus for our analysis:

(1)   Stephen (AuE): I wasn't a particularly good high school student but I found university was such a different environment.

Step 2: Determine the lexical units
The basic unit of analysis in MIPVU is the individual lexical unit. In most cases, the lexical unit corresponds to the orthographic unit, what is in layman's terms referred to as a *word* (as a consequence, we henceforth use the terms *lexical unit* and *word* interchangeably). Steen et al.'s (2010b) MIPVU protocol outlines a number of exceptions to this one-to-one correspondence between lexical unit and single-unit word, along with detailed guidelines for lexical demarcation. This protocol, however, was created by linguists and (mainly) for linguists, who frequently require an extremely precise definition of what a lexical unit is. Researchers from other disciplines may not require such finely graded analysis, and we therefore recommend a less detailed means of lexical demarcation, through reliance on dictionary codification.

In this way, for example, we count 17 words in sentence (1): *I, was, n't [not], a, particularly, good, high school, student, but, I, found, university, was, such, a, different, environment.* Here we see that *high school* is considered as one lexical unit, even though it consists of two orthographic words; the reason for this is that it is codified as such in our primary reference dictionary, the *Macmillan English Dictionary for Advanced Learners* (MM).[5] Such a simplification through reliance on a quality dictionary should not seriously affect any findings, although we do recommend that researchers be forthright in explaining how they demarcated lexical units, to facilitate any future comparability studies.[6]

Step 3: Determine the contextual meaning of each lexical unit
To demonstrate steps 3 to 6, we focus on the word *environment* as it appears in the context of sentence (1). Consulting the Macmillan dictionary, we find that the contextual meaning of *environment* in Stephen's statement corresponds to the first sense entry for the noun in the dictionary:
    MM1:[7] "the place in which people live and work, including all the physical conditions that affect them."

Step 4: Determine if there is a more basic meaning for each lexical unit
The more basic meaning for *environment* is its most concrete sense, and corresponds to the dictionary's second sense entry for the noun:

MM2: "the natural world, including the land, water, air, plants, and animals, especially considered as something that is affected by human activity."

Step 5: Decide if the basic and the contextual meaning of each lexical unit can be contrasted but understood by comparison
The contextual meaning of *environment* relates to social and cultural conditions of a place, in this instance the university where the student Stephen follows his educational pursuits. The more basic meaning of *environment* concerns external, physical factors of a geographically situated place comprising ecological elements such as air, water, soil, organisms, and so on that surround and interact with the survival of all living organisms. These two meanings contrast (i.e., there is a noticeable difference between the contextual and the basic meaning) and they can be understood by comparison (i.e., consideration of similarities and differences): we can understand the social and cultural conditions of a place in terms of a geographically situated place with interactive, living organisms.

Step 6: Label each lexical unit as metaphorical when the answer to step 5 is yes
The basic and contextual meanings of *environment*, in this situated context of understanding, can be contrasted and understood in terms of a comparison of similarities. Therefore, the lexical unit *environment* is labeled as metaphorical. More specifically, it is an indirect metaphor, evoking a referent that differs from its basic "direct" meaning.

DISCUSSION

How much metaphorical language did we identify? The boxplots in Figure 14.1 show a comparison of the frequency of metaphorical content words (nouns, lexical verbs, adjectives, and adverbs) in the Australian English transcriptions and the Norwegian transcriptions (i.e., the number of metaphorical content words / the total number of content words, per text). Here we see that the median in both sets of text is almost identical: 16.5% and 16.3% respectively. Even though there is more non-metaphorical language than metaphorical language, metaphor is clearly ubiquitous in the recorded videos from both countries. This finding aligns with that of other empirical investigations into metaphor frequency, such as Steen et al. (2010b) and Nacey (2013).

According to results from the Shapiro–Wilk test, the frequencies of metaphorical lexical words in both the Australian English and Norwegian texts are normally distributed (For AuE, $W=0.95$, $p{\approx}0.54$; for Norw, $W=0.97$, $p{\approx}0.43$). The assumptions for normality thus being met, an independent two-tailed Welch's t-test was performed to compare the metaphorical frequencies of content words in the Australian and Norwegian sets of videos. The results indicate that we cannot reject the null hypothesis that there is no significant difference ($N=30$, $t=0.19$, $p{\approx}0.85$). As can be seen in the boxplots, the quantitative differences in terms of numbers of identified metaphors

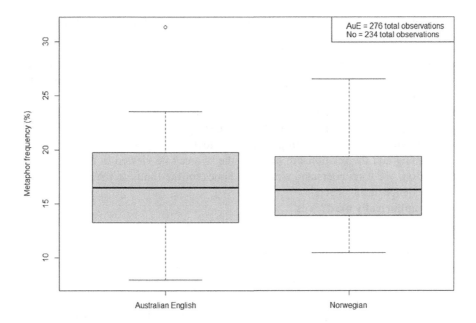

Figure 14.1   *Frequency of metaphorical lexical words in the Australian (AuE)*
            and Norwegian (Norw) samples

in the two sets of videos are minimal. When it comes to quantitative measures, both groups therefore appear to be using metaphor to an equal extent.

As far as content is concerned, we find a number of similarities in the metaphors students and graduates employ. The examples we provide here for discussion concern the broad metaphorical theme of AN OBJECT. First, we identify a recurring similarity between the Australian and Norwegian students when discussing their career aspirations. Both English *dream/dreams* and their Norwegian correspondents *drøm/drømmer* demonstrate conventional usage of metaphor when the entity under discussion is less tangible and more abstract. Consider sentences (2) and (3), where Matthew, an Australian student studying a Bachelor of Commerce, and Amund, a Norwegian student studying a Bachelor of Product Design, talk about their future aspirations in terms of a mental object:

(2)   Matthew (AuE): I suppose my *dream* job is to become an accountant.
(3)   Amund (Norw):[8]

Min	*drøm*	er	å	bli	bil.designer
my	*dream*	be.PRS	to	become.INF	car.designer

"My *dream* is to become a car designer."

Looking at Matthew's statement in example 2, MIPVU identifies the lexical unit *dream* to be a metaphor as follows:

- **Contextual meaning**: In this context, the meaning of the noun *dream* corresponds to MM2 "something good that you hope you will have or achieve in the future."
- **Basic meaning**: The basic meaning of the noun *dream* is MM1 "something that you experience in your mind while you are sleeping."
- **Contextual vs. basic meaning**: The contextual meaning contrasts with the basic meaning and the relationship between the two can be viewed in terms of comparison. We can understand a person's hopes for the future in terms of a mental experience during sleep.
- **Metaphorically used?** Yes.

Identification of the metaphorical word *dream* may form the foundation of analysis of how the conceptualization of a future career as a mental object (i.e., CAREER IS A MENTAL OBJECT) influences productive or innovative thinking by a student grappling with career options or ambitions. Acceptance of the metaphor may enable students to visualize themselves in a variety of careers, enabling exploration and reflection without direct physical engagement. However, the *dream* metaphor may sometimes be a handicap because it is an idealized version entailing students with unlimited options that does not necessarily align with real-life capabilities or constraints. Instead, the *dream* metaphor could be reappropriated as a story metaphor enabling students to talk about future opportunities and thereby develop or change their narrative based on personal identity construction.

A second similarity in our two datasets is the conceptualization of higher education and/or the studies pursued by the Australian and Norwegian students as AN OBJECT with an inside and an outside. Lakoff and Johnson (1980) identify the container image schema as a recurring metaphor with a schematic meaning related to activities and states including the physical experience of being "in" and "out." The situated use by the students indicates an agency or preparedness to go forth. This pattern is evident in statements (4) and (5) where the student Kate, an indigenous Australian studying a Bachelor of Psychology, and Lise Helen, a Norwegian student studying orthopaedics, talk of the transition from being "in" education to going "out" to working life:

(4)   Kate (AuE): It is sort of exciting to think that I can go *out* there and change things.

(5)   Lise Helen (Norw):

Vi	er	derfor	veldig	etter.trakt-a	*ut*	i	arbeids.liv-et
we	be.PRS	therefore	very	after.wish-PTCP	*out*	in	work.life-ART.DEF.N

"We are therefore very attractive *out* in working life."

This conceptualization of movement in or out of a container-like object may be grounded in the metaphor "environment" used by both groups of students to describe education and the learning context or situation as seen in the following two examples:

(6)   Stephen (AuE): I found university was such a different *environment* [Stephen, AuE]

(7)   Magnus (Norw):

Noe	av	de	best-e	med
some	of	the.PL	best-PL	with
studie-t	er	det	god-e	lærings.*miljø*-et
study-ART. DEF.N	be.PRS	the. ART.DEF.N	good-N	learning.*environment*-ART.DE.N

"One of the best thing with the studies is the good learning *environment*."

Although the Australian and Norwegian students often used metaphor in similar ways to discuss their education or future after university, we also observe some differences between them. For instance, our small pool of videos indicates a possible difference in metaphorical "taking" expressed in the discourse of Australian and Norwegian students. Both English *take* and its Norwegian correspondent *ta* are conventionally used as metaphors when the entity being taken is abstract rather than concrete, as we see sentence 8, where Stephen talks about hopes for his future career. Here, Stephen uses a construction whereby he proposes "taking" an abstract entity—knowledge as a psychological resource—and doing something further with it. We see this same pattern in Kate's statement in sentence (9) discussing the positive benefits of her education for her working life; she too "takes" knowledge—resources-in-hand—and does something with it, reflecting Lent's (2013) description of preparedness:

(8)   Stephen (AuE): In my future, I'd like to *take* what I've learnt from anthropology and combine it with my law career.

(9)   Kate (AuE): Already I'm able to *take* a lot of what I know and put it back into the community.

By contrast, we find no such pattern in the Norwegian testimonials. Consider sentence (10) where the student Daniel, studying for a bachelor's in engineering, electronics, and ICT, says he can "take" jobs, and sentence (11) where Niosha explains that he has "taken" a degree:

(10) Daniel (Norw):

Du	kan	med	denne	utdanning-en
you	can	with	this.M	education-M
her	*ta*	mange	forskjellig-e	jobb-er
here	*take.INF*	many	different-PL	jobb-PL

"You can *take* [idiomatic: *get*] many different jobs with this education."

(11)   Niosha (Norw):

Jeg	ha-r	ta-tt	bachelor	i	revisjons.fag
I	have-PRS	take-PTCP	bachelor	in	auditing.subject

"I have *taken* [idiomatic: *earned*] a bachelor's in auditing."

Both Daniel and Niosha have employed the Norwegian verb *ta* in a conventionally appropriate manner. Neither these metaphors, nor those of Stephen and Kate, bear any of the hallmarks of deliberate use of figurative speech, whereby one intentionally employs metaphor to change the perspective of the interlocutor. Instead, they illustrate an important point in Lakoff and Johnson's CMT, that we frequently use metaphor in conventional ways when expressing ourselves; indeed, it would be difficult to avoid metaphor, in any language. However, a cross-cultural comparison such as ours has the potential to reveal nuances that may otherwise prove elusive. For example, we see here that whereas Stephen and Kate "take" X for a particular purpose, both Daniel and Niosha "take" X more or less as a means in itself. Hence, metaphor analysis facilitates access to situational and context-specific meanings.

It should be noted, however, that there is nothing inherent in the Norwegian language that would preclude Norwegians from using the verb *ta* in a pattern mirroring that of the Australian statements. Absence of any such Norwegian examples might simply be the result of the relatively small dataset we have compiled for the present exploratory study. Further research is required to uncover whether this difference is due simply to sample size, or whether it reflects a real difference in the ways in which Australian and Norwegian institutions of higher education and/or their students talk (and perhaps think) about education, career, and future working life. Nevertheless, our identification and analysis of metaphorical language in the students' testimonials in these promotional videos helps to illuminate personal or organizational conceptions. In addition, it offers the potential to cross-culturally compare and contrast the discourse in light of current research comparing national cultures in shaping the outcomes of career proactivity (e.g., Smale et al., 2019) and notions of career success (e.g., Shen et al., 2015). The analysis could also be used to compare with postulated metaphors of career to generate conceptual insight about a participant group—students and graduates—that remains largely unexplored in current literature of metaphor and vocational psychology.

CONCLUDING THOUGHTS

In this chapter, a social constructivist perspective was followed that calls attention to language, narrative, and storying to understand and inform the reality of career and working life. This perspective emphasizes the interpersonal and social existence of individuals through personal and social narratives. In applying MIPVU to this small study of student testimonials used for promotional purposes by an Australian and Norwegian university, we found the conventional use of indirect metaphors to be far more frequent than use of direct metaphor such as similes, analogies, and so on. These results draw attention to the ubiquity of metaphor in the language students use to talk about educational choices and career plans but also suggest that they are not consciously attending to the target concept (e.g., CAREER) in terms of the source domain (e.g., AN OBJECT).

The MIPVU versions used in this study make possible the reliable identification of metaphor in real language situations free of propositions of conceptual structures, cognitive processes, and products. In doing so, identified metaphors can provide a "tool through which career counselors may conceptualize and define their work" (McMahon, 2007, p. 274). From such a basis, an analysis of metaphorical language may indicate a conceptual bridge that helps scaffold communication to enhance awareness and build understanding of career-life preparedness. When metaphorical expressions are identified and explicitly discussed, or developed collaboratively, they can advance the client/counselor, student/professor, or applicant/employer relationship. For example, practitioners can identify metaphors in their own or client's communication and then evaluate the capacity of those metaphors to enhance (or not) the clarification of career goals, motivate education and career planning activities, or support individuals' adjustment to new education or work contexts that advance adaptability, resilience, and coping.

Vocational psychology that considers career behavior, decision-making, and development continues to benefit from insights drawn from culturally diverse narratives and collective experiences of career success. However, metaphor analysis as a method for the investigation of "notions of collective experience of careers, or collective criteria for career success" remains infrequent in the literature as Inkson (2007, p. 6) points out and an empirical procedure for identification appears altogether absent. Future research that draws from diverse international environments and collects data from different demographic groups (e.g., students and graduate-level employees) to examine metaphor use in narratives of career and working life can potentially reveal unacknowledged variation in the concept of career. The beauty of MIPVU is its potential for adaptability across languages for the identification of metaphor, providing a springboard for linguistic and conceptual analysis that offers a robust foundation for empirical studies of metaphorical language use in vocational psychology.

NOTES

1. The capital letters follow convention dictating the mnemonic naming of systematic sets of correspondences in our conceptual system as TARGET-DOMAIN IS SOURCE-DOMAIN (Lakoff, 1993, pp. 207 & 209).

2.   A third type of metaphor may also be identified with MIPVU: implicit metaphors consisting of cohesive grammatical or semantic links that refer back to recoverable metaphors. Examples of implicit metaphors are demonstrative pronouns (e.g., *that, this*) that refer to an indirect metaphor. Although they contribute to the overall metaphor density of a given text, they are less interesting for the type of discourse analysis for the present study.
3.   See here: http://www.vismet.org/metcor/documentation/relation_to_metaphor.html.
4.   The videos, analyzed data and R code are available at our Open Science Framework project page. We also provide a template for metaphor identification for scholars to adapt for their own research. Please see https://osf.io/bk32q/.
5.   This is a contemporary, corpus-based learners' dictionary and was also the primary reference dictionary for the developers of MIPVU. It may be freely accessed here: http://www.macmillandictionary.com.
6.   Note that we employed the complete original version of MIPVU in our analysis, rather than the simplified version we recommend here. In doing so, we came to realize that the MIPVU demarcation instructions would present an unnecessarily prohibitive barrier for use by non-linguists.
7.   The number following the dictionary abbreviation–here and elsewhere in our chapter– identifies the particular sense in the entry being referred to.
8.   All renditions of Norwegian examples into English follow the Leipzig Glossing Rules. See https://www.eva.mpg.de/lingua/pdf/Glossing-Rules.pdf.

REFERENCES

Blount, B. (2014). Situating cultural models in history and cognition. In M. Yamaguchi, D. Tay, & B. Blount (Eds.), *Approaches to language, culture, and cognition* (pp. 271–298). Basingstoke, Hampshire: Palgrave Macmillan.

Bowdle, B. F., & Gentner, D. (2005). The career of metaphor. *Psychological Review, 112*(1), 193–216.

Burgers, C., Kronijn, E. A., & Steen, G. J. (2016). Figurative framing: Shaping public discourse through metaphor, hyperbole and irony. *Communication Theory, 26*(4), 410–430.

Cornelissen, J. P., Oswick, C., Thøger Christensen, L., & Phillips, N. (2008). Metaphor in organizational research: Context, modalities and implications for research—introduction. *Organization Studies, 29*(1), 7–22. https://doi.org/10.1177/0170840607086634

Creed, A., & McIlveen, P. (2017). Metaphor identification as a research method for the study of career. *International Journal for Educational and Vocational Guidance, 18*(1), 27–44.

El Sawad, A. (2005). Becoming a lifer? Unlocking career through metaphor. *Journal of Occupational and Organizational Psychology, 78*(1), 23–41.

Frank, R. M., Dirven, R., Ziemke, T., & Bernárdez, E. (Eds.) (2008). *Sociocultural situatedness* (Vol. 35). Berlin, Germany: Walter de Gruyter.

Gentner, D., & Markham, A. B. (1997). Structure mapping in analogy and similarity. *American Psychologist, 52*(1), 45–56.

Gibbs Jr, R. W. (Ed.) (2008). *The Cambridge handbook of metaphor and thought*. Cambridge, UK: Cambridge University Press.

Inkson, K. (2004). Images of career: Nine key metaphors. *Journal of Vocational Behavior, 65*(1), 96–111.

Inkson, K. (2006). Protean and boundaryless careers as metaphors. *Journal of Vocational Behavior, 69*(1), 48–63.

Inkson, K. (2007). Career and metaphor. In K. Inkson, N. Dries, & J. Arnold (eds) *Understanding careers: The metaphors of working lives* (pp. 1–26). London, UK: Sage Publications.

Inkson, K., & Amundson, N. (2002). Career metaphors and their application in theory and counseling practice. *Journal of Employment Counseling*, *39*(3), 98–108.

Inkson, K., Dries, N., & Arnold, J. (2015). *Understanding careers: Metaphors of working lives*. London, UK: Sage.

Kövecses, Z. (2005). *Metaphor in culture: Universality and variation*. Cambridge, UK: Cambridge University Press.

Kövecses, Z. (2010). *Metaphor: A practical introduction*. Oxford, UK: Oxford University Press.

Krippendorff, K. (2017). Three concepts to retire. *Annals of the International Communication Association*, *41*(1), 92–99.

Lakoff, G., & Johnson, M. (1980). *Metaphors we live by*. Chicago, IL: University of Chicago Press.

Lakoff, G. (1993). The contemporary theory of metaphor. In A. Ortony (Ed.), *Metaphor and Thought* (2nd edition). Cambridge: Cambridge University Press, pp. 202–251.

Landau, M. J., Meier, B. P., & Keefer, L. A. (2010). A metaphor-enriched social cognition. *Psychological Bulletin*, *136*(6), 1045–1067.

Lengelle, R., Meijers, F., & Hughes, D. (2016). Creative writing for life design: Reflexivity, metaphor and change processes through narrative. *Journal of Vocational Behavior*, *97*, 60–67.

Lent, R. W. (2013). Career-life preparedness: Revisiting career planning and adjustment in the new workplace. *The Career Development Quarterly*, *61*(1), 2–14.

McIlveen, P., & Creed, A. (2018). Counseling case formulation as metaphor. In A. Di Fabio & J. L. Bernaud (Eds.), *Accountability in post-modern guidance and career counseling narrative interventions: A review of case studies and innovative qualitative approaches* (pp. 77–86). Cham, Switzerland: Springer International Publishing.

McMahon, M. (2007). Metaphor and career counseling. In K. Inkson (Ed.), *Understanding careers: The metaphors of working lives* (pp. 270–297). Thousand Oaks, CA: Sage.

Mignot, P. (2000). Metaphor: A paradigm for practice-based research into 'career'. *British Journal of Guidance & Counselling*, *28*(4), 515–531.

Morgan, G. (2006). *Images of organisation*. Thousand Oaks, CA: Sage.

Nacey, S. (2013). *Metaphors in learner English*. Amsterdam, NL: John Benjamins.

Nacey, S., Dorst, A. G., Krennmayr, T., & Reijnierse, W. G. (Eds.) (2019). *Metaphor identification in multiple languages: MIPVU around the world*. Amsterdam/Philadelphia: John Benjamins.

Nacey, S., Greve, L., & Johansson Falck, M. (2019). Linguistic metaphor identification in Scandinavian. In S. Nacey, A. G. Dorst, T. Krennmayr, & G. Reijnierse (Eds.), *Metaphor identification in multiple languages: MIPVU around the world* (pp. 138–158). Amsterdam/Philadelphia: John Benjamins.

Savickas, M. L. (2011). Constructing careers: Actor, agent, and author. *Journal of Employment Counseling*, *48*(4), 179–181.

Shen, Y., Demel, B., Unite, J., Briscoe, J. P., Hall, D. T., Chudzikowski, K., ... & Fei, Z. (2015). Career success across 11 countries: Implications for international human resource management. *The International Journal of Human Resource Management*, *26*(13), 1753–1778.

Smale, A., Bagdadli, S., Cotton, R., Dello Russo, S., Dickmann, M., Dysvik, A., ... & Rozo, P. (2019). Proactive career behaviors and subjective career success: The moderating role of national culture. *Journal of Organizational Behavior*, *40*(1), 105–122.

Steen, G. J., Dorst, A. G., Herrmann, J. B., Kaal, A. A., & Krennmayr, T. (2010a). Metaphor in usage. *Cognitive Linguistics*, *21*(4), 765–796.

Steen, G. J., Dorst, A. G., Herrmann, J. B., Kaal, A. A., Krennmayr, T., & Pasma, T. (2010b). *A method for linguistic metaphor identification: From MIP to MIPVU* (Vol. 14). Amsterdam, NL: John Benjamins.

Super, D. E. (1957). The preliminary appraisal: In vocational counseling. *Journal of Counseling & Development, 36*(3), 154–161.

Super, D. E. (1963). *Career development: Self-concept theory.* New York, NY: College Entrance Examination Board.

Super, D. E. (1980). A life-span, life-space approach to career development. *Journal of Vocational Behavior, 16*(3), 282–298.

Whiston, S. C., Lindeman, D., Rahardja, D., & Reed, J. H. (2005). Career counselling process: A qualitative analysis of experts' cases. *Journal of Career Assessment, 13*(2), 169–187.

15. Mixed methods in careers research: contradictory paradigms or desired approach?

Jelena Zikic and Viktoriya Voloshyna

INTRODUCTION

We study careers from several disciplinary perspectives, from psychology and sociology to economics and political science (Arthur, Hall, & Lawrence, 1989). This interdisciplinary attention makes career studies fascinating but also complex and in need of some conceptual clarity (Baruch, Szűcs, & Gunz, 2015). Moreover, some would agree that the careers field lacks an overarching career model or a grand career theory (e.g., Iellatchitch, Mayrhofer, & Meyer, 2003; Savickas, 2012). Second, traditional career models focusing on organizational careers (i.e., progress through organizational hierarchy), are less and less likely due to the instability of the labor market, restructuring, and globalization to name just a few of the forces that have impacted our career trajectories (Baruch & Bozionelos, 2010). Thus, contemporary careers scholarship attempts to capture this dynamic and constantly evolving nature of careers through some new terms and concepts. Yet equally important are the types of research questions and accompanying methodology seeking to address this dynamic and diversified career landscape. In this context, our methodological approaches should be able to accompany the growing complexities of the phenomena we study (Molina-Azorin, Bergh, Corley, & Ketchen, 2017). In this chapter, we describe why a *mixed method* approach to studying career phenomena may be of special value given our field's stage of development and the above-mentioned intricacies.

Mixed method is a methodological approach that focuses on collecting, analyzing and mixing both quantitative and qualitative data in a single study (Creswell & Plano Clark, 2007). Thus, when using a multi method approach the researcher should focus on how the integration of two methods will exceed the sum of the individual qualitative and quantitative components. Thus, we propose that for careers studies in particular there are multiple benefits to be gained from integrating different methodologies into one study. Since it will produce insights that go beyond one single approach and will appeal to the developing and diverse nature of career concepts and career theories at different stages of maturity. In this chapter, we first introduce the mixed method approach followed by the description of the career field and its dominant methods and paradigms. Next, we describe in detail two examples of the mixed method approach in career studies and its associated benefits. Finally, we briefly conclude with recommendations to career scholars wishing to pursue a mixed method approach in their studies.

DEFINING MIXED METHODS

Mixed methods research combines quantitative and qualitative data, concepts, and techniques within a single study (Molina-Azorin, 2012; Creswell & Plano Clark, 2007). Each type of data is collected and guided by its own principles and ideologies. Specifically, quantitative data involves gathering predominantly numerical information, traditionally collected through surveys and guided by the quantitative empirical tradition (Creswell, 1994). In contrast, the collection of qualitative data is driven by the qualitative research design focusing on gathering textual or open-ended data (Strauss & Corbin, 1998) through in-depth interviews, observation, or focus groups for example (Crane, Henriques, & Husted, 2018). The analysis of this type of data is usually done by aggregating words/text into categories and presenting ideas based on the analysis of the narratives, interviews, or written cases (Creswell, 2003).

Traditionally, there has been some skepticism about the possibility of integrating quantitative and qualitative types of data in one study. These criticisms were based on the fact that "different methods manifest different paradigms, thus fundamentally different beliefs and assumptions about the nature of the studied phenomenon" (Gioia & Pitre, 1990, p. 585). For example, quantitative data collection is traditionally guided by the *positivist (functional) paradigm*, assuming objective nature of reality and researcher's independence from what is being researched (Creswell, 1994). As Bryman (1984) notes, the positivist paradigm is preoccupied by operational definitions, causality, and generalizability of the research results. In contrast, the qualitative data collection is guided by the *interpretive paradigm*, which assumes subjective reality, dependent on the researcher who instead of generalizing the results, attempts to preserve and emphasize the unique, or emic perspective of the informants (Gioia & Pitre, 1990). As a result of these seeming incompatibilities between fundamental assumptions guiding these two research traditions, researchers may sometimes shy away from combining them and applying them in a single study (Lincoln & Guba, 2000).

Furthermore, this incompatibility thesis posits that quantitative and qualitative research paradigms including their associated methods cannot and should not be mixed (Johnson & Onwuegbuzie, 2004). According to this view, these paradigms are fundamentally "incommensurable," thus, emphasizing the main role of the researcher to maintain the paradigm as a coherent whole (Lincoln & Guba, 2000). For example, quantitative purists believe that researchers should be detached and uninvolved with the object of the study (Johnson, Onwuegbuzie, & Turner, 2007). Similarly, qualitative purists insist that quantitative and qualitative researchers use distinct language (Tashakkori & Teddlie, 2015) and have different inquiry aims in terms of the nature of knowledge or "mutually exclusive axioms" (Johnson & Onwuegbuzie, 2004).

On the other hand, proponents of the mixed method approach offer strong arguments for integration between the positivist and interpretivist/constructivist perspectives (Feilzer, 2010). The proponents of the mixed method approach state that even if methods belong to different paradigms it is possible to establish convergence between methods; specifically, through a mixed method approach the researcher is better able to elaborate and provide richness in understanding of the given phenomena, as well as initiate and identify new interpretations and future research questions (Green, Caracelli, & Graham, 1989). The proponents of mixed methods suggest that the research question not the assumptions should guide the combination of methods and approaches (Creswell, Plano Clark, Gutmann, & Hanson, 2003). More importantly, when focusing on the phenomenon that needs to be investigated from the different perspectives, the mixed methods design allows the researcher to overcome the biases and limitations (Green et al., 1989) of each method alone.

Thus, the focus on methodological triangulation in the mixed method approach, whereby the researcher is able to collect both quantitative and qualitative data (Molina-Azorin & López-Gamero, 2016) is in many ways seen as superior, enhancing our ability to more fully understand phenomena under study and to better address our research questions (Morse, 1991). In career studies, as mentioned above, the ability to combine two perspectives through a multi method approach, that is to study, for example, how individuals enact careers in a more dynamic environment, will be especially beneficial. Namely, mixed methods will allow career scholars to combine the emic perspective of the individual careerist with the more positivist view of career phenomena by measuring and verifying specific relationships.

Molina-Azorin and López-Gamero (2016) integrated several types of triangulation in mixed methods designs into a useful typology. This typology is built on two main dimensions, namely the *sequence* dimension vs. the *priority* of data collection. Specifically, the type of data (i.e., qualitative vs. quantitative) being collected first can happen at the same time (i.e., concurrent, simultaneous or parallel design) or introducing information in phases, that is sequential or two-phase design. Second, one can give equal priority to both types of data (i.e., equivalent status) or instead emphasize one over the other (i.e., dominant status). This ladder decision will depend on the research question, practical issues related to data collection, or the need to understand one form of data before proceeding to the next. This dimensionality allowed the division of mixed methods studies into four groups that differ according to the type of design researchers apply (Figure 15.1) (more detailed description provided by Molina-Azorin, 2012; Johnson & Onwuegbuzie, 2004).

Therefore, it is important to understand how researchers make decisions about the priority and the sequence of qualitative vs. quantitative design. For example, priority of the method might be considered on the basis of values and beliefs of the researcher or his/her worldview (Creswell & Plano Clark, 2007). Those who are inclined towards more naturalistic inquiry admit domination of the qualitative method in their approach. As a result, they may choose the exploration/discovery, inductive approach as a priority in order to understand the subjective reality (Johnson & Onwuegbuzie,

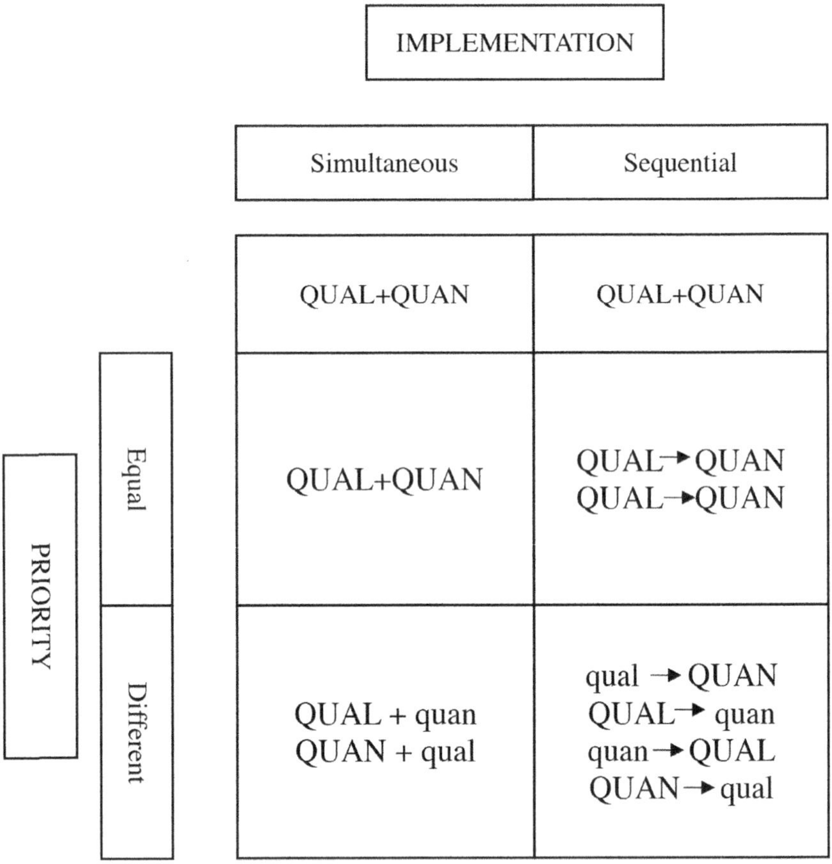

IMPLEMENTATION

	Simultaneous	Sequential
	QUAL+QUAN	QUAL+QUAN
Equal	QUAL+QUAN	QUAL→QUAN QUAL→QUAN
Different	QUAL + quan QUAN + qual	qual →QUAN QUAL→ quan quan→QUAL QUAN→qual

PRIORITY

Source: Molina-Azorin (2012).

Figure 15.1   Types of mixed methods design

2004); they may use quantitative methods as secondary and supportive type of information that is to complement, or clarify initial qualitative findings.

On the other hand, those who are inclined towards traditional more positivist approaches, admit domination of quantitative methods. They may choose the positivist quantitative research method as their primary tool in search of a more objective explanation of reality; in this scenario, the use of qualitative methods would be seen as a secondary instrument of data collection and analysis perhaps to elaborate or accompany quantitative findings. Finally, the decision about methodology domination is also guided by the rationale that one method can "offset limitations of another method" (Turner, Cardinal, & Burton, 2017, p. 244).

In conclusion, the combination and priority of methods should be guided by several factors: by the research question(s), the state of the current theory, and by the purposes of the study. In addition, research questions and methods are also reciprocally interrelated. For example, contrary to quantitative research, research problems suitable for qualitative research are typically less structured, as qualitative research is broad in nature and key concepts usually come from the data (Strauss & Corbin, 1998). Therefore, the exploratory nature of the problem assumes that the researcher will search for the method that will bring further exploration, opportunity of flexibility, and freedom (Agee, 2009).

CAREERS STUDIES: POSITIVIST PARADIGM

Careers are the product of the interaction of individuals with organizations as well as broader society (Collin, 1998). Career is typically defined as a sequence of a person's work-related experiences over one's lifetime (Arthur, 2008). Careers researchers also propose that careers can be objectively understood and measured (Khapova, Arthur, & Wilderom, 2007) as a sequence of jobs and statuses that individuals engage in as they perform a series of organizational moves. If examined through this "classic scientific approach" belonging to the positivist philosophical tradition (Collin, 1997), career is seen as a sequence of positions unfolding over time and adhering to the idea that careers and all career-related phenomena should be studied empirically (Collin, 1998) and measured as independent statistical constructs (Collin & Young, 1986). Thus, career-related concepts become measurable variables that can be compared with the norms of the wider population allowing researchers to establish cause and effect relationships (Collin, 1998) between measurable variables. In this manner, the positivist research tradition somewhat decontextualizes individuals, treating them as independent from the environment in which their careers unfold (Collin, 1997), thus seeking to study careers rationally and objectively.

While acknowledging the existing debate about the nature of careers and what type of logic, inductive or deductive, should be applied to career studies, "there is still tendency towards positivistic approaches in career theory" (Cohen, Duberley, & Mallon, 2004). Careers researchers most often rely on deductive reasoning, and typically collect data from representative samples by distributing questionnaires and seeking to generalize the results to an aggregated population. These studies attempt to describe the population under study and in general use established objective measures and normative methodological designs in order to test and describe reality (Cohen et al., 2004).

To obtain a more detailed understanding of how careers researchers approached their subject area in terms of method used, we examined articles that were published in two main career outlets: *Career Development International* and *Journal of Vocational Behaviour* between 2010 and 2019 (Figure 15.2). Overall, the analysis revealed that in fact the majority of career-focused articles relied on the positivistic paradigm. Careers research in these journals focused on empirical testing of the relationships between independent career variables and various objective and subjective career outcomes such as career success, career choice, or career satisfaction.

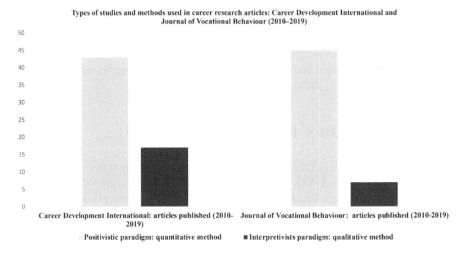

Figure 15.2   Methods used in career research articles

In general, positivist career researchers used two groups of theories to formulate research questions and initiate the process of inquiry. The first group of theories are career-related theories and frameworks. Among these we distinguish more mature theories and frameworks, such as life span development model, social construction career theory (Savickas, 2013), boundaryless career framework (Arthur & Rousseau, 1996; Sullivan & Arthur, 2006) and the protean career model (Hall, 2004) to name a few. Others, however, are in earlier stages of development, such as, for example, the kaleidoscope career model (Sullivan & Baruch, 2009). More mature theories and frameworks allowed for using validated measures to test the proposed models and relationships; while newer career theories required more triangulation to elaborate and better understand these career phenomena (Molina-Azorin et al., 2017). The second group of theories we found used in careers research are mature psychological or sociological theories (social capital theory, human capital theory, expectancy theory, person–environment fit theory) that allow for testing ideas even with rel-atively small sample sizes and are concerned with fundamental concepts such as career behavior, affect, attitudes, and personality.

In fact, a large number of careers studies constructed their research questions based on influential and mature psychological theories (Sandberg & Alvesson, 2011), which do not necessarily belong to the careers field per se. Studies identified underdeveloped research areas (Alvesson & Sandberg, 2011) and applied these theories in order to respond to these gaps; for example, furthering our understanding of career barriers, mobility or employability and studied these in relation to various career attitudes and motivation (Doherty, Dickmann, & Mills, 2010; Zhang, Hirschi, Herrmann, Wei, & Zhang, 2015; Lin, 2015; Kostal & Wiernik, 2017) or personality and its impact on career planning or career success (Presbitero, 2015; Joo & Ready, 2012). Yet another group of studies relied on social cognitive career theories to understand, for example, how socialization mechanisms may impact career adaptability across generations (Garcia, Restubog, Ocampo, Wang, & Tang, 2019). Contrary to that, some studies were narrowly focused on an identified research gap based on theories and approaches that belong to the careers field solely. For example, how protean career attitudes influence employability (Lin, 2015), or the role of career control and career dialogue in predicting employability (Veld, Semeijn, & van Vuuren, 2016).

Finally, based on this brief inquiry into the type of method and paradigms used in career studies, several criticisms remain. For example, researchers lament the theoretically heterogeneous nature of career studies (Spurk, Hirschi, & Dries, 2019) as well as its overreliance on the measurement (Hyde, 2000). Others highlight that classic assumptions about stability and security of individual careers cannot be relied upon anymore (Savickas, 2005), proposing that core concepts in career theories must be reframed to fit the new economy. Similarly, researchers note that current theoretical models have been created to predict relatively stable relationships. These criticisms are based on the fact that individuals do not operate within a stable context and that career decision-making processes do not happen in isolation from external influences. As a result of careers becoming more complex and unpredictable (Akkermans & Kubasch, 2017), as well as the need for grand career theory, it is proposed that greater attention should be placed on the benefits of the qualitative paradigm; that is eliciting career stories/in-depth career narratives which are much more likely to explore the rich career context and multiple influences on our careers. Specifically, qualitative inquiry, as a way of "further exploring, and broadening the existing emphasis on positivist study of career phenomena will enrich quantitative findings collected in our career research so far" (McMahon, Watson, & Lee, 2019, p. 420).

CAREERS THROUGH THE LENS OF INTERPRETIVISTS

In contrast to the positivist view of career as an objective sequence of work opportunities, the interpretivist paradigm defines career as "a subjective construction that imposes personal meaning on the past memories, present experiences, and future aspirations by weaving them into a life theme" (Savickas, 2005, p. 43). As a result, interpretive research focuses on subjectively guided career behavior that emerges through a meaning making process (Collin, 1998; Savickas, 2005). Creating and giving meaning is unlikely to be understood through measuring simple cause and effect relationships. In other words, in this tradition, career is best understood through "biographical reflexivity" that is told through stories (Savickas, 2005).

Thus, according to the interpretivist tradition we ought to study individuals as agents that actively generate and interpret career knowledge as they socially construct reality where their careers unfold. Based on this reasoning, the career enactment process involves individuals who construct and co-construct the meaning of the organizational and other career environments they function in. Therefore, career as an interpretive concept is not measurable but rather it is a subjectively expressed entity which constantly unfolds and changes. When we analyze career meanings that individuals reflect on, these experiences are unique and cannot be directly observable, operationalized or validated (Gephart & Richardson, 2012).

Some interpretivists will deny any objective nature of the career phenomenon, considering careers mainly as a product of the human mind; others will try to bring some objective assumptions into their career inquiries (Gubrium, Holstein, Marvasti, & McKinney, 2012). This latter group, also known as "interpretive objectivists" try to understand participants' subjective world and their implicit meanings, however, at the same time they try to bring objective scientific concepts and employ analytic methods to create rigor and objective knowledge (Gubrium et al., 2012). For example, they would analyze participants' interpretations of careers (i.e., own feelings, emotions, and aspirations), and through a series of analytical procedures interpretive objectivists will transform these descriptions into scientific concepts (Strauss & Corbin, 1990). Thus, in this case, their research on career phenomena is driven by subjective experiences on the one hand, which are then transformed into scientific concepts that emerged during the analysis. As a result, "interpretive objectivists" actively use qualitative methods in order to understand career behavior and then inductively produce new career theories (Gephart & Richardson, 2012).

Qualitative method is present in a much smaller proportion of careers research published in the two sources we examined for the period of ten years: *Career Development International* and *Journal of Vocational Behaviour* between 2010 and 2019. Closer examination of these studies shows that authors used non-numerical types of data and applied various qualitative techniques for data analysis. These studies typically used semi-structured interviews, thus by collecting non-numerical data, one was able to explore the patterns of meaning in career stories and allow for a more holistic view of careers (Laud & Johnson, 2012; Omair, 2010).

For example, some qualitative career studies investigated subjective perceptions of career challenges of women in various cultural contexts, thus taking into consideration context as an important aspect of one's career experience. The research questions focused on how women constructed their careers, overcame related challenges, and enacted their careers within the specific contexts (Afiouni, 2014; Omair, 2010; O'Neil, Hopkins, & Sullivan, 2011; Cho, Park, Han, & Ho, 2019; Al-Asfour, Tlaiss, Khan, & Rajasekar, 2017; Kim, Jang, & Baek, 2019). A majority of studies collected data through in-depth semi-structured interviews allowing for a more holistic understanding of participants' careers (Laud & Johnson, 2012; Omair, 2010). In analyzing this type of data, researchers used such tools as thematic data analysis, case analysis, qualitative content analysis, and narrative career analysis, among others (see studies provided above as examples).

Other studies explored perceptions of the career development process (e.g., Harman & Sealy, 2017) and studied career ambitions and challenges in early career stages, for example. Similarly, Lewis, Harris, Morrison, and Ho (2015) focused on the interplay between life-stages and career transitions for women within the organizations; while Usinger and Smith (2010) explored social construction of the career development processes. These studies used qualitative case analysis and thematic data analysis that allowed for hierarchical organization of data without necessarily building a process model.

The sampling procedures in qualitative career studies show that researchers are not primarily motivated by the prospect of generalizing from the experiences of their participants, but rather they are seeking to "explore the range of opinions" through obtaining rich information from diverse participants. This approach can shed the light on the phenomenon from different angles as the researcher is able to explore different career experiences and perspectives (e.g., Walsh, Fleming, & Enz, 2016). Most commonly, career researchers relied on purposeful sampling (e.g., Clarke, 2015), that is, choosing informants that can illuminate unique phenomena under study, while less often researchers relied on theoretical sampling techniques. For example, the study of Petriglieri, Petriglieri, and Wood (2018) used purposeful sampling by choosing the informants strategically (Patton, 2002), that is, the experience of previous participants guided the search of subsequent participants; through semi-structured interviews this study examined individuals' identity responses when they cannot follow continuous and stable careers.

In general, as has been shown above, traditional qualitative design reveals peoples' lived experience within the specific context (Cho et al., 2019). However, even though the main purpose of qualitative research methods is to bring new concepts and theories into light, reviewed career studies instead appealed to the existing theoretical constructs (i.e., career success, career stages); and through self-narration uncovered how these are reflected in individuals' careers stories. Unfortunately, there was little attempt to initiate the development of explanatory new theories of basic career processes (Starks & Brown Trinidad, 2007).

As a result, it has been reinforced that career studies are in need of a grand theoretical framework and a number of career terms still exist without being captured by any such grand career theory (Baruch et al., 2015). For example, career boundaries, career attitudes, and career behavior are closely connected to career mobility and boundaryless career concepts, which have been heavily studied from psychological and sociological perspectives, however, these still have not been intertwined into one coherent theory and continue to stay fragmentedly described without a grand theoretical approach. Thus, in the future, qualitative methods may serve as a much-needed methodological tool that will focus on the study of new career phenomena and concepts that offer a potential for establishing more mature and comprehensive career theories. Qualitative career studies, as part of the mixed methods research design, have significant potential to serve as a bridge between quantitative methods, that is, to increase one's ability to define, explain and put forward new ideas and dimensions of the phenomena under the study (Molina-Azorin et al., 2017).

TWO EXAMPLES OF MIXED METHOD RESEARCH IN THE CONTEXT OF CAREER STUDIES

In studying job loss and coping, most studies examine it through the quantitative method, seeking to understand which variables may influence the speedy return to work (e.g., Kanfer, Wanberg, & Kantrowitz, 2001). These studies typically explore the job search process and focus on the measurable employment outcomes. However, less is known about the actual transition stage and the kinds of meanings that the unemployed may experience during these highly challenging times. While job loss is one of the most stressful life events, we know much less about the sense making process of displaced individuals and how it may shape one's career decisions at the time and eventually the return to work. Thus, in order to go beyond just how quickly the unemployed individuals find reemployment, the current study was designed to first of all expand our knowledge on the "how" related to the coping stage at the individual level and second, to test some of these newly established relationships in the quantitative phase, thus triangulate the two methods.

The focus of the initial stage of the project involved in-depth interviewing and research questions around how displaced individuals make sense of the job loss in the context of their life and career. This part of the mixed method research focused on the exploratory paradigm, seeking qualitative understanding of the job loss and coping experience, seeing it more holistically and focusing on the emic view, that is, respondents' accounts of the transition experiences. As a result, the study was planned in a way that the qualitative paradigm would precede the quantitative stage as this would offer new insights beyond what quantitative approach could obtain alone. Another benefit for triangulating qualitative and quantitative design in this context is the need to understand the mechanisms underlying quantitative results up to date, that is, to explore this phenomenon in a partially new territory (i.e., sense making in the midst of the unemployment transition). Thus, by focusing on the qualitative findings first, the researcher seeks to elaborate on the job loss phenomena; that is, to triangulate by expanding the breadth and range of inquiry and to expand existing research on how individuals cope post job loss. Specifically, we expand the reach of either method alone by enriching our understanding of the complex unemployment and coping phenomena; one, by obtaining an in-depth look into the transition experience and two, by testing and measuring the impact of significant coping relationships, thus extending the inquiry into different components.

At the start of this qualitative study, the researcher was much less interested in seeking answers to how the unemployed obtain reemployment, such as specific job search strategies they pursue (typically done through quantitative methods), rather the focus was on the lived experiences of the unemployment (Richardson & Zikic, 2007). After conducting just over 30 in-depth semi-structured interviews, which were inductively analyzed, the results revealed interesting new knowledge of the coping with job loss experience. For example, experience of job loss was identified as a major theme and parts of the interviews when participants mentioned the difficulty they experienced were coded as "career exploration" node or "blessing disguise" node. While respondents spoke at length about the challenges related to being unemployed, sometimes even the stigma attached to their status, many also spoke about rediscovering themselves and the positive side of job loss. Specifically, the routine schedule and the constant focus on working was often preventing these individuals from realizing their true self in terms of their interests and work preferences. Thus, the qualitative study uncovered new ways in which job loss and unemployment may lead to positive outcomes, such as exploring other more suitable work options for example and/or finding ways to fulfill personal interests and goals. Along the same lines, some unemployed realized that they were not spending enough time with their families, or the transition even led them to discover a new hobby. Many of the unemployed decided to engage in career planning and related job search that led them in a somewhat new career direction. This ability to reflect on their life and career prompted them to engage in some conscious career exploration, as to what it is they may want to do next and how any future work role may fit with their work–life needs. As a result, qualitative inquiry allowed researchers to understand those hidden and even positive meanings of the unemployment transition.

As a result of these qualitative findings, the next step was to conduct a quantitative study that would confirm and test some of the relationships that emerged in the initial, qualitative stage of this research. In this way, following the basic rule of the mixed method design, we seek to obtain further insights that exceed the sum of the individual qualitative and quantitative components (Molina-Azorin et al., 2017). Specifically, the quantitative study was able to test the types of career behavior that emerged from the qualitative findings and how these may affect reemployment outcomes. Thus, we focused on specific and measurable questions around whether career exploration and career planning behaviors versus job search behavior assist job seekers in finding a job, but more importantly, which type of behavior may lead to a better job.

Next, career adaptability theory (which focuses on career behaviors related to coping with transitions) as well as job search as self-regulation served as the foundation of the qualitative study; the survey was designed to test job seekers' behaviors at two points in time. Once during their unemployment transition and again nine months later, hoping to measure some reemployment outcomes (i.e., focusing on the type of outcomes that may emerge from various activities that job seekers will engage in during their transition). In this quantitative study we used established scales for measuring job search activities, career planning, and career exploration activities (self and environmental dimensions). We also included two important antecedents of these behaviors that were evident in prior models of job search as well as confirmed in our interviews, that is, the amount of social support as well as individuals' confidence (i.e., self-efficacy) in their ability to conduct various job search and career behaviors. In addition, many of these relationships have been tested in the context of job search during school to work transition, but less was known about transitions of mid-career professionals and especially in relation to obtaining a better-quality employment. Quantitative data confirmed and further clarified many of the findings from the qualitative study conducted earlier; for example, that external career exploration and career planning do in fact enhance one's ability to find a better-quality job, while self-exploration had a negative relationship with job quality. This ladder result could perhaps be explained by some of the qualitative findings. For example, self-exploration and reflection may lead one to seek more work–life balance and choose work opportunities that allow for that, while not necessarily seen as better-quality employment, but rather allowing for better quality of time with the family/outside of work. Thus, by combining methods, the outcome was better than doing either alone; one, we were able to learn about in-depth transition experiences that expand current models and knowledge beyond just job seeking and speedy reemployment; moreover, through quantitative analysis we were able to confirm these, obtain measurable results and further obtain another perspective on these relationships.

The second example of a mixed method study shows a case where the two types of data were given equal priority and collected at the same time. It involved a study of migrant career transitions and understanding the causes and experiences of underemployment. In this research, the author sought to extend the breadth and range of inquiry by using different methods for different inquiry components (Green et al., 1989; Molina-Azorin et al., 2017). Specifically, qualitative data was collected in order to understand one side of the phenomena; how foreign professionals, skilled migrants in particular, experience underemployment in highly regulated versus unregulated fields in the local labor market. While on the other hand, the quantitative study was conducted to understand how skilled migrants, specifically in the unregulated group, may overcome some of the underemployment challenges through proactive career behaviors. Thus, in-depth qualitative interviews were conducted with about 20 professionals in each of the groups (i.e., 20 foreign doctors, highly regulated group, and 20 IT professionals, unregulated profession). This study used the extreme case comparisons in terms of comparing one highly regulated profession (i.e., medical doctors) to an unregulated profession (IT professionals). The research question guiding this part of the study was focused on how skilled migrant professionals in each of the professional groups experience underemployment; specifically, how this transition and often downshifting in their career affects their sense of self, that is their professional identity. In this phase of the study, the researcher sought to explore individuals' perceptions of the following: the structural barriers inherent in each of the occupations but also how foreign professionals in each occupation proactively managed these barriers while seeking to establish continuity in terms of their professional identity.

As a result, the qualitative findings allowed the researcher to obtain an in-depth understanding of how underemployment is experienced for each group of professionals and idiosyncrasies involved due to different levels of barriers and strength of the professional identity. It was clear that the strength of the original professional identity was a major obstacle in how these professionals approached the challenges. Specifically, foreign doctors identified so strongly with their original profession and understandably had much harder time envisioning themselves in any other type of role. Instead, they focused most of their efforts on re-entering the medical profession but often without much success due to extreme occupational closure (Zikic & Richardson, 2016). On the other hand, the qualitative data shows a very different identity experience for IT professionals whose barriers to entry were much more manageable and often related to their soft skills such as language skills and communication.

In parallel, the quantitative study was being conducted to understand in more detail the role of proactive career behaviors of the unregulated group of professionals specifically, and how they navigate the local labor market in order to regain professional status. At the start of the study, it was known that the unregulated group (i.e., IT professionals) would be studied quantitatively as well in terms of their labor market entry and strategies used to regain employment; however, the highly regulated professionals, often unable to re-enter their profession, could best be understood by qualitative inquiry into their professional identity struggles and inability to become doctors again. Thus, qualitative data together with the quantitative data meant to complement our understanding of how established professionals in two occupations experience a major career transition in the host country, but more specifically how they actively manage their underemployment experience.

In this case, the mixed method allowed the researcher to obtain a much richer and more holistic understanding of a complex phenomenon than either approach alone. Specifically, while understanding the subjective experiences of each group of professionals through qualitative inquiry clarified specific barriers and the type of identity work for each group, the quantitative data allowed for clarifying, measuring and testing for specifying proactive career behaviors that may improve employment quality (i.e., battle underemployment) for foreign professionals in the unregulated group. As a result, the quantitative study was guided by the career self-management perspective while also including measures of specific objective barriers in the labor market. Thus, together, by assessing barriers as well as active career behaviors this study provided broader understanding of how, through career self-management behaviors, foreign professionals may avoid underemployment and instead find employment that is more commensurate with their qualifications and experience.

CONCLUSION

As career studies are evolving and growing in complexity, researchers must pay special attention to the best methodological approach that fits the context and allows for research questions to be properly addressed. While coherent conceptualization of "mixed methods" with its distinct identity did not emerge until the 1980s, in many disciplines mixed method research design has since been recognized as the third methodological movement. Yet, in organizational studies mixed method is not as institutionalized and formalized (Hesse-Biber, 2010); however, despite the term perhaps not being applied or used that often, the integration of research methodologies dates back with its own history in organizational research to Van Maanen (1979). Currently, mixed method research design practices are solidified and there have been special issues on mixed methods in journals as well as interdisciplinary journals focused on mixed methods and even international mixed method association (e.g., Special issue *Organizational Research Methods*, 20(2), 2017).

Thus, we feel that the key to using a mixed method design for career scholars should be determining the core reason for collecting both forms of data by providing a clear rationale to study the interrelationships between the quantitative and qualitative phases; particularly for how and when data are to be collected (Creswell et al., 2003). Finally, it is also important to note that mixed method design also requires more extensive time, resources and effort on the part of the researcher as they need to develop a broader range of skills that span both qualitative and quantitative paradigms, which may be contrary to some scholars' training (Niglas, 2009). As a result, the researcher must be motivated to develop a broader set of skills or to assemble a team that could conduct this kind of study together. However, the benefits of enriching our methodological toolbox by engaging in this type of research often surpasses the costs, as the researcher is able to study the topic of choice while having an adaptive toolkit and the ability to compare, extend and integrate results.

To conclude, mixed method research design is nevertheless highly relevant for career studies. As described above, our field presents overreliance on the quantitative, positivist paradigm and is still in need of a grand career theory; as a result, there is even more reason to consider conducting mixed method studies as a way to address these challenges and obtain a more informed understanding of career related phenomena by combining two perspectives. Specifically, in-depth qualitative knowledge will allow career researchers to obtain a subjective, emic perspective, thus the ability to extend and enrich our current theories. At the same time, complementing this qualitative paradigm with a more traditional quantitative and positivist method will allow for objective tests of the new relationships that may have emerged from the interpretivist study. As a result, careers researchers will be better equipped to provide more valid, and comprehensive knowledge by learning from two very important perspectives in one study. Finally, given the long-standing debate between subjective versus objective career focus, mixed methods also offer the opportunity to pay equal attention to each dimension as well as to triangulate these two perspectives in one study.

REFERENCES

Afiouni, F. (2014). Women's careers in the Arab Middle East: Understanding institutional constraints to the boundaryless career view. *Career Development International, 19*(3), 314–336. http://dx.doi.org.ezproxy.library.yorku.ca/10.1108/CDI-05-2013-0061

Agee, J. (2009). Developing qualitative research questions: A reflective process. *International Journal of Qualitative Studies in Education, 22*(4), 431–447. 10.1080/09518390902736512

Akkermans, J., & Kubasch, S. (2017). Trending topics in careers: A review and future research agenda. *Career Development International, 22*(6), 586–627. https://doi.org/10.1108/CDI-08-2017-0143

Al-Asfour, A., Tlaiss, H. A., Khan, S. A., & Rajasekar, J. (2017). Saudi women's work challenges and barriers to career advancement. *Career Development International, 22*(2), 184–199. http://dx.doi.org.ezproxy.library.yorku.ca/10.1108/CDI-11-2016-0200

Alvesson, M., & Sandberg, J. (2011). Generating research questions through problematization. *Academy of Management Review, 36*(2), 247–271. https://doi-org.ezproxy.library.yorku.ca/10.5465/amr.2009.0188

Arthur, M. B. (2008). Examining contemporary careers: A call for interdisciplinary inquiry. *Human Relations, 61*(2), 163–186. 10.1177/0018726707087783

Arthur, M. B., Hall, D. T., & Lawrence, B. S. (Eds.) (1989). *Handbook of Career Theory.* Cambridge: Cambridge University Press.

Arthur, M. B., & Rousseau, D. M. (1996). Introduction: The boundaryless career as a new employment principle. In M. Arthur & D. M. Rousseau (Eds.), *The Boundaryless Career: A New Employment Principle for a New Organizational Era* (pp. 3–20). New York: Oxford University Press.

Baruch, Y., & Bozionelos, N. (2010). Career issues. In S. Zedeck (Ed.), *APA Handbooks in Psychology®. APA Handbook of Industrial and Organizational Psychology, Vol. 2. Selecting and Developing Members for the Organization* (pp. 67–113). Washington, DC: American Psychological Association. https://doi.org/10.1037/12170-003

Baruch, Y., Szűcs, N., & Gunz, H. (2015). Career studies in search of theory: The rise and rise of concepts. *Career Development International, 20*(1), 3–20. http://dx.doi.org.ezproxy.library.yorku.ca/10.1108/CDI-11-2013-0137

Bryman, A. (1984). The debate about quantitative and qualitative research: A question of method or epistemology? *British Journal of Sociology, 35*(1), 75–92.

Cho, Y., Park, J., Han, S. J., & Ho, Y. (2019). "A woman CEO? You'd better think twice!" Exploring career challenges of women CEOs at multinational corporations in South Korea. *Career Development International, 24*(1), 91–108.

Clarke, M. (2015). Dual careers: The new norm for Gen Y professionals? *Career Development International, 20*(6), 562–582. http://dx.doi.org.ezproxy.library.yorku.ca/10.1108/CDI-10-2014-0143

Cohen, L., Duberley, J., & Mallon, M. (2004). Social constructionism in the study of career: Accessing the parts that other approaches cannot reach. *Journal of Vocational Behaviour, 64*(3), 407–422. 10.1016/j.jvb.2003.12.007

Collin, A. (1997). Career in context. *British Journal of Guidance and Counselling, 25*(4), 435–446.

Collin, A. (1998). New challenges in the study of career. *Personnel Review, 27*(5), 412–425.

Collin, A., & Young, R. A. (1986). New directions for theories of career. *Human Relations, 39*(9), 837–853.

Crane, A., Henriques, I., & Husted, B. W. (2018). Quants and poets: Advancing methods and methodologies in business and society research. *Business and Society, 57*(1), 3–25. 10.1177/0007650317718129

Creswell, J. W. (1994; 2003). *Research Design: Qualitative and Quantitative Approaches.* Thousand Oaks, CA: Sage Publications.

Creswell, J. W., & Plano Clark, V. L. (2007). *Designing and Conducting Mixed Methods Research.* Thousand Oaks, CA: Sage Publications.

Creswell, J. W., Plano Clark, V. L., Gutmann, M. L., & Hanson, W. E. (2003). Advanced mixed methods research designs. In A. Tashakkori & C. Teddlie (Eds.), *Handbook of Mixed Methods in Social and Behavioral Research* (pp. 209–240). Thousand Oaks, CA: Sage Publications.

Doherty, N., Dickmann, M., & Mills, T. (2010). Mobility attitudes and behaviours among young Europeans. *Career Development International, 15*(4), 378–400. http://dx.doi.org.ezproxy.library.yorku.ca/10.1108/13620431011066259

Feilzer, Y. M. (2010). Doing mixed methods research pragmatically: Implications for the rediscovery of pragmatism as a research paradigm. *Journal of Mixed Methods Research*, *4*(1), 6–16. 10.1177/1558689809349691

Garcia, P. R. J. M., Restubog, S. L. D., Ocampo, A. C., Wang, L., & Tang, R. L. (2019). Role modeling as a socialization mechanism in the transmission of career adaptability across generations. *Journal of Vocational Behaviour*, *111*, 39–48.

Gephart Jr, R. P., & Richardson, J. (2012). Qualitative research methodologies and international human resource management. In M. Harris (Ed.), *Handbook of Research in International Human Resource Management* (pp. 29–52). London: Psychology Press.

Gioia, D. A., & Pitre, E. (1990). Multiparadigm perspectives on theory building. *Academy of Management Review*, *15*(4), 584–602.

Green, J., Caracelli, J., & Graham, W. F. (1989). Toward a conceptual framework for mixed-method evaluation designs. *Educational Evaluation and Policy Analysis*, *11*(3), 225–274.

Gubrium, J. F., Holstein, J. A., Marvasti, A. B., & McKinney, K. D. (Eds.) (2012). *The Sage Handbook of Interview Research: The Complexity of the Craft*. London, UK: Sage Publications.

Hall, D. T. (2004). The protean career: A quarter-century journey. *Journal of Vocational Behaviour*, *65*(1), 1–13. 10.1016/j.jvb.2003.10.006

Harman, C., & Sealy, R. (2017). Opt-in or opt-out: Exploring how women construe their ambition at early career stages. *Career Development International*, *22*(4), 372–398. http://dx.doi.org.ezproxy.library.yorku.ca/10.1108/CDI-08-2016-0137

Hesse-Biber, S. N. (2010). *Mixed Methods Research: Merging Theory with Practice*. New York, NY: Guilford Press.

Hyde, K. F. (2000). Recognising deductive processes in qualitative research. *Qualitative Market Research: An International Journal*, *3*(2), 82–90. http://dx.doi.org.ezproxy.library.yorku.ca/10.1108/13522750010322089

Iellatchitch, A., Mayrhofer, W., & Meyer, M. (2003). Career fields: A small step towards a grand career theory? *International Journal of Human Resource Management*, *14*(5), 728–750. 10.1080/0958519032000080776

Johnson, R. B., & Onwuegbuzie, A. J. (2004). Mixed methods research: A research paradigm whose time has come. *Educational Researcher*, *33*(7), 14–26. 10.3102/0013189X033007014

Johnson, R. B., Onwuegbuzie, A. J., & Turner, L. A. (2007). Toward a definition of mixed methods research. *Journal of Mixed Methods Research*, *1*(2), 112–133. 10.1177/1558689806298224

Joo, B. K., & Ready, K. J. (2012). Career satisfaction: The influences of proactive personality, performance goal orientation, organizational learning culture, and leader–member exchange quality. *Career Development International*, *17*(3), 276–295. 10.1108/13620431211241090

Kanfer, R., Wanberg, C. R., & Kantrowitz, T. M. (2001). Job search and employment: A personality–motivational analysis and meta-analytic review. *Journal of Applied Psychology*, *86*(5), 837–855. http://dx.doi.org.ezproxy.library.yorku.ca/10.1037/0021-9010.86.5.837

Khapova, S. N., Arthur, M. B., & Wilderom, C. P. M. (2007). The subjective career in the knowledge economy. In H. Gunz & M. Peiperl (Eds.), *Handbook of Career Studies* (pp. 114–130). Thousand Oaks, CA: Sage Publications.

Kim, N., Jang, S. Y., & Baek, P. (2019). Career chance experience of Korean women workers. *Career Development International*, *24*(1), 74–90.

Kostal, J. W., & Wiernik, B. M. (2017). A meta-analytic investigation of demographic differences in protean, boundaryless, and proactive career orientations. *Career Development International*, *22*(5), 520–545. http://dx.doi.org.ezproxy.library.yorku.ca/10.1108/CDI-08-2017-0139

Laud, R. L., & Johnson, M. (2012). Upward mobility: A typology of tactics and strategies for career advancement. *Career Development International, 17*(3), 231–254. 10.1108/13620431211241072

Lewis, K. V., Harris, C., Morrison, R., & Ho, M. (2015). The entrepreneurship–motherhood nexus: A longitudinal investigation from a boundaryless career perspective. *Career Development International, 20*(1), 21–37. http://dx.doi.org.ezproxy.library.yorku.ca/10.1108/CDI-07-2014-0090

Lin, Y. C. (2015). Are you a protean talent? The influence of protean career attitude, learning-goal orientation and perceived internal and external employability. *Career Development International, 20*(7), 753–772. http://dx.doi.org.ezproxy.library.yorku.ca/10.1108/CDI-04-2015-0056

Lincoln, Y. S., & Guba, E. G. (2000). Paradigmatic controversies, contradictions and emerging confluences. In N. K. Denzin & Y. S. Lincoln (Eds.), *Handbook of Qualitative Research* (2nd ed., pp. 163–188). Thousand Oaks, CA: Sage Publications.

McMahon, M., Watson, M., & Lee, M. C. (2019). Qualitative career assessment: A review and reconsideration. *Journal of Vocational Behaviour, 110*, 420–432.

Molina-Azorin, J. F. (2012). Mixed methods research in strategic management: Impact and applications. *Organizational Research Methods, 15*(1), 33–56. 10.1177/1094428110393023

Molina-Azorin, J. F., Bergh, D. D., Corley, K. G., & Ketchen Jr., D. J. (2017). Mixed methods in the organizational sciences: Taking stock and moving forward. *Organizational Research Methods, 20*(2), 179–192. 10.1177/1094428116687026

Molina-Azorin, J. F., & López-Gamero, M. D. (2016). Mixed methods studies in environmental management research: Prevalence, purposes and designs. *Business Strategy and the Environment, 25*(2), 134–148. 10.1002/bse.1862

Morse, J. M. (1991). Approaches to qualitative-quantitative methodological triangulation. *Nursing Research, 40*(2), 120–123.

Niglas, K. (2009). How the novice researcher can make sense of mixed methods designs. *International Journal of Multiple Research Approaches, 3*(1), 34–46.

Omair, K. (2010). Typology of career development for Arab women managers in the United Arab Emirates. *Career Development International, 15*(2), 121–143. http://dx.doi.org.ezproxy.library.yorku.ca/10.1108/13620431011040932

O'Neil, D. A., Hopkins, M. M., & Sullivan, S. E. (2011). Do women's networks help advance women's careers? Differences in perceptions of female workers and top leadership. *Career Development International, 16*(7), 733–754. http://dx.doi.org.ezproxy.library.yorku.ca/10.1108/13620431111187317

Patton, M. Q. (2002). *Qualitative Research and Evaluation Methods. Integrative Theory and Practice.* Thousand Oaks, CA: Sage Publications.

Petriglieri, G., Petriglieri, J. L., & Wood, J. D. (2018). Fast tracks and inner journeys: Crafting portable selves for contemporary careers. *Administrative Science Quarterly, 63*(3), 479–525. https://doi-org.ezproxy.library.yorku.ca/10.1177/0001839217720930

Presbitero, A. (2015). Proactivity in career development of employees: The roles of proactive personality and cognitive complexity. *Career Development International, 20*(5), 525–538. http://dx.doi.org.ezproxy.library.yorku.ca/10.1108/CDI-03-2015-0043

Richardson, J., & Zikic, J. (2007). The darker side of an international academic career. *Career Development International, 12*(2), 164–186. https://doi.org/10.1108/13620430710733640

Sandberg, J., & Alvesson, M. (2011). Ways of constructing research questions: Gap spotting or problematization? *Organization, 18*(1), 23–44. 10.1177/1350508410372151

Savickas, M. L. (2005). The theory and practice of career construction. In S. D. Brown & R. W. Lent (Eds.), *Career Development and Counseling: Putting Theory and Research Work* (pp. 42–70). Hoboken, NJ: John Wiley.

Savickas, M. L. (2012). Life design: A paradigm for career intervention in the 21st century. *Journal of Counselling & Development*, *90*(1), 13–19. http://dx.doi.org.ezproxy.library .yorku.ca/10.1111/j.1556-6676.2012.00002.x

Savickas, M. L. (2013). Career construction theory and practice. In R. W. Lent & S. D. Brown (Eds.), *Career Development and Counseling: Putting Theory and Research to Work* (2nd ed., pp. 144–180). Hoboken, NJ: John Wiley.

Spurk, D., Hirschi, A., & Dries, N. (2019). Antecedents and outcomes of objective versus subjective career success: Competing perspectives and future directions. *Journal of Management*, *45*(1), 35–69.

Starks, H., & Brown Trinidad, S. (2007). Choose your method: A comparison of phenomenology, discourse analysis, and grounded theory. *Qualitative Health Research*, *17*(10), 1372–1380. 10.1177/1049732307307031

Strauss, A., & Corbin, J. (1990). *Basics of Qualitative Research*. Thousand Oaks, CA: Sage Publications.

Strauss, A., & Corbin, J. (1998). *Basics of Qualitative Research Techniques*. Thousand Oaks, CA: Sage Publications.

Sullivan, S. E., & Arthur, M. B. (2006). The evolution of the boundaryless career concept: Examining physical and psychological mobility. *Journal of Vocational Behaviour*, *69*(1), 19–29.

Sullivan, S. E., & Baruch, Y. (2009). Advances in career theory and research: A critical review and agenda for future exploration. *Journal of Management*, *35*(6), 1542–1571.

Tashakkori, A., & Teddlie, C. (2015). Overview of contemporary issues in mixed methods research. In A. Tashakkori & C. Teddlie (Eds.), *Handbook of Mixed Methods in Social and Behavioural Research* (pp. 1–42). Thousand Oaks, CA: Sage Publications.

Turner, S. F., Cardinal, L. B., & Burton, R. M. (2017). Research design for mixed methods: A triangulation-based framework and roadmap. *Organizational Research Methods*, *20*(2), 243–267. 10.1177/1094428115610808

Usinger, J., & Smith, M. (2010). Career development in the context of self-construction during adolescence. *Journal of Vocational Behaviour*, *76*(3), 580–591. 10.1016/j.jvb.2010.01.010

Van Maanen, J. (1979). The fact of fiction in organizational ethnography. *Administrative Science Quarterly*, *24*(4), 539–550.

Veld, M., Semeijn, J. H., & van Vuuren, T. (2016). Career control, career dialogue and managerial position: How do these matter for perceived employability? *Career Development International*, *21*(7), 697–712. http://dx.doi.org.ezproxy.library.yorku.ca/10.1108/CDI-04 -2016-0047

Walsh, K., Fleming, S. S., & Enz, C. A. (2016). Give and you shall receive: Investing in the careers of women professionals. *Career Development International*, *21*(2), 193–211. http:// dx.doi.org.ezproxy.library.yorku.ca/10.1108/CDI-04-2015-0059

Zhang, C., Hirschi, A., Herrmann, A., Wei, J., & Zhang, J. (2015). Self-directed career attitude as predictor of career and life satisfaction in Chinese employees: Calling as mediator and job insecurity as moderator. *Career Development International*, *20*(7), 703–716. http://dx .doi.org.ezproxy.library.yorku.ca/10.1108/CDI-06-2015-0090

Zikic, J., & Richardson, J. (2016). What happens when you can't be who you are: Professional identity at the institutional periphery. *Human Relations*, *69*(1), 139–168. 10.1177/0018726715580865

Index

Printed and bound by CPI Group (UK) Ltd, Croydon, CR0 4YY

16/04/2025